CONTEMPORARY BRITISH POETRY

Contemporary British Poetry

Essays in Theory and Criticism

Edited by
James Acheson and
Romana Huk

State University of
New York Press

For permission acknowledgments, see p. 401. Every effort has been made
to trace all copyright holders, but if any have been inadvertently
overlooked the publishers will be pleased to make the necessary
arrangements at the first opportunity.

Published by
State University of New York Press

© 1996 State University of New York

For information, address the State University of New York Press,
State University Plaza, Albany, NY 12246

Production by Bernadine Dawes • Marketing by Fran Keneston

Library of Congress Cataloging-in-Publication Data

Contemporary British poetry : essays in theory and criticism / [edited
    by] James Acheson and Romana Huk.
        p.   cm.
    Includes bibliographical references and index.
    ISBN 0-7914-2767-6 (acid-free paper). — ISBN 0-7914-2768-4 (pbk.)
: acid-free paper)
    1. English poetry—20th century—History and criticism—Theory,
etc. 2. English poetry—20th century—History and criticism.
I. Acheson, James, 1947– . II. Huk, Romana, 1959– .
PR 611.C66 1966
821'.91409—dc20   96-5029
                                                       CIP

1 2 3 4 5 6 7 8 9 10

CONTENTS

PREFACE

Editing a book like *Contemporary British Poetry: Essays in Theory and Criticism* is a risky business, since the tradition behind it is replete with attempts at comprehensive mapping of named terrains. We were aware from the start that any full accounting for Britain's contemporary poetry scene would now be even less possible than it ever was, given how much has been happening in the very variegated field of these "poetries" and how little room we have between the covers of our collection. Competing with our desire to bring readers up to date with changes that have occurred over the last twenty years—changes that have received less attention than they deserve, particularly in literary circles outside the U.K.—was our desire to demonstrate some of the new ways that established figures more familiar to our audience are currently being (re)read; therefore, the book's time frame has also broadened beyond any possibility of inclusiveness, treating poems that range from, say, Donald Davie's or Ian Hamilton Finlay's work of the 1950s and 1960s to the new poems of Benjamin Zephaniah and Carol Ann Duffy. Yet we feel that the book's strengths lie not so much in its having drawn a tidy circle around its topic but rather in its forays into new textual territories, both poetic and critical; in other words, the widely ranging approaches taken by our essayists assume no set audience and contribute to no "evenness" of tone or theoretical/rhetorical register for the book as a whole. We felt that our topic demanded that we take the risk of substituting variety for conformity, due to the different readerships that these poetries currently enjoy and the relatively neglected status of several of them. We accepted, for example, and not without concern, that some essays would focus singly on well-known poets with a critical tradition behind them, exploiting the latitude that such foundations afford for pursuing specific theoretical arguments, while others—such as the ones on black British poetry and poetry by women—would be more descriptive and of a "survey" nature in order to introduce the majority of our readers to both the poets and the major issues in their newly (and belatedly) formulating critical ground. Our book is bound to demonstrate the limitations inherent in projects of this kind; we hope nonetheless that it will move readers to investigate further not only the poems and poets discussed here, but also works by the many fine writers who happen to receive no mention along the way. As we write this, near the end of 1995, British poetry is experiencing a boom—an explosion of new talents, many fine small- and large-press publications, and a resultant rekindling of audience interest. *Contemporary British Poetry: Essays in Theory and Criticism* offers a stepping-stone to that scene, as well as an invitation and a provocation for others to produce further work in response to the vitality they find there.

Introduction

Romana Huk

In recent years a number of fine collections of critical essays on Anglo-American modern and contemporary poetry have appeared, among them David Murray's *Literary Theory and Poetry: Extending the Canon*, whose focus spans the century, and Antony Easthope and John O. Thompson's *Contemporary Poetry Meets Modern Theory*, which devotes approximately one third of its space to current British work.[1] Another very recent arrival is Manchester University Press's 1993 volume *New British poetries: The scope of the possible* (ed. Robert Hampson and Peter Barry), whose narrowed focus on several strands of formally innovative poetries provides the space for some substantial and, in some camps, long-awaited theoretical exploration (which I will return to in a moment). But not since Carcanet Press's *British Poetry since 1970: a critical survey* (ed. Peter Jones and Michael Schmidt, 1980)—an update on their earlier book edited by Grevel Lindop and Michael Schmidt, *British Poetry since 1960: a critical survey* (1972)—has a volume exclusively focusing on a wide range of contemporary British "poetries" appeared, and never has there been such a book produced by an American press or written by an international group of writers. My coeditor and I have attempted to demonstrate something of the variety of possible conversations to be encountered on recent British poetry; we have done so by following (if rather loosely and, at times, critically) in the footsteps of Carcanet's editors, offering our readers some updates on new developments in poetry since Jones and Schmidt's 1980 volume, as well as a number of rereadings of the contexts and writers that volume featured (or neglected to feature) from new perspectives in critical theory and contemporary philosophy. Everything about our volume bespeaks variousness and not definitiveness: readers will

1

find in its pages a number of differing critical and theoretical languages at work that articulate what we believe are accessible if at times clashing views of the poetry, the poets, and their "postmodern" historical moment.

What *is* made certain by our volume is that much has changed since Peter Jones and Michael Schmidt wrote their introduction to *British Poetry since 1970*—both in terms of the sensibilities of the poets emerging on the scene since then and the means by which that scene and its predecessors have become represented by critics, academics, and (as a consequence) publishers. For example, the well-respected poet/critic Blake Morrison could write, in the Carcanet volume (and with his tongue only partly in cheek), that a rough sketch of the young poet of the 1970s would picture him—"for 'he' is still more likely to be the case"—as emerging from the professional or middle classes ("or if it is working class we are less likely to hear about this than we would have been in the 60s"); he would have attended grammar school and then gone on to university ("probably Oxford or Cambridge") and would "certainly have read English Literature."

> His politics are on the whole quietly conservative, and where they intrude into the poetry at all, it is as a kind of nostalgic liberal humanism. . . . He has a surprisingly strong respect for "traditional" forms, even strict meter and rhyme.[2]

This nonpolemical writer nostalgic for premodernist paradigms for poetry is, of course, the kind of poet readers of British poetry will recognize as belonging to the "Movement"—represented, perhaps most famously, by Philip Larkin and Donald Davie—which emerged during the 1950s and took good enough hold of the poetry scene to weather the cultural revolution of the 1960s (with its proliferation of new, radically "popular" poetic forms corresponding to social and moral upheaval) and come out ostensibly on top again in the 1970s. The Movement's judgment of the 1960s would no doubt be in sympathy with the retrospective judgment offered by the editors of the Carcanet volume that during that decade there were too many (and too "different") kinds of poetries emerging at once and far too rapidly for critical sorting: "The 1960s were spoiled by excess of opportunities and choices and by paucity of generously stringent critics."[3]

By contrast, recent anthologies of poetry like *the new british poetry* and

The New Poetry [4]—both of which allude by name to A. Alvarez's now legendary anti-Movement anthology, *The New Poetry*[5]—define and celebrate the
current scene as being, like its supposedly emergent correlative in cultural
politics, "pluralized" and undefinable, as the editors of *The New Poetry* make
clear:

> Throughout the century, the hierarchies of values that once made
> stable poetics possible have been disappearing. In the absence of
> shared moral and religious ideals, common social or sexual *mores*
> or political ideologies, or any philosophy on the conduct of life,
> plurality has flourished.[6]

Not everyone is equally pleased about or convinced by the new poetic
"democracy"[7] and the plurality of its forms and voices, as reviews in central
poetry journals like *PN Review* have made clear.[8] But other long-standing
poetry reviewers and theorists like Terry Eagleton remind us that the situation is at least increasingly one in which "the *marginal* becomes somehow
central"[9]—a situation that has been fostered as much by the ascendency of
certain kinds of literary theory and criticism as by the compelling presence
of growing numbers of women poets, black poets from a range of differing
cultural communities, poets writing out of postcolonial experience or sub-
merged traditions in Scotland and Wales, regional and working-class poets,
and poets of all inflections writing in experimental, oppositional and/or
"poststructuralist" forms.

It is in fact arguable—and several essays in our volume present this
view—that there is no such thing as the much-discussed "*new* pluralism"
but rather a newly seen or newly acknowledged pluralism. Theorists, critics,
teachers, and, in turn, their readers and students are now being *trained* to
train a critical eye on literary history's occlusions: the women poets crowd-
ing behind Blake Morrison's hypothetical "he" in the 1970s, some of whom
are discussed in this book by Claire Buck; the black artists anthologized in
liminal publications such as James Berry's *Bluefoot Traveller: An Anthology of
Westindian Poets in Britain* back in 1976,[10] some of whom are discussed here
by Alastair Niven; the triply marginalized female black poets *not* included
in anthologies like Berry's but finally published in *A Dangerous Knowing* in
1985, and discussed here by C. L. Innes; the neomodernist or, as the authors

of *New British poetries* call them, the "Poetry Revival" poets who, as they claim, were edited out of British literary history until the 1980s[11] and who are discussed in our book by Edward Larrissy and John Matthias; such lists go on.

The crisis that the acknowledgment of all these differing artists on the poetry scene precipitates is primarily a crisis for conventional criticism because it is, in large part, one of judgment (and therefore power). Particularly in the first three examples above, "otherness" demands another kind of apprehension apart from the "standard"—one that the critic who is not from the social or cultural positioning at hand must learn yet remain always outside of, and one whose presence in the arena makes any final comparisons of "worth" between the different poetries difficult and even offensive. Postmodernism's method of revising Yeats's ominous line that "the center cannot hold" to read "the center *should* not hold" (meaning that it should be dismantled to reveal what it by definition marginalizes or suppresses) forces "judges" of poetry to look self-critically at their criteria for judgment and robs them of all tacitly granted authority. The continuing resistance to these poetries—demonstrated even by those anthologies that announce their circumspection—cannot easily be separated from resistance to the present era's indeterminacies and destabilizations of order and power that have aided in enabling the emergence of "plurality" by calling the very idea and ideal of cultural unity into question.

Such challenges become much more complex when one considers, as many of our essayists do, strategies recently practiced by poets of all positionings that launch threats at an even deeper stronghold of the liberal humanist tradition: its conception of the free-standing, unified "self," and that self's power to act through rather than as an instrument of language. Ironically, the same theories that fostered critical interest in marginalized voices have thrown them and all others under suspicion; the impossibility of escaping formation by dominant structures of thought embedded in language itself causes "voice" to become the site for a new sort of struggle in poetry. At stake are revised understandings of subjectivity and its relation to the public sphere; the pervasiveness of such issues, both thematically and formally, in recent poems is such that Peter Middleton in his essay in *New British poetries* feels safe in drawing a dichotomy between "dominant poetries and those where subjectivity is put into question."[12] The new consciousness of the mediation of seemingly self-generated feelings and thoughts by ascendant forces in culture and history through language has of course had a profound effect particularly on the lyric—that supposed haven of the "private" self—but also on other forms, including narrative poetry and even elegy. One need only note the differences between the essays in *British Poetry since 1970* and the ones in this volume to realize that the writing of both poetic and critical work has as a result undergone a sea-change, though one produced, unlike Shakespeare's, by processes of *de*mystification from what have been perceived as various kinds of sorcery and illusion induced by the standard cultural narrative.

Middleton and the writers of *New British poetries* claim that the inevitable politicization of poetry that accompanies such recognitions about the self and language caused those Eric Mottram refers to as descendants of "the 1950s Axis orthodoxy"—or the Movement conglomerate "Conquest-Fraser-Larkin"—to actively exclude the poets that they understood to be harbingers of it.[13] *New British poetries* specifically identifies those expressly excluded as being the poets of *A Various Art* and *the new british poetry* or those poets who, according to the book's major argument, are described as having grown, like the language-centered poets of the United States, out of roots in an Anglo-American modernist tradition running back through Ashberyesque developments to Basil Bunting, David Jones, Hugh MacDiarmid, and (across the water) Charles Olson, Gertrude Stein, William Carlos Williams, and (ultimately) Ezra Pound: poets including such diverse figures as Roy Fisher, J. H. Prynne, Allen Fisher, Elaine Feinstein, Veronica Forrest-Thomson, Tom Pickard, Tom Raworth, and many more recently acclaimed poets mentioned in the book's lists of perceived adherents and sympathizers. The "return to Pound" after his long literal and figurative exile could, one might argue, only be comfortably accomplished (or written about) in a context such as the present, in which the individual's complicity in systemic cultural and intellectual violence is newly understood as the inevitable result of coming to being in language; thus it might be that in an interesting twist and reversal of literary history, Pound can be found by the authors of *New British poetries* to be in some ways no more politically reprehensible than his less forthcoming "Axis" accusers:

Pound's fascism provides an excuse for ignoring his poetry, perhaps precisely because his "disastrous career"[14] raises unavoidably
the question of the relations between poetry, history and politics,
a question that Eliot's poetry or Larkin's occludes and mystifies.
On the other hand, the tradition that Crozier mentions [in the
introduction to *A Various Art*], which includes poets like Oppen,
Zukofsky and Olson, repudiates Pound's fascism through an engagement with the issues of politics and poetics.[15]

Accepting that their hands are "always already" dirty in the Derridean sense—
and that poetry is equally and inescapably permeated by not only politics
and history but the history of *poetic* politics—the poets currently drawn to
this particular strain of often highly theoretical poststructuralist art are able
to recuperate Poundian political forays and "process" forms. Their reassertion
of a vital link between contemporary British poetry and such modernist
traditions has become the cornerstone joining an important new version of
postmodernism's genealogy with the articulation of an increasingly disjunctive formal aesthetics—not too distantly related to that of the American
L=A=N=G=U=A=G=E poets—involving poetry in the politics of discourse.
In our volume, Edward Larrissy discusses more specifically the tensions
present between an American and native British modernist influence on
such poets, focusing his readings on three who appeared in *A Various Art*:
J. H. Prynne, Andrew Crozier, and Veronica Forrest-Thomson. Theorizing
that the British have practiced "only intermittently" the strain of "Romantic objectivism" that characterizes American projectivist art and other open
forms, Larrissy brings the "knowing self-consciousness about discourse" he
understands to undergird native neomodernism into seemingly unlikely
dialogue with "organic" and process forms, locating a new hybrid at the
intersection between modern Anglo-American trends.

The various readings, rereadings, and recontextualizations of poets
writing at the juncture between modernist and postmodernist eras offered
by Edward Larrissy, Antony Easthope, and John Matthias in this volume
form interesting (if unplanned) complements for one another. Antony
Easthope also calls up the "anti-Romantic" vision that has characterized
British poetry (after a short tenure of neo-Romanticism in the 1940s) in
order to trace the glimmer of postmodern perception that it made possible

in Donald Davie's early poems—those still wavering on the near side of the love/hate relationship with Ezra Pound's poetics demonstrated in Davie's critical work. With a "deliberately polemical intention," Easthope attributes "the failure of Englishness" to move, at that time, in the direction of such perceptions to "the undertow" of the dominant empirical tradition, which for decades held much of English poetry and philosophy back from engagement with ideas like those breaking on shore in mid-century France in the work of Lacan, Barthes, Althusser, Foucault, and others. Matthias, writing here about Roy Fisher (whom he included in his "neomodernist" anthology, *23 Modern British Poets*),[16] raises questions similar to Easthope's concerning the empirical tradition and poetry, only in this case his concern is with the way in which that tradition has tended to read Fisher's work— usually perceiving him as a "realist," particularly after the publication of "City," his long poem in an urban setting. Returning to what Fisher might have meant when he said in a 1973 interview that in his work he portrays "the discontinuous self," Matthias suggests that an "equivocal 'I'" as opposed to an "empirical 'I'" is at work in the poems—or an "I" that becomes part of each construction it makes out of what it perceives in modernist, "vorticist" fashion. Between the lines of Fisher's work, as Matthias discusses it, readers are able to glimpse pivotal arguments about authorship and language that were occurring in the background at the time, revolutionizing literary theory and causing/reflecting new directions in poetry as well.

Rather than "transvalu[ing]" the works discussed in them—turning them into proofs for literary theory, as the editors of *British Poetry since 1970* feared critical writings might do to poems that surrender to such explication—the essays in this volume that are focused on the oeuvres of well-established poets like Fisher invoke new thought in order to reinvestigate poems for workings that could not be perceived from what our predecessors valued: "perspectives provided by precedent."[17] For example, Nicholas Zurbrugg reconsiders the work of iconoclast Ian Hamilton Finlay—whose creations vanished into tradition's critical pigeonhole for concrete (meaning formally and therefore, the assumption goes, thematically radical) poetry—as evolving not only out of the experiments of modernism's avant-garde artists, and their "foreground[ed] signifier,"[18] but also out of complex, not simply "radical," responses to one form of 1960s anti-Movement poetry, the "confessionalist"

poem. Zurbrugg likens Finlay's reconception of the poetic image to Roland
Barthes's reconceptions of the sign in his phases of structuralist and
poststructuralist thought, suggesting that Finlay engages self-consciously
with the uncontrollable slippage of images through visual and textual history yet uses that knowledge to resist *both* the innocent use of language as
self-expression *and* concrete poetry's becoming "a mere typographic game"
or dalliance with what postmodern theorists have termed "simulacra"—
overwritten images, figures, and forms that have lost the significance they
may have once held in historical context. The fall of the hypostatic image
from myth into textual history also becomes the focus of Paul Giles's essay
on the equally long, interrelated careers of Ted Hughes and Thom Gunn.
Giles discusses both poets' early immersion in the mid-century American
modernist search for "architectonic synthes[es]" of the national experience
within new/old mythic frameworks, and their gravitation away from mythic
symbolism "into history," through ironic uses of what Paul de Man described
as the allegorical trope to indicate not mythic but linguistic prior constructions of meaning. Giles's reading of the significance of particularly Gunn's
subsequent use of formal meters opens the field for the arguments that R. K.
Meiners, Linda Kinnahan, and I attempt to make concerning the importance of reconceived methods of formalist reading in a poststructuralist age.

Until recently in Britain, a poem's adherence to conventional syntax
and structures would almost routinely be interpreted as a sign of its acceptance, at least by and large, of the traditional moral and ethical structures
of centralized English culture that historically gave rise to or adapted such
forms. Donald Davie put the equation most baldly in an early articulation
of Movement aesthetics when he drew correlations "between the laws of
syntax and the laws of society, between bodies of usage in speech and in
social life, between tearing a word from its context and choosing a leader
out of the ruck."[19] Certainly much recent formal work does indeed demonstrate allegiance to the cultural order. However, given the gradual development of new sets of questions concerning the construction and imprisonment of subjectivity by linguistic and rhetorical structures, a new kind of
"formality" can be discerned as having offered an effective (and indeed,
some argue, the *only*) means of not only expressing a poet's awareness of
the ineradicable influence of those structures but even of constructing, despite if necessarily *through* them, possible means of resistance. In Geoffrey

Hill's case, critics suggesting the presence of such an awareness in his work have remained opposed by those who would read his as an essentially conservative poetry, given its formality and obsession with the traditional themes of religion, war, and imperial history. In our volume, Meiners re-views both Hill's themes and forms as inherited elements of the poet's own construction in action, suggesting that his is a *formal* thematics: one in which the *contradictions* between the "site" for Hill's work—"in the shit" of linguistic history—and the oft-noted purity and chiseled beauty of his forms are what give rise to any available "meaning." In my own essay for the volume I attempt to contextualize similar strategies at work in the poems of Tony Harrison and Jon Silkin, both of whom were writing, like Hill, in Leeds at the beginning of the cultural/linguistic revolution, though theirs is poetry more overtly charged with working class and minority issues. By retrieving several fragments of the argument (which ranged from midcentury to the 1970s) over the changing nature of *littérature engagée* and its future in the postmodern arena, I attempt to draw relationships between developing poetic/formal and political philosophies and to understand their intersection as the generative matrix for a new form of "poetry of the committed individual."

Clearly any commitment to recovering the experience of the suppressed and unrepresented must become enormously vexed in the present theoretical climate; the art of "revolt" is for many less simple than it might have seemed in the 1960s. Certainly increasing numbers of women writers have found it difficult to continue what Claire Buck describes as the "Radical Feminist search for an authentic female nature" such as it might have been before patriarchal/discursive manipulation of it, though the idea is obviously an attractive one given that it binds women together in relation by identity, as a political force. Reconstructing the debate between early essentializing forces in feminist poetry and those writing from "marginalized" positions within it—Wendy Mulford and Denise Riley, for example, and those whose various poststructuralist awarenesses precluded participation in quite the same goals—Buck begins to rectify the "general failure to examine the place of the body of this work" in postwar cultural studies. Keeping an eye on the differing dynamics operant in American feminist poetry, she also discusses some reasons for "the difficulty about establishing a significant role for poetry [in Britain] as a mode of feminist cultural politics."

Taking up opposing problems raised, more recently, by the emergence of what some refer to as "postfeminism" in British women's poetry, Vicki Bertram engages frankly with what she understands to be its covert conservative politics of "judgment" leading women directly back into the textual confines of the liberal humanist tradition instead of toward its goal somewhere beyond gender politics. In her problematization of "the search for evaluative criteria" conducted by poets like Fleur Adcock and Carol Rumens, who have both edited influential new anthologies of women's poetry, Bertram deconstructs the reemergence of words like *universal* in discussions of feminine aesthetics as well as the resurrection of disparaging representations of the earlier feminist poets discussed by Buck, suggesting that such "new" developments leave us "no nearer having a satisfactory context within and against which poetry by women can be read and enjoyed than we were in the 1950s." The perpetuation of midcentury divisions between politics and poetry in British women's writing (made evident, ironically, by its politics of anthologization and exclusion as exposed by Buck and Bertram) has contributed to the isolation into which such work has been cast, particularly by American readers and critics, whose frequent misconception is that "there is nothing interesting or experimental happening in British women's poetry."

With the help of a transported context from the United States, Linda Kinnahan revises some of these misconceptions in a reading of the poetry of Carol Ann Duffy, which she sees as being no less (only differently) innovative and oppositional in its British context than the disruptive forms that have tended to be developed by North American women poets emerging out of organic traditions into the postmodern landscape of L=A=N=G=U=A=G=E poetry. Reconsidering Duffy's "more accessible form" as "mark[ing]," perhaps even more significantly than the disturbing displacements in signification of her North American neighbors, "an . . . engagement with [rather than a departure from] social discourse," Kinnahan locates formal strategies in Duffy's work that redraw the writer's individual and even gendered agency in the act of negotiating linguistically with her own selfhood as a construction "aware of its constructedness or its own grammar." Such awareness renews rather than precludes "feminism" or "commitment" in poetry, and formal readings such as Kinnahan's help to refute the charge of "nihilism so often leveled as criticism at poststructuralist interrogations of the humanist, autonomous self."

Of course the process of interrogating selfhood becomes even more complex for the "multicultural" poet, whose models involve constructs from outside dominant western European traditions. The desire to give voice to those constructs, and to counter-colonize British poetry with one's own "nation-language," have for such poets understandably preceded any desire to "enact a process of self-deconstruction." Instead, images from South Asian mythologies, as well as Caribbean and African rhythms of reggae and rap, calypso and blues, have, as they have in the United States, accompanied the sounding of "other" vital communities gathering force, like feminist contingents, alongside the dominant one. Aware of their liminality—or "rejection," as Alastair Niven more strongly puts it—and intent upon collectivity rather than fragmentation in the face of it, many poets have chosen to develop their own native forms of "performance poetry" that, like little else heard in Britain for hundreds of years, speak of models of communal selfhood rather than bourgeois individualism. Others, as Niven discusses them, work over a wide, exploratory range, encountering an equally wide range of problems—ones not limited, of course, to newly incoming peoples. As Fred D'Aguiar writes in his contribution to the *New British poetries*, the first and very bloody riots that occurred in the 1980s arose from the frustration of a "generation of British-born and bred blacks [who] had come of age only to find that Britishness did not include them."[20] Niven discusses the emergence of black writing "Out of the Margins," as it was put in a recent, grandscale celebration in London (hosted by the Arts Council, for which Niven serves as literature director); beginning with pioneering figures like James Berry and E. A. Markham, he brings readers up to date on some of the newest young writers, many of whom have not yet fought their way in from the "outside."

As an influential artist and critic, D'Aguiar also stirs up controversy when he writes that he is "not sure how much mileage is to be had out of seeing [the] wellspring of black women's writing as so different from what black men are writing that it merits separate treatment."[21] Others like Susheila Nasta have lamented the fact that the latter tends to subsume the former and that in Britain, unlike in the States, no body of criticism has been developing alongside the gathering number of black women's texts.[22] In our volume, C. L. Innes discusses a number of good reasons for the "separate treatment" of multicultural women poets who, as she makes clear, are particularly sensitive to issues of difference—both those tentatively dismissed by D'Aguiar in the above quotation and those overlooked or downplayed in the interest of feminist solidarity. Standing at the vanishing point of any new representation of either their culture (dominated by the black male's image) or their sex (dominated by the white western female's image), multicultural women poets importantly illustrate in their work the impossibility of, and potential dangers inherent in, essentializations about selfhood or womanhood.

Also included in the contemporary project of asserting and exploring cultural differences—as well as the effects sustained by the subject *made* subject to another culture's domination—are the poets of Scotland and Wales, where retrievals of native language and tradition long subsumed by English culture and its centrifugal forces often prompt comparison with those of postcolonial nations. In Scotland, as Cairns Craig writes, the "obliterating effects" of post–World War II consensus politics have slowly given way, enabling poets to experience the 1980s as "a decade of deepening and intensifying awareness of the difference of Scottish culture from English." Some of those differences, recovered not only from modernism's strong nationalist drive in the work of Hugh MacDiarmid and others but also from much older political and religious traditions, encourage, as in postcolonial poetry, a revaluation of community identity and "rejection of the individualist ethics of Thatcherism." Such recastings of identity are never seamless, as Linden Peach suggests by examining changes in constructions of Welshness given their partial dislocation from traditional roots in the landscape and regional mythology and their relocation among less-stable realms for identification. Reading in Welsh poetry a coming to terms with postmodern, industrialized Wales, with its "electronic spaces," gender fault lines, and truncated cultural memory, Peach describes a process within it that he identifies, borrowing a term from theorist Edward Soja, as "reterritorialization"—the reclamation of a sociospatial understanding of self through rereadings of the ways in which power relations have all along been inscribed in "'the apparent innocent spatiality of social life.'"

The recognition on the part of these poets, and indeed so many of the poets discussed in this volume, of the situatedness of selfhood—perceived, paradoxically, alongside the recognition that "[i]ncreasingly, modern identities are being shaped by a process that is both multilayered and international"—makes the return to a "poetry of place" seem particularly necessary now, if for a new set of reasons. Recovering some sense of the ways in which places map out *selves* rather than vice versa and of the ways in which constructed spaces perpetuate, through learned means of perceiving them in language, the influence of long unwritten histories of power relations, dominations, occlusions, and subtle persuasions allows the postmodern poet a new terrain within which to operate—one so critically fashioned by metonymic language and spatial metaphors that poetry's figurative medium becomes, arguably, one of the best for exploring its design. Counteracting the depthless, decorative, "fetishized" use of history in some strains of postmodern art, such poetry attempts to recompose itself in dialogue with the past—resurveying, in the case of Scotland and Wales, constructs of national identity made particular by the cultural web that draws "lines," signs, and boundaries all about where they are.

To summarize where British poetry in generalized terms seems to stand, at this or at any given moment in contemporary history is, as the above outline of this book's various topics and arguments is intended to make clear, an impossible and misguided task. Even as I make the sort of mildly descriptive/prescriptive, generalized statement that I do above concerning revised notions of a "poetry of place," at my back I hear the objections of poets like Adrian Clarke and Robert Sheppard who, in the afterword to their anthology *Floating Capital: New Poets from London* write that the "deadening . . . obsession with 'place' has been superseded by a willingness to deal with the materials that are readily to hand or impose themselves in the act of writing"[23]—or by a poetry in which attention has "shifted from referent to signifier" in ways equally conversant with recent theory but with somewhat different goals. Again, as I suggested at the outset of this introduction, such poetries have been as marginalized in recent literary history in Britain as many other-cultural and other-national poetries; therefore I feel compelled to say with care that although a number of key issues have demanded response across the spectrum of contemporary poems, given the challenges presented by postmodern philosophy to conventions like the lyric voice and traditional narrative—even the seemingly simple use of the sign itself—it is no longer possible to characterize developments decade by decade as has been customary in criticism about British poetry. That kind of construction is now perceived as being far too simple and exclusionary to accommodate the diversity of the scene since midcentury, if it ever indeed accommodated any decade without distortion. Perhaps I can only venture to say that the current poetry scene in Britain demands renewed attention from readers and critics alike because, on its relatively small but widely varied, internationalized stage, it is richly enacting the breakdown of older orders and newly responding to the sorts of postcolonial and postpatriarchal as well as "postmodern" instillations that have in differing vocabularies spelled the fates of many other cultural/political structures in our *fin-de-siècle* world. The stir has had efflorescent results in poetry; we hope that our collection conveys some of that excitement, and that both the limitations and the strengths of our volume will work in tandem to inspire others to join in the ensuing conversation about contemporary British poetry.

Notes

1. David Murray, *Literary Theory and Poetry: Extending the Canon* (London: Batsford, 1989); Antony Easthope and John O. Thompson, eds., *Contemporary Poetry Meets Modern Theory* (Toronto: University of Toronto Press, 1991). Objection may well be made to my use of the word *British* here, given that the book being described includes work on Seamus Heaney, who *has* objected to being subsumed under its cultural heading. Our book does not include work on Irish or Northern Irish poets, simply for reasons of space; still, we apologize to readers who take issue with our title, given that we include essays on Scottish, Welsh, and "multicultural" poets writing from hyphenated positions within those national boundaries.

2. Blake Morrison, in *British Poetry since 1970: a critical survey*, ed. Peter Jones and Michael Schmidt (Manchester, England: Carcanet Press, 1980), 142.

3. Jones and Schmidt, *British Poetry since 1970*, ix.

4. Gillian Allnutt, Fred D'Aguiar, Ken Edwards, and Eric Mottram, eds., *the new british poetry* (London: Paladin, 1988); Michael Hulse, David Kennedy, and David Morley, eds., *The New Poetry* (Newcastle: Bloodaxe Books, 1993).

5. A. Alvarez, *The New Poetry* (Harmondsworth, England: Penguin, 1962).

6. Hulse, Kennedy, and Morley, *The New Poetry*, 15.

7. Ibid., 16.

8. See, for one example, Neil Powell's review in *PN Review* 19, no. 6 (July–August 1993): 58–59; see also "The New Poetry: A Symposium," in *Poetry Review* 83, no. 2 (summer 1993): 4–33.

9. Terry Eagleton, "Comment," *Poetry Review* 79, no. 4 (winter 1989–90): 46 (emphasis added).

10. James Berry, ed., *Bluefoot Traveller: An Anthology of Westindian Poets in Britain* (London: Limestone, 1976).

11. These poets were, however, anthologized by John Matthias in the United States in *23 Modern British Poets* (Chicago: Swallow Press, 1971).

12. Peter Middleton, "Who am I to speak? The politics of subjectivity in recent British poetry," in *New British poetries: The scope of the possible*, ed. Robert Hampson and Peter Barry (Manchester, U.K.: Manchester University Press, 1993), 119.

13. Hampson and Barry, *New British poetries*, 32, 23.

14. This phrase is quoted from Donald Davie's *Pound: The Poet as Sculptor* (New York: Oxford University Press, 1964), 244.

15. Hampson and Barry, *New British poetries*, 7.

16. Matthias, *23 Modern British Poets*. See note 11 above.

17. Jones and Schmidt, *British Poetry since 1970*, xxi.

18. Adrian Clarke and Robert Sheppard, eds., *Floating Capital: New Poets from London* (Elmwood, Conn.: Poets and Poets Press, 1991), 122.

19. Donald Davie, *Purity of Diction in English Verse* (London: Chatto & Windus, 1952), 99.

20. Fred D'Aguiar, "Have you been here long? Black poetry in Britain," in Hampson and Barry, *New British poetries*, 59.

21. Ibid., p. 69.

22. "Publishing" (debate), "Out of the Margins: African, South Asian and Caribbean Writers in Britain," Arts Council/South Bank Centre, London 1993. Nasta is the founding editor of *Wasafiri*, a well-known journal devoted to black writing.

23. Clarke and Sheppard, *Floating Capital*, 122.

CHAPTER ONE

Donald Davie
and the Failure
of Englishness

Antony Easthope

A family with the wrong members in control—that, perhaps, is as near as one can come to describing England in a phrase.

—George Orwell (1941)

Despite a deliberately polemical intention, this essay is written, as they say, more in sorrow than in anger. Sorrow because it mourns a poetic talent that, I shall argue, never fulfilled its promise, but anger also because, as I shall try to suggest in this space, what did most to suffocate that talent was the dominant tradition in English culture, particularly as that tradition focuses on poetry.

The Case in Favor

We may begin by considering two poems. The first is the title piece of Donald Davie's volume *A Winter Talent* (1957):

Lighting a spill late in the afternoon,
I am that coal whose heat it should unfix;
Winter is come again, and none too soon
For meditation on its raft of sticks.

Some quick bright talents can dispense with coals
And burn their boats continually, command

17

> An unreflecting brightness that unrolls
> Out of whatever firings come to hand.
>
> What though less sunny spirits never turn
> The dry detritus of an August hill
> To dangerous glory? Better still to burn
> Upon that gloom where all have felt a chill.[1]

Two kinds of individual, the Stoic and the Romantic, contrast in several ways. Romantics use up their own energies ("burn their boats") or even make a *gesture* of doing so because they do so "continually," Stoics conserve themselves and their stocks like "coal"; whereas Romantics act ("dispense," "command," "turn") with "unreflecting brightness" in unconsidered spontaneity (or apparent spontaneity), Stoics are committed to "meditation" and so to action that claims the authority of an infinitive ("to burn"); Romantics are all feeling (or pretend to be so), Stoics think. And of course a distinction is assumed between two versions of masculine sexuality, hardly recondite, between the prematurely exhausted Romantics with their quick "firings" and the long, slow burn of the Stoic.

The contrast opens onto another layer of meaning at which the two kinds are demarcated by conceptions of the subject/object relation. They, the Romantics, are characterized by their misrecognition of subject and object as a unity in which each mirrors the other—as "sunny spirits" (subject) they seem to achieve fulfillment in relation to an equally sunny "August hill" (object), a unity made even closer if these "spirits" (alcohol?) set fire to the "dry detritus," igniting equally it and themselves. The "I" of the poem is also a subject posed in a relation of some correspondence with the objective world—lighting a taper (for a fire in the grate or, more likely, his pipe), he sees *himself* as the material being burned. But this dependence on the other matches an independence from it, for, once released, his "heat" will defy the winter just as human "meditation" stands over against the cycle of the seasons. Similarly, in the third stanza, when burning "Upon that gloom where all have felt a chill," the flame of his life defines itself against the universal cold of death, even while another meaning ("to burn / Upon," meaning to "be burned upon") suggests that—cold performing the work of fire—he is finally consumed by this ultimate chill. Though technically the gender of the speaker is unmarked (except, no doubt, by the pipe smoking), he is unmistakably defined as masculine by the whole tone and manner.

Refusing the Romantic dyad in which subject becomes object, "A Winter Talent," then, explores the nature of human dependence and independence from what Heidegger writes of as the contingency of "Being There." Consciousness on its "raft of sticks" is always already materially situated—in the body, in a world not of its choosing. Meditation can free itself from inauthenticity only to the extent that it deliberately embraces its own being towards death and chooses to look into the gloom "where all have felt a chill." So in terms of thematic assertion, so also in terms of textual operation. Whereas Romanticism follows the convention of seeking an ever spontaneous, ever original expression for its feelings, the language of this poem, in relative contrast, accepts its own textuality. It openly reaches back via Milton on his blindness ("and that one talent . . .") to such well-known precedents as Shakespeare's "Sonnet 73" ("That time of year thou may'st in me behold"), with its allusions to life as a fire that burns "on the ashes of his youth." Its quatrains with their elaborate rhymes ("afternoon" / "soon," "unfix" / "sticks") also hark back to Eliot's highly wrought stanzaic poems of 1920 ("Sweeney Erect," "A Cooking Egg"). Recalling the work of Walter Savage Landor, Davie's poem, in its carefully worked artifice, sustained deictic syntax, self-conscious development of metaphor, and premeditated shifts between polysyllabic rapidity ("meditation," "unreflecting") and ponderous monosyllables ("that gloom where all have felt a chill"), rather than treating language and the signifier as a mere vehicle for feeling, acknowledges the dependence of idea on sound, intention upon language.

That may be somewhat of a "best case" made for the poem. But if it errs on the side of generosity, that only makes the next move more unsettling. For here, seventeen years later, is "Lancashire," a poem from *The Shires* (1974):

> My father was born in Horton
> In Ribblesdale—the highest
> Signal-box in England
> He'd say, but he was biased.
>
> Though Horton is in Yorkshire,
> The Ribble flows to the west.

> I have imagined that river
> With awful interest:
>
> Dark gullies, sobbing alders
> Must surely mark its course;
> It rolls and rounds its boulders
> With more than natural force[2]

The poem, in fact, continues in this vein, mentioning "Lancashire witches," "Catholic gentry" in the Civil War, a feeling of oppression in "Liverpool, Manchester, Salford," but there is really not much point in quoting any more (if in doubt, the reader could recite over to him- or herself again that third verse). An entirely conventional (that is, ideologically complicit) view of England as significant regional counties or shires draws on picture post-card clichés to protract a fantasy of England as "country" (not city—Manchester and Salford are oppressive), along with the history of the gentry, all in a poetic discourse that might well be called "Neo-Georgian." If "A Winter Talent" is by Donald Davie, "Lancashire" must be by another poet of the same name.

Postwar Contexts

Before turning to a second poem from the collection *A Winter Talent* for confirmation of what the poet could do at that time, I want to suggest some of the possibilities of "A Winter Talent" by relating that text to its contemporary context or to some versions of that.

Of these versions, the most obvious is that of "The Movement," especially the poets D. J. Enright, Kingsley Amis, Elizabeth Jennings, Philip Larkin, and Donald Davie included in the anthology *New Lines* (1956), edited by Robert Conquest, who defends these poets in his introduction. Blake Morrison, in his history of the group, writes, "The identity of the Movement has, it seems, transcended both the group and the decade, coming to stand for certain characteristics in English writing—rationalism, realism, empiricism—which continue to exert their influence today."[3] Morrison's belief that rationalism and empiricism are compatible, perhaps even the same thing, is mistaken, though it is a mistake characteristic of the Movement and its thinking at that time. Despite this, we can agree that "A Winter Talent" takes sides with thought and consideration as opposed to the irrationalism of the "quick bright talent" (figured, in contemporary poetry circles, very much as the Dylan Thomas who had his last drink in New York in 1953).

But in doing this, the anti-Romanticism of "A Winter Talent" engages with another tradition in another context, just because it sets a distance between itself and Romanticism. If Romanticism—or one major and continuing strand of it—is persuasively captured by René Wellek in his definition of it as "that attempt, apparently doomed to failure and abandoned by our time, to identify subject and object, to reconcile man [sic] and nature,"[4] then this early text of Davie's firmly rejects the presumed identity of subject and object, the human and the nonhuman. It follows clearly enough in the footsteps of Ezra Pound, who in 1912 famously proposed that the "perfect symbol is the natural object" and that the symbolic meaning should not *replace* a literal sense of the object as it is presented in the everyday world.[5] This can be expanded a little because Pound's principle carries a long way. If a poem says, "I wandered lonely as a cloud," then subject (I) and object (cloud) are united in a higher term, loneliness, presumed to be common to them both and constituting a single, symbolic domain; if, however, a hawk is conceded a literal meaning as an object in the everyday, *apart* from the usual connotations it has acquired subjectively for human beings (ferocity, rapacity, nobility, and so on), then subject and object are not subsumed together—human consciousness falls inside the circle of Being rather than comprehending it.

A poem that almost programmatically follows Pound's dictum is Charles Tomlinson's "Hawks," from *Written on Water*.[6] The poem keeps moving between an assertion of the difference between hawk and human, on the one hand, and "what we share with them" on the other. Against the fantasy that hawk nature mirrors human nature, it emerges that what we share with them is not rapacity but the biological necessity to mate and rear young; the pair of hawks "After their kind are lovers." (I suspect Tomlinson learned this irony from Pound's concluding poem in the "Cathay" sequence ["To-Em-Mei's 'The Unmoving Cloud'"]—when the speaker does finally imagine he is in communication with the birds they don't want to hear about him, they want to talk about their problems.) After noting the shared genetic disposition between us and them, the poem goes back the other way to assert "we cannot tell what it is they say." It all adds up to a devastating riposte to the sentimental banalities of Ted Hughes's hawk poems.

There is a problem here that cannot be avoided. Both the "literal" meaning (a hawk as a hawk) and the "symbolic" meaning (hawk as rapacity) exist as they are experienced by human beings, so how is one to fulfill Pound's anti-Romantic program by discriminating them? Because the real exists only at one with itself, outside representation, the real can only be represented precisely *as* representation, a human construction, and so not as itself. How then can an effect of the real be given? A main strategy here, one most fully deployed by the poetry of Wallace Stevens, is to sustain a set of subjective meanings that are obviously derived from an objective setting alongside but askew from a rendering of the objective setting itself, so that the effect of the real comes to be represented in the gap between them, as it were. Thus in "The Snow Man" a subjective attitude of stoical unsentimentality is staged through a set of metaphors ("a mind of winter," being "cold" of heart) in an asymptotic relation to the rendering of a winter landscape in the everyday. Or, more relevantly as an influence on Davie's "A Winter Talent," there is what happens in "Montana Pastoral," a poem by J. V. Cunningham, published in 1942. Again dismissing the sentimental cast of mind that seeks to co-opt object to subjectivity ("I am no shepherd of a child's surmises"), this poem develops a rendering of an objective landscape—summer, grasses, dryness, wheat for threshing—but concludes by finding in this pastoral arcadia anything but happiness, finding instead a subjective possibility expressed in images of winter:

> Through the warm dusk I drove
> To blizzards sifting on the hissing stove,
>
> And found no images of pastoral will,
> But fear, thirst, hunger, and this huddled chill.[7]

Davie's apparent reliance on Cunningham goes much further than just the use of the same concluding word. "A Winter Talent" also works by contrasting heat and cold, human heat and nonhuman coldness, but again like "Montana Pastoral" it marks the distance between subject and object by acknowledging the dependence of subject on object alongside a degree of independence for the subject. Human beings, one might say, cannot find meaning except in terms derived from the rest of nature, but that meaning and those terms do not coincide with nature.

There is, however, a third and even more suggestive context within which Davie's early poetry might be read. When I went to university in 1958, the two most intellectually fashionable books were *Being and Nothingness* by Sartre and Kerouac's *On the Road* (yes, children, once upon a time Europeans thought of the United States as the land of Freedom and Democracy, and Vietnam was still called "Indo-China"). Deriving from the writings of Nietzsche, Husserl, and Heidegger, existentialism in the postwar world spread well beyond its serious philosophic enactment in Sartre. For example, the masculinist (and racist) hero of Camus's *The Outsider*, first published in 1942, is said to go to his death happy in that he could lay his "heart open to the benign indifference of the universe."[8] Originating in the 1930s, this popularized existentialism is arguably symptomatic of a much wider cultural movement in the West, one that would include—and be evidenced by—French films such as Marcel Carné's *Le jour se lève* (1939), in which Jean Gabin holes up in an attic with Arletty until the police finally get him, or the Hollywood genre of film noir in which, typically, a hard-bitten, wised-up, and laconic hero endures attack from anonymous others without expecting to be better treated, least of all by the woman he is tempted to trust. Though his tone is a long way from that of Camus's Meursault or of Humphrey Bogart in a Chandler adaptation, the speaker of "A Winter Talent" shares their stoical disabusement and acceptance of, if not the "indifference of the universe," at least of contemporary urban society.

At stake in such existentialism is not simply a macho ethic or the nature of the universe or the alienations of twentieth-century Western capitalism. Rather, it is the issue of *humanism*, as the novelist Alain Robbe-Grillet showed in an article translated into English and published in the *Evergreen Review* in 1959. Humanism rejects "solidarity between the human spirit and the world" in favor of an acceptance that "'Things are things, and man is only man.'"[9] Humanism, occupying that same transcendental space as Christianity, affirms a "metaphysical pact" between people and things—as, for example, Robbe-Grillet suggests, in the use of metaphor.[10] Even a casual reference to "a village 'crouching' in the hollow of a valley" assumes that human feelings find their natural correspondence in the world, whereas to say that the village was "situated" in the hollow of the valley would not. Saying "No" to this humanism, Robbe-Grillet determines that he will "record the separation between an object and myself."[11]

It is not quite as simple as that, for the reason already suggested (for us the real always exists in our representations). But Davie's early poetry certainly forms a parallel to Robbe-Grillet's manifesto proclamation of the need to demonstrate a distance between subject and object. Davie does it, though, not so much by eschewing metaphor as by setting two forms of representation alongside each other so that their difference might annotate what separates the real from its representation. Before going on to look at the limitations of Davie's project, here—to give further substance to the argument—is how we might read another text from *A Winter Talent*, "The Priory of St Saviour, Glendalough":

> A carving on the jamb of an embrasure,
> 'Two birds affronted with a human head
> Between their beaks' is said to be
> 'Uncertain in its significance but
> A widely known design.' I'm not surprised.
>
> For the guidebook cheats: the green road it advises
> In fact misled; and a ring of trees
> Screened in the end the level knoll on which
> St. Saviour's, like a ruin on a raft,
> Surged through the silence.
>
> I burst through brambles, apprehensively
> Crossed an enormous meadow. I was there.
> Could holy ground be such a foreign place?
> I climbed the wall, and shivered. There flew out
> Two birds affronted by my human face.[12]

The poem begins with an object, a carving in a place, that immediately is translated into a form of subjectivity, a meaning ("Two birds affronted . . .").

There is a small problem about the word "affronted" because it might trans-late one of two terms from heraldry, either *affronté*, animals with heads *facing* each other, or *affrontée*, facing forward. My sense is that the guide-book description has the two heads facing each other holding a human head in between (nature surrounding the human and tearing at it?), whereas "affronted" in the last line of the poem suggests two birds facing forward to the human face that frightens them. The represented speaker's ironic skepticism about the uncertainty of the inscribed text ("I'm not surprised") is confirmed by something like a parable in the second stanza. The visitor gets lost trying to follow written directions to the tourist attraction, just as, by analogy, the hope of finding a transcendental guarantee "out there" for human aspirations is disappointed (if the "guidebook" is the Bible, the "knoll" is Golgotha, and "St. Saviour's" the Cross with Christ).

Though armed by doubt against the promises of the transcendental, the pilgrim visitor presses on and finds *less* than he expected (an unmistak-ably masculine tone again). Suspense builds across the first-person singu-lar—"I burst," "I was there," "I climbed"—but the climax comes from some-where else, not "there" where the "I" is, but "There" where something other is, which "flew out"—the two birds frightened by this intrusion. But we already know about these two birds and the human face, for they are a "widely known" representation, as deeply coded in human convention as a heraldic device. The lines therefore produce an unnerving effect, like count-ing stairs down in the dark and finding an unanticipated step. Although this happens in a poem, not outside, the coincidence between the two forms of text—the "subjective" heraldic meaning and its "objective" realization in an event—lends extraordinary stress to their difference and separation. By this textual effect, the "Two birds" of the last line are rendered so uncanny, so other, it is as though they enter the poem from the real. In this respect the poem, by giving people what Charles Tomlinson wrote of as an awareness of the mystery of a universe "bodied over against them,"[13] trenches upon contemporary existentialism, rejects what Robbe-Grillet calls the "metaphysical pact," and says "No" to humanism defined as an ontology in which a material world finds its center in the human essence it reflects.

But . . .

Or does it? We may read back from consequences in order to assess causes, and here the contrast between what ensues from Sartre and existentialism in France and what emerges from early Donald Davie and the poetry of the Movement in England should give pause to any overconfident identification of "A Winter Talent" with a text of the *nouveau roman*. The narrative of what happens in France can be briefly told very much as a working out and working through of the logic of what was already on that agenda by 1960. If (human) Being There is only part of the Being that encompasses it, if our existence is provisional and not given as an essence, then the question follows ineluctably: how did this sense of Humanity get to be there and how does it work? What are the structures—a question from the early 1960s—of which Humanity is an effect? And if we are constructed—a question especially after 1968—how may we be transformed? From this inquiry, pursued collectively in the writings of Claude Lévi-Strauss, Jacques Lacan, Michel Foucault, and Jacques Derrida (among others), two conclusions become matters of principle—that the real cannot be known except as it is represented, and that the individual human subject cannot be simply identified as a punctual "I," because the ego is an effect of a process, at once ideological and unconscious.

No such set of questions and answers developed in England after 1960. "Poststructuralism," as it has been named on this side of the Channel, had to be largely imported from Paris. In England that whole problematic continues to have a dubious and oppositional status in relation to the dominant culture[14] and is either ignored in the main organs of the public sphere or vilified in ignorance as some French intellectual equivalent to mad cow disease. While the attempt to establish poststructuralism outside certain academic enclaves failed in England, the poetry of the Movement, from origins quite as marginal and academic, has expanded since the 1950s to acquire a dominant position in English culture today. As Andrew Crozier argues in a modestly phrased but strongly convincing analysis, "the present-day canon has its roots in the Movement."[15]

Whereas the literary tradition of the United States is always looking for the Great American Novel, English culture (in its dominant mode), disparaging the novel with its disturbingly social overtones, has hoped instead for the Great English Poet, a new name to slot into the line that runs Shakespeare and Milton and Wordsworth and . . .? Since 1950, the number one spot has been occupied first by Philip Larkin, then by Ted Hughes, and now by Seamus Heaney, each promoted for largely conjunctural reasons. Larkin was first noticed through his association with the Movement, and though the others were not, they became candidates because they write a *kind* of poetry the Movement made possible.

For the Movement was able to hold back the persistent threat of poetic modernism, so clearing the path for Larkin/Hughes/Heaney (and the other Hs, Hill and Harrison, who have figured in the frame merely for scattering some modernist verbal glitter on a foundation of solid Hardy). In his introduction to *New Lines* (1956), Robert Conquest attacks the use in the poetry of the 1940s of "images of sex and violence"; on this Andrew Crozier comments:

> What Conquest goes on immediately to say, however, suggests that his quarrel is not just with the poetry of the forties but with most of twentieth-century writing: "When a condition of this sort takes hold it sometimes lasts for decades. The writers remembered later are odd eccentrics—the Kiplings and Hardys." Announcing "a general tendency, perhaps of lesser talents," rather than a collection of individual eccentrics, Conquest is implicitly claiming that the Movement, the poetry of the fifties, represents a return to literary standards inscribed in social normality.[16]

I would disagree with Crozier's diagnosis only by adding that it was—ironically—the Left poets of the 1930s (Day Lewis, Spender, and others) who, by rejecting elitist modernism in the name of the people, were able to reinstate liberal humanism, so providing a necessary condition for the reactionary postwar insularity Crozier acutely diagnoses.[17] It is a question, then, of the continuity of a national poetic tradition, as opposed to the potential disruption of that tradition instigated by poetic modernism.

Empiricism

The tradition of English national culture is empiricist.[18] That is, it assumes an epistemological scenario in which the real is conceived to exist in itself as object such that it can be known more or less directly by the unprejudiced observer, a subject posed in correspondence to that object as equally given and free-standing. Modernism endangers this scenario at each point. For modernism the real is in question, any means for representing the real has its own materiality, and the subject—far from being given—is in process (and if this description makes modernism sound like poststructuralism, it is because poststructuralism as a conceptual movement, following the track of Hegel's owl of Minerva, caught up with what was inherent in the aesthetic practices of modernism a generation after the event). Modernism can be defined in other ways, but this shorthand summary enables us to inspect the English poetic tradition for any cracks caused by the modernist upheaval. There are remarkably few. After the Left poets of the 1930s, it was a relatively easy task for the Movement to restore the status quo ante, to clear a path back to the English poetic tradition before 1914.

The poetry of the Movement, says Conquest in 1956,

> is empirical in its attitude to all that comes. This reverence for the real person or event is, indeed, a part of the general intellectual ambience (insofar as that is not blind or retrogressive) of our time. One might, without stretching matters too far, say that George Orwell with his principle of real, rather than ideological honesty, exerted, even though indirectly, one of the major influences on modern poetry.[19]

As Conquest makes clear, at issue is not just an *empirical* reliance upon facts but an *empiricist* notion that the real exists unproblematically "out there." Previously I have extended maximum sympathy to the early Davie as exemplifying a possible break with the Romantic tradition, but now a limit must be set to this sympathy and that writing must be defined otherwise.

"Refusing the Romantic dyad in which subject becomes object, 'A Winter Talent' explores the nature of human dependence and independence from what Heidegger writes of as the contingency of 'Being There.'" Well, yes, but Romanticism, as Paul de Man rightly redefined it, based itself as much on acknowledgment that (regrettably) subject and object were in fact separate as it did in the occasional ecstatic celebration of their supposed union.[20] Marking a separation between subject and object does not necessarily push the Davie poem out of the Romantic tradition, nor does dramatizing a sense that the real is over against the subject as the "Two birds" are in the last line of "The Priory of St. Saviour, Glendalough."

Hard to settle satisfactorily from the side of the object, the problem becomes clearer from the side of the subject if we ask, with Robbe-Grillet, whether humanism comes into doubt or not. Posed like this, a simple—and traditional—answer rapidly emerges. The "I" in both these early Davie poems is the good old English transcendental ego, the "I" that surveys the world with splendid confidence from a position of supposed exteriority, reflects upon it (or meditates), and masters what it sees. An unreflectingly free-standing ego is assumed and enacted in the secure positionality of "I am that coal," "I'm not surprised," "I was there," "I climbed." And one does not have to go all the way down the road with accounts of *écriture féminine* to find these (hysterical) denials of insufficiency traditionally masculinist.

A necessary—though not sufficient—condition for this "I" is the use of meter. In the poetry of the Movement, a traditional formal and metrical pattern serves a double purpose, something on which Andrew Crozier comments again: "Traditional forms . . . define the space in which the self can act with poetic authority, while at the same time, in the absence of assurances provided by conventionally felt poetic experience, they secure the status of the text."[21] So, the conventional iambic pentameter of "A Winter Talent" and "St. Saviour" not only supports the would-be autonomous "I" but also binds the texts back into the English post-Renaissance tradition. Hence, we need to revise the earlier judgment that the intertextuality of "A Winter Talent" foregrounded its textuality in favor of the view that it really worked to bury the poem more deeply inside the inherited poetic discourse.

Englishness

As happens so often, it is those features conventionally regarded as marginal and formalist that most reveal how a text is operating—as for instance here with meter. Although Donald Davie as a critic had written with insight and sympathy in *Ezra Pound, Poet As Sculptor* (1965) of the modernist compulsion to break from the pentameter into free verse, his views on his own poetic practice are surprisingly reactionary:

> The metrical and other habits of English verse seem to me to be in no sense "arbitrary" but rather to be rooted in the nature of English as a spoken and written language; I see no other explanation of the fact that the rules which, say, Mr. Amis and Mr. Graves observe are the rules which have governed ninety per cent of English poetry for more than 500 years.[22]

This is not true. The four-beat line of Old and Middle English is more "rooted in the nature of English" than is the Romance import of iambic pentameter, and it is continued in ballads, nursery rhymes, and work songs down to the football chants of the 1990s (for his "ninety per cent of English poetry," Davie is counting only the poetry of the gentry). But the polemical stance serves adequately as a way to reject modernism twice over—it blocks out modernism and free verse while it also keeps a channel clear back past modernism to the English post-Renaissance tradition.

In 1973 that project becomes a manifesto commitment for Donald Davie when he publishes *Thomas Hardy and British Poetry*. Its avowed aim, after clumsily dismissing modernism in the early pages with a vague appeal to the way Pound and Eliot reject liberal politics, is to affirm that the "most far reaching influence" on English poetry "of the last fifty years" has been "not Yeats, still less Eliot or Pound, not Lawrence, but *Hardy*."[23] Here is where I would locate the main responsibility for what went wrong, what led the poetic talent of the early poems to run away into the sands of *The Shires* and the Psalms in paraphrase. The undertow of Englishness proved too strong for someone not resolved to oppose it.

The national culture is in jeopardy when Robert Conquest, in a 1963 defense of the Movement, dismisses the possibility that some American poets might be models for English poetry:

> The British culture is receptive to immigration, if not to invasion; but it remains highly idiosyncratic. It is part of our experience, and

for that no one else's experience, however desirable, can be a substitute.[24]

"Modernists go home": Conquest not merely advocates Englishness, he
enacts its main procedures in his advocacy. To defend English national culture, he appeals to individuals who simply experience Englishness as a direct access to the real, and this is the method of empiricism. It is the same
appeal that Davie in the same year makes in defending Larkin's poetry (and
reprints in his book on Hardy): "we recognize in Larkin's poems the seasons
of present-day England, but we recognize also the seasons of an English
soul—the moods he expresses are our moods too, though we may deal with
them differently."[25] So there it is—the real is English, and Englishness is the
real. Landscape is there (English), Larkin's poetry is there (English), but we
are him (through direct recognition) and he is us and we are the "English
soul." It is a long way from "meditation on its raft of sticks" and what that
might have become. The tradition of English national culture is empiricist,
putting a Lockeian "I experience, therefore I am" in the place of a Cartesian
cogito. Modernism makes such empiricism impossible both by refuting empiricism in principle and by evidencing, through its mere force and preva-
lence, that empiricism has had its day. In limited ways some of the early
poetry of Donald Davie (and Charles Tomlinson, though his work has only
been mentioned on the sidelines here) begins to unpick the empiricist tradition, at least, by exploring the contingencies of the individual subject, its
situatedness. And this tendency moves far enough away from the English
inheritance to touch ways of thinking at the time best expressed in Sartre's
influential rereading of Heidegger. When we review that moment, though,
a fork on the road appears. For while the Parisian avenue took it away from
humanism into poststructuralism, the poetry of the Movement made way
for the present-day canon of Larkin, Hughes, Heaney, etc. for a return to
humanism, empiricism, and the triumph of the experiential self. Failing to
break on through to the other side, Davie's trajectory was sucked back into
the orbit of traditional Englishness, a poetic Englishness that can keep open
its lifeline back to Hardy and beyond only by constantly warding off the
"invasion" (Conquest's word) of modernism. The dominant mode, in which
Davie's work soon becomes incorporated, remains—strictly—a version of
prewar poetry (pre–First World War, that is): Neo-Georgian. In the phrase

of Charles Bernstein, the American L=A=N=G=U=A=G=E poet, it becomes
the British High Anti-Modernist Tradition.

Notes

1. Donald Davie, *A Winter Talent and Other Poems* (London: Routledge & Kegan
Paul, 1957), 47.

2. Donald Davie, *Collected Poems* (Manchester: Carcanet, 1990), 258.

3. Blake Morrison, *The Movement: English Poetry and Fiction of the 1950s* (Oxford:
Oxford University Press, 1980), 9.

4. René Wellek, "Romanticism Re-examined," in *Romanticism Reconsidered,* ed.
Northrop Frye (New York: Columbia University Press, 1963), 133.

5. Ezra Pound, *Literary Essays* (London: Faber, 1963), 9.

6. Charles Tomlinson, *Written on Water* (Oxford: Oxford University Press,
1972), 12.

7. J. V. Cunningham, *The Exclusions of a Rhyme* (Denver: Alan Swallow,
1960), 37.

8. Albert Camus, *The Outsider* (Harmondsworth, England: Penguin, 1961), 120.

9. Alain Robbe-Grillet in *Evergreen Review* 9 (summer 1959): 99–100.

10. Ibid., 105.

11. Ibid., 101–2 and 116.

12. Davie, *A Winter Talent,* 60.

13. Charles Tomlinson, "The Middlebrow Muse," *Essays in Criticism* 7 (April
1957): 215.

14. For further discussion of this subject, see Antony Easthope, *British Post-Structuralism: Since 1968* (London: Routledge, 1988).

15. Andrew Crozier, "Thrills and Frills: Poetry As Figures of Empirical Lyricism,"
in *Society and Literature, 1945–1970,* ed. Alan Sinfield (London: Routledge, 1983), 207.

16. Ibid., 211–12.

17. See my "Traditional Metre and the Poetry of the Thirties," in *1936: The Sociology of Literature,* ed. Francis Barker et al. (Colchester: University of Essex Press,
1979), 324-43.

18. See Perry Anderson, "Origins of the Present Crisis," *New Left Review* 23 (Janu-
ary/February 1964): 26–53; Tom Nairn, "The English Working Class," *New Left Review*
23 (March/April 1964): 43–57; and Tom Nairn, *The Break-up of Britain: Crisis and Neo-
Nationalism* (London: New Left Books, 1977).

19. Robert Conquest, ed., *New Lines* (London: Macmillan, 1956), xiv–xv.

20. See Paul de Man, *Blindness and Insight,* 2d rev. ed. (London: Methuen, 1983).

21. Crozier, "Thrills and Frills," 206.

22. Donald Davie, *Ezra Pound: Poet As Sculptor* (London: Routledge & Kegan Paul, 1965), 8.

23. Donald Davie, *Thomas Hardy and British Poetry* (London: Routledge & Kegan Paul, 1973), 3.

24. Cited in Crozier, "Thrills and Frills," 214.

25. Davie, *Thomas Hardy and British Poetry*, 15.

CHAPTER TWO

The Poetry of
Roy Fisher

John Matthias

One cold evening in the winter of 1980 I drove with Roy Fisher through a landscape of abandoned factories, empty warehouses, and uncollected refuse past the ruins of the railway station in South Bend, Indiana. He was in town to give a reading at the University of Notre Dame and, as I discovered to my considerable surprise, was about to spend the first night of his life outside of England.

As we talked about cities—Birmingham, Chicago, London, Indianapolis—lines and phrases from his work surfaced in my mind that led me, partly in jest and partly with a fascinated sense of what I took to be a near identity between the setting of a poem and the scene in which we found ourselves, to label, as it were, things and places that we passed along the road by quoting bits of *City*. At the same time, I had the odd feeling that I was looking at familiar objects, not through the windshield of a moving car, but through the glass above some labeled trays exhibited for an ambiguous purpose in an industrial museum of the mind—one like Fisher would later, in actual fact, imagine in a section of "Diversions," where the works of a foundry patternmaker—shapes for "drains, gears, / furnace doors, [and] couplings"—mime "the comportment / of the gods in the Ethnology cases."[1] As we passed the station, coming on it just exactly as one does upon the station in *City*—"suddenly in its open prospect out of tangled streets of small factories"[2]—I had the uncanny sense that Fisher had, on his first night out of England, fallen from the sky directly into his best-known poem.

Because the language of *City* seems sometimes to describe the decayed industrial topography of Studebaker Corridor in South Bend—an area where auto manufacturing produced at first a prosperous, small Detroit and then, following the bankruptcy of Studebaker in the 1960s, a few square miles of hulking, empty buildings and unlighted streets—one's memory of the poem could make it for a moment an example of that realism many seek to find in it, and that two other early Fisher poems, "For Realism" and "The Memorial Fountain," might seem to validate. The remembered language seemed to match, or correspond to, aspects of the bleak urban landscape through which we drove in many of the same ways it might have had we been driving through the streets of Birmingham instead, leading me to point and quote (though also to hallucinate the glassed, sealed, and labeled trays in that industrial museum of the mind).

But Fisher has talked about confronting a topography as "an indecipherable script with no key" when he went to work on *City*, about "a perceptual environment for which no vocabulary needed to exist," about "floating real things into a fictive world" and "exploring inner space rather than in any way attempting to do justice to a place as itself." More than the actual city of Birmingham, Fisher thought of Rilke's Paris and Kafka's Prague, towns in paintings by Kokoschka and Paul Klee, the tiny hilltop cities in the backgrounds of paintings by Italian primitives.[3] This does not suggest the imagination of a realist. Perhaps Fisher was more the poet of the glass case— or even the Large Glass—than he was the Laureate of postindustrial Birmingham.[4] And maybe his urgent desire to *construct* complex configurations out of language aligned him with assumptions absolutely antithetical to realism—those of the philosophers and cognitive psychologists who believe, as one of them says, that "knowledge does not reflect an 'objective' ontological reality, but exclusively an ordering and organization of a world constituted by our experience," and who agree with Piaget when he says that "Intelligence organizes the world by organizing itself."[5] Fisher's "indecipherable script" had found its key when he had made from his perceptual environment a vocabulary and conceptual construction by floating real things into a fictive, inner space. This, by his account, was *City*. And yet the critics talked of it as if it were a photograph—or even a place that one could go and visit. And I myself was pointing to it out the window as we drove to Fisher's reading in a place where he had never been.

Fisher was in town partly because I had included *City* in *23 Modern British Poets*, an anthology that appeared in 1971. My intention in that book was to demonstrate the existence of an indigenous British modernism by anthologizing work by David Jones, Hugh MacDiarmid, and Basil Bunting (all of whom were still living in the early 1970s), and by following that up with selections from the poetry of, among others, Fisher, Charles Tomlinson, Christopher Middleton, Ian Hamilton Finlay, Gael Turnbull, Christopher Logue, Matthew Mead, Ken Smith, Peter Whigham, Lee Harwood, John Montague, Nathaniel Tarn, and Tom Raworth. Some of these poets, and perhaps Roy Fisher himself, would now be called "postmodern" rather than "modern" by many critics. But in 1971, the term *postmodern* was just beginning to rear its head, and I thought of my twenty-three as representing an extension and development of mainstream Anglo-American modernism.

I had come to *City* as to a kind of demythologized *Waste Land*, and wanted to see it as a link between the fully mythologized work of David Jones and the nominalistic constructions of Lee Harwood and Tom Raworth. Toward the end of *City*, Fisher writes that "each thought is at once translucent and icily capricious," calling this "A polytheism without gods,"[6] and I also liked to think of my reader remembering the polytheism *with* gods of Christopher Logue's *Patroclia* and *Pax*, his versions from Homer that appeared in the anthology, where Apollo, dressed as Priam's brother, strolls with Hector for a while, and Logue writes in amazement (or Homer matter-of-factly): "think of it: They stand like brothers, man and god, / Chatting together on the parapet that spans the inner gate."[7] From living gods to icily capricious and translucent thoughts: it defined a kind of range.

When Fisher read at Notre Dame, however, celebrating that initial night away from England, he did not read from *City*. More than a decade had passed since the publication of the Fulcrum Press *Collected Poems* of 1969, and after *Matrix*, *The Cut Pages*, and *The Thing About Joe Sullivan*, one began to wonder if the radically hermetic *Ship's Orchestra* might not have prefigured more in the later Fisher than did *City*, and without forcing the choice of whether to toss that herring *realism* from one's analytic net or consume it as an hors d'oeuvre. Still, *City* had begun the critical discussion, and by 1981 it had already led to something of a critical debate. While I return to an early moment in that debate, into which I was drawn by virtue of having included *City* in *23 Modern British Poets,* and then go on to look at certain key poems of the 1970s that anticipate *A Furnace*, I should leave Roy Fisher where I best remember him—playing jazz piano at a party following his reading—"jamming sound against idea / hard as it can go," as he says about Joe Sullivan[8]—while another guest of the university, also in town to read, watched and listened and smiled enigmatically, making the rest of the audience, though not the pianist, about as uncomfortably conscious of a perceptual environment as possible. It was John Cage.

Although even John Cage may ultimately be seen to have more in common with Roy Fisher than have Thomas Hardy and Philip Larkin, Donald Davie's polemical *Thomas Hardy and British Poetry* of 1973 attempts to secure Fisher's work for a native British tradition, stemming from Hardy and leading to Larkin, that, civic-minded and politically responsible, involves "an apparent meanness of spirit, a painful modesty of intention, and extremely limited objectives."[9] There has been little avoiding Davie's influential book in discussions of Fisher, and nearly every commentary on his work addresses it at one point or another. It is particularly difficult for me to pass it by, because my anthology is the one that Davie has in mind in his "Afterword for the American Reader" when he talks about "anthologies of British poetry since 1945" that are "now on offer to the American reader" but that leave out Philip Larkin and are hostile to the native, Hardyesque tradition.[10] There was, in fact, no conspiracy of anthologies in 1970; there was just my book—still, alas, the last anthology of exclusively British poetry to be published in the United States. And however inadequate it may have been in some respects, I *do* think it placed Fisher's work in the proper context—with poetry, by those whose names were listed earlier, that is modernist, experimental, and wide open to a range of influences from abroad.

Davie finds Fisher's concerns to be "social" rather than "human," his sentiments to be anti-Lawrencian in their derivation from a realism that "sees intensities and ecstasies . . . only as so many dangerous distractions," and his work through the Fulcrum Press *Collected Poems*, and particularly in *City*, to be a kind that excludes tragedy in favor of pathos. Facing a real world in the real Birmingham, Fisher, Davie feels, tells hard truths: "One responds to [a section of prose quoted from *City*] as one responds to Larkin's 'Whitsun Weddings': This is how it is!" And, like Larkin, Davie's Fisher is "fully aware of the bargain he is striking [in denying tragedy to render pathos], and he agrees to its humiliating terms."[11] But Fisher's concerns are almost entirely cognitive and aesthetic. Both tragedy *and* pathos seem beside the point, as does the distinction between content that is social and content that is human. And although Fisher is no D. H. Lawrence—a mistaken affinity invalidating much of J. D. Needham's initial response to Davie in an article of 1975—he has intensities of his own and is not a Larkinesque poet of defeat, settling for what Davie calls a "hobbit-world of reduced expectation."[12]

Thomas Hardy and British Poetry was written before the publication of *Matrix, The Cut Pages, The Thing About Joe Sullivan*, or *A Furnace*. But Davie did have *The Ship's Orchestra* and "Three Ceremonial Poems" before him, and he did not like them at all. Here perhaps we arrive at the crux. Although Davie is willing to admire the technique of "making strange" in a poem like "As He Came Near Death," he recoils sharply when "the full battery of resources" that Fisher has derived from Russian modernism is deployed. Fisher has called himself at various times a "1920s Russian modernist," and Davie's point is that Fisher's allegiance to a nondiscursive poetics in *The Ship's Orchestra* and "Three Ceremonial Poems" is, in his view, "mannered, wasteful, and perverse." Specifically, in the case of "Three Ceremonial Poems," such a poetics—deriving, Davie supposes, chiefly from the practice of Mandelstam and Pasternak—prevents Fisher from making definitive judgments.[13]

But Fisher is not, whether in "Three Ceremonial Poems," *The Ship's Orchestra*, or *City*, in the business of making definitive judgments. He is in the business of building fictive verbal structures, sometimes definitive and sometimes indeterminate. And if we are to invoke the poetics of Acmeism or the theories of Victor Shklovsky,[14] we should also consider that other Russian modernism—the modernism of constructivists like Malevich and Tatlin, together with their Bauhaus contemporaries and assemblagist successors—because Fisher has always been deeply influenced by visual art, and, when he describes his work, it is more frequently by way of an analogy with painting, printmaking, or music than by way of comparison with the practice of other poets. Instead of viewing *City* as a discursive mix of verse and prose that seeks to arrive at a judgment about life in Birmingham, it would be better to see it as Fisher does himself—as an assemblage in which a fictive world is made from the signs and names of real things (*GI*, 34). Both assemblage and constructivism use materials out of the real world to make an object that has never existed in that world before, an object that does not reflect or represent it but takes its place in it, fits beside or among the very objects from which it has taken the materials out of which it has been made, but as a thing apart.

Although the dominant idiom of the several at work in *City* differs substantially from those of *The Ship's Orchestra* and "Three Ceremonial Poems," nonetheless passages from all three works could be interchanged in such a way as to severely test a reader's sense of how strange "making strange" can get before it grows to be "mannered, wasteful, and perverse" or seems to crop up in an inappropriate context.[15] (Had Fisher played in a ship's orchestra for twenty years without ever setting foot on land, and had he only seen photographs of Birmingham in a book, which of his two major early works would critics confidently call "mimetic," and which "hermetic"?) Fisher's assemblage in *City* is made from a wide range of English idioms— from the sharply denotative to the weirdly surrealistic—and not, of course, from things. The figures gathering objects and materials in the section called "Starting to Make a Tree" are making a *physical* assemblage in an irregular, radial form (like *City* itself) from "a great flock mattress," "two carved chairs," "chicken-wire," "tarpaulin," "a smashed barrel," "lead piping," and "leather of all kinds," while Fisher is making an assemblage out of those words (the words in quotes), along with others. More than that, some of the parts that comprise the larger assemblage of *City* as a whole are themselves, as parts, discursive. But the final effect of the work is neither that of discourse nor of a form, as Davie insists, with a center, nor indeed of a judgment being rendered or a message being delivered about the politics or social history of British urban life. The effect is stranger, finally, than much in Mandelstam and Pasternak because *City* really does have the *feel* of assemblage in visual art—as described, for example, by Lawrence Alloway.

> Its source is obsolescence, the throwaway material of cities, as it collects in drawers, cupboards, attics, dustbins, gutters, waste lots, and city dumps. Objects have a history: first they are brand new goods; then they are possessions, accessible to few, subjected, often, to intimate and repeated use; then, as waste, they are scarred by use but available again. . . . Assemblages of such material come at the spectator as bits of life, bits of the environment. The urban

environment is present, then, as the source of objects, whether transfigured or left alone.[16]

Fisher's objects, whether imported from Birmingham, other cities, literature, or works of art,[17] are usually much larger than those identified by Alloway or those collected in "Starting to Make a Tree"—they are typically buildings, street lamps, statues, oil drums, viaducts, cisterns, girders, buses, and windows—but the mind moves among them as the eye moves among the objects of a Louise Nevelson sculpture or, to return to my drive through Studebaker Corridor, among objects under glass in an assemblage as defined by anthropology, "a group of artifacts found together in a closed context of association."[18]

I think Roy Fisher had probably read *Thomas Hardy and British Poetry* by the time he gave his interview to Jed Rasula and Mike Erwin in the year of its publication (1973). More recently, he has objected to Davie's treatment of his work in an interview with Robert Sheppard and in a letter to John Ash,[19] but even in 1973 he must have had in mind Davie, or at least a critic of the same temperament, when he referred to "quite skilled readers who will very characteristically go at my work from the representational end or the end which appears to have morality in it" (*GI*, 25). It is extremely interesting that in the same interview Fisher reveals that an earlier book by Davie, *Ezra Pound: Poet As Sculptor*, provided a source for the very aspect of his work that these skilled readers are bent on exaggerating—the representational, or the realist (*GI*, 32). Now I have not intended in what I have written thus far to suggest that a mimetic impulse does not exist in Fisher, only that its job is usually the production of parts that take their place in configurations in which the effect of the whole is nonmimetic, as in assemblage or constructivist art. But it is necessary now to qualify this claim by considering the nature of the subject in Fisher's work, the "I" that perceives, creates, moves among his images, and, finally, becomes itself an object in an overall design.

I mentioned at the outset the titles of two early poems, "For Realism" and "The Memorial Fountain." In the latter, the speaker looking at the fountain describes himself as "a thirty-five-year-old man, / poet / by temper realist . . . / working to distinguish an event from an opinion." In the *Grosseteste* interview, Fisher tells us that he was looking at two things when he wrote "The Memorial Fountain"—"a very vulgar thing," the fountain, that was "an actual reality which looked fictive," and passages in Davie's book on Pound in which Davie "makes a good deal of play with ideas about realism," saying that "there's something of a joke going on." The joke had to do with the fact that "what I was portraying was already rendered, that the rendering was real" (GI, 32), and certainly, too, with the fact that this realist, looking at passages in Davie, was not, or not any longer, the sort of representational writer whose realism Davie might want to sponsor—and later would think he had in the chapter on Fisher in *Thomas Hardy and British Poetry*.

In a recent article, John Ash describes the speaker of the poem as "a realist for whom realism is no longer adequate," quoting from an earlier moment in the *Grosseteste* interview where Fisher says, "I find it a bit of an irritation to make fictive things which look fictive in order to show that I am not merely a brute documentary writer." And so he "plays with" a landscape that "didn't need to be rendered fictive since it WAS so."[20] But the interest here is really in the subject, the speaker, the observer who, in the companion poem, writes about what is required "For Realism." And I think the orientation of this observer is best approached as Fisher suggests we approach a passage in "Five Morning Poems from a Picture by Manet," taking it as a "sort of sortie or sally from which I've withdrawn, or withdrew pretty quickly" (GI, 22).

All of this is to say that the observer in the early poems, including *City*, is a less stable figure than we might suppose. Davie takes the speaker in *City* to be the poet himself speaking in his own voice, finding there to be no grounds "for thinking that the 'I' of the poem is a persona behind which the poet conceals himself."[21] Fisher, on the other hand, sees the observer as "dramatized" and as "wedging himself into a Byronic posture" in which he "speaks as if afflicted in his sensibilities" (GI, 36). Peter Barry has said that neither in *City* nor in "The Handsworth Liberties" (the first sections of which were published in the same *Grosseteste* pamphlet that contains the interview) does Fisher avoid turning people into specimens, or things.[22] But Fisher does not attempt to avoid this, and indeed the subject—the "I" that is responsible for the process—is the most conspicuous specimen in the poem, correctly identified by Barry as the Romantic solitary, the "I" as an "eye," looking (as it does, disembodied, from the cover of Fisher's *Collected Poems*), but also seen, objectified, thinged (as it also is on the cover).

> I . . . see no ghosts of men and women, only the gigantic ghost of stone . . .
>
> I . . . see people made of straws, rags, cartons . . . kitchen refuse . .

> I stare into the dark . . .
>
> I see . . . as it might be floating in the dark . . .
>
> I have often felt myself to be vicious, in living so much by the

eye . . .

> I want to believe I live in a single world. That is why I am keeping my eyes at home while I can. The light keeps on separating the world like a table knife: it sweeps across what I see and suggests what I do not. The imaginary comes to me with as much force as the real, the remembered with as much force as the immediate. The countries on the map divide and pile up like ice-floes . . . I feel only a belief that I should not be here.[23]

But being "here"—there, in the assemblage—is the condition required for arriving at what may be *City*'s most radical, and of course unforeseen, anticipation of *A Furnace*: the implication that we cannot know objective reality at all; that we inhabit our minds and know what they have built; that we are the process of our building and are also all the bricks. That is why "each thought is at once translucent and icily capricious." And if Pound thought the gods were eternal states of mind and that they manifest themselves when such states of mind take form, then Fisher's "polytheism without gods" is a remarkable way to describe the transience of his observer's thoughts, which partly form the multifaceted assemblage in which he is himself assembled, the parts of which—if something must be imitated—may yet mime, like the works on exhibit of that foundry patternmaker in "Diversions," "the comportment of the gods," whom the observer's polytheism does without.

But Fisher is not entirely happy with the speaker/observer in *City* because, although not identical with the autobiographical, social self—what Fisher calls, following Michael Hamburger, the "empirical self"[24]—he "hasn't got the discontinuous self . . . which I would claim to have portrayed in later writing" (*GI*, 36). Also, of course, the experience of the dramatized speaker/ observer overlaps—doubtless through exaggeration—with certain aspects of Fisher's own experience. Although Fisher wishes, in retrospect, that he had not created such a romantic/dramatic presence in *City*, he does not want his poems spoken by the voice of the empirical self, either. Of "The Entertainment of War," that section of *City* in which the speaker probably comes closest to reproducing specific details of Fisher's autobiographical past, Fisher says that these stanzas "about some of my relatives getting killed in an air raid" are "the thing most untypical of anything I believe about poetry that I ever wrote" (*GI*, 25). And in "The Poplars," he writes of needing "to withdraw / From what is called my life / And from my net / of assembled desires" both in order "to know" adequately the objects, represented here by the poplars, that he would engage in his writing—he will learn that he cannot "know" them, although he can fit them into his constructions well enough—and also to avoid becoming "a cemetery of performance" in his life outside his art.

One way of "withdrawing from his life" is to create a dramatic persona and externalize it in his poetry, something that Fisher feels he has done, if not in "The Entertainment of War" and "The Poplars," then in most of the rest of *City*. Another way is constantly and consciously to probe away at the empirical self in an attempt to locate a cognitive self, as it were, buried beneath it and then "try to steer a sufficiently agile course [that you] may be able to see the back of your own head" (*GI*, 33). This is a matter, in Rimbaud's terms, of locating the "I" that is being thought, rather than the "I" that is thinking. In "Of the Empirical Self and for Me" Fisher writes,

> In my poems there's seldom
> any *I* or *you*—
>   you know me, Mary;
>   you wouldn't expect it of me—[25]

and many of the shorter poems on this subject are almost jokes, poems that Peter Barry has called the poet's "wry explanations of why he must remain in the corner he has written himself into."[26] But I'm certain that Fisher regards this corner not, as Barry implies, as one that constrains him as a poet, but rather as the very corner he must inhabit to be free to understand constraint itself and to write the kind of poems he wishes to compose. As he has said in the *Grosseteste* interview, "[It] seems to me a very honorable thing to try . . . to catch time or the limits of the perceptive field at [their] tricks of limiting consciousness of the world" (*GI*, 33). But how, exactly, is this to be done, and what new kinds of forms emerge from the processes adopted after *City* and the *Collected Poems* of 1969? The journey to *A Furnace*, Fisher's masterpiece and his revision of *City*, is a long one, with major stages on the way recorded in "The Cut Pages," "Stopped Frames and Set Pieces," "Metamorphoses," "Matrix," "Handsworth Liberties," "Diversions," "New Diversions," and "Wonders of Obligation," the eight cycles that I think comprise Fisher's most important work after *City* and *The Ship's Orchestra*, and before *A Furnace*. It will be useful, however, before looking at three of these cycles, to consider a very recent poem about the empirical self in order to understand why Fisher's later constructions are so bent on excluding it.

> Often it will start without me and come soon to where I once was
> whereupon I am able for a while to speak freely . . .
> >   I have never chosen
> to speak about what I have
> myself said, seldom of what I have done.
> Though these things are my life
> they have not the character of truth I require.
>
> . . . .
> Often it will start without me. More truthfully
> other than without me it wouldn't, I have to be away . . .
> >   taking that walk is compulsory, for
> there's something about me
> I don't want around at such moments—maybe
> my habit of not composing . . .
>
> . . . .
> Whatever I start from
> I go for the laws of its evolution,

> de-socializing art, diffusing it
> through the rest till there's no escaping it. Art talks
>
> of its own processes, or talks about the rest
> in terms of the processes of art; or stunts itself
> to talk about the rest in the rest's own terms
> of crisis and false report—entertainment,
> that worldliness that sticks to me
> so much I get sent outside
> when the work wants to start[27]

For the poetry, the work of art, to begin, the empirical self must be somehow gotten round, sent on a walk, outwitted. Otherwise, it will take over the process of writing and talk about itself, socialize art, grow worldly, discuss the evening news. "The Lesson in Composition," the poem from which I have quoted, appears among the most recent work in *Poems 1955–87*, echoing the notion that "the poem has always / already started" from "If I Didn't," in *The Thing About Joe Sullivan*, and anticipates a key passage from the beginning of *A Furnace*:

> Something's decided
> to narrate
> in more dimensions than I can know
> the gathering in
> and giving out of the world on a slow
> pulse . . .[28]

What is involved here, I think, is a freeing of *poiesis* in the cognitional self through a kind of Heideggerian openness to language that augments Fisher's openness to perceptual stimulation, even to the point of hallucination, leading to an art that goes about its proper work, that "talks of its own processes, or talks about the rest / in terms of the processes of art," and to the effacing of the autobiographical, social, empirical "I" that does not know, to borrow the conclusion of Fisher's poem for Michael Hamburger, "the language / language gets my poems out of."[29] What "will often start without me," what "has always already started," the "something" that "has decided to narrate," is an active process that Fisher seeks to enter in various ways and, moreover, one that leads him to a place in which his experience of the process is intensified and deepened—a place first discovered in the isolation and fear of a youthful illness that he now identifies as the location of his imagination, combining "a sense of lyrical remoteness with an apprehension of something turbulent, bulky, and dark."[30] The methods of entry into the process—and through it to the place—vary from work to work, but they may be seen to begin afresh after the 1969 *Collected Poems* in the rapid association of improvisation and to end in the high artifice of Vorticist construction.

It was through an improvisational piece, "The Cut Pages," that Fisher managed to work his way through a severe writing block that had cut off composition entirely between 1966 and 1970. In some ways, the practice of improvisation is related to the automatic writing with which he had experimented as early as 1956 after having been introduced to the work of Americans like Zukofsky, Creeley, and Olson, the effect of which was intended "to get me out of my own way." In an introductory note to *The Cut Pages*, Fisher tells us that the improvisations in the title piece are intended "to give the words as much relief as possible from serving in planned situations; so the work was taken forward with no programme beyond the principle that it should not know where its next meal was coming from. It was unable to anticipate, but it could have on the spot whatever it could manage to ask for. This method produced very rapid changes of direction"[31]— and certainly also got rid of the empirical "I."

The method in "The Cut Pages" suggests not only an analogy with Fisher's experience of playing jazz, in which, when one musician takes over the improvisation from another or begins to work variations on a known theme, the music "has always already started," but also Heidegger's notion of language speaking through our listening when, as Gerald Bruns has said, "nothing gets signified . . . but things make their appearance in the sense of coming into their own."[32] It is difficult to quote effectively from "The Cut Pages," but this is the way the work begins:

> Coil   If you can see the coil hidden in this pattern, you're
>   colour-blind
>   Pale patterns, faded card, coral card, faded card,
>   screen card, window fade

Whorl   If you can see this word and say it without hesitation
you're deaf
Then we can get on with frame

Frameless Meat rose, dog-defending, trail-ruffling[33]

Once the improvisation, the listening that has given access to a process, produces materials out of which to build a form, serial construction gets under way, a construction that Fisher regards to be methodical and systematic—"self-branching and self-proliferating," he calls it (*GI*, 34)—but different from the "additive" technique first explored in *The Ship's Orchestra* and developed in "Matrix," "Handsworth Liberties," and other cycles.[34] But in "The Cut Pages," as in these other works, Fisher characteristically creates a model of certain precincts of the place to which the process leads and in which it continues to unfold, that mental space discovered in his illness— and later identified with very early memories unlocked by words—characterized by "lyrical remoteness and an apprehension of something turbulent, bulky, and dark."

The way this works will become clearer by looking at "Handsworth Liberties," a poem that at first glance would seem to have much in common with *City*. It represents a process analogous to the one in full view in Fisher's recent "Home Pianist's Companion," in which, in the course of actual piano improvisations, what appears to be "a disorder of twofold sense"—visual images asserting themselves as the pianist concentrates on his playing—turns out in fact to be "an order thinking for me as I play." The act of listening to his own playing projects "an image trail" for the pianist across "what looked like emptiness" all the way to "the utterly forgotten,"[35] a vestigial figure from a lost time who resurfaces also in *A Furnace*, "primitively remembered, / just a posture of her, an apron, / a gait." But the analogous process is hardly in full view in the "Handsworth Liberties." For some time, in fact, it was deliberately hidden.

Fisher described his method of composition in the Handsworth poem only after it had been in print for five years.[36] It derived, it seems, from a sequence of associations that developed between certain recorded performances of music and the mental images that, in each case, came into his mind when he first heard them. All of the images are associated with various locations in the Handsworth area of Birmingham as it existed in his youth. Eddie Condon's "Home Cooking" produced "a pleasant sunny morning on the stretch of grass outside what was then Holmes's Garage at the junction of Church Lane and Grove Lane"; Billy Banks's "Spider Crawl" had its existence "somewhere in the air of a leafy and peaceful suburban street called Butler's Road, viewed from the north-east"; Beethoven's *Arietta* and its variations from the piano sonata *Opus 111*—for not all the music consisted of jazz improvisations—were "tucked up under the branches that used to overhang a long-disappeared set of railings" a little way along the same road that elsewhere contained Ralph Vaughan Williams's "Fantasia on a Theme of Thomas Tallis."[37] And so on.

In the poems, Fisher provides a small gallery of sixteen mental snapshots, the process that has "always already started" when he hears the music having given access to one precinct of his mental space—call it "Handsworth, Birmingham"—out of which the images, not quite of "places," more like "the backgrounds and marginal details of photographs and postcards,"[38] issued as language: on Butler's Road, at the junction of Church Lane and Grove Lane, tucked under the branches that used to overhang a set of railings. The character of the listening is different here from what it amounts to in "The Cut Pages," but it is still listening. And the individual scenes lead downward toward the penultimate, all of them pointing finally toward that zone that is "turbulent, bulky, dark, and lyrically remote."

> No dark in the body
> deep as this
>   even though the sun
> hardens the upper world.
>   A ladder
> climbs down under the side
> in the shadow of the tank
> and crosses tarry pools.
>   There are
> metals that burn the air;
> a deathly blue stain

> in the cinder ballast
> and out there past the shade
> sunlit rust hangs on the still water.[39]

Like "Matrix," which preceded it, "Handsworth Liberties" has to do with
"getting about in the mind" and locating there materials in a visual memory
that is, Fisher says, "hallucinatory to a stupefying degree" (*GI*, 21). The scenes
in the cycle, cut off for the reader from a music that the poet does not cease
to hear, arrange themselves in silence. But we are involved, without our
fully knowing it, with Fisher's listening, his "diffusing of art through all the
rest [of experience] till there is no escaping it," his "talk about the rest in
terms of the processes of art," and his search for a self that is thought by
language that "will start without me and come soon to where I once was."

"Matrix," the title sequence of Fisher's 1971 volume, is as deceptive in
the initial impression it makes as the "Handsworth Liberties" and grows
even stranger than the later poem when we understand the manner in which
the poet enters a process that has already begun when he starts to write. At
first glance, the ten sections look like brief descriptive pieces treating a coastal
area that seems to include islands, inlets, shingle, gardens, paths, and so
on—a kind of seaside parallel to one's first impression of the urban "scenes"
in "Handsworth Liberties." But again we are dealing with a mental rather
than an actual physical place, and again also with a configuration that involves "the diffusing of art through all the rest [of experience] till there is
no escaping it." This is how Fisher describes the work's origin:

> The sequence of ten poems called "Matrix," from which the book
> takes its name, is probably the most developed piece of work in
> verse I have done, a comparatively rich mix of allusions and sen-
> sory imagery. Some while ago, without warning, I had one of those
> curious near-hallucinatory experiences in which one is able to stand
> outside one's mind and watch its oddly assorted memories quickly
> reprogramming themselves to make new forms. On this occasion
> there was a rain of images which seemed to be joining one another
> according to some logic of their own. They were nearly all to do
> with works of art; and I could see impressions from Bocklin, Claude

> Monet, Thomas Mann and lurid tourist souvenirs from Japan, among many others, forming up into relationships which I should never have presumed to try to impose on them consciously. The complex collective image they made was still present after some months had passed, and the poems of the sequence are a sort of tour of its interior.[40]

The looking (as from the outside) at the mind's display becomes a listening when the language of Mann's *Dr. Faustus* mingles with the names of things in Monet, Bocklin, and postcards from Japan, in the dictation of Fisher's muse as mental programmer and tour guide. There is, that is to say, an element of automatism once again implicit in this process. But "Matrix" is also, according to Fisher (writing, of course, before the composition of *A Furnace*), "the most developed piece of work in verse I have done," and the development involves the construction of individual units from the "complex collective image," which he describes elsewhere as the breaking up of—or separating out of details from—something like an immensely complex color slide or stained glass window (*GI*, 21).[41] There is an externalization, through language, of the mental images and an objectification of them through austerities of form that once again recall the Russian Constructivists and anticipate the Vorticist affinities of *A Furnace*. As Marjorie Perloff writes about an early Malevich, quoting Roman Jacobson on Khlebnikov, Fisher's cycle manifests characteristics of *nanizyvanie*, "the conjoining of motifs which do not proceed on the basis of logical necessity but are combined according to the principle of formal necessity, similarity or contrast" and has the effect "of dispelling the autonomy of the lyrical I," a version of the self no less problematic for Fisher than the despised empirical "I."[42] (One could also apply the notion of *nanizyvanie* to the work of Fisher's frequent collaborator, Tom Phillips, whose illustration appears on the cover of *Matrix*.) In the cycle, the lyrical "I," which otherwise might speak—or, God help us, even sing—is effectively dispelled in favor of an implied cognitive self whose perceptions are broken down, sorted out, and labeled through the agency of Mann, Bocklin, and Monet. In the "Handsworth Liberties" a version of the "I" appears twice (in sections 12 and 13), but in the most equivocal way possible, where "Travesties of the world / come out of the fog / and rest at the boundary" leading (in section 12) to the conclusion that "I shall go with them / sometimes / till the journey dissolves under me," and where Fisher writes (in section 13) of a slope in the mist: "I / never went there / Someone else did, and I went with him." Through various contortions in the poems of the 1970s and early 1980s, Fisher seeks to see, through the eyes of this equivocal "I" and through the agency of artworks, "the back of [his] own head" (as he has it in the *Grosseteste* interview) and, in a manner analogous to that of *City*, to make the perceiver a fundamental property of the thing perceived, even as the thing perceived becomes a fundamental process in the perceiver's act of writing, always already begun. As he writes in a poem to Tom Phillips:

> Caught sight of myself
> in the monitor
>
> The world looked like itself
> I looked like it too
> not like me
> as if I was
> solid or something
> . . . .
> It's not hard to look busy
> from behind[43]

In what is perhaps the most impassioned moment in the *Grosseteste* interview, Fisher returns to the sources of his art in jazz, painting, and printmaking, saying that "I very often turn to people who do a very small thing and do it again and do it again and do it again and vary and vary and vary" (*GI*, 30). He cites the musicians Pee Wee Russell, Jess Stacey, and Eddie Condon, and also the three minutes available to such musicians on one side of a 78 rpm record—brief takes and retakes, music that "fills and exhausts, fills and exhausts," something that becomes "a life" (*GI*, 31). And he turns again to the printmakers and illustrators—ultimately to Paul Klee—for what can surely be taken as an analogue to the "additive method" in the cycles that I have examined as typical of his work leading from *City* to *A Furnace*:

> Again you do a thing, and you haven't exhausted it, you haven't inflated it, and you do it again, same size. You do a thing which is slightly different, you turn it backwards, do it again, nothing is wasted. You stick to what you first thought of, you do it again. This appeals to me enormously. The idea of Klee working away at things, having a theory, and doing many variants, many alphabets, many grids, and having an apparently inexhaustible source of statements and restatements which are like frames, like hours, like days, very simple conceptions. I like that. (*GI*, 31)

This would also seem to describe Fisher himself at work. And the artist's rage "to make visible with charged energy," as Klee wrote from the Bauhaus, rather than merely seeking "to render the visible," is Fisher's rage.[44] It takes him just about as far from the poetics of Philip Larkin as it is possible to be.

Fisher has said that he seeks to avoid allowing his cycles to "solidify" or to "turn into a collection of colour slides" by stalking up on "a perceptual field jammed solid with sensory data" and breaking it up into mobile, unstable parts (*GI*, 21). Nonetheless, if I were to posit an analogy for the cumulative effect of typical Fisher sequences and cycles consistent with his statement about Paul Klee, it would be something like a slide show—the "Handsworth Liberties" he called "a gallery of sixteen mental snapshots"— or an exhibition of prints that would come to mind. In a very early poem, Fisher wrote of looking out a window "that holds what few events come round / like slides, and in what seems capricious sequence," and there is something of that feeling in an initial reading of the "Glenthorne Poems," "Matrix," "Handsworth Liberties," "Diversions," "New Diversions," and, in a rather different way, the earlier "Stopped Frames" and "Seven Attempted Moves." But repeated readings show us that these sequences are far more systematic than capricious—sufficiently systematic in the poet's convoluted treatment of cognition that we might even be reminded of the subject-object relationship in a work of M. C. Escher's, such as *Print Gallery*, an etching in which the observer, a man at an exhibition of prints, is ultimately found to be standing inside the same work of art he is viewing. About this etching Francisco Varela has drawn the following conclusions—conclusions that it is tempting to apply to Fisher in his sequences and cycles:

We find ourselves in a cognitive domain, and we cannot leap out of it or choose its beginnings or modes. . . . In finding the world as we do, we forget all we did to find it as such, entangled in the strange loop of our actions through our body. Much like the young man in the Escher engraving "Print Gallery," we see a world that turns into the very substratum which produces us, thereby closing the loop and intercrossing domains. As in the Escher engraving, there is nowhere to step out into. And if we were to try, we would find ourselves in an endless circle that vanishes into an empty space right in its middle.[45]

"No system describes the world," Fisher writes of a projected film at the end of "Metamorphoses," and one must be consistent on this point, turning from his poems that can be thought about as if they were a run of slides or prints lining up to form an Escher loop to the "system" of the double spiral in *A Furnace*. But Fisher's vortex in this magnificent poem, like the works of the foundry patternmaker in section 18 of "Diversions," from which I quoted very early in this essay, *engages* the world it cannot describe by virtue of fulfilling analogous "conditions of myth":

> it celebrates origin,
> it fixes forms for endless recurrence;
> it relates energy to form;
> is useless in itself;
>
> for all these reasons it also attracts
> aesthetic responses in anybody
> free to respond aesthetically;
> and it can be thought with; . . .

One thing that Fisher wants to think about in *A Furnace* is time, and he tells us in a preface that the sequence of the poem's movements "is based on a form which enacts, for me, the equivocal nature of the ways in which time can be thought about. This is the ancient figure of the double spiral, whose line turns back on itself at the centre and leads out again, against its own incoming curve."[46]

Were there space left to do so, I think we might profitably extend the several connections made thus far between Fisher's work and the Constructivist-Bauhaus-Assemblagist aesthetic by listening to the turning of the double spiral in *A Furnace* as an elegiac backward-looking version of the forward-striding double spiral of Tatlin's famous Tower, the wooden model for his "Monument to the Third International," and answer to Eiffel's engineers, which looked with such optimism into the industrial-communal future, but which was never built and which, as much now as in the time of his Icarus glider, is an emblem of something archaic in the way of human aspiration. Of Tatlin, too, as of the foundry patternmaker, Fisher might have said: *"Everything cast in iron / must first be made of wood."* And that such casts might mime "the comportment / of the gods in the Ethnology cases."

What there is just space enough to do is to indicate that Fisher's examination of the subject-object relationship in the context of a process that has "always already started" reaches its fullest development in this book. It would take an essay the length of what I have already written to explain the workings of so complex a poem, but I can suggest a few continuities by glossing the titles of the first two parts, "Calling" and "The Return," by way of extending for a few lines a passage from the "Introit," quoted earlier:

> Something's decided
> to narrate in more dimensions than I can know
> the gathering in
> and giving out of the world on a slow
> pulse, on a metered contraction
> that the senses enquire towards
> but may not themselves
> intercept. All I can tell it by
> is the passing trace of it
> in a patterned agitation of
> a surface that shows only
> metaphors. Riddles. Resemblances
> that have me in the chute
> as it meshes in closer, many modes
> funnelling fast through one event, . . .[47]

From this passage, the subject (the speaker, the "I"), which is clearly part of the process under observation—those "resemblances that have [him] in the chute" of the vortex—emerges, "having eased awkwardly / into the way of being called," in section 1. At the level of narrative, this calling comes to an urban man from Gradbach Hill, a mysterious corner of North-West Staffordshire that includes Lud's Church and its legendary connection with *Sir Gawain and the Green Knight*, and thus suggests initiation and change. I also take this calling to suggest both the perfectly traditional notion of a poet's being called to practice his or her craft and the calling into existence of an internal energy externalized in the figure of the vortex and of the impulse to "make identities," which Fisher says in his preface acknowledges "a primary impulse in the cosmos."[48] In cosmological terms—and the poet has gone to school for this poem on the visionary novels of John Cowper Powys, to whom it is also dedicated—Fisher's Heraclitean cauldron, through which all lines of his vortex pass, explodes the matter of what was Birmingham into something like a verbal analogue to an expanding universe. *City*, in comparison, is a steady state.

In a brilliant and so far unpublished essay on *A Furnace*, Andrew Crozier makes some observations that will help me to conclude.[49] He remarks that although philosophically Fisher is not a realist, neither is he a nominalist, "for he is not concerned with real existences as such but with the signs they make by which they can be evoked. His interest in knowledge concerns cognitive modes rather than positive knowledge, and he sees its boundary fluctuating with intention. The laws of the Newtonian universe— the laws of the heavy industrial processes, and the commerce they served, that lie in ruins throughout *A Furnace*—fail to describe the involution of time and space in the mind's conjunction with the world." Where I disagree with Crozier—and where I must end—is in his contention that the mind's conjunction with the world in this poem does not "arrive, finally, at a heterodox mysticism." It seems to me that it does. "The Return," which no one, to my knowledge, has traced back to Ezra Pound's early poem of the same title or to Yeats's use of it in *A Vision*, is uncanny in its dealings with the dead. If in "Calling" the subject moves outward on the double spiral, in "The Return" the dead—the objects in this section of the subject's thought—return to earth along the incoming curve, grounded in the present by the act of being "called" into the memory of the subject, himself "called" into the infinite reaches of the cosmos by the objects of his thought. The poem is about the return of the dead, as Yeats thought Pound's poem was.[50]

> Whatever breaks
> from stasis, radiance or dark
> impending, and slides
> directly and fast on its way, twisting
> aspect in the torsions of the flow
> this way and that,
>   then suddenly
> over,
>   through a single
> glance of another force touching it or
> bursting out of it sidelong,
>
> doing so
> fetches the timeless flux
> that cannot help but practise
> materialization,
>
> .   .   .   .   .   .
>
> and it fetches
> timeless identities.
>
> .   .   .   .
>
> *like dark-finned fish embedded in ice*
> *they have life in them that can be revived.*
>
> .   .   .   .
>
> Something always
> coming out, back against the flow,
> against the drive to be in,
>   close to the radio,
> the school, the government's wars;
>
> the sunlight, old and still,
> heavy on dry garden soil,

and nameless mouths,
events without histories, voices,
animist, polytheist, metaphoric,
coming through; . . .[51]

Although these mouths, beings, and voices—including Fisher's own dead among his family and early neighbors—have "no news," they have a life in this poem in the poet's memory as disturbing as the politics of the dead in the life of the living in journeys to the underworld in Homer, Virgil, and Pound:

They come anyway
to the trench,
the dead in their surprise,
taking whatever form they can
to push across.[52]

It may seem ironic, given the way I began this essay, that I want to end by saying that it is probably Donald Davie, more than any other living critic, who is equipped to grapple with both the function of the vortex and the metaphysics in *A Furnace*. Davie the Poundian is not the same critic who wrote *Thomas Hardy and British Poetry*, and his approach to "Ideas in *The Cantos*," in his Modern Masters series volume on Pound could be usefully applied to analogous issues in *A Furnace*. His reluctance to write about the later Fisher—there is nothing on his work in Davie's recent *Under Briggflatts*—is a loss for Fisher's poetry, for Fisher's readers, and probably for Davie himself.[53]

Notes

1. Roy Fisher, "Diversions," part 18, in *Poems 1955–87* (Oxford: Oxford University Press, 1988), 138.

2. Roy Fisher, "City," in *Poems 1955–87*, 21.

3. Roy Fisher, *19 Poems and an Interview* (Pensett, Staffordshire: Grosseteste Press, 1975), 15, 17, 18. The interview was conducted on 19 November 1973 by Jed Rasula

and Mike Erwin, and it is the best source available for getting a sense of Fisher's intentions in his work up through at least the "Handsworth Liberties," nine parts of which appear among the 19 poems. It is subsequently referred to in notes as *Grosseteste Interview* and in text as *GI*.

4. The "Large Glass" refers, of course, to Marcel Duchamp's "The Bride Stripped Bare by Her Bachelors, Even." In "Then Hallucinations," the prose sequel to the 1962 Migrant Press edition of *City*, the following sentence appeared: "This city is like the Bride of Marcel Duchamp; and when she is stripped the Glass needs to be broken and carted away." Quoted in Peter Barry, "Language and the City in Roy Fisher's Poetry," *English Studies* 3 (1986): 234.

5. Ernst Von Glaserfield, "An Introduction to Radical Constructivism," in *The Invented Reality* (London and New York: W. W. Norton, 1984), 24. Had I not been such a realist on my drive through Studebaker Corridor, Fisher's language might have stimulated a sequence of perceptions that seemed to "fit" rather than to "match" or "correspond to" what we passed. Von Glaserfield writes: "The metaphysical realist looks for knowledge that matches reality. . . . In the epistemologist's case it is . . . some kind of 'homomorphism' [that concerns him], which is to say, an equivalence of relations, a sequence, or a characteristic structure—something, in other words, that he can consider the same, because only then could he say that his knowledge is of the world. . . . If, on the other hand, we say that something fits, we have in mind a different relation. A key fits if it opens the lock. The fit describes a capacity of the key, not of the lock" (21–22). Fisher sought a key for a topography presenting itself as "an indecipherable script." Such a key might fit in several locks—in Birmingham or elsewhere.

6. Fisher, "City," 29.

7. Christopher Logue, "Patroclia," in *23 Modern British Poets*, ed. John Matthias (Chicago: Swallow Press, 1971), 170.

8. Fisher, "The Thing About Joe Sullivan," in *Poems 1955–87*, 152.

9. Donald Davie, *Thomas Hardy and British Poetry* (London: Routledge & Kegan Paul, 1973), 11.

10. Ibid., 188.

11. Ibid., 152–72.

12. J. D. Needham, "Some Aspects of the Poetry of Roy Fisher," *Poetry Nation* 5 (winter 1975): 74–87.

13. Davie, *Thomas Hardy*, 166–67.

14. Along with Davie's argument, see Peter Barry, "Language and the City in Roy Fisher's Poetry," *English Studies* 67, no. 3 (June 1986): 234–49. Barry summarizes Shklovsky's famous doctrine by saying that "what literature does is to make us see reality as if for the first time by subverting our habitual modes of perception and 'making strange' things to which we have become so accustomed that we no longer really perceive them at all." This is certainly one of the things that Fisher is some-

times up to in his poems, and it is frequently discussed by his critics. But I am primarily interested in something rather different.

15. The following, for example, is from *The Ship's Orchestra*, not *City*: "Swung from the arms of the gaslamp that was the only light in the street; a street greenish black, among factories. The long linen sack was twisted round and round and was unknotting itself in slow revolutions, with all the weight at the bottom. As it turned, the moisture caught the light, coming through the fabric from top to bottom, but not dripping." And this is from *City*: "The creature began to divide and multiply . . . I could see people made of straws, rags, cartons, the stuffing of burst cushions, kitchen refuse . . . a long-boned carrot-haired girl with glasses, loping along, and with strips of bright colour, rich, silky green and blue, in her soft clothes. For a person made of such scraps she was beautiful."

16. Quoted in William C. Seitz, *The Art of Assemblage* (New York: Doubleday, 1961), 73.

17. John Ash insists in "A Classic Postmodernist" (*Atlantic Review*, n.s., 2 [autumn 1979]: 46) that Fisher's Birmingham is also Baudelaire's Paris and "the hallucinatory Petersburg of Andrei Bely and Aleksandr Blok (which is also Mandelstam's 'Petropolis'). Against all odds, Birmingham has become an aspect of Fisher's ideal, 'Pan-European city of art.' This is a triumph of art, but the triumph is accompanied by a sense of loss: the real city, the whole, escapes."

18. Allan Bullock and Oliver Stallybrass, *The Harper Dictionary of Modern Thought* (New York: Harper and Row, 1977), 39.

19. In the Sheppard interview, *Turning the Prism: An Interview with Roy Fisher* (London: Toads Damp Press, 1986), Fisher said, "I wasn't aware that [Davie had] exactly written about my work in that book," and to Ash he wrote that he was no part of a tradition ending with "a full house for Philip Larkin" (Ash, "A Classic Postmodernist," 44).

20. Ash, "A Classic Postmodernist," 46.

21. Davie, *Thomas Hardy*, 171.

22. Barry, "Language and the City," 246.

23. Fisher, "City," 21, 23, 27, 28 and 29.

24. See Michael Hamburger, *The Truth of Poetry* (New York: Harcourt Brace, 1969), chapters 2–4. Hamburger identifies this self as "the everyday person, the citizen and employee, the family man" and even the *"poet maudit* who might well have no servant to do his living for him" (58).

25. Roy Fisher, "Of the Empirical Self and for Me," in *Poems 1955–87*, 125.

26. Barry, "Language and the City," 248.

27. Roy Fisher, "The Lesson in Composition," in *Poems 1955-87*, 185–86.

28. Roy Fisher, "Introit: 12 November 1958," in *A Furnace* (Oxford and New York: Oxford University Press, 1986), 3.

29. Roy Fisher, "Style," in *Poems 1955–87*, 143.

30. *Contemporary Authors*, s.v. "Roy Fisher."

31. Roy Fisher, *The Cut Pages* (London: Fulcrum Press, 1971), 6–7.

32. Gerald L. Bruns, *Heidegger's Estrangements* (New Haven and London: Yale University Press, 1981), 164.

33. Fisher, *The Cut Pages*, 13.

34. Fisher has said that *The Ship's Orchestra*, "along with a lot of things I do," was rigorously composed in an additive form. That is, each section was written in an attempt to refer only to what I had already written in that work, and without any drive forward at all" (*GI*, 14). An improvisational work must obviously involve a "drive forward," however sharp its turns and "changes of direction."

35. Roy Fisher, "The Home Pianist's Companion," in *Poems 1955–87*, 168–69.

36. Roy Fisher, "Handsworth Compulsions," *Numbers* 2, no. 1 (spring 1987): 24–28.

37. Ibid., 25.

38. Ibid., 27.

39. Roy Fisher, "Handsworth Liberties," part 15, in *Poems 1955–87*, 123–24.

40. Jacket note to *Matrix* (London: Fulcrum Press, 1971).

41. Cf. the beginning of "Calling" in *A Furnace*, where the stained glass window of a church, broken by a pick handle or a boot, has been "cobbled / into a small / new window beside the Dee."

42. Marjorie Perloff, *The Futurist Moment* (Chicago: University of Chicago Press, 1986), 150.

43. Roy Fisher, "Correspondence," in *Poems 1955–87*, 94–95.

44. Paul Klee, "Creative Credo," in *Theories of Modern Art*, ed. Herschel B. Chipp (Berkeley: University of California Press, 1970), 182.

45. Francisco J. Varela, "The Creative Circle: Sketches on the Natural History of Circularity," in *The Invented Reality*, 320.

46. Fisher, preface to *A Furnace*, vii–viii.

47. Fisher, "Introit," 3–4.

48. It is also a genetic calling, in which the double vortex functions as the DNA molecule: "The ghosts' grown children / mill all day in the Public Search Office / burrowing out names for their own bodies. . . . Genetic behaviour, / scrabbling, feeling back across the spade-cut / for something; the back-flow of the genes' / forward compulsion. . . ."

49. This essay, "Signs of Identity," was originally intended for a Donald Davie Festschrift. An abbreviated version is scheduled for publication in *PN Review*. Crozier's anthology, *A Various Art* (Manchester: Carcanet Press, 1987), in a sense picks up where *23 Modern British Poets* ended, anthologizing Fisher's work with poetry by, among others, Anthony Barnett, David Chaloner, Veronica Forrest-Thomson, John James, Tim Longville, Douglas Oliver, J. H. Prynne, John Riley, Iain Sinclair, and Crozier himself. The passage is quoted with the author's permission.

50. It is also, like parts of "Calling," about a return to Nature and the country-side.

51. Fisher, part 2 of *A Furnace*, 11–14.

52. Ibid., 18.

53. My essay was written in 1992. Although Donald Davie died in 1995 at about the time this book was going to press, I have not revised the final paragraph. The dialogue, insofar as there is a dialogue going on here, was with a living critic. Davie's loss to British poetry and criticism is a very great one.

CHAPTER THREE

Poets of *A Various Art:*
J. H. Prynne,
Veronica Forrest-Thomson,
Andrew Crozier

Edward Larrissy

I

It is tempting to find a tendency among the poets who appear in
A Various Art, an anthology of some of the best to have made a kind of
name for themselves in British small presses and small magazines since the
1960s.[1] The editors, Andrew Crozier and Tim Longville, chose their title
precisely by way of disclaiming an overarching tendency. Yet they themselves are understandably willing to hazard a few generalizations; and all of
the most important of these include the word "American." Throughout the
sixties, much interest had been focused on American music, painting, and
writing, on American art in general.[2] In the particular case of poetry there
was a shift away from the tradition of "Pound and Eliot" toward that of
"Pound and Williams"—a coded reference to Olson and the Black Mountain
poets.[3] And, finally, there was the example of American poets taking their
fates into their own hands by starting their own publishing houses and
journals.[4] It does not require the most rigorous reading of this anthology
to confirm the impression that, formally, most of these poets are to a greater
or lesser degree influenced by the American metaphor of "open form."

Yet the editors are right to emphasize variety. Granted, many of these
poets write "open-ended" stanzas and poems or other "open" forms where
lines or stanzas move around the page in expressive ways. But only intermittently does this volume accord with Olson's Romantic objectivism, or

with his mistrust of "words, words, words" and their interposition between poet and living experience. The reason is hinted at by the editors, who refer to "different procedures and affective states of language": not all these poets, but many of them, employ language with a biting expressiveness or a knowing self-consciousness about discourse, which are beyond the ken of Olson's theories and of his practice. The overall impression, though not everywhere confirmed, is of a meeting and a tension between two currents in modernism: one the specifically American, which espouses a dynamic notion of the objective and seeks radical formal methods, but often undemonstrative diction, to embody it; the other, which is cognizant of the materiality of language and discourse, and is at least congruent with the insights of structuralism and poststructuralism, if not actually indebted to them. In some cases, notably that of Jeremy Prynne, the two currents flow strongly together, and the tension is usually fruitful. In general, the great interest of some of these poets resides in a kind of high typicality. That is to say, here are further developments in a tension between two areas of exploration that have characterized Anglo-American modernism since its inception; and here is some of the most considered poetic theory and practice in the English-speaking world. In what follows I should like to look at three poets who exemplify different reactions to the tension I have identified.

II

In his approach to stanzaic form and lineation, Prynne is clearly indebted to Olson. Where stanzas are employed, the sense runs fluidly through, with a careful consciousness of the emphasis created by line endings and beginnings. Unlike Olson, however, Prynne deploys the full variety of syntax; he often uses precise and varied punctuation; and he gives his poems a rounded shape, with firm beginnings and with endings of conclusive or resonant closure. When these characteristics consort, as they fairly often do, with elements of discursiveness (which are perhaps encouraged by certain aspects of Olson), one feels the ghostly presence of the poetic essay. Ghostly: for this presence has to live with elements of calculated indeterminacy that render it fuzzy, especially in the matter of identifying links between images and gauging the precise reference of pronouns. The establishment of a putative context or an internal coherence is deliberately impeded. But one is frequently offered hints that it may be possible. When one combines this realization with the apprehension of the poems' roundedness and address, one may be reminded, in a very general way, of Ashbery's half-proffered but endlessly deferred naturalization.

Nevertheless, the point about Olson offers a convenient way into both Prynne's practice and his preoccupations. Olson's intent, as recorded in "Projective Verse," was to permit the text to become a record of the poet's energy in process. But "Composition by Field" is not merely an attempt to find a quasi-scientific terminology for making a poem that is "a high energy-construct and, at all points, an energy-discharge."[5] It is also a reference to the poet's venturing into a field and going by a "track": "From the moment he ventures into FIELD COMPOSITION—puts himself in the open—he can go by no track other than the one the poem under hand declares, for itself."[6] The idea of the poem's proceeding by a track, or of tracing the track of the poet's consciousness, is present also in Prynne. One sees it in lineation and stanza form, as I have suggested, but also in the constant deployment, in many poems, of rhetorical devices intended to convey spontaneous reflection—exclamation, rhetorical question, and so on. And, finally, it appears as a theme in some of the poems: "Even / in this modern age we leave tracks, as we / go" ("Frost and Snow Falling" [*VA*, 242/*P*, 70]). At this point one can see a suggestion of how "tracking" is so fundamental an aspect of the individual consciousness that it is also a much-ignored aspect of social consciousness, though one that, Prynne seems to think, will increasingly be recognized. In "Aristeas, in Seven Years" (*P*, 89–95) he records the journey of a Pontic Greek into the Asian territories of the Scythians and other peoples professing shamanistic religions. I think Donald Davie is right to see as relevant to an interpretation of this poem the fact that "it seems to be the case that the shaman's dream journey is not up or down a vertical axis as in Dante, or even in Homer, but along the level."[7]

To put this matter of "tracking" more abstractly, the production of knowledge has a heuristic and tentative aspect, even when it is considered as a social production. For Prynne, it is a matter of looking at knowledge and at consciousness, both in their social and their individual aspects. This is suggested in the ringing phrase with which he begins "Die a Millionaire (pronounced 'diamonds in the air')" (*P*, 13–17): "The first essential is to take knowledge / back to the springs." From one point of view, this is a desideratum about capturing the process of the formation of knowledge in the individual mind; from another, it enjoins an archaeology of the dominant social forms of knowledge. The radical poetic relevance of this is that the poem can become an exploration of the way in which consciousness intersects with, or discovers itself in, the social discourses that are to hand. So that although the phenomenological notion of *epoché* (the bracketing off of dubious, socially acquired significations) might offer a suggestive analogy with Olson's theories, it will not meet the case with Prynne's practice. For the latter, Heidegger's insistence both on the importance of language, and on the time-bound character of interpretation, seems more apt, especially because he is nonetheless wedded to a return to "those primordial experiences in which we achieved our first ways of determining the nature of Being."[8] Heidegger also espouses the critique and "destruction" of inauthentic language. This position does seem to offer a suggestive parallel with a certain doubleness in Prynne: seeking origins, but always aware that one's sense of them is conditioned by the present; deliberately exploring the ways in which contemporary technical discourses (scientific, legal, economic) imbue subjectivity, but at the same time subjecting elements in them to a critique that is sometimes scurrilous, sometimes indignant.

To pick up another fundamental aspect of the "tracking" idea: an accessible way of approaching the presentation of subjectivity in some of Prynne's poems is simply to think in terms of another variant on the stream of consciousness. Thus, in "Thoughts on the Esterhazy Court Uniform," which can be read as thoughts occurring as the poet climbs a hill, one comes across these lines, which are fairly characteristic in temper and function:

> I know I will go back
> down & that it will not be the same though
> I shall be sure it is so.

> (*VA*, 248/*P*, 98)

However one may regard this kind of thing, it is true that some of the long poems from *Kitchen Poems* (1968), *The White Stones* (1969), and *Brass* (1971), which are in any case among Prynne's most accessible works, become more approachable when considered as the movement of the mind on the spot. But these poems also suggest a way in which one might want to qualify that statement: as we have suggested, they ask to be read as discursive poems, or at least this is an aspect of them that cannot be ignored. Sometimes the sinews of argument become the most salient, or the only, level of coherence in the poem. Thus, in "Sketch for a Financial Theory of the Self," one encounters lines such as these, which are as characteristic as the foregoing:

> 4.   The name of [need] is of course money, and
> the absurd trust in value is the pattern of
> bond and contact and interest—just where
> the names are exactly equivalent to the trust
> given to them.
> > Here then is the purity of
> > pragmatic function:
> > we give the name of
> > our selves to our needs.
> > We want what we are.
>
> (*VA*, 233-34/*P*, 20)

One might conclude that an important strain in Prynne's work is the attempt to portray intellection, not purely in the form of traditional discursive conventions, but as it occurs to a consciousness: "The depiction of thinking" is a phrase that springs to mind. But thinking at this phase of immediate intellection is subject, Prynne seems to say, to the abrupt intuitions of the image-making faculty. For this reason, one of the difficulties about reading his poems is that of decoding chains of imagery that might begin to assert themselves with an air of inscrutable self-evidence; for to explain them in the poem would be to move away from the edge of emerging thought. Yet persistence by the reader repays the effort. One of the pleasures offered is the play of image linking.

But here one touches on another point of self-reflexivity. For just as the movement of the poem (formal level) exhibits a particular instance of the mind's "tracking" (a subject at the thematic level), so does the difficult gesture

toward image-pattern (formal level) exhibit that doubtful drift toward coherent views, which it is one of Prynne's chief aims to explore and question
(at the thematic level).

The most obvious version of the ideal of coherence and order is that
which derives its warrant from some explicit notion of the transcendent. In
"Sketch for a Financial Theory of the Self," Prynne suggests that in the modern world—probably the post-Renaissance world—ethical and personal values have increasingly been displaced from their position in a metaphysically
grounded scheme and have come to take much of their color from the
apparent congruence with them of financial value. But something of the
affect associated with the transcendent ("the sky") still attaches itself to the
commodities money can buy ("silk"), and the desire for the transcendent
persists in a world that cannot believe in it:

> The qualities as they continue are the silk
> under the hand; because their celestial
> progress, across the sky, is so hopeless & so
> to be hoped for. I hope for silk, always, and
> the strands are not pure though the name
> is so. The name is the sidereal display, it
> is what we *know* we cannot now have.
>
> (*VA*, 233/*P*, 19)

Yet, in a typically guarded stance, Prynne calls into question any easy return to faith: "the stars are names and the / names are *necessarily* false." On
the other hand, "the city does need, / the sky," and "the names" (interpretation, including metaphysical interpretation) are "just / the tricks we / trust,
which / we choose." Interpretation is unavoidable but is a product of historically defined social need, and it is misleading to think of it in terms of
objective truth.

Desire for a lost sense of the transcendent, and for the role that such
a sense has played in buttressing coherence of identity or worldview, are
constant themes in Prynne's work. In "The Holy City," the transcendent is
"Jerusalem" (*P*, 43). In "Thoughts on the Esterhazy Court Uniform," it appears as the idea of a founding origin: "we make / sacred what we cannot
see without coming / back to where we were" (*VA*, 247/*P*, 98). Unfortu-

nately, in the process we lose our appreciation of the actual and the momentary. Nor can we really get back to an innocent origin. Yet, paradoxically, it seems that we need the idea that we can do so in order to go forward in our track through the world. On these terms we make an image of our progress in "music." We appreciate the order of "music," but we know that it has lost its metaphysical foundation for us. There is a particular irony in this for us moderns:

> Music is truly the
> sound of our time, since it is how we most
> deeply recognize the home we may not
> have: the loss is trust and you could
> reverse that without change.
>
> (*VA*, 248/*P*, 99)

To return to the shape of Prynne's poems, his music is intended to instantiate an oscillation between the coherence offered by argument and image pattern, on the one hand and, on the other hand, unassimilable effects, or ones that are hard to assimilate. This oscillation corresponds to the need for interpretation weighed against the fact that there will always be that which cannot be accounted for in any interpretation.

In view of these features of Prynne's composition and themes, it is hard to agree completely with Peter Ackroyd, who, in *Notes For a New Culture*, asserts that Prynne's language "does not have any extrinsic reference. There is only a marginal denotative potential since the language aspires towards completeness and self-sufficiency."[9] There are certainly some poems, such as those in *High Pink on Chrome* (1975), that vigorously obstruct naturalization, whether by putative context or internal coherence. Yet the notion that any use of language completely lacks reference seems to me to be highly problematic in principle. And certainly even Prynne's most difficult poems tease the reader with possible naturalizations by context, like, for instance, the idea of a packed lunch eaten in the country in "What he says they must do is" (*VA*, 265/*P*, 254). Elizabeth Cook has the better view of his work as a whole when she says that he "has his way of seeing the world as vitally interconnected."[10] This quite rightly implies that he believes the world can be seen—subject to the ironic qualification that we are only enabled to do so by founding our seeing in suspect notions of coherence. Thus, one reason why scientific discourse figures so largely among Prynne's registers is simply that he places some credence in its descriptions. But Cook's point about the "interconnected" may help one to notice how Prynne can transfer the language of science to the description of emotional states in a transposition slightly reminiscent of Blake's reuse of Newtonian and other scientific terms. In Prynne, the rationale is presumably that we live so much amid the discourse of science that such a transposition can provide an authentic language for certain modern states of mind:

> See him recall the day by moral trace, a squint
> to cross-fire shewing fear of hurt at top left; the
> bruise is glossed by 'nothing much' but drains
> to deep excitement. His recall is false but the charge
> is still there in neural space, pearly blue with a
> touch of crimson.
>
> ("Of Movement Towards a Natural
> Place" [VA, 262/P, 221])

Veronica Forrest-Thomson is nearer the mark than Ackroyd when she explains Prynne's poetic force in terms of "minute attention to technical detail . . . together with tendentious thematic obscurity."[11] The last phrase is her term for what the reader feels as possible but deferred and difficult theme construction. She takes Prynne's "Of Sanguine Fire" (VA, 174–78) as an example of what she means. It is a difficult poem, not least because, as she asserts, "the constant movement from one implied external context to another does not allow consistent development of image-complexes over several lines; they appear momentarily only to disappear again."[12] This is a sign of virtue for Forrest-Thomson, who makes it clear in her notably lively theoretical book that she holds to an extreme version of the view that poetry is not in the language-game of conveying information. She sees this as a fact entailing a difficult future for poetry as it seeks to ward off, by cunning resistance to "Bad Naturalization," the threat from mimetic modes of writing. "Bad Naturalization" is swift and linear sense making in terms of "external" context. Her account of Prynne seems to me to be obviously partial:

there are sufficient examples of the seriousness with which he takes right apprehension of things, however difficult this may be to achieve. Probably he intends even his most rebarbative work to be recuperated to a significant degree into statements about the world, though in such cases Forrest-Thomson's account seems to me to be truer to the reader's experience, whatever the intention may have been. But it is instructive and not surprising that there should be a spectrum of this kind among interpretations of Prynne: Ackroyd seeing him in terms of the autonomy of language, Cook as revealing the connectedness of the world, and Forrest-Thomson somewhere in between these two positions. For Prynne's work exhibits in a deeply pondered and developed form that tension between the two currents of modernism to which I referred above: that is, between an American-influenced objectivism about the process of things and, on the other hand, self-consciousness about form and discourse.

III

Forrest-Thomson's theories are more radical than her poems. This is certainly the impression conveyed by the brief selection in *A Various Art*, and it is one that is confirmed in the very handsome 1990 *Collected Poems and Translations*, published by Allardyce Barnett.[13] The poems from her first collection *Language-Games* (1971) are playful, discursive essays. Much of the playfulness derives either from the ironic placing of quotations or from the ironic handling of word position or lineation in a verse practice broadly within the William Carlos Williams tradition. There is an apologetic British intellectual's humor about these poems that, combined with their narrowness of register, offers the kind of easy naturalization that is expressly denigrated in her critical theories. But a change of form and aspect occurs in the work she produced in the remaining years before her premature death in 1975, and it is from this period that the editors of *A Various Art* draw their selection. These poems intermittently display characteristics admired in her critical work, such as "tendentious thematic obscurity," the image cluster, even capital letters at the beginning of lines—a healthy sign of "artifice," apparently. Such preferences put her at odds with some of the more lucid and straightforward tendencies of Anglo-American modernism—but not, she deems, with the work of John Ashbery or Sylvia Plath, whom she much admires, as, indeed, she does the capital-free Prynne.

Yet the names Ashbery, Plath, and Prynne suggest a radicalism that is not fully in evidence in her poetry, though one must allow for some very fine work, such as that to be seen in one of her best and most justly admired poems, the short lyric "Pastoral," which I here quote in full:

> They are our creatures, clover, and they love us
> Through the long summer meadow's diesel fumes.
> Smooth as their scent and contours clear however
> Less than enough to compensate for names.
>
> Jagged are names and not our creatures
> Either in kind or movement like the flowers.
> Raised voices in a car or by a river
> Remind us of the world that is not ours.
>
> Silence in grass and solace in blank verdure
> Summon the frightful glare of nouns and nerves.
> The gentle foal linguistically wounded
> Squeals like a car's brakes
> Like our twisted words.
>
> (*VA*, 117/*CP*, 72)

The poem can be read thematically in terms of a proposition that, arguably, is a paradox: nature, including vegetative nature, is akin to us, is gentle, and loves us; whereas words and technical creation (and perhaps these are related) are in some way not human and are dangerous to us and to our natural kindred. The poem displays all the elements of artifice prized by its author. There is linkage by phonic patterning: "creatures," "clover," "love us." There is ambiguity: "Jagged are names and not our creatures" means either "Names are jagged and they are not our creatures" or "Names are jagged; but our creatures (like clover and foals) are not jagged." Clusters of imagery are fairly obvious: for instance, there is a chain formed by "diesel fumes," "voices in a car" and "a car's brakes," representing the intrusion of the nonnatural. Finally, there is thematic complexity sufficient to undermine confidence in our first thematization. The most obvious sign of this complexity is to be found in the lines that declare that pastoral silence is itself what summons "the frightful glare of nouns and nerves." We may then feel free to note that the squeal of the foal sounds like what may, conceivably, be helping to wound it: it sounds like a car's brakes and, for that matter, "like our twisted words." Looking back across the poem, we may then note that the diesel fumes are in the meadow all the time, and that though the raised voices may well be in a car, they may just as easily be by a river. How deep does this thematic miscegenation go? There is the suggestion that it goes quite deep: that words, though they may look unnatural, express natural pain; and that at one level the foal is not equine, but is a young human person who has entered the world of language, which is itself a moment of being wounded, perhaps precisely by that confusing, disabling, and poignant disjunction of world and words that is close to the heart of the poem's subject.

This is a fine poem. But although it is as good as the work of Empson, whom Forrest-Thomson much admires, one might ask how far it transcends his poetic. Other poems of this period appear conservatively discursive. Apart from a more straightforward approach to lineation and the presence of capitals at line beginnings, they remind one of the chatty, facetious intellectualism of *Language-Games*. These lines from "Cordelia, or 'A poem should not mean, but be'" (1974), are fairly characteristic. A negative view might claim that they constitute a partial refutation of the poem's title:

> I with no middle flight intend the truth to speak out plain
> Of honour truth and love gone by that has come back again
> The fact is one grows weary of the love that comes again.
> I may not know much about gods but I know that
> Eros is a strong purple god
> And that there is a point where incest becomes
> Tradition. I don't mean that literally;
> I don't love my brother or he me.

> (*VA*, 121/*CP*, 104)

One should probably do the author the courtesy of being guided by the title. In that case the poem is trying to enact, as well as speak about, weariness with love. The question might still be whether, even when one grants this possibility, the achievement is very notable when it is compared with the scope, lucidity, and trenchancy of the theory.

IV

The sense of a possible disjunction between language and experience is also present in the work of Andrew Crozier, whose collected poems are published by Allardyce Barnett with the title *All Where Each Is*.[14] One of the editors of *A Various Art*, he is also, of the three poets discussed here, the one most obviously indebted to the William Carlos Williams tradition in point of a certain undemonstrative manner and an attentive deference to the experience or the object combined with an ideology of language as properly representational. In "The Veil Poem," for instance, we are told that

> This is
> the ordinary world, naturally incomplete and
> in no wise to be verbally separated
> from your picture of it. For words
> are the wise men's counters, they do but
> reckon with them, but they are the money
> of fools.
>
> (*VA*, 75/*AW*, 121)

The notion, and even something of the cadence, are reminiscent of Wordsworth:

> Words are but under-agents in their souls;
> When they are grasping with their greatest strength
> They do not breathe among them.
>
> *The Prelude* (1805), 272–74

Another passage from *The Prelude* is in fact quoted at an earlier point in Crozier's poem. Of course, it is common enough to find Wordsworth accepted as the first "poet of reality," even by Anglo-American poets who abhor certain aspects of Romanticism. But in point of fact, the implications of the two passages are different. Crozier asserts a right relationship between words and the world. Wordsworth, though he would also desire something under that description, in this passage asserts a supraverbal level of thought. But this notion, too, may have influenced Crozier. For although "wise men" may use words well, there are better signs to be had than can be found in most uses of language. Thus, in "Two Robin Croft," jars of pussy willow become the spontaneously found sign of a wedding anniversary. The poem concludes: "Everything that might be said comes into this / We need no other sign than this branch gives" (*VA*, 70/*AW*, 92). Words imbued with egotism say nothing that will endure:

> Add your name to the glass
> through which you witnessed this
> time soon mists over it.
>
> (VA, 85/AW, 229)

It is futile to inscribe one's identity in what should properly be a transparent medium. And yet the figure of the watcher through glass suggests also alienation, even as it proffers itself as potentially accurate observation. The figure itself, but also this duplicity in it, is reminiscent of the work of George Oppen, whom Crozier much admires.[15] In general, Crozier's is a poetry of the isolated consciousness, even where, as is often the case, he writes unaffectedly, and sometimes movingly, of personal tenderness.

In line with his mistrust of egotistical language, Crozier wishes to encourage an attitude of deference towards the world, announcing, for instance, with a degree of satisfaction, that he "cannot dominate" a tree ("The Veil Poem" [*VA*, 72/*AW*, 114]). In his literary criticism, he finds contemporary British poetry to be vitiated by an alliance of the "lyric self" with an intrusively "figurative" technique.[16] The result is a poetry of "small verbal thrills" or "bravura display."[17] Heaney and Craig Raine are seen as extreme exponents of this tradition. Tomlinson's poetry, on the other hand, provides evidence "that language might be compatible with what it refers to rather than necessarily appropriated to the special register of the poet's sensibility."[18] Yet such compatibility does not entail the annihilation of the self so much as the right, living relationship of the self with the world:

> all language is truth
> though a bed of dry leaves when evaporation
> ceases and our words turn and fall
> flickering with our life upon the earth
> ("Pleats" [*VA*, 82/*AW*, 182])

The self that lives, through language, a direct relationship with the world is true and is itself to be seen in terms of growth and vitality. The self that dominates and uses language as a vehicle of domination is not a part of life. We are back among thoughts that owe something to Wordsworth and Coleridge, but also to Williams and Olson.

Our words, then, have the potential to come alive to the extent that they are the reflex of a lively interaction with the universe. And this is true for the good reason that we are part of the universe and are bound up with its life:

> But the creation of something alive in the cosmos
> in which we express our delight, being ourselves
> alive, is indeed miraculous, though not a chance
> imposition on some bleakly available background.
> We are the daily miracle of clouds and snow
> with a little extra armature of coal and soot.
> ("The Life Class" [*VA*, 76/*AW*, 139])

This life is best conceived as a process not to be arrogantly segmented by the ego. Just as a jar of pussy willow may do better than words to mark an anniversary, so, in "High Zero," "The advance of happiness / is never an anniversary" (*VA*, 84/*AW*, 222). This realization goes with another: "There is never / a last thing," and "There is always a page or carpet beyond / the arch, not hidden, green to the touch" (*VA*, 74/*AW*, 120). It is better to go onward with the process, appreciating the humble or unexpected beauty of the present:

> It is a February evening
> the nights are drawing out and I love you
> driving your car so attentive to the hazards of traffic
> while I observe the passing skyline which so exactly
> defines the way your hair falls onto your shoulders
> alert to whatever should show up next.
>   ("February Evenings" [*VA*, 69/*AW*, 91])

This evocation of the present, or of successive presents, has its stylistic correlative in Crozier's fondness for unpunctuated flows, in which one is constantly discovering new qualifications of preceding statements and is frequently uncertain of the precise interrelationship of the array of clauses. This is an exploitation of one of the possibilities of Olsonian poetics. Crozier has taken it as far as anyone. It is perhaps for this reason, by an apparent paradox, that Crozier seems at times happier than most of the poets in his anthology to permit the ghost of the iambic pentameter to linger. The series of unpunctuated sonnets called "Half Artifice," though metrically very free, contains some resonant pentameter lines, as at the end of "Evaporation of a Dream" (*VA*, 94/*AW*, 297): "Scorn and regret condense out of the air / Earth's empty case as full as life was full." The title of the series helps to make my point; Crozier is ready to compromise with artifice to the extent that artifice is ready to engage with process, for instance, by abandoning punctuation and strict meter. The resulting forms themselves constitute a sign: a sign for signification as properly arising out of an engagement with life.

V

The questions and choices of principle involved in writing poetry in Britain today are too complicated and, perhaps, disheartening for the discussion of three courageous avant-garde poets to be made to yield many general lessons. One can say that all of them set out with some kind of positive response to the post-Williams tradition of American poetry, and that all three seem to feel, sooner or later and in varying degrees, that this offers too naive a view of language and artifice. Forrest-Thomson's theories, which go furthest in this direction, are surely too slighting of the truth-functional claims of poetic propositions, though they do offer a sharp set of tools for examining the aesthetic effect in poetry, particularly modern poetry. Her practice, however, has, perhaps, less to add to our understanding. It is to the practice of Prynne and Crozier that contemporary poets will turn if they wish to seek models capable of encompassing more diverse areas of thought and experience than can be treated in the modes that have prevailed until recently with British publishers and reviews. Prynne fruit-fully combines a modern sense of experience as process with a conviction that science can come in aid of feeling and a postmodern awareness of the power of discourse. The results are rich, complex, and as powerfully original as any poetry written in the English-speaking world in this century. Yet it seems unlikely that they can ever achieve a wide readership. It is as if Prynne were happy to be rebarbative in an age of barbarous commercialism and to find a fit audience, though small.

Crozier is also responding to a climate in which, as he sees it, the domi-nant modes of poetic production pander to a facile and sensationalist taste for the translation of experience into striking metaphor. As we have seen, he has both Heaney and Craig Raine in his sights. Unlike Prynne, though, Crozier is accessible enough. His is another way, that of attempting to write as if poetry were still capable of finding a wide audience, without trivializing either its subject or its means. Some may come to feel that these serious, attentive, and undemonstrative explorations of contemporary experience speak to their condition more fully than any Metaphor Man can do.

Notes

1. Andrew Crozier and Tim Longville, eds., *A Various Art* (1987; reprinted Lon-don: Paladin, 1990). All quotations are from the Paladin edition; page numbers will be given in the text, preceded by *VA*. I shall also be quoting from J. H. Prynne's *Poems* (Edinburgh: Agneau 2, 1982); page numbers will be given in the text, prefaced by *P*. In some cases, the same poems appear in both collections, and, for the convenience

of the reader, I shall give both page numbers. Other poems appear in only one of the two collections, for which a single page number will be given.

2. Crozier and Longville, *A Various Art*, 12.

3. Ibid.

4. Ibid.

5. Charles Olson, in *Selected Writings*, ed. Robert Creeley (New York: New Directions, 1966), 16.

6. Ibid.

7. Donald Davie, *Thomas Hardy and British Poetry* (London: Routledge & Kegan Paul, 1973), 128.

8. Martin Heidegger, *Being and Time*, trans. John Macquarrie and Edward Robinson (London: SCM Press, 1962), 44.

9. Peter Ackroyd, *Notes For a New Culture* (London: Vision Press, 1976), 130.

10. Elizabeth Cook, "Prynnes's Principia," *London Review of Books,* 16 September–8 October 1982, 15.

11. Veronica Forrest-Thomson, *Poetic Artifice: A Theory of Twentieth-Century Poetry* (Manchester: Manchester University Press, 1978), 142.

12. Ibid., 145.

13. Veronica Forrest-Thomson, *Collected Poems and Translations* (London, Lewes, and Berkeley: Allardyce Barnett, 1990). Hereafter, page numbers of quotations from this work will be given in the text, preceded by *CP*. As with Prynne, page numbers of her poems that appear in *A Various Art* will also be given.

14. Andrew Crozier, *All Where Each Is* (London and Berkeley: Allardyce Barnett, 1985). Hereafter, page numbers of quotations from this work will be given in the text, preceded by *AW*. As with Prynne and Forrest-Thomson, page numbers of poems that appear in *A Various Art* will also be given.

15. Andrew Crozier, "Inaugural and Valedictory: The Early Poetry of George Oppen," in *Modern American Poetry*, ed. R. W. (Herbie) Butterfield (London and Totowa, N.J.: Vision Press, 1984), 142–57.

16. Andrew Crozier, "Thrills and Frills: Poetry as Figures of Empirical Lyricism," in *Society and Literature 1945–1979*, ed. Alan Sinfield (London: Methuen, 1983), 199–233.

17. Ibid., 229, 230.

18. Ibid., 231.

CHAPTER FOUR

Poetry and the Women's Movement in Postwar Britain

Claire Buck

Feminist Poetry in Postwar Britain

In his 1962 anthology of contemporary British poetry, *The New Poetry*, A. Alvarez claimed to be "simply attempting to give my idea of what, that really matters, has happened to poetry in England during the last decade."[1] What really mattered, in Alvarez's view, had nothing to do with women poets. The anthology was all male. In 1966, his revised edition included Sylvia Plath and Anne Sexton under the American section, which offered his model of a desirable direction for poetry to take in Britain; it was, in his description, "poetry of immense skill and intelligence which coped openly with the quick of [the poets'] experience, experience sometimes on the edge of disintegration and breakdown."[2] Still no British women poets were included. It was, in fact, to be thirteen years before the publication of Lilian Mohin's *One Foot on the Mountain: An Anthology of British Feminist Poetry, 1969–1979* was to assert the place of women poets as women in British postwar culture.[3] Two significant anthologies, Cora Kaplan's *Salt and Bitter and Good: Three Centuries of English and American Women Poets* (1975) and *The Penguin Book of Women Poets* (1978), had paved the way for Mohin by highlighting the systematic exclusion of women poets from literary history.[4] But neither of these anthologies included much contemporary poetry or focused substantially on British poetry.

Mohin's groundbreaking anthology was followed by a spate of anthologies, such as the Virago anthology *Bread and Roses: Women's Poetry of the*

Nineteenth and Twentieth Centuries, edited by Diana Scott (1982); *The Faber Book of Twentieth Century Women's Poetry,* edited by Fleur Adcock (1987); Carol Rumens's *Making For the Open: The Chatto Book of Post-Feminist Poetry 1964–1984* (1985); and Barbara Burford's *A Dangerous Knowing: Four Black British Women Poets* (1985).[5] The titles of these anthologies acknowledge the central role of the women's movement in altering the map of both contemporary and earlier poetry, but they also signal one of the tensions that has been present in discussions of women's writing since the 1970s: What is the relationship between feminist writing and women's writing? Indeed this tension is inscribed in the Virago anthology in the division between the two final sections: "'The Meeting': On Reading Contemporary Poetry 1920–1980," which includes poets like Jenny Joseph, Elaine Feinstein, U. A. Fanthorpe, and Anne Stevenson, and "'The Renaming': Poetry Coming from the Women's Liberation Movement 1970–80," which includes Mary Dorcey, Judith Kazantzis, Astra, Michèle Roberts, Stef Pixner, and Alison Fell. Thus, a slightly older generation of contemporary women poets who are broadly sympathetic to the ideas of feminism, despite Stevenson's famous refusal of the label "feminist poet,"[6] are divided off from poets who are categorized by means of their identification with the women's movement. Some, but by no means all, of the latter group reappear in *the new british poetry* (1988).[7] The inclusion of the new postcolonial writing in Britain, of feminist poetry, and of examples of the British avant-garde made this anthology the first to map the challenges in the 1970s and 1980s to the myth of a new postwar cultural consensus of the kind that Alvarez's anthology essentially represents.[8]

However, these poets are still unknown outside Britain and are hardly known within Britain. The women poets who are best known and tend to represent contemporary British poetry of the 1970s and early 1980s are Anne Stevenson, U. A. Fanthorpe, Elaine Feinstein, Fleur Adcock, and Jenny Joseph.[9] This is in striking contrast to the impact of women's movement poetry in the equivalent period in the United States, where poets such as Adrienne Rich, Audre Lorde, Judy Grahn, Marilyn Hacker, Alice Walker, and Marge Piercy have given poetry a central place within the women's movement, and are themselves well known both inside and outside the movement. Adrienne Rich is regularly taught at American universities and colleges, whereas the British feminist poets listed above have very little currency within British higher education. The focus of my discussion of British feminist poetry will, therefore, be on the very real marginality of that poetry in contemporary British culture. I will attempt to give an account of the relationship of feminist poetry to postwar British culture that demonstrates how the specific historical and cultural location of those poets explains the limits on the place that this poetry could achieve in Britain, within both feminism and the mainstream poetry establishment. In addition, however, I will discuss the significance of a general failure in recent critical accounts of postwar British poetry to examine the place of this body of work.

Before embarking on this account, however, something needs to be said about the category that I am setting up here: feminist poetry of the 1970s and 1980s in Britain. This is by no means a self-evident category, and I am not concerned to make claims for its self-consistency or to discover whether the poets whom I include can still be said to belong to it. Neither am I attempting to establish a fixed division between poetry that is feminist and poetry that is not. The interest of that particular distinction lies, in my view, in the process by which different writers and editors draw it, and in the implications of what gets included and excluded, rather than in seeking a particular place where the line can be drawn. The feminist poetry I will be discussing was to a large degree presented as such, at the time, by the poets themselves. Their work appeared in identifiably feminist contexts such as *Spare Rib, Red Rag, Writing Women,* and *Distaff,* and during the 1970s many of them published collectively as feminists. *Licking the Bed Clean: Five Feminist Poets* (1978) would be one example; it includes the work of Alison Fell, Stef Pixner, Tina Reid, Michèle Roberts, and Ann Oosthuizen.[10] These poets also define their writing practice as feminist, engendered by their involvement in feminist writers' groups and their relationship to the women's movement.

The relative cohesion of this grouping of feminist poets needs, however, to be framed by an awareness of its exclusions, which were often those of the women's movement of the time. Wendy Mulford and Denise Riley are poets whose uncertain relationship with the women's movement poets working and publishing together in the late 1970s raises questions about the emerging definition of a feminist poetics. Both define their work in feminist contexts, and Riley's collection *Dry Air* appeared in the Virago series in 1985.[11] However, their self-proclaimed allegiance to a modernist concentration on formal and linguistic experiment, together with a very explicit use of poststructuralist theory, set their work somewhat at odds with the work of poets published in *One Foot on the Mountain*.

It is, however, the publishing history of black poets such as Merle Collins, Grace Nichols, Jackie Kay, Barbara Burford, and Amryl Johnson that highlights even less subtly their exclusion from the early British women's movement. For example, Barbara Burford outlined the difficulties of publishing for black women in the 1985 anthology *A Dangerous Knowing: Four Black Women Poets*: "Racism in the publishing industry has insured this invisibility by ignoring black women's creativity and denying them access to publishing, so many black women have been reluctant to name themselves as poets."[12] The publication of this anthology of black women poets by Sheba, a feminist press, ironically recalls Cora Kaplan's comment about the rationale for anthologies of women's poetry: "It is male anthologists, after all, who have made women poets inaccessible to the common reader and, ironically, created the need for collections such as this one."[13] Similarly, Grace Nichols's first collection, *i is a long memoried woman,* was published by Caribbean Cultural International (Karnak House) rather than by a feminist press, in 1983.[14] The Virago Poets series followed suit the following year with Nichols's *The Fat Black Woman's Poems* (1984).[15] The use of terms like *British* or *Britain* to group poets tends, therefore, to obscure the centrality of immigration, migrancy, and the aftermath of British colonialism in the postwar period; this impacts on the poets of the women's movement with whom I will be dealing, as well as on the Caribbean, Asian, and Irish women poets who represent the postcolonial experience.

Feminist Poets in the British Women's Movement

I want to turn now to the specific location of feminist poets within the contemporary women's movement of the 1970s and the aesthetic principles that issued from it. Emergent in Britain at the end of the 1960s, the contemporary women's movement was fueled by the work of women in the Campaign for Nuclear Disarmament, the Vietnam Solidarity Campaign, and left-wing groups such as International Socialism and the International Marxist

Group. By 1969 seventy women's liberation groups were operating in London, and in 1970 the first National Women's Liberation Workshop was attended in Oxford by six hundred women. At that conference, demands were formulated for equal pay, equality of opportunity, equal access to education, twenty-four-hour nurseries, free contraception, and abortion on demand. Later conferences in the 1970s extended these demands to include legal and financial independence for women, the end to discrimination against lesbians, and freedom from intimidation by violence or sexual coercion. These later demands demonstrated a greater interest in sexuality and the growing influence of radical feminism in the British women's movement.[16]

Writers and poets were involved with the women's movement from the start. Michèlene Wandor, playwright, poet, and feminist critic, describes joining a women's liberation group in north London in 1969 and attending the Oxford conference in 1970. As Wandor puts it, "beginning to write seriously coincided more or less exactly with my discovery of a political involvement which meant something to me. Creative and critical writing developed as my efforts to understand and be part of, [sic] feminism and socialism developed."[17] Another poet, Michèle Roberts, writes, "I came out as a poet when I found the Women's Liberation Movement in 1970 and realized that I wasn't mad so much as confused and angry."[18] Similarly, the art historian Rozsika Parker, writing about her involvement with *Spare Rib* in the early 1970s, draws attention to the interrelationship between feminist politics, theoretical analysis, and art practice: "Had it not been for the re-emergence of feminism in the late 1960s I would have undoubtedly abandoned my ambition to write. Feminism produced a radical critique and reassessment of the relationship between artist, critic and audience, while transforming art practice itself. And, of crucial importance for me, feminism offered a new forum for women writers—*Spare Rib*."[19]

This emphasis on the role of feminist publishing is important. The work that appeared in the 1970s was often self-published, as, for example, in the case of *Licking the Bed Clean* (1978);[20] published by collectives such as the Women's Literature Collective, which published a collection called *Seven Women* in 1976; and produced by small radical and feminist presses, such as Playbooks 2, who published *Cutlasses and Earrings* in 1977, and Onlywomen Press, who were responsible for *One Foot on the Mountain* (1979).[21] In these and other retrospective accounts of women writers' engagement with feminism, the women's movement is depicted as being liberating for women writers. Libby Houston, a member of Michael Horovitz's underground poets of the 1960s and only later associated with feminism, describes the sheer sexism of the British poetry scene: "In that immediate scene I was the only woman I met reading—was it just because I was living in the thick of it?—though there were some in e.g. Liverpool or others published in *New Departures* up-market of myself. But I always identified with the boys."[22] This identification did not prevent her from being asked to do the clerical and administrative work of running Horovitz's reading agency, Poetry in Motion. Wandor, in an equivalent vein, describes the very male-centered poetry scene of the "late 1960s—early 1970s," where she "felt uncomfortable at being (mostly) the only woman poet—the other women around the posts were wives or groupies, and [she] always felt a bit odd in relation to both camps."[23] For confirmation, one only needs to think of the absence of British women poets from Alvarez's *New Poetry,* which was reissued in 1966.

In addition to the experience of being literally isolated as a woman writer within the poetry scene of the time, a more profound sense of dislocation consequent on the return of middle-class women to the home and family after the war is registered by Michèle Roberts: "increasing alienation from myself and from the view of femininity purveyed by the late 1950s/ early 1960s culture drove me and my writing underground; I stopped being honest with myself and others about what I felt, and tried to please, and kept my poems, my authentic records, secret."[24] Roberts's description of her sense of alienation, prior to the women's movement, was theorized in the mid 1970s at the Patriarchy Conference of 1976 by Cora Kaplan in her controversial keynote address, which was subsequently published as "Language and Gender" in *Papers on Patriarchy.*[25] Kaplan argues that "social silence as part of the constitution of female identity—i.e., subjectivity—is a crucial factor in her handling of written language."[26] Using a Lacanian psychoanalytic model of analysis, which met with a mixed reception at the time, Kaplan suggested that women's unease with writing, particularly with public genres,

> is intimately connected . . . with the way in which women become social beings in the first place, so that the very condition of their accession to their own subjectivity, to the consciousness of a self

which is both personal and public is their unwitting acceptance of the law which limits their speech. This condition places them in a special relation to language which becomes theirs as a consequence of becoming human, and at the same time not theirs as a consequence of becoming female.[27]

Whether or not Roberts would agree with this account—and her distrust of the Lacanian account of femininity is wittily expressed in the poem "women's entry into culture is experienced as lack"[28]—Kaplan's paper represented an important strand in cultural feminism at the time, which was recognized by the poets themselves.[29] The work of feminist critics and theorists was a necessary element in the development of new ideas about the relationship of gender, politics, and writing and in the creation of a culture sympathetic to feminist poetry.

The Aesthetics of Consciousness-Raising

The poetry that flourished within the context of the new women's movement was characterized by a clear fidelity to its political ideals translated into a poetics concerned with cultural critique, an accessible language and form, and the expression of women's personal experience. The poetry of *One Foot on the Mountain* is representative of this particular aesthetic, bringing together a body of work that was originally produced and published in feminist contexts. In my discussion, I will therefore largely focus on work published in this anthology.[30] The dominant voice in these poems is first-person, and the subject matter women's day-to-day lives and experiences; a minority of poems in *One Foot on the Mountain* use a third-person voice. A poem by Astra, "coming out celibate," exemplifies these characteristics. The poem opens with an abstract generalization:

> like men
> so many women cannot imagine
> > friendship creativity existence
> > without sexuality
> or what passes for sexuality[31]

However, the poem roots this political and theoretical issue about the effects of normative ideas about sexuality on contemporary women's lives in personal experience and the anecdotal:

> so that when i say
> > i am celibate
> smiles of embarrassment appear
> and the subject is quickly changed
>
> i am awarded
> > pity or contempt or simply bewilderment
> that i should not do
> > sexual things with and to
> > another person
> preferably of the other gender
> but anyway with someone for god's sake
> since it's
> "abnormal/unnatural/undesirable/and especially immature"
> not to be dependent on someone
> some of the time
> for sexual satisfaction[32]

The register is an assertively accessible language of statement and the anecdotal, displaying an allegiance to a spoken rather than to a written register ("for god's sake"). The demand for accessibility is also represented by the decision to use a free-verse form, a choice shared by virtually every poet in the anthology and endorsed by Mohin's skeptical approach, in the introduction, to "traditional academic standards of poetic craft."[33]

Personal experience, that of being subject to the normalizing judgments of others, "awarded / pity or contempt or simply bewilderment," is also central to the poem as a way of grounding a feminist political debate about sexuality. As such, it is given the function of authenticating the political point of the poem: the need for women to move beyond a self-definition delimited by their place in either a domestic, a sexual, or a romantic couple. Indeed, Astra is praised by Angela Hamblin, in a poem called "To Astra," for "your search / for authenticity."[34] The place of the personal is, however, qualified to some degree. The lowercase first-person pronoun, for example, also used by Angela Hamblin, Anna Wilson, and many others, signals a caution about this self that matches Virginia Woolf's parody of the masculine "I" in *A Room of One's Own*: "a shadow seemed to lie across the page. It was a straight dark bar, a shadow shaped something like the letter 'I.' One began dodging this way and that to catch a glimpse of the landscape behind it."[35] Woolf's witty portrait of the consequences of a masculine entitlement to a confident sense of self and to literary authority links these poets' use of a lowercase "i" to Kaplan's account of the very different position of men and women in relation to language. Kaplan's use of Lacanian theory to demonstrate a relationship between the masculine privilege of the phallus and the "straight dark bar" of "the letter 'I'" suggests the significance of Astra's and Hamblin's subtle attempt to alter the terms of the personal and the self as an alternative to asserting women's claim to identity on this masculine model.

The use of free, indirect style—"i just need to meet the right person don't i?"—also allows Astra to blur the distinction between external attitudes and their internalization. This blurring brings the poets into dialogue with contemporary feminist theory, allowing them to move beyond the assertion of an autonomous and individualist model of subjectivity to an exploration of the way identity emerges from within a linguistic and social nexus. It is the poem's dramatization of the relationship between inside and outside, however, that allows a feminist self to be established as distinct and different from those attitudes and judgments that Astra defines as distorting.

> celibacy is about choosing one's own
>   life style
>   friendships
>   ways of
>   working doing being
> and putting them all together
> at different times[36]

Thus, the "self" is distinguished and specified in terms of a particular feminist agenda of self and liberation, in which the self is individualized but

distinguished from a negatively conceived model of selfhood with a capital
"I." In "To Astra," Hamblin delineates this different self of feminism:

>   what i recognise
>   in you—is
>   what i see in myself
>
> Recognition—
>   i guess that's
>   what it's all
>   about
>   i really know
>   you
>   woman-friend
>   and i like what
>   i know.[37]

Instead of the poem's establishing a clear distinction between self and other
as the ground for a self-contained and authoritative selfhood, the "i" and
"you" are defined as essential to each other's existence. The "i" here depends on, and is produced through, interdependence. "Recognition" and
identification with another woman become supports for selfhood and self-
respect as a woman. A set of new terms is established here that opposes a
masculine and individualist model of selfhood with a model conceived in
terms of relationship and a feminist political community.

These poetics and models of the self and experience emerge from the
1970s' emphasis on consciousness-raising as a key political strategy for feminists. "Consciousness raising groups, the basic stuff of Women's Liberation,"
writes Mohin, "have been putting flesh on the bones of the idea that the
personal is political, that our individual experiences have social significance,
are important on a world political scale."[38] Mohin's description of consciousness-raising parallels *The Redstockings Manifesto* in the United States: "we
regard our personal experiences as the basis for an analysis of our common
situation."[39] The status of the personal is a touchstone of authenticity because "we cannot rely on existing ideologies as they are all products of male
supremacist culture."[40] Women's movement poetry, of the kind I am dis-

cussing here, operates, on this model, as a sustained form of cry, as consciousness-raising came to be called within the women's movement. Every kind of day-to-day experience, and women's feelings about the experiences, are included and explored in the poems: work, friendships with women, domesticity and family relationships, abortion, childbirth, and sexual relationships—heterosexual and lesbian—all become appropriate subject matter for poetry. The impact of this reformulation of the traditional territory of poetry can be gauged by the response of the two thousand television viewers who wrote in to Channel 4, to ask where they could find the poems that the feminist group The Raving Beauties performed on its opening night in 1982:

> "In The Pink"'s reception, and the spate of letters we received after it was broadcast, showed that we had tapped a source of feeling common to thousands of women. . . . In discussing the truth of the poetry we were of course discussing our own truth.[41]

However, this aesthetic of personal experience elicited criticism on the grounds that the poems were a form of unmediated experience, "'primal scream' writing: slabs of raw experience," as Fleur Adcock says in her introduction to *The Faber Book of Twentieth Century Women's Poetry*, "untransformed by any attempt at ordering and selection."[42] Anne Stevenson similarly characterizes early feminist poetry in the following terms: "Vengeance, self-immolation, man-hating and blood were the themes of the angry women who followed Sylvia Plath."[43] These criticisms underestimate the degree to which these writers take up the confessional model inherited from Plath and Anne Sexton and reformulate it as a poetics of consciousness-raising in which women's personal experience becomes central to the poetry, but only insofar as its status as private and individual experience is challenged by means of a feminist political perspective.[44] The reception accorded to Sexton by the English literary establishment indicates how inhospitable British literary culture was likely to be to a poetry grounded in women's personal experience. Her *Transformations* (1972), for example, was greeted by the *Times Literary Supplement* as work that "might be expected to appeal to a fairly sophisticated but undemanding American adolescent."[45] And, in 1975, Stevenson wrote in the *New Review* that "sensitive students, seeking a meaning in life, or a justification of their own abnormality in American society, turn to poetry as an alternative to reality—and a way of redeeming themselves, at the same time, from social insignificance."[46] These judgments were made despite, or perhaps were a nervous response to, the fact that Sexton's poetry sold very well in the United Kingdom. They also indicate the context of judgments about the kinds of experience, language, and sensibility that were deemed appropriate to contemporary poetry in Britain and that were rooted in white, middle-class codes of behavior and writing. Caroline Gilfillian's explicitly celebratory approach to menstruation—

> the brilliant
> red blood clot that remained and
> flowered with transparent petals
> into the water
> .   .   .   .   .   .
> blood tasting sweet
> smelling fresh of
> vagina skin and uterus
> this is the blood
> we are taught to hate[47]

—with its implicit reference to lesbian eroticism, blatantly refused the terms of these judgments.

The terms of Adcock and Stevenson's rejection of a poetry based on unmediated personal experience include a desire to advocate a humanism in which sexual difference would be transcended. This breeds a discomfort with the particular mode in which feminist poetry deals with the relationship of power and gender. Because Stevenson herself writes poetry that explicitly engages with issues of gender and power,[48] her criticism in the *New Review* suggests the depth of her allegiance to a poetry espousing a moderate rationality, similar perhaps to the temperate reasonableness demanded by such Movement poets as Donald Davie and Philip Larkin. It is this allegiance that lies behind her and Adcock's mobilization of an ideal of good poetry and the structuring value of art in opposition to unmediated experience.

Their criticisms fail, however, to recognize the call to reformulate and reposition personal experience, which is central to consciousness-raising. For instance, Caroline Halliday uses Adrienne Rich's *Of woman born: Motherhood as Experience and Institution*[49] to explore personal feelings about the possibility of having children, childbirth, and all that it implies about a woman's relationship to her body:

> This chapter is about pain.
> Or is it about labour?
> Work/birth,
> worn hands, or
> the farmed body of a woman.
> I do not want to read this future of mine,
> beautiful contusion of pain.
> The hidden thought beneath the skin.[50]

Here, Halliday uses Rich's model in *Of woman born*—where she juxtaposes personal journals with anthropology, medical history, and politics to investigate the ways in which the representation of motherhood and its social organization "has alienated women from our bodies by incarcerating us in them."[51] Rich's perspective and words are both the occasion for the poem and the framework that allows Halliday to reposition personal experience within a context that allows her to explore its meanings. Rich offers a language as well as a context (the nexus in which labor is both work and childbirth, for instance), so that personal experience is taken up within a feminist discourse that grants it significance and authenticity but that also permits its analysis:

> The consciousness raising process is one in which personal experiences, when shared, are recognized as a result not of an individual's idiosyncratic history and behavior, but of the system of sex-role stereotyping. That is, they are political, not personal, questions.[52]

The whole presentation of *One Foot on the Mountain* emphasizes a consciousness-raising framework. In addition to defining consciousness-raising in the introduction, Mohin discusses the significance of women's writing groups that "have made a large contribution to feminist poetry . . . we have begun to help each other to write, to write for each other, to influence, to criticize, to destroy barriers and intimidations and old standards, and to construct new working methods."[53] Similar acknowledgment of the productive exchange allowed by these groups comes from the writers' groups who published *Tales I Tell My Mother*[54] and *Licking the Bed Clean*. Mohin specifically extends the role of the groups to that of the anthology: "The work in this book comes out of connections we are making, a collective sense of effort and of discovery. We intend to tell each other everything we can, every secret, because we know this intimate difficult exchange makes a difference, is the process of change."[55] The anthology is framed as part of "a dynamic which insists upon discussion and response." Each poet's work is then presented with both a biography written by its subject and a photograph reiterating the emphasis on feminism's relationship to women's personal experience.[56] Thus, the book becomes a version of a consciousness-raising group.

However, by the early 1980s the limits of the consciousness-raising process had become the focus of feminist debate about the status and meaning of women's personal experience, which is reflected in the work of feminist critics and poets influenced by poststructuralism. In particular, a critique of the terms of women's personal experience that underpinned the aesthetic of *One Foot on the Mountain* emerged in the writing of two poets who were never included in the anthology, Mulford and Riley. Mulford, in her essay "Notes on Writing: A Marxist/Feminist Viewpoint," which first appeared in *Red Letters* in 1979,[57] picks up the tensions that exist in consciousness-raising. That is, the value of women's experience, expressed in *The Redstockings Manifesto* as authentically theirs in an ideologically distorting world, conflicts with the recognition, in the extract from *Radical Feminism*, that personal experience is not the result of "an individual's idiosyncratic history."[58] Mulford implicitly addresses this tension using the work of Althusser and Lacan: "Who was this 'I' speaking? What was speaking me? How far did the illusion of selfhood, that most intimate and precious possession, reach? How could the lie of culture be broken up if the lie of the self made by that culture remained intact?"[59]

These are some of Mulford's questions that emerge in her poetry and in Riley's as a careful scrutiny of the ways in which self and experience are embedded in language. Although committed to a feminist politics, Mulford defines her project as "different from" the practice of most women because "I insist with other modernist writers . . . that for the writer revolutionary practice necessitates revolutionary practice in the field of the signifier."[60] That is, language, rather than women's experience, becomes central.

Riley's poem, "A note on sex and 'the reclaiming of language,'"[61] explicitly addresses the dangers of assuming any kind of authenticity about women's experience or about a utopian ideal that postulates an essential femininity undistorted by patriarchal impositions. Riley's metaphor for woman is the immigrant returning to her native land:

> The Savage is flying back home from the New Country
> in native-style dress with a baggage of sensibility
> to gaze on the ancestral plains with the myths thought up
> and dreamed in her kitchens as guides
>
>   She will be discovered
> as meaning is flocking densely around the words seeking a way
> any way in between the gaps, like a fertilization

The "baggage of sensibility" and the "native-style dress" signal the fantasy of authenticity that is involved in the search for what is truly female. The locale that Riley establishes for "the work" of feminism is that of the intersection point between language and identity:

>   The work is
> e.g. to write 'she' and for that to be a statement
> of fact only and not a strong image
> of everything which is not-you, which sees you
>
> The new land is colonised, though its prospects are empty
>
> The Savage weeps as landing at the airport
> she is asked to buy wood carvings, which represent herself [62]

Riley's investigation of what Kaplan calls "that grim conjunction of self 'in' and 'out' of society that the literary inscribes"[63] effectively denaturalizes the terms *identity, gender,* and *experience.* The quotation marks around the pronoun *she* and the use of the word *savage* for woman signal how far identity and gender are products of language. The woman in the poem discovers not a true self but representations from which she is so far removed that they are up for sale. Riley's strategy lies primarily with her use of multiple discourses. The shift between a language of nativism and primitivism—the source of the poem's gender metaphors—and the poststructuralist theoretical discourse of the third stanza allows her to criticize the radical feminist search for an authentic female nature. However, because the use of this language implies the dangers of eliding the differences of race and ethnicity through an appeal to a universal notion of female experience, the choice to use it is by no means coincidental or uncritical. Here the danger is framed as a problem about language, in which the effects of the growth of a black immigrant population in postwar Britain surface in the structural metaphors of the poem. The co-optation of the metaphors to a feminist project, which does not yet specifically engage race, is problematic because the conflation of gender and race denies the specificity of the colonial experience. But because this language does not reappear elsewhere in Riley's work, its use in her poem is arguably part of her critique. Nonetheless, Riley never makes this criticism explicit through the theoretical discourse of the poem in the way that she does with gender, so that the enactment of the gesture of co-optation within "a note on sex" verges uncomfortably on a repetition of the colonization process.

Riley's focus on the poststructuralist concerns of language and sexual difference place her, with Mulford, in opposition to the main trajectory of feminist poetry in both the 1970s and the 1980s. This is particularly so because the more effectively the poems disempower the "self," the less they have an "obligation to the law of legibility."[64] Thus, Riley's verse is exemplary of how feminism can use avant-garde poetry to investigate the effect of ideologies of gender and the self within a poetics and politics of representation. But the result is of necessity a "difficult" poetry, although the demands it makes on the reader, the nature of its refusals and explorations, are essential to its project. However, these demands, and the nature of their works' critique of experience, have also left Riley and Mulford marginal to an already marginal feminist poetics. Their critique nevertheless found parallels within an increasingly influential body of feminist academic theory, which shared the focus on language and representation and in the 1980s was dedicated to a refusal of what was seen as the essentialist project of radical feminism. Mulford, herself, points to a potentially fruitful relationship "between women working in the theoretical field and those producing certain kinds of contemporary fiction and poetry, both here and in America."[65] Her complaint is that Marxist/feminist academics influenced by poststructuralist theory were working on nineteenth- and early-twentieth-century literature, rather than reading contemporary poetry.[66] However, it is not the case that the poetry represented in *One Foot on the Mountain*, and continued in the work of poets such as Fell, Kazantzis, Roberts, and others, is in any simple sense restricted by the limits of a consciousness-raising model of personal experience, despite the weight of this theoretical critique.

Judith Kazantzis, for example, mixes the personal voice with poetry that critiques and reworks cultural myths, such as the biblical story of Noah's ark or the Greek Medea—"princess of the high I.Q."—who becomes an emblem for feminist modes of resistance and for the transgression of traditional ideals of femininity.[67] Notably, in "Medea," Kazantzis uses an assertive personal mode of address tied to a contemporary register: "Medea, mother of witches / drawn by dragons in your getaway car / you got the rough edge of the world."[68] In consequence, although the poem depends on classical allusion, the characterization of the speaker links the subject matter to women's personal experience and accedes to the demand for accessibility.[69] In this instance, and equally in the case of "personal experience," poems about menstruation, abortion, women's sexual pleasure, lesbian sexuality, and other taboo subjects, the impact is the result of the poems' intervention into literary traditions and norms rather than the unmediated expression of women's experience. That is, it is not that the poems reflect experience that exists outside of or prior to its expression in the poem. Rather, as Jan Montefiore's book, *Feminism and Poetry,* makes clear, experience is written in terms of available conventions or its representation.[70]

Montefiore, in her analysis of Alison Fell's "Girl's gifts" makes this point clearly. She shows how Fell uses flowers to represent female sexuality and creativity in the poem: "I mould petals, weave stems, with love / my little finger inches in the folds: / it is done, red and gold."[71] But the flowers "are not innocently 'there,' devoid of the traditional symbolism which determines the limit of their possible meanings."[72] Rather, the poem reworks the traditional identification of women's sexuality with flowers within a specifically feminist discourse about women's culture and creativity. This, Montefiore argues, is done within a "Romantic inheritance . . . apparent in the way the child's perceptions, as much as or more than her actions, focus the poem."[73] Literary and philosophical traditions thus provide limiting frameworks for the poem, as well as being subject to critical revision. "Girl's gifts" represents, too, the juncture between fantasy and sexuality that became central to a feminist critique of consciousness-raising's neglect of the role of the unconscious (in, for example, Elizabeth Cowie's "Fantasia").[74]

Psychoanalysis, that is, offered feminist theorists a model of subjectivity that, because it was founded on the repression of a heterogeneous, infantile sexuality, could not be conceived of in terms of a fixed or innate gender identity. Fell's poem is, however, precisely a representation of that juncture and not a failure to acknowledge the degree to which sexuality and desire refuse a coherent and stable model of gendered identity. Montefiore describes the poem as representing "itself as part of women's culture of making, sharing and enjoying, in which the process of creation is valued more than the artefact."[75] That said, the poem also creates an undercurrent of unease to do with its representation of a temporality that interweaves adult sexuality with infantile eroticism. On the one hand, the poem memorializes a moment of childhood, which for poet and reader is past. On the other hand, it mixes in the present continuous tense of fantasy—"I am making a flower basket"—with the conditional tense: "I would lick the green leaf, taste the bronze / and yellow silk of my snapdragon." The poem ends, too, with the final promise of the gift giving: "I will carry it . . . It will lie, perfect, in her wrinkled palm / I will cross the grass and give it." The poem registers an infantile eroticism—"my little finger inches in the folds"—but frames it with the consciousness of being watched: "a shadow in the window is my mother / cooking, watching."[76] The assertion that the gift is "secret" combines with self-consciousness to introduce an element of sexual transgression into the positive female sensuality and creativity created by the poem, taking it beyond a simple celebration of women's culture or female sexuality. Thus, women's personal experience may be the chosen ground for the poems in *One Foot on the Mountain,* but this does not mean that the poet's treatment of experience is naive.

"This revisionist need to write poetry"

So far, I have concentrated on the nature of the aesthetics developed by feminist poets within the context of the women's movement. In the final section of this article, I want to return to the question of the marginal status of the poetry, whether grounded in women's personal experience or in a poststructuralist investigation of language and sexual difference. This marginality is arguably more obvious now than it was in the later 1970s and early 1980s, at the point of feminism's initial impact on traditional literary values. Moreover, these poets remain peripheral to feminist literary criticism, as well as to a mainstream cultural and literary scene. Recent feminist work on contemporary poetry has concentrated more on U.S. poets like Rich and Lorde and increasingly on Caribbean and South Asian British poetry.[77] And even though individual poets—for example, Liz Lochhead, Alison Fell, Gillian Allnutt, Michèle Roberts, and Mary Dorcey—may claim recognition, a focus on their merits as individuals threatens to return us to a model of literary quality that leaves unaddressed the relationship of feminist poetry's marginality to the particular imperatives of British postwar culture. More fundamentally, the values and meanings that attach to poetry in Britain can be seen to place a limit on what claims can be made for the centrality of poetry within feminism.

Kaplan's paper, "Gender and Poetry," which I discussed earlier, specifies the dilemma that faced contemporary feminist poets at the time. She states that "Poetry is a privileged metalanguage in western patriarchal culture," and although it "is increasingly written by members of oppressed groups . . . its popular appeal is so small in western society today that its shrinking audience may make its elitism or lack of it a non-issue." But, she goes on to suggest that its lack of popularity has not undermined "its status and function in high culture."[78] An awareness of this contradiction has been echoed in the writing of British feminist poets, both at the time Kaplan wrote her paper and since. The way in which Wandor, Mohin, Scott, Riley, and others write about the need to create a new feminist writing practice is never entirely at ease with the idea of choosing to write poetry.

It is here that the cultural location of feminist poetry in Britain emerges as most clearly different from that of poetry in the U.S. women's movement, even despite the influence of the United States on British feminism.

In the United States, a very clear concept of the role and value of poetry emerged out of the women's movement, articulated principally by Adrienne Rich, Audre Lorde, and Judy Grahn. Poetry was, on the one hand, a form of social and cultural critique, engaged in exposing the role of patriarchal language in constructing the world for women—what Rich calls "a criticism of language," which could "let us see and hear our words in a new dimension."[79] On the other hand, poetry is a specialized language with a privileged relationship to the unconscious, if not actually a language of the unconscious: "Poetry is too much rooted in the unconscious; it presses too close against the barriers of repression," and "Poetry is above all a concentration of the *power* of language, which is the power of our ultimate relationship to everything in the universe. It is as if forces we can lay claim to in no other way, become present to us in sensuous form."[80] It is not my purpose to discuss the assumptions about subjectivity, language, and poetry that are articulated here, but rather to note Rich's confidence in the possibility of making such claims for poetry's importance to the women's movement.[81]

Such a confidence, I would argue, can be attributed very largely to two features of U.S. culture. It emerges from the professionalization of the poet's role within the academy in the United States; the Iowa Writers' Workshop arose, for example, out of the University of Iowa's graduate creative-writing program, which was established in the 1930s. Second, there is an identifiable mainstream tradition of poetry allied to democratic ideals in the United States that could underwrite the claim that poetry was the natural language of a radical politics. June Jordan, for example, exploring the role of the poet as an African American woman, can lay claim to Walt Whitman as forebear of her own "aspiration to a believable collective voice and . . . broadly accessible language,"[82] despite her recognition of the dangers of speaking for groups or individuals who have been deprived of access to literary culture. Jordan's allegiance to a poetic tradition that represents an "egalitarian sensibility" is also informed by an international perspective peculiar to her location as a black woman. Pablo Neruda, Agostino Neto, Gabriela Mistral, Langston Hughes, Margaret Walker, and Edward Brathwaite are all poets she names, with Whitman in opposition to a narrowly rationalist, academic, and elite tradition represented by Emily Dickinson, Ezra Pound, T. S. Eliot, Wallace Stevens, Robert Lowell, and Elizabeth Bishop. Although other women poets, like Rich, for example, might quarrel about the inclusion of Dickinson in the list of the elite, the global perspective generated through the place of women of color in the U.S. women's movement was influential for white feminist poets, such as Rich, in a way that it could not be in Britain in the 1970s because of its history of imperialism and colonialism. The presence of an alternative democratic tradition meant that the assertion of a meaningful cultural role for poetry in the U.S. women's movement did not need to be as qualified and hedged by the consciousness of its elitist, high-culture value, in the way that it did in Britain.

Neither of these features was operative in Britain. Insofar as it has happened at all, the professionalization of the poet's role came much later in Britain. Moreover, the state promotion of literature through the Arts Council and Public Broadcasting (for example, through the BBC Third Programme *New Soundings* and *First Reading,* radio programs designed to popularize poetry in the 1950s) represented a clear dedication to high-culture ideals.[83] As Raymond Williams put it: "I thought that the Labour government [of 1945] had a choice: either for reconstruction of the cultural field in capitalist terms, or for funding institutions of popular education and popular culture that could have withstood the political campaigns in the bourgeois press that were already gathering momentum."[84] That is, any serious attempt to reformulate the relationship of class, value, and culture was passed up in favor of a model of good culture, which meant, in practice, a middle-class "high culture." Moreover, the precursors of a democratic mainstream tradition in verse (for example, Wordsworth) who might have been available to British women poets in the 1970s were too clearly embedded within a literary canon evidently antidemocratic in its premises. Alternatively, they were already spoken for, as in the case of Blake who had been named by Michael Horovitz and the underground poets in *Children of Albion: Poetry of the Underground in Britain,* an anthology that was no more hospitable to women than *The New Poetry.*

By contrast with either Horovitz's claim for a "poetry that jumps the book"[85] or the confidence of the U.S. feminists, feminist poets in postwar Britain rarely articulate a confident program for the revolutionary effectiveness of their poetry. Instead, it is possible to detect a persistent discomfort with having elected to "do" feminist politics in such an elite mode as poetry. Wandor humorously evokes this feeling in "Masks and Options": "a difficult paradox: in life I was placing bets on feminism, and yet in art I was being rejected by people I took to be my comrades. I remember one political meeting where a woman renounced all poetry as moribund. I went home mortified by this revisionist need to write poetry, which simply wouldn't go away."[86] This same ambivalence is much more subtly evident in the introductions to both *One Foot on the Mountain* and *Bread and Roses*. Mohin uses an epigraph from Robin Morgan that, in line with Rich's views quoted above, presents poetry as a "dangerous force" that "can move mountains" and "create the rage, the longing, the joy, the courage, the consciousness to make real revolutions." This is the model of poetry that Mohin elaborates in her introduction, describing poetry as a privileged cultural space where the transgressive can be expressed. Appropriately, the transgressive is defined as the gesture whereby the "ordinary fabric of our lives" is made significant. Poetry is also the ideal medium, she suggests, for the feminist task of changing language "so that it reflects our experience of the world" as women.[87]

However, this rearticulation of a U.S. radical feminist model of poetry is accompanied by a need, common to a number of accounts of women's poetry, to justify the choice of genre. Mohin states that "the nature of most women's lives, of course, makes any written work more likely to come out in short form, as we snatch moments from what we are supposed to be doing as mothers, as wives, as workers at the bottom of the heap. Poetry has traditionally been the place to state condensed and particular perceptions . . ."[88] The idea, put baldly, that poetry is an appropriate form for women writers because they can stir the pot with one hand while they write with the other, recurs, for example, in the introduction to the Raving Beauties' anthology, *In the Pink* (1983).[89] Its purpose lies in the display of a consciousness about the conditions of an "ordinary" woman's life, and in an acknowledgment of material determinants on literature, in the most conventional sense of the economic and social. It belongs with a cluster of similar statements that do the job of establishing the political credentials of this feminist promotion of poetry, such as statements about accessibility. The need for this justification can also, however, be read as an indication of an unease with poetry as a political form that cuts against the other claims Mohin makes for the genre.

Diana Scott also struggles with the knowledge that "most serious present-day poets are working in a situation where public recognition of poetry as a serious art form no longer exists," even though "as a poet, I believe that the experience of creating poetry is valuable, exciting, and worthy of attention."[90] The way that she offers her introduction to *Bread and Roses* as a beginner's guide for the "reader newish to poetry" demonstrates this tension. The notes represent an important acknowledgment that literary culture is not immediately available or accessible to all, but they also place Scott as the privileged possessor of this cultural capital. Hence, her tone is uncertain (for example, the reference to the "newish" reader), and her recommendations about the purpose of the notes are severely qualified: "You may wish to read them now, or to refer to them while you are reading the poetry, or to read them after you have read the poetry, or not to read them at all. They are there to be used, just like the poetry, by the reader, and in the reader's own way."[91] Significantly, her construction of an alternative relationship between reader and poetry is based on the validation of personal experience and response. This is echoed in the way that she handles the relationship between literary excellence or value and contemporary writing: "Writing for many of us, puts self-expression first and sets aside considerations of 'sounding like literature'. This is how it should be, for if all we could think about was the creation of literature many of us would never be able to start." Nonetheless, she admits: "I found that what worked in the context of a collection that consisted largely of 'literary' material, was to use feminist material of some 'literary quality.'"[92] In each case, Kaplan's point that poetry is inevitably embedded in assumptions about the superior value of high culture can be seen to conflict with the explicit feminist politics of the editor.

One key factor behind this difficulty about establishing a significant role for poetry as a mode of feminist cultural politics lies with the particular relationship of feminism to the Left in Britain. This is not so much a question of the internal divisions between radical feminism and socialist feminism that were so important in the 1970s;[93] rather, it concerns the aesthetic models available for a feminist writing practice and their connection to debates about the proper focus of cultural critique and analysis. Both Wandor and Mulford describe the difficulties that faced them. For Wandor, the aesthetic norms for both feminist and socialist work of the early 1970s were defined by socialist realism and agitprop: "There was an idea that art was only valuable when it was in the service of politics, when it went out to find a mass audience, raised their political consciousness, roused them to political action," and "mass accessibility was the only thing that justified art."[94] Her poetry was "dense, jagged, 'modernist,'" by implication inaccessible and "difficult"; but arguably it was in the nature of "all poetry" to be "moribund" and "revisionist." Women's writing groups provided Wandor and others with a forum in which to explore questions about "what 'feminist poetry' is or should be, either as regards form or content"—whether the poems had to "clearly contain an awareness of feminist struggle and change"; was the poetry "'right on' in relation to the Women's Movement," or "is it art?" All these questions were discussed in their writers' group by the five feminist poets who published *Licking the Bed Clean*.[95] Out of these groups emerged more confidence in the desirability of forming an aesthetic appropriate to feminism but not necessarily rigidly prescriptive. "Toeing an ideological line," writes Judith Kazantzis, "can have the writer of imagination lock herself into a 'constipating little cage of lies' in the end."[96] Increasingly, too, this confidence found support in the work of academic feminist literary critics.

Nonetheless, the work of feminist poets remains somewhat peripheral, not only to critical accounts of contemporary poetry but also within accounts of the history of cultural feminism. A look at Bea Campbell and Anna Coote's *Sweet Freedom* or Elizabeth Wilson's *More than Half the Sky* reveals another aspect to the relationship of the Left to feminist cultural politics. Their accounts concern not the literary products of the women's movement, but the possibilities for a feminist critique of popular media, mass-market romance fiction, the pornography industry, and advertising. Here we see the impact on the women's movement of the British Marxist tradition of cultural studies. Janet Batsleer et al., in *Rewriting English*, drew attention to the division that existed between cultural studies and literary criticism at the Birmingham Centre for Cultural Studies. "In its much firmer engagement with Marxism and, rather differently, with feminism, it had turned to an interest in cultural manifestations and speculative developments that was not by any means hospitable to the idea of literature, as that word would be understood in a university English department." The study of literature gives way here to the study of "literary-critical ideologies and discourses, and their institutional locations and forms of power."[97] Although

Rewriting English is one of the few books that does offer some discussion of British feminist poetry, in a chapter called "Remembering: feminism and the writing of women," the emphasis of the cultural studies project on discourse rather than on literature tends to undermine the basis of the rationale argued for poetry, by poets and editors like Scott and Mohin, as a privileged language of the unconscious and of radical politics. Thus, the formulation of a cultural politics within universities and on the Left essentially contributes to an inhospitable climate for a poetry of feminist political commitment.

In conclusion, it would be easy to overstate the marginality of feminist poetry in the 1970s and 1980s. And it is important to stress that the British women's movement was a productive context for women writers. The coming together of street and cultural politics around gender was, I have shown, crucial to many women poets of the period, and it is notable that Onlywomen Press has managed to keep *One Foot on the Mountain* in print. Moreover, poets such as Fell, Roberts, Dorcey, and Kazantzis have continued to publish individual collections. Nonetheless, it would be difficult to argue that poetry ever achieved the status and centrality as a "revolutionary" language that it achieved in the United States. The particular cultural context in Britain, the relationship of feminism to the Left, and the theoretical paradigms of cultural studies and poststructuralist critical theory placed severe limitations on the significance that could be claimed by the poets represented in *One Foot on the Mountain*. The poetry was squeezed from all sides: reliant on a model of women's experience that was increasingly under attack, it was also a genre associated with high-culture values and, on the face of it, of a decidedly minority appeal. Yet it challenged traditional literary values. As a result, it has been easy for cultural and literary criticism in the present to ignore British feminist poetry as a body of work. Other categorizations have become more important and have received more attention—in particular, black, migrant, and Irish women's poetry. In view of the historical invisibility of these categories of writing, this is hardly surprising. Yet I want to end by suggesting that the ease with which this has happened is problematic and that it is important to ask what this failure of critical attention to women's movement poetry represents. The answer is beyond the scope of this chapter, if only because there is no single constituency of readers, critics, or publishers who are guilty of this neglect. However, there is a common pattern of reluctance to engage with specific elements of British postwar culture and feminist history.

The publication of the *Selected Letters of Philip Larkin, 1940–1985* in 1992 provoked a storm of controversy because of the letters' casual racism and sexism.[98] Lisa Jardine, Professor of English at the University of London, summed up the controversy thus:

> The row over the Larkin Letters is in the end about whether we are right to turn our attention to a cultural centre which reflects the diversity and richness of contemporary multi-racial Britain, and to draw our contemporary values from that rich vein. Or whether to dig with nostalgic memories of a "great" Britain that (perhaps) once was, and to spend the fading years of British imperial glory trying to persuade our children that everything of value lies behind us.[99]

Here, Jardine's call for critical attention to postcolonial and migrant writing in Britain is a welcome corrective to the conservatism of many English departments and much literary culture. However, there is a danger of exoticizing "the diversity and richness of multi-cultural Britain" and making a few writers representative of selective groups. In addition to promoting and supporting writing from a range of cultural backgrounds, there also remains the task of examining the interconnections among *all* the various histories of contemporary culture. Our reluctance to look back to 1970s British feminist poetry includes a discomfort with the role of white, middle-class feminism. I would argue that it is necessary to investigate this history, and the constructions behind terms such as *white* and *middle class,* precisely in order to avoid an exoticization of the "migrant" or the "multiracial."

Moreover, the category of "women's experience," which is so central to women's movement poetry, is still troubling to British academics, feminist or otherwise. The rejection of feminist poetry as adolescent, lacking in decorum, and unmediated by formal expertise characterizes the response of feminist criticism as much as it does that of Stevenson and Adcock. This has in part to do with the continued pervasiveness of a particular kind of English poetic sensibility that Larkin is often taken to represent. But it has also to do with the potency and resistance of the category of women's experience. This was represented to me by my own comic unease when last week a woman student, neither immature nor theoretically naïve, told me of her intense excitement at reading *One Foot on the Mountain*. To her, the appeal to "women's experience" is still powerful. I have argued earlier in this chapter for a reading of the poetry that does not condescend to its theoretical naïveté but that, rather, examines the terms in which personal experience is represented. By insisting on the significance of women's movement poetry as part of both a feminist history and a history of British culture, I hope to arrive at a parallel reading of my own poststructuralist unease.

Notes

1. A. Alvarez, *The New Poetry* (London: Penguin, 1966), 17.

2. Ibid., 28–29.

3. Lilian Mohin, ed., *One Foot on the Mountain: An Anthology of British Feminist Poetry, 1969–1979* (London: Onlywomen Press, 1979).

4. Cora Kaplan, *Salt and Bitter and Good: Three Centuries of English and American Women Poets* (London: Paddington Press, 1975); Carol Cosman, Joan Keefe, and Kathleen Weaver, eds., *The Penguin Book of Women Poets* (Harmondsworth, England: Penguin, 1978).

5. Diana Scott, ed., *Bread and Roses: Women's Poetry of the Nineteenth and Twentieth Centuries* (London: Virago, 1982); Fleur Adcock, ed., *The Faber Book of Twentieth Century Women's Poetry* (London: Faber & Faber, 1987); Carol Rumens, *Making for the Open: The Chatto Book of Post-Feminist Poetry 1964–1984* (London: Chatto, 1985); and Barbara Burford, *A Dangerous Knowing: Four Black Women Poets* (London: Sheba Feminist Publishers, 1985), vii.

6. Anne Stevenson, "Writing as a Woman," in *Women Writing and Writing about Women*, ed. Mary Jacobus (London: Croom Helm, 1979).

7. Gillian Allnutt et al., eds., *the new british poetry* (London: Paladin, 1988).

8. For useful discussions of this idea of cultural consensus in postwar Britain, see Andrew Crozier, "Thrills and Frills," in *Society and Literature 1945–1970*, ed. Alan Sinfield (London: Methuen, 1983); and also Alan Sinfield, *Literature, Politics and Culture in Postwar Britain* (Oxford: Basil Blackwell, 1989).

9. It is worth noting here that Adcock is from New Zealand and Stevenson from the United States, and that a number of the poets who appeared in *One Foot on the Mountain* were Americans living in Britain.

10. Alison Fell et al., *Licking the Bed Clean: Five Feminist Poets* (London: Teeth Imprints, 1978).

11. Denise Riley, *Dry Air* (London: Virago, 1985).

12. Burford, *A Dangerous Knowing,* vii.

13. Kaplan, *Salt and Bitter and Good,* 11.

14. Grace Nichols, *i is a long memoried woman* (London: Caribbean Cultural International, Karnak House, 1983).

15. Grace Nichols, *The Fat Black Woman's Poems* (London: Virago, 1984).

16. For fuller accounts of the British women's liberation movement, see Elizabeth Meehan, "British Feminism from the 1960s to the 1980s," in *British Feminism in the Twentieth Century,* ed. Harold L. Smith (Amherst: University of Massachusetts Press, 1990), 189–204; Anna Coote and Bea Campbell, *Sweet Freedom* (London: Picador, 1982); Sheila Rowbotham, Lynne Segal, and Hilary Wainwright, *Beyond the Fragments: Feminism and the Making of Socialism* (London: Merlin Press, 1980); and David Bouchier, *The Feminist Challenge* (London: Macmillan Press, 1984).

17. Michèlene Wandor, "Masks and Options," in *On Gender and Writing,* ed. Michèlene Wandor (London: Pandora Press, 1983), 5.

18. Michèle Roberts, "Questions and Answers," in Wandor, *On Gender and Writing,* 64.

19. Rozsika Parker, "Art, Feminism and Criticism," in Wandor, *On Gender and Writing,* 89.

20. See note 10 for bibliographic details.

21. *Seven Women* (London: Women's Literature Collective, 1976); Michèlene Wandor and Michèle Roberts, eds., *Cutlasses and Earrings* (London: Playbooks, 1977); see note 3 for bibliographic details of *One Foot on the Mountain.* Although feminist presses played a crucial role in fostering women's writing, poetry, in line with mainstream publishing trends, occupied a much smaller place in their lists than did fiction.

22. Libby Houston, "On Being a Woman Poet," in Wandor, *On Gender and Writing,* 44. Stevie Smith is an important exception to both Houston's and Wandor's characterization of the poetry reading circuit.

23. Wandor, *On Gender and Writing,* 6.

24. Roberts, "Questions and Answers," 46.

25. Cora Kaplan, ed., *Papers on Patriarchy* (Brighton: PDC and Women's Publishing Collective, 1976).

26. Ibid., 27–28.

27. Ibid., 29.

28. Michèle Roberts, *The Mirror of the Mother: Selected Poems 1975–1985* (London: Methuen, 1986), 27.

29. See Fell et al., *Licking the Bed Clean,* 1–2, where Kaplan is quoted at length.

30. I am taking this anthology as representative of a particular trend in feminist poetry. Many of the poets published in it continued to write and publish work that would not necessarily fit with this trend. Moreover, I have been able to discuss only a tiny minority of the numerous poets whose work fits within my category. My choice of poets and poems to discuss is not made on the basis of individual literary quality

or significance, these being exactly the criteria that make it impossible to consider women's movement poetry satisfactorily.

31. Astra, "coming out celibate," in Mohin, *One Foot on the Mountain*, 37–38.

32. Ibid., 37.

33. Mohin, introduction to *One Foot on the Mountain*, 5.

34. Angela Hamblin, "To Astra," in Mohin, *One Foot on the Mountain*, 17.

35. Virginia Woolf, *A Room of One's Own* (London: Grafton Books, 1977), 95.

36. Astra, "coming out celibate," 38.

37. Hamblin, "To Astra," 18.

38. Mohin, introduction to *One Foot on the Mountain*, 1.

39. *The Redstockings Manifesto* (New York: Redstockings, 1979), 5.

40. Ibid.

41. Fanny Viner, introduction to *In the Pink: The Raving Beauties Choose Poems from the Show and Many More*, ed. Raving Beauties (London: Women's Press, 1983), 11–13.

42. Adcock, introduction to *Faber Book of Twentieth Century Women's Poetry*, 13.

43. Anne Stevenson, "Review," *Times Literary Supplement*, 15 July 1983.

44. An immediate example of Sexton's influence on feminist poetry in Britain is Barbara A. Zanditon's "The Big Tease Lady Playing Games with Death," dedicated to Anne Sexton, in Mohin, *One Foot on the Mountain*, 40.

45. Cited in Diane Wood Middlebrook, *Anne Sexton: A Biography* (Boston: Houghton Mifflin, 1991), 364.

46. Anne Stevenson, "Is the Emperor of Ice Cream Wearing Clothes?" *New Review*, 17 August 1975, 43, cited in ibid.

47. Caroline Gilfillian, [Untitled], in Mohin, *One Foot on the Mountain*, 46.

48. See, for example, Anne Stevenson, *Correspondences: A Family History in Letters* (Oxford: Oxford University Press, 1974).

49. Adrienne Rich, *Of woman born: Motherhood as Experience and Institution* (New York: W. W. Norton, 1976), 13.

50. Caroline Halliday, "Reading 'Of woman born,' by Adrienne Rich," in Mohin, *One Foot on the Mountain*, 58.

51. Rich, *Of woman born*, 13.

52. Adrienne Rich, "Consciousness Raising," in *Radical Feminism*, ed. Anne Koedt, Ellen Levine, and Anita Rapone (New York: Quadrangle Books, 1973), 280–81.

53. Mohin, *One Foot on the Mountain*, 5.

54. Zoe Fairbairns, Sara Maitland, Valerie Miner, Michèle Roberts, and Michèlene Wandor, *Tales I Tell My Mother: A Collection of Feminist Short Stories* (London: Journeyman Press, 1978).

55. Ibid., 6.

56. Alison Fell continues to use the idea of contextualizing her poems with biographical prose introductions in *The Crystal Owl* (London: Methuen, 1988).

57. Wendy Mulford, "Notes on Writing: A Marxist/Feminist Viewpoint," *Red Letters* 9 (1979); reprinted in Wandor, *On Gender and Writing*, 31–41.

58. *The Redstockings Manifesto*, 5.

59. Ibid., 31.

60. Ibid., 32.

61. Denise Riley, "A note on sex and 'the reclaiming of language,'" in *Dry Air*, 7.

62. Ibid.

63. Cora Kaplan, *Sea Changes: Essays in Culture and Feminism* (London: Verso, 1986), 72.

64. Mulford, in Wandor, *On Gender and Writing*, 5. Mulford is here quoting Hélène Cixous in an interview with Christiane Makward in *Substance* 13 (1976).

65. Ibid.

66. Exceptions to this would be Cora Kaplan, *Papers on Patriarchy*; Jan Montefiore, *Feminism and Poetry: Language, Experience, Identity in Women's Writing* (London: Pandora Press, 1987); Alicia Suskin Ostriker, *Stealing the Language: The Emergence of Women's Poetry in America* (Boston: Beacon Press, 1986); and the work of Vicki Bertram. The work of Montefiore and Ostriker did not appear, however, until the second half of the eighties and was concentrated on American more than on British poetry.

67. Liz Lochhead and Judith Kazantzis both follow in Sexton's footsteps in their revisions of fairy tales and myths.

68. Judith Kazantzis, "Medea," in Mohin, *One Foot on the Mountain*, 121.

69. See Ostriker, *Stealing the Language*, 210–40, and Montefiore, *Feminism and Poetry*, 38–56, for good discussions of what Ostriker calls "revisionist mythology."

70. Montefiore, *Feminism and Poetry*, 1–25.

71. Alison Fell, "Girl's gifts," in Mohin, *One Foot on the Mountain*, 12.

72. Montefiore, *Feminism and Poetry*, 19.

73. Ibid.

74. Elizabeth Cowie, "Fantasia," *m/f* 9 (1984): 71–104.

75. Montefiore, *Feminism and Poetry*, 19.

76. Fell, "Girl's gifts," 1-12.

77. See Liz Yorke, *Impertinent Voices: Subversive Strategies in Contemporary Women's Poetry* (London: Routledge, 1991); Patrick Williams, "Difficult Subjects: Black British Women Poets," in *Literary Theory and Poetry: Extending the Canon*, ed. David Murray (London: B. T. Batsford, 1989), 108–26; Merle Collins, "Themes and Trends in Caribbean Poetry," in *The Empire Writes Back* (London: Methuen, 1980). Vicki Bertram's work on contemporary women's poetry in Britain is an exception in its concern with the women's movement poets whom I discuss.

78. Kaplan, "Gender and Poetry," in Kaplan, *Papers on Patriarchy*, 21.

79. Adrienne Rich, *On Lies, Secrets, and Silence: Selected Prose, 1966–1978* (London: Virago, 1980), 248.

80. Ibid., 175, 248.

81. See Margaret Homans, *Women Writers and Poetic Identity* (Princeton: Princeton University Press, 1980), and Montefiore for good discussions of the underlying assumptions.

82. June Jordan, *Civil Wars* (Boston: Beacon Press, 1981), xxiv.

83. Blake Morrison, *The Movement: English Poetry and Fiction of the 1950s* (Oxford: Oxford University Press, 1980), 42–47.

84. Raymond Williams, cited in Sinfield, *Postwar Britain*, 50.

85. Michael Horovitz, *Children of Albion: Poetry of the Underground in Britain* (Harmondsworth, England: Penguin, 1969), 323.

86. Wandor, "Masks and Options," 16.

87. Mohin, introduction to *One Foot on the Mountain*, 1.

88. Ibid.

89. "I have always been someone who tried to squeeze the impossible into each day, determined to be at once a good mother, wife, friend, teacher, actress; so reading became a luxury. I read poetry because it was brief, but satisfying" (Anna Carteret, *In the Pink*, 16).

90. Diana Scott, introduction to *Bread and Roses*, 17, 1.

91. Ibid., 1.

92. Ibid., 190.

93. See Segal, *Beyond the Fragments*, for a full account.

94. Wandor, "Masks and Options," 5–6.

95. Fell et al., *Licking the Bed Clean*, 1–3.

96. Judith Kazantzis, "The Errant Unicorn," in Wandor, *On Gender and Writing*, 26.

97. Janet Batsleer, Tony Davies, Rebecca O'Rourke, and Chris Weedon, *Rewriting English: Cultural Politics of Gender and Class* (London: Methuen, 1985), 3.

98. *The Selected Letters of Philip Larkin, 1940-1985*, ed. Anthony Thwaite (London: Faber & Faber, 1992).

99. Lisa Jardine, "Saxon Violence," *Guardian*, 2 December 1992, 20.

CHAPTER FIVE

Ian Hamilton Finlay
and Concrete Poetry

Nicholas Zurbrugg

"Some questions require to be answered."
"You must ask me whatever you wish.
—Those things strung on the knotted string
You are staring at, are fish."
"Fish?—I thought they were socks."
He wrote me all down in his book.

As these lines from Ian Hamilton Finlay's early poem "O.H.M.S." indicate, his poetic vision is voluntarily metaphorical and mistrustful of ministerial rhetoric.[1] Finlay's mature work is equally resistant to the critic's compulsion to write it "all down" in their book; indeed, as Finlay himself has acknowledged, it is not his intention to be "an easy artist."[2]

Finlay's poetry is not "easy," for a number of reasons. First, its very form—extralinear groupings of words, or words and images—takes the average reader by surprise. It is far easier to make naive jokes about the term *concrete poetry* than to trace this genre's artistic origins. Second, the fact that Finlay's explorations of this form span several media, such as the printed page, the card and poster, the folio of prints, the three-dimensional installation, and the allegorical garden, makes it difficult for one to place Finlay's work in familiar categories. Commenting upon "the small crisis of classification" brought about by the "bewildering variety of forms in which the work of Ian Hamilton Finlay has appeared," his fellow poet Thomas A. Clark notes how Finlay has variously been identified as "'the father of concrete poetry,' a gardener, a sculptor or (the current solution) simply an 'artist,' taking that word as a hold-all for any odd or unpredictable behavior."[3]

A third reason for one's sense of difficulty before Finlay's work is its very compression. Frequently Finlay's compositions synthesize and distill a number of associations and require considerable additional information in order to be fully understood. So far as Finlay is concerned, accompanying texts by the critic offer a solution to this problem. Familiarity with the thematic and aesthetic evolution of Finlay's work also facilitates its accessibility.

As becomes evident, Finlay's ethical and aesthetic integrity continually challenges public taste and expectations by integrating imagery and allusions in unexpected ways. Defending his use of classical references, for example, Finlay's "More Detached Sentences on Gardening in the Manner of Shenstone" (1984) characteristically observes: "As public sex was embarrassing to the Victorians, public classicism is to us."[4] Proving precisely this point, Finlay's use of classical references, and his contemporary "translations" of classical references, have repeatedly provoked widespread critical debate. Whereas the Italian art historian Achille Bonito Oliva argues that the return to classical allusion in the seventies and eighties is characterized by art that "lets the image ride without asking where it comes from or where it is going, following drifts of pleasure,"[5] Finlay's work of the last two decades considers the past and present function of images with exemplary independence, imagination, and moral seriousness.

Pondering, for example, upon the most appropriate iconography for terror in the late twentieth century, Finlay observes: "If war-galleys were a main subject of sculpture in Roman gardens, why should not stone aircraft carriers—representations of our modern Imperial navies—be thought proper in ours?"[6] Finlay's argument here evokes two fundamental aspects of his mature poetics: the attempt to work within, and yet also to update, traditions of classical imagery and the attempt to evoke this imagery with maximum visual immediacy and contemporaneity by employing word and image in sculptural terms—in this instance, within the context and the tradition of the ornamental, allegorical garden.

Finlay's unexpected defense and deployment of images, such as the aircraft carrier, might at first seem too unfashionable and unfathomable to take seriously. Like W. H. Auden, when faced with examples of verbal/visual texts, one might at first be tempted to reply, "I'm sorry, but that's not poetry."[7] Or, like the architectural historian Charles Jencks, one might well initially argue that Finlay's most recent work resists definition. Applauding the "challenging impulse" of Finlay's work, but also rather gingerly appraising it as "wonderfully mad but just," Jencks concludes: "The media is so mixed—including photos, pamphlets, sculpture, gardens, art works, model battleships and engraved stones—as to defy any simple marketing strategy New York City might come up with."[8]

Neither Auden's rather traditional sense of the parameters of poetic practice nor New York City marketing strategies offers very helpful guides to Finlay's innovative oeuvre. Although Finlay's themes are usually eminently traditional, his choice of imagery and of media are often highly surprising and, to many, highly disconcerting. Paradoxically, perhaps, Finlay is best defined as a neoclassical avant-gardist: a poet and artist working from past traditions across present and evolving media. In this respect, he is not so much iconoclastic as pluralist. His innovations are not attempts to ridicule or eliminate the past but, rather, attempts to extend past traditions in contemporary ways. As the American composer John Cage suggests in "Experimental Music" (1957), innovation need not necessarily prompt critical indifference or ire. "The coming into being of something new does not by that fact deprive what was of its proper place. Each thing has its own place; and the more things there are, as is said, the merrier."[9]

Cage's enthusiasm for creative innovation and for the avant-garde tradition in art hinges upon his conviction that inventive art preserves "flexibility of mind" and prevents artists from falling prey to the orthodoxies of "government and education."[10] Like Cage's music, Finlay's poetry typifies the way in which many of the most innovative artists of the late twentieth century have extended their initial practice across adjacent art forms, following the example of the poets, artists, and musicians of the early-twentieth-century avant-garde movements, such as Futurism and Dadaism.[11]

English literary criticism has often been slow to recognize the positive potential of the early-twentieth-century avant-garde, preferring instead the familiar academic verse that Michael Hamburger deplores as "a by-product of literary criticism, full of literary allusions and—what is much worse—of a piddling wit, a trivial ingenuity that cries out for the applause of learned colleagues."[12] In his British Council survey, *Poetry Today, 1960–1973*, Anthony Thwaite, for example, dedicates a little over three pages to "extreme experimentation," makes no mention of Finlay's poetry, and rather condescendingly confides that "[though] my own attitude is that such work is culturally marginal it deserves to be treated with something other than contempt: it is a sign of *homo ludens*, and its ingenuities are sometimes genuinely mind-stretching."[13]

Finlay's work may well appear "marginal" if the tradition sketched above by Hamburger is considered "central," and if the critic nurtures insular rather than international values. If one's model for great English poetry is poetry that, in Stephen Spender's terms, conveys "the feeling that the poet lives in this landscape, has always lived in this landscape," thereby "making a virtue of the unexcitingness of England" and "insisting on the quietness of England,"[14] then poetic experimentation based upon the early-twentieth-century avant-garde will undoubtedly seem extremely "marginal" at first sight. Finlay's achievement, however, is to resolve this tension by creating a *formally* experimental poetry that—initially, at least—celebrates "the quietness" of seafaring and pastoral life in Scotland.

As the French sound poet and artist Henri Chopin remarks, literary criticism frequently fails to take adequate account of what one might term the multimedia sensibility.

> For me, the problem is that most people are completely unaware of the real quality of twentieth century creativity. Even in the nineteenth century, for example, Victor Hugo was perhaps a better graphic artist than a poet, Baudelaire was also both a very great graphic artist and poet. Paul Valéry was just as interested in drawing as in poetry. If we now turn to the Italian Futurists, for example, Luigi Russolo was a painter, a composer and an inventor. Albert-Birot was a typographer, a sculptor, a poet and a dramatist. Arp was the same—several disciplines. Seuphor too. Throughout the twentieth century, all of these categories have exploded.[15]

Turning to the problem of categorizing his own practice—"the question of whether or not Chopin should be categorised as a composer or as a poet"— Chopin concludes: "the best critical solution seems to be to suggest that as a result of this research, the frontier between poetry and music no longer exists."[16] In much the same way, Cage's research suggests the way in which the frontiers between music, text, and theater become insignificant, and Finlay's research suggests, in turn, the ways in which hypothetical divisions between poetry, painting, and sculpture have become increasingly irrelevant to art practices since the seventies.

It is instructive to compare differing critical responses to the kind of inter-arts experimentation championed by Chopin, Cage, and Finlay. Rather simplistically associating experimentation with iconoclasm, Anthony Thwaite muses: "'Divisions between the arts are breaking down,' as Bob Cobbing has written: to some, the contemplation of destruction is itself a form of enjoyment—even a form of art—though in a century that has seen as much destruction as ours such tastes should surely be repugnant."[17]

Focusing instead upon the concrete poem's explicit formal cohesion, Jonathan Raban's *The Society of the Poem* (1971) mischievously proposes that concrete poems

> Stand in relation to the central body of contemporary English and American poetry much as the sacking-and-scrubbed-deal Health Food restaurant does to the steak house. They self-consciously exemplify the virtues of impoverishment and deprivation.

In Raban's terms, concrete poems are somehow guilty of "the puritanical air of righteous minimalism" and, at worst, consist of "elegant examples of the craft of the typographer," posing as it were as "the very last unpolluted goods that could be salvaged from the ruins of corrupted language."[18]

Raban's generalizations are both perceptive and deceptive. Even though the concrete poem obviously is a minimal, restrained genre, its minimal restraint is no more symptomatic of axiomatic semantic impoverishment or deprivation than the haiku or the imagist poem. Rather, as another of Finlay's earliest critics, the concrete poet Dom Sylvester Houédard, proposes: "Concrete poems can be dull amusing grand satirical playful sad—anything except epic."[19]

Not surprisingly, Finlay's most perceptive early critics were almost always interested in both poetry and art, and they usually practiced what they preached. Discussing concrete poetry and the potential of experimental typography in *Typography/Basic Principles* (1966), John Lewis enthusiastically argued: "When this kind of typography is handled by a poet, we

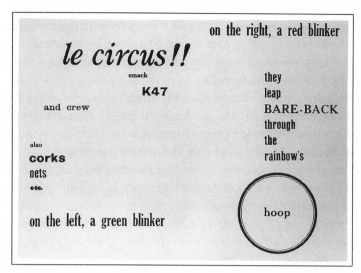

Fig. 5.1. Ian Hamilton Finlay, "Poster Poem" (1964)

come nearest to *my* understanding of what typography is all about . . . not only the sense of the words but the look of the printed word on the page."[20]

Lewis's comments upon Finlay's "Poster Poem" offer particularly valuable analysis of the way in which the poem's typographical, semantic, and semiotic metaphors "double" its levels of allusion. Remarking that Finlay's evocation of a fishing scene "has parodied the old-fashioned typographic circus poster," Lewis observes:

> The imagery is doubled so that the fishing smack K47 is compared to a little circus pony and vice versa, for ponies and fishing smacks are fat, sturdy, and staunch. The colored blinkers of the pony become the port and starboard navigation lights of the smack. The rainbow in its reflection in the sea is the hoop through which the pony jumps, or the boat sails.[21]

Although it is certainly the case that many of Finlay's poster poems consciously parody or echo *popular* visual traditions, such as the circus poster, it is also evident that his *poetic* orchestration of the poster format elaborates and refines many of the more visual, *artistic* experiments with text and typography of the early-twentieth-century avant-garde. As the poet and artist

Brion Gysin puts it, "Writing is fifty years behind painting," in the sense that many of the literary experiments of the past three or four decades belatedly adapt ideas first explored by the artists of the early twentieth century.[22]

This tendency suggests that postmodern literary experiments, such as the concrete poetry, sound poetry, and cut-up poetry movements of the years since the Second World War, are not so much developments in opposition to the modernist avant-garde as they are the highly positive developments that Dom Sylvester Houédard describes as "the reincarnation of pre–WW/1 creativities in the post–WW/2 world." Tracing the origins of this kind of positive postmodern avant-garde creativity, Houédard attributes concrete poetry's verbal-visual aesthetic to two modernist groupings:

> POETS who use layouts to reinforce poetic ideas (Marinetti Mayakovsky) or make pictures with type (Apollinaire); ARTISTS who use type to create messages as much pictorial as literary (Schwitters Picabia van Doesburg Lissitzky Boccioni).[23]

Even though all the above poets and artists "reinforce" words with typographic layout or create pictures with words and letters, and thus anticipate many aspects of concrete poetry, the specific ambitions of the pioneer concrete poets are best understood as belated literary counterparts to the ideals that the De Stijl painter Theo van Doesburg and the Dadaist Hans Arp associated with "concrete art."

Van Doesburg's manifesto "Art Concret" (1930) proposes a rigorously nonreferential art that would "exclude lyricism, dramatism, symbolism, etc." and "be constructed entirely from plastic elements, that is to say planes and colors."[24] Published in the same year, van Doesburg's notes on "elementarism," in the last issue of *De Stijl*, similarly advocate an "approach to universal form" based upon "the calculation of measure, direction and number . . . the basis of the pyramid."[25] Arp's manifesto, "Abstract Art, Concrete Art" (1942), likewise proposes "a denial of man's egotism," arguing that art should "remain anonymous and form part of nature's great workshop."[26]

Although concrete art was subsequently championed by the Swiss artist Max Bill, as "a non-individualistic approach to so-called art problems,"[27] and in 1960 became firmly established in Bill's exhibition *Concrete Art: Fifty Years of Development*, it was not until 1954 that the poet Eugen Gomringer— Bill's secretary for the years 1954–58—published one of the first concrete poetry manifestos, "From Line to Constellation." Here, Gomringer proposed that poetry, too, might offer a strictly nonindividualistic approach to the fundamental elements of language.

In Gomringer's terms, concrete poetry would constitute "a reality in itself and not a poem about something or other." "Perceived visually as a whole as well as in its parts," this sort of elementary textual composition was conceived of as "an arrangement, and at the same time a play-area of fixed dimensions,"[28] within which the reader's eye could freely roam—or "play"—across its extralinear structure. Emphasizing its formal, material qualities, Gomringer's subsequent manifesto, "Concrete Poetry" (1956), specified that the concrete poem should function first and foremost as "a linguistic structure" rather than as "a valve for the release of all sorts of emotions and ideas."[29] To some extent, then, concrete poetry anticipates the equally linguistic structural values advocated by Roland Barthes in the mid sixties in essays such as "The Death of the Author" (1968), in which Barthes also more or less claimed that texts were play-areas of fixed dimensions, where "everything is to be *disentangled*, but nothing *deciphered*."[30]

Although Finlay's early concrete poems and associated writings espouse a similarly impersonal aesthetic, his subsequent work, particularly his overtly political and ethical texts of the eighties, indicate a far more complex range of references. Barthes's later writings, especially his essays on photography in *Camera Lucida* (1981), also look beyond structural and social codes to the more personal evocations that Barthes associates with "punctum,"[31] or deep, uncodifiable responses to the photographic image.

In this respect, what Raban might term the "puritanical air of righteous minimalism" in both Finlay's and Barthes's early writings is perhaps best understood historically, as a reaction against the excessively subjective and authorial emphasis of writing and criticism in the sixties. Barthes, for his part, argued that the "image of literature to be found in contemporary culture" was "tyrannically centred on the author, his person, his tastes, his passions."[32] In much the same way, Finlay's early enthusiasm for concrete poetry's ordered, impersonal aesthetic grew from his increasing impatience toward the pervasive anxiety that he associated with "anguish poems" and "self poetry."[33]

As Jeff Nuttall emphasizes in *Bomb Culture* (1968), much English and American art, fiction, and poetry in the early sixties seemed haunted by intimations of impending personal and global calamity. Citing the painting of Francis Bacon and the novels of William Burroughs as exemplars of an era in which "art itself has seldom been closer to its violent and orgiastic roots," Nuttall amusingly relates that

> As Francis Bacon's *Figure In A Landscape* caused a schoolgirl to faint on the floor of the Tate Gallery, so *The Naked Lunch* actually caused at least one unprepared square to vomit on the carpet. . . . It depicts the world and existence as a nightmare obscenity and it describes accurately how we felt the world to be at that point.[34]

Finlay's early concrete poems are a considered reaction against this kind of indulgent, confessional creativity. Writing to Dom Sylvester Houédard in the early sixties, Finlay comments: "The new poetry will be a poetry without the word 'I.' It will be silent, and will be a sign of peace and sanity. I think the poets should bear the anguish of not writing anguish poems. I think self poetry is bad, now."[35] Explaining that his own poems tend either to be playfully referential, in the sense that Derain's *fauve* paintings used bright color to evoke the intensity of summer landscapes, or to evoke abstract spirituality, in somewhat the same way that Malevich's suprematist squares and rectangles aspired to convey pure feeling, Finlay adds: "My own concrete poems are of two kinds—one corresponding to *fauve* painting (in feeling) and one to suprematism. They are not ambitious. I try to make them exact."[36]

As Finlay explains in a letter of 17 September 1963 to the French concrete poet Pierre Garnier, his search for exactness of expression began with "the extraordinary (since wholly unexpected) sense that the syntax I had been using . . . had to be replaced with something else" that might allow the poem to "'make it,' possibly, into a state of perfection." For Finlay, the concrete poem's orderly extralinear syntax best approximated to this ethically and aesthetically desirable sense of order.

"Concrete" by its very limitations offers a tangible image of goodness and sanity; it is very far from the now-fashionable poetry of
anguish and self. . . . It is a model of order, even if set in a space
which is full of doubt. . . . I would like, if I could, to bring into this,
somewhere the unfashionable notion of "Beauty," which I find
compelling and immediate, however theoretically inadequate. I
mean this in the simplest way—that if I was asked, "Why do you
like concrete poetry?" I could truthfully answer "Because it is beautiful."[37]

Finlay's impulse toward an extralinear "model, of order" continually
surfaces in his first collection of poems, *The Dancers Inherit the Party* (1960).
One way or another, the poems in this collection all seem to approximate
to the more concise "small but intense and tightly bound systems of relationships" that M. L. Rosenthal associates with his first concrete poems.[38]
    "Angles of Stamps," for example, rather ponderously dwells upon the
codes of stamps and other amorous inscriptions upon envelopes, reflecting:

> Stick a stamp at an angle on a letter
> It means a kiss, yes, but what sort, is it a torn
> Kiss, sweet kiss, anguished, cool as water
> Rowan-burning kiss or kiss as pure as hawthorn?
>
> *(D, 12)*

Whereas this poem ends conclusively, with "A crooked stamp means a kiss
and so do little crosses," Finlay's one-word poems in *Air Letters* (1968) jux-
tapose—rather than articulate—the relationship between amorous signs and
abbreviations and pastoral images. The title "The Windmill's Poem" prefigures the text "X," and the title "The Sunset's Poem" prefigures the text
"S.W.A.L.K."[39]
    Such poems are not Finlay's strongest works, and are perhaps most
interesting as exploratory texts—or as a kind of expeditionary gesture within
a new genre. Compared with the final lines of Philip Larkin's "Money,"
these poems might not even seem to *be* poems, in the sense that they appear
to say so little, whereas Larkin's lines seem to say so much:

It's like looking down
From long french windows at a provincial town,
The slums, the canals, the churches ornate and mad
In the evening sun. It is intensely sad.[40]

Reconsidered in terms of Finlay's work, however, it might be argued that
Larkin's lines say *too* much. Not content with the notion of a provincial
town, Larkin lists slums, canals, and churches. Not content with churches,
he qualifies them as "ornate and mad." Not content with recording this
vision touched by evening sun, he adds: "It is intensely sad."

By contrast, Finlay spares the reader such qualifications and judgments
as "provincial," "ornate and mad," and "intensely sad" and offers the reader
the implied relationship between evening sun and a loving kiss, or the
implied correspondence between a kiss and a windmill's sail silhouetted
against the skyline. Arguably, there is a certain spirit of generosity in Finlay's
restraint: his texts await realization via the reader's imagination, rather than
offer the reader a textual fait accompli, adjectives and all, rhymes and all.

Another poem in *The Dancers*, entitled "The One-Horse Town," initially
appears closer in spirit to Larkin's "Money," until one realizes that rather
than offering a detailed cityscape with particular emotional overtones, the
poem employs the clichés of description and Wild West narrative in order
to conflate the connotations of its title and text.

A little one-horse town . . . I asked, "Where
is this?" The Sheriff told me, "Dobbin."
The evening sun went down.

(*D*, 48)[41]

United under a generic "evening sun," the whimsical connotations of
this poem's American and rural English vernacular might well have been
reduced to "THE ONE-HORSE TOWN/ *Dobbin*" in Finlay's subsequent collection of one-word poems, *Stonechats* (1967). Setting one-word "texts" beside
complex, crossword clue-like preparatory titles, this volume invites the reader
to trace the implicit connections linking such condensed models of metaphorical order as "'THE BOAT'S BLUEPRINT/ *water*"; "THE CLOUD'S ANCHOR/

swallow"; "ONE (ORANGE) ARM OF THE WORLD'S OLDEST WINDMILL/
autumn.'"[42]

Finlay's typographic and visual imagination is perhaps most obviously
evident in "Scene," a poem that rather curiously places the geometric imagery of triangles, squares, and ellipses within rhyming couplets, describing, rather than typographically transcribing, the angular aspect of rain,
distant trees, and so on.

> The fir tree stands quite still and angles
> On the hill, for green Triangles.
> Stewing in its billy there
> The tea is strong, and brown, and Square.
> The rain is Slant, Soaked fishers sup
> Sad Ellipses from a cup.
>
> > (D, 46)

Some four years after the publication of "Scene," Finlay's typewriter
poems, *Telegrams from my Windmill* (1964), demonstrated that he had finally
found a way to present the kind of typographic vision outlined in "Scene"
within more impersonal, extralinear terms. Abandoning the Larkinesque
tone of lines such as "soaked fishers sup / Sad Ellipses from a cup," and
condensing "fir tree," "hill," "angles," and "green Triangles" into a single,
immediate verbal/visual composition, "fir/far," typifies the concision of
Finlay's early concrete vision.

It is precisely this kind of highly condensed and more or less instantly
assimilable presentation of different concepts and relationships that Finlay's
concrete poems perfect. Both typographically, in terms of the perspectival
relationship of the word *fir* leading from left and right to a distant central
horizon, and semantically, in terms of the sonic distinction between *fir* and
far, this poem dynamically synthesizes the verbal/visual energies of two
seemingly simple words.

Such "exact" ideogrammatic structures could not be more distant from
the studied subjective intensity of lines like Ginsberg's: "I saw the best minds
of my generation destroyed by madness"; Lowell's "My mind's not right";
Plath's "Daddy, daddy, you bastard, I'm through"; and Mitchell's "I smell
something burning, hope it's just my brains."[43] Not surprisingly, Finlay

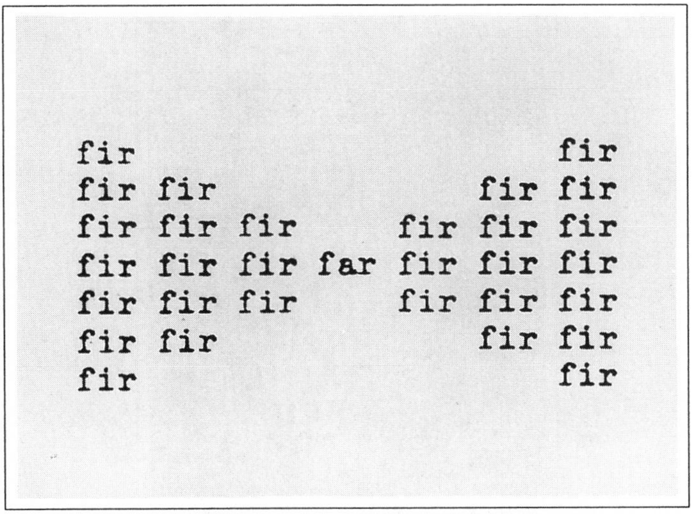

```
fir                          fir
fir fir                  fir fir
fir fir fir          fir fir fir
fir fir fir  far fir fir fir
fir fir fir          fir fir fir
fir fir                  fir fir
fir                          fir
```

Fig. 5.2. Ian Hamilton Finlay, "fir/far" (1964)[44]

himself soon argued for slightly more complex expression, proposing by
the mid sixties that "the simplicity achieved by concrete . . . is only going
to *remain* possible if we can get back to metaphor."[45]

Something of this metaphorical ambition becomes clear when one considers Finlay's poem poster "Star/Steer" of 1966. As Stephen Bann comments,
this poem, drawn from the world of seafaring, is not so much an ideogrammatic synthesis of the spatial relationship of a natural scene, as a fusion of
"two distinct interpretations or viewpoints in the serpentine structure of the
poem." Discussing the way in which the position and typography of the poem's
final word, "steer," corresponds in position and typeface to the ninth of a
series of twelve successive repetitions of the word "star" rising above it, Bann
points out that although the poem might evoke both "the relationship of star
to steersman" (in terms of the star seemingly being "caught in the rigging of
the ship") and the more general "winding course plotted by the steersman"
(in terms of several stars delineating this course), "The strength of the work
comes from both of these images and from neither, since beyond the intri-
cacies of the printed word and the metaphor of the ship at sea there is the
intimation of our own course to be chosen, and our own star to steer by."[46]

If Finlay's early concrete poems and his found poems of the sixties
celebrated relatively timeless metaphorical visions, his work of the early

Fig. 5.3. Ian Hamilton Finlay, "Star/Steer" (1966)[47]

seventies becomes increasingly concerned with specifically contemporary
subject matter. A text introducing his folder *Headlines/Pondlines* (1969)—a
series of poems illustrated by drawings by John Furnival—explicitly defends
"the tradition of describing ponds" as "a largely uncorrupted one" and offers
what one might think of as consciously atemporal haiku-like renderings of
prosaic journalist "headlines" in "pondlines" such as: "GREAT FROG-RACE
A FLOP" and "pebble ROCKS POND."

In much the same way, Finlay's folder, *FISHING NEWS, NEWS* (1970),
combines miraculous titles with mundane extracts from *FISHING NEWS*,
transforming the banality of local headlines into such magical tales as "FROM
'THE METAMORPHOSIS OF *FISHING NEWS*' (1)/ 'SHETLAND BOATS TURN
TO SCALLOPS'" and "FROM 'THE ILLUMINATIONS OF *FISHING NEWS*'/
'OCEAN STARLIGHT TOWED OFF ROCKS.'"[48]

By contrast, the more historical focus of Finlay's work of the seventies
is typified by "homage to gomringer" (1972), a poem-print made with the
artist Ron Costley that relates the formal and thematic purity and dignity

Fig. 5.4. Ian Hamilton Finlay, with John Furnival, "pebble ROCKS POND" (1969)[49]

of Gomringer's poetics to the structural and mechanical purity and effi-
ciency of the Second World War German battleship, the *Prinz Eugen*. Discussing his decision to evoke such contemporary references, Finlay comments:
"The appearance of the warship in my work signifies the rejection of purity
as inconsequentiality in favor of purity as commitment."[50]

This sense of "commitment" is best understood in terms of Finlay's
transition from atemporal, universal motifs to more immediate, contemporary questions. "homage to gomringer," like "Star/Steer" certainly juxtaposes related concepts. But whereas "Star/Steer" relates predominantly
general images and, at most, asks rather general questions regarding the
viewer's own points of reference, "homage to gomringer" invites the reader
to consider the poetry of the seventies in terms of a precise historical event.

Introducing the historical event to which "homage to gomringer" refers, in terms of the ethical allegory "underpinning" this work, Stephen

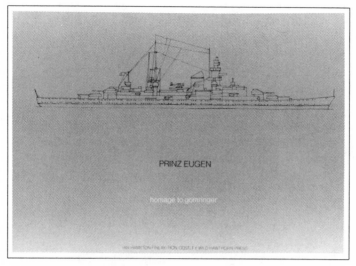

Fig. 5.5. Ian Hamilton Finlay, "homage to gomringer" (1972) with Ron Costley[51]

Bann comments that "when its dedicated German crew handed over the warship at the end of the Second World War, ten out of eleven engines were working. But by the time that the Americans had sailed the *Prinz Eugen* to Honolulu, only one of these was still in operation. The same thing has happened, Finlay implies, to the 'Cruiser Concrete Poetry'."[52]

Considered at face value, this poem-print appears to celebrate the rigorous design of both the *Prinz Eugen* and of Eugen Gomringer's poetry. Considered more precisely, however, in terms of the specific historical fates of the *Prinz Eugen* and of concrete poetry as a movement, "homage to gomringer" may also be read as a more satirical work that ponders the fates of its subjects. By the late sixties, concrete poetry had proliferated both aesthetically and geographically and, in Gomringer's terms, had frequently become "a mere typographic game."[53] Expressing much the same reservations, Finlay declined to contribute to John Sharkey's *Mindplay: An Anthology of British Concrete Poetry* (1971), explaining that this decision was at least partially motivated by his sense of being "outside and uninvolved in what is happening now."[54]

Depending upon their aesthetic and existential priorities, poets and critics either bewailed the "coarsening and vulgarisation" of purist concrete poetry or hailed its mutation into "fascinating new shapes" that permitted

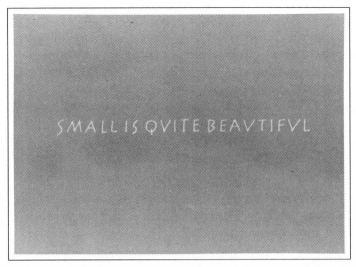

Fig. 5.6. Ian Hamilton Finlay, "Small is Quite Beautiful" (1976) with Ron Costley[55]

"work in other dimensions."[56] Acknowledging that "concrete poetry is no longer what it was thought and made at the beginning," Gomringer himself pragmatically concluded: "But so has grown up something else and there is no sorrow."[57] Finlay's "homage to gomringer" is perhaps most notable as a work that at once evokes both Finlay's nostalgia for the purist restraint of early concrete poetry and his concern that his poetry should look beyond "purity as inconsequentiality."

Not simply an affirmation of Finlay's initial admiration for the "quite beautiful" appeal of purist concrete poetry (in which small clusters of words addressed the lyrical ambiguity of modest observations), "Small is Quite Beautiful" (1976) also signals his subsequent determination to address still more "Beautiful" "Big" issues. These "Big" issues are above all concerned with the decline of contemporary culture and focus upon the ethical, spiritual, and artistic values that Finlay sensed to be under threat from the increasingly secular mentality of the seventies and eighties. In Finlay's terms, little metaphors are quite beautiful but moral battles are still more so.[58] Very simply, "Small is Quite Beautiful" damns overly minimal texts with faint praise and—by implication—suggests that formally minimal texts should address thematically maximal issues. As Finlay points out in a letter of 23 December 1992, the deplorable cancellation of his French Bicentenary project raises the most challenging questions regarding contemporary cultural politics and ethics. "What has to be understood is a MECHANISM OF DENUNCIATION, how evil that phenomenon is, how its VOCABULARY may change (Gentile or Jew or whatever) but how its essence, the bullying of the defenceless, remains the same."[59]

If Finlay's early works, such as his collection *Tea-leaves & Fishes* (1966), self-consciously restricted their focus to "Non-Alcoholic Beverages, Certain Flowers, Certain Trees," and other "proper subjects for poetry," within a general, timeless context, his texts, prints, and installations of the last two decades defend the same orderly ideals in a far more contemporary, interventionist manner.[60] To the surprise of both Finlay and his admirers, perhaps, his work of the eighties precipitated two major public confrontations: his dispute with the Strathclyde Regional Council in 1983 and his ill-fated dealings with the French Ministry organizing the Bicentennial celebrations of 1989.

The first of these disputes occurred when the Strathclyde Regional Council requested Finlay to pay commercial rates for the "Garden Temple" that he had built in the grounds of his farm at "Little Sparta." The Strathclyde Regional Council considered this temple to be a commercial gallery, displaying and distributing his work. Finlay replied that it was "a non-profit building with a spiritual purpose" and should therefore be exempt from commercial rates.[61] When the council threatened to enforce sales of Finlay's work to recuperate unpaid rates, Finlay took "whatever action seemed lyrically appropriate" and "defended" his property with "works of art that this culture understands, imitation tanks, checkpoints and minefield posters."[62]

The "Battle of Little Sparta" rapidly became something of a cause célèbre, and in a number of lengthy features in the national press Finlay insisted that his parodic hostilities arose not so much "about rates" as "about whether the spirit has any place in the world." Claiming that "The Council . . . refused . . . to accept the term 'garden temple' because it is not on its computer programme,"[63] Finlay transformed this parochial dispute into a more open-ended critique of bureaucratic logic. While the director of the Scottish Arts Council, Tim Mason, urged the Strathclyde Regional Council to postpone its actions against Finlay, on the grounds that "The question of the rating of the garden temple and the warrant sale is causing concern not only in Britain but overseas," Finlay published a series of posters declaring "DEATH

Fig. 5.7. Ian Hamilton Finlay, "A View to the Temple" (1987), *Documenta 8*

TO STRATHCLYDE REGION" and reproclaiming a series of Saint-Just's revolutionary maxims, such as: "LONG LAWS ARE PUBLIC CALAMITIES" and "THE WARS OF LIBERTY MUST BE CONDUCTED WITH RAGE."[64]

Four years later, Finlay's contribution to the major European art exhibition *Documenta 8* presented similar sentiments in a three-dimensional installation work entitled *A View to the Temple* (1987), a row of four monumental guillotines, blades inscribed with such maxims as "Terror is the piety of the Revolution," set before a distant temple.[65] Classical values, Finlay seemed to suggest, require stern sacrifices.

Finlay's enthusiasm for the French Revolution led to his subsequent invitation to design a commemorative garden invoking "the two main aspects of the Revolution, the titanic and the pastoral,"[66] as part of the celebrations marking its Bicentennial. Describing the allegorical purpose of this project, Finlay relates:

What I planned was a central area of grass, exactly the size of the seated area in the Assembly. Round the edge would be placed wild stones, and on these would be carved, continuously in the Roman manner, a beautiful inscription from Michelet about the Rights of Man. These stones would double as seats, and between them were to be miniature cherry trees; in summer the students or whoever could pick cherries, which would allegorise the Rights of Man.[67]

Here, as in other recent works, Finlay was clearly concerned to find iconic equivalents for past values. Far from sharing the prevalent critical perception that the postmodern period is one in which "visual depth and systems of interpretation fade away," and that apparently witnesses "the abolition of . . . historical depth,"[68] Finlay's work continually illustrates how historical and visual "depth" may be retranslated—and reaffirmed—metaphorically by the verbal-visual poet and artist. Ironically, public outcry concerning Finlay's choice of contemporary iconography in preceding works of the eighties led to the abrupt cancellation of his Bicentennial project.

This extraordinary decision arose principally from the incapacity of Finlay's French critics to understand how he could meaningfully employ Nazi insignia in sculptures such as *OSSO*, a work of the mid eighties exhibited in both Paris and Liverpool. As Christopher McIntosh and Katherine Kurs explain, *OSSO* consists of three blocks of marble: the first uninscribed, the second inscribed graphically, the third inscribed textually.

The second bears the carved double lightning flash symbol of the SS, representing savage nature, with the concluding fragment having an 'O' added at each end to give *OSSO*, the Italian word for bone. This is complemented by another work consisting of a set of perfect cubes representing art.[69]

Misunderstanding Finlay's allegorical logic (his evocation of the cruelty of nature in terms of the "SS" sign and his evocation of aesthetic order in terms of "perfect cubes"), misrepresenting *OSSO* as a monument to the SS, and irked, perhaps, by his increasing profile in the Paris art world, where he had recently exhibited four times in a single year, a number of European critics and journalists accused Finlay of having Nazi sympathies—and, still

Fig. 5.8. Ian Hamilton Finlay, *OSSO* (second block)[70]

more curiously, "of having served in the *Waffen-SS*."[71] According to one Dutch newspaper, "the real Finlay died in Spandau and . . . the man now living at Little Sparta is Rudolf Hess."[72]

Although agreeing with Finlay that these grotesque charges were simply "a campaign of misinformation," the French Ministry cancelled Finlay's Bicentennial project, purporting that "the campaign was so scurrilous and of such an extent that it had to give in to it."[73] Finlay responded with "Bicentenary Tricolor" (1989), a poem-print made with the artist Gary Hincks, depicting a tricolor inscribed "LIBERTY FOR SOME," "EQUALITY FOR SOME," "FRATERNITY WITH SOME."

Among contemporary writers, artists, poets, and theorists, Ian Hamilton Finlay stands out among those positive postmoderns who have consistently advocated positive cultural values with integrity and innovation. Despite volume upon volume of apocalyptic theory insisting that present times

Fig. 5.9. Ian Hamilton Finlay, "Bicentenary Tricolor" (1989), with Gary Hincks[74]

witness the demise of "master narratives," the death of authorial originality, and the disappearance of all authenticity,[75] Finlay's innovative orchestrations of word and image have repeatedly demonstrated that metaphorical meditations upon the conflict between order and disorder may still have considerable social, historical, political, spiritual, and aesthetic impact.

As Stephen Bann suggests, Finlay's most recent works carry conviction above all in terms of their sensitivity to "historical destiny."[76] Like all great art, the best of Finlay's seemingly simple texts take us by surprise, force us to rethink our condition, and, as John Cage suggests with reference to the white paintings of Robert Ryman, leave us "with a renewed sense of joy, and even a joy close to a change of mind."[77]

Put another way, Finlay's particular gift seems to be that of framing affirmative insights within the *doubled* cultural register of statements such as "MAN IS BORN PIOUS, BUT IS EVERYWHERE A SUBSCRIBER TO *PRIVATE EYE*", an avowal that, as Bann remarks, "turns the famous first sentence of Rousseau's *Social Contract* into a tract for our own irreverent times."[78]

So long as the reader is capable of discerning the implicit "tract" between Finlay's lines—or between Finlay's words and images—then these lines and words and images, more than many others of our time, deserve our continued contemplation. As Mike Weaver advised almost thirty years ago: "Finlay is the only genuinely experimental poet we have: we had better look to him."[79]

Notes

1. Ian Hamilton Finlay, *The Dancers Inherit the Party* (1960; reprint, London: Fulcrum, 1969), 13. All quotations are from this edition; page numbers are given in the text, prefaced by *D*.

2. Ian Hamilton Finlay, conversation with the author, spring 1988. This is not to suggest that Finlay's relationship toward critics is voluntarily antagonistic; rather, his reluctance to be an "easy" artist signals his antipathy to facile, populist art and poetry. If Finlay's work resists critical analysis, it is because it explores new discursive possibilities that are irreducible to familiar expectations but that are suggestive of new frames of reference and analysis.

3. Thomas A. Clark, "The Idiom of the Universe," *PN Review 47*, vol. 12, no. 13 (1985): 55.

4. Ian Hamilton Finlay, "More Detached Sentences on Gardening in the Manner of Shenstone," *PN Review 42*, vol. 11, no. 4 (1984): 20.

5. Achille Bonito Oliva, *Trans-Avant-Garde International*, trans. Dwight Gost and Gwen Jones (Milano: Giancarlo Politi Editore, 1982), 66.

6. Finlay, "More Detached Sentences," 19.

7. W. H. Auden, conversation with the author, spring 1973.

8. Charles Jencks, *Post-Modernism: The New Classicism in Art and Architecture* (London: Academy Editions, 1987), 121–94.

9. John Cage, *Silence* (Cambridge: MIT Press, 1966), 11.

10. John Cage, "Conversation with Stephen Montagu" (1982), in *Conversing with Cage*, ed. Richard Kostelanetz (New York: Limelight, 1988), 238.

11. For further discussion of the impact upon late-twentieth-century poetry of Futurism and Dadaism, see my articles, "Marinetti, Boccioni, and Electroacoustic Poetry: Futurism and After," *Comparative Criticism*, no. 4 (1982): 193–211; and "Towards the End of the Line: Dada and Experimental Poetry Today," in *Dada Spectrum: The Dialectics of Revolt*, ed. Stephen Foster and Rudolf Kuenzli (Madison, Wisc.: Coda Press, 1979), 226–48.

12. Michael Hamburger, unpublished text of 1969, quoted by Michael Horovitz, in "Afterwords," in *Children of Albion: Poetry of the Underground in Britain*, ed. Michael Horovitz (Harmondsworth, England: Penguin, 1969), 317.

13. Anthony Thwaite, *Poetry Today, 1960–1973* (London: Longman, 1973), 69. The second edition of Thwaite's book offers a still more sparing version of his original comments.

14. Stephen Spender, interviewed by Peter Stitt, *Paris Review*, no. 77 (1980): 142–43.

15. Henri Chopin, interviewed by Nicholas Zurbrugg, in *Henri Chopin*, ed. Nicholas Zurbrugg and Marlene Hall (Brisbane: Queensland College of Art Gallery, 1992), 53.

16. Ibid.

17. Thwaite, *Poetry Today*, 67.

18. Jonathan Raban, *The Society of the Poem* (London: Harrap, 1971), 109.

19. Dom Sylvester Houédard, "Concrete Poetry and Ian Hamilton Finlay," *Typographica*, no. 8 (December 1963): 50.

20. John Lewis, *Typography/Basic Principles: Influences and Trends since the Nineteenth Century* (1966; London: Studio Books, 1967), 71. Finlay's "Poster Poem" (1964) is reproduced in Lewis (p. 73) and in the most comprehensive survey of Finlay's work, Yves Abrioux's excellent *Ian Hamilton Finlay: A Visual Primer*, with introductory notes and commentaries by Stephen Bann (Edinburgh: Reaktion Books, 1985), 75.

21. Abrioux, *Ian Hamilton Finlay*, 71–73.

22. Brion Gysin, "Cut-Ups Self-Explained" (1958), in William S. Burroughs and Brion Gysin, *The Third Mind* (London: John Calder, 1979), 34. Despite such exceptions as Eliot's *The Waste Land,* Gysin emphasizes the way in which avant-garde artists of the early twentieth century comprehensively explored the compositional potential of collage, montage, and permutation fifty years before the writers of the early postmodern avant-gardes systematically applied these methods. In this respect, concrete poetry, cut-ups, and permutated texts, along with various kinds of visual and sonic montages dependent on new printing and recording techniques, finally bring literature up to date with the experimental vision of avant-garde modernist art. At the same time, the self-consciously international quality of these movements' explorations of visual, extralinear texts gives them a distinctively postmodern chronological and conceptual character. The multimedia techniques deployed by such work similarly evince an inimitably postmodern technological register. All of these developments typify the relatively neglected positive impulse within the postmodern literary avant-garde.

23. Houédard, "Concrete Poetry and Ian Hamilton Finlay," 47.

24. Theo van Doesburg, "Art Concret" (1930), quoted in "Concrete Art," in *The Oxford Companion to Twentieth Century Art*, ed. Harold Osborne (Oxford: Oxford University Press, 1981), 123.

25. Theo van Doesburg, "elementarism," *De Stijl*, final number (1930); trans. R. R. Symonds, in Hans L. C. Jaffe, *De Stijl* (London: Thames & Hudson, 1970), 238.

26. Hans Arp, "Abstract Art, Concrete Art" (1942), in *Theories of Modern Art: A Source Book by Artists and Critics,* ed. Herschel Browning Chipp (Berkeley: University of California Press, 1968), 390.

27. Max Bill (1974), quoted in Sheldon Williams, "Max Bill," in *Contemporary Artists*, ed. Colin Naylor and Genesis P-Orridge (London: St. James Press, 1977), 111.

28. Eugen Gomringer, "From Line to Constellation" (1954), trans. Mike Weaver, *Hispanic Arts* 1 (winter–spring 1968): 67.

29. Eugen Gomringer, "Concrete Poetry" (1956), trans. Irene Montjoye Sinor, *Hispanic Arts* 1 (winter–spring 1968): 67–68.

30. Roland Barthes, "The Death of the Author" (1968), in Roland Barthes, *The Rustle of Language*, trans. Richard Howard (New York: Hill & Wang, 1986), 53–54. Finlay's later work from the early seventies, like the later work of Barthes in *Camera Lucida* (1981), explores more pluralistic subject matter and media than the verbal text and could be considered either "postconcrete" or "poststructuralist" in temper. In much the same way, both Gomringer's and Finlay's early poems, and Barthes's essays of the late sixties, share a "concrete" or "structuralist" concern with elementary relationships between words. Although modernist artists such as van Doesburg and Arp investigated the "concrete" or "structural" relations in the fine arts, literary and analytical variants of the structuralist impulse seem to be a chronologically postmodern development of the 1950s and 1960s. Both the concrete and structuralist impulses in poetry and theory, and their postconcrete and poststructuralist successors, constitute central *conceptual* shifts within the postmodern mentality (as opposed to those *technological* innovations brought about by the new electronic media that have been explored more systematically by poets and artists associated with "text-sound" composition and performance art). Although structuralist and poststructuralist claims suggest that modernist cultural aspirations are negated by the postmodern condition, the compositions of concrete poets, postconcrete poets, text-sound poets, and performance poets all indicate ways in which postmodern cultural practices *extend* and *fulfill* modernist cultural aspirations in terms of new conceptual and technological developments. As subsequent pages will indicate, Finlay's affirmation of ethical values stands in striking contrast to what Félix Guattari has called the ethical "abdication" of most facets of postmodern theory and mass postmodern culture (conversation with author, Québec, summer 1991).

31. Roland Barthes, *Camera Lucida: Reflections on Photography*, trans. Richard Howard (New York: Hill & Wang, 1981), 51.

32. Barthes, "The Death of the Author," 50.

33. Ian Hamilton Finlay, quoted by Houédard, in "Concrete Poetry and Ian Hamilton Finlay," 60.

34. Jeff Nuttall, *Bomb Culture* (1968; London: Paladin, 1972), 9, 108.

35. Ian Hamilton Finlay, quoted by Houédard, in "Concrete Poetry and Ian Hamilton Finlay," 60.

36. Ibid.

37. Ian Hamilton Finlay, letter to Pierre Garnier, 17 September 1963, in *Hispanic*

Arts 1 (winter–spring 1968): 84. See Kasimir Malevich's manifesto, "Suprematism" (1927), in Chipp, *Theories of Modern Art*, 341–46, for an outline of Malevich's values. As Malevich notes, "Under Suprematism I understand the supremacy of pure feeling in creative art"—a purity that Malevich associates with "a blissful sense of liberating nonobjectivity" as opposed to "the falsity of the world of will and idea" (p. 342). Finlay's sense of the "goodness" of concrete poetry similarly discounts the world of "anguish and the self." Once again, Finlay's ideals typify the ethical integrity that one might associate with the positive impulse within postmodern culture, as opposed to the ethical neutrality or nihilism of apocalyptic postmodern theory. As becomes evident, those who associate postmodern culture with neutrality or nihilism tend to overemphasize the significance of mass culture and tend to neglect less obvious examples of positive postmodern creativity.

38. M. L. Rosenthal, *The New Poets: American and British Poetry since World War II* (New York: Oxford University Press, 1967), 206.

39. Ian Hamilton Finlay, *Air Letters*, with drawings by Robert Frame (Nottingham: Tarasque, 1968), unpaginated. "X" obviously denotes a kiss, and "S.W.A.L.K." is the abbreviation for "sealed with a loving kiss."

40. Philip Larkin, "Money," in *High Windows* (London: Faber & Faber, 1974), 40.

41. "Dobbin" is the English colloquial name for a horse. By juxtaposing it with the Americanism "one-horse town" and an allusion to "The Sheriff," Finlay accommodates the new within the old, bridging continents with minimal wordplay.

42. Ian Hamilton Finlay, *Stonechats* (Edinburgh: Wild Hawthorn Press, 1967), unpaginated. Collected in Abrioux, *Ian Hamilton Finlay*, 86.

43. Allen Ginsberg, "Howl," in *Howl and Other Poems* (1956; San Francisco: City Lights, 1976), 9; Robert Lowell, "Skunk Hour," *Life Studies* (1956; New York: Farrar, Straus & Giroux, 1968), 90; Sylvia Plath, "Daddy," in *Ariel* (1965; London: Faber & Faber, 1972), 56; Adrian Mitchell, "To Whom It May Concern," in *Out Loud* (London: Cape Goliard, 1968), unpaginated.

44. Ian Hamilton Finlay, *Telegrams from my Windmill* (Edinburgh: Wild Hawthorn Press, 1964), unpaginated. Collected in Abrioux, *Ian Hamilton Finlay*, 137.

45. Ian Hamilton Finlay, quoted by Stephen Bann, in "Introduction," *Beloit Poetry Journal* 17 (fall 1976): 5.

46. Stephen Bann, notes accompanying Ian Hamilton Finlay's "Star/Steer" (Nottingham: Tarasque, 1966), unpaginated folding page.

47. Ian Hamilton Finlay, "Star/Steer," poem-print (Nottingham: Tarasque, 1966); also collected in Ian Hamilton Finlay, *Honey By the Water*, with an afterword by Stephen Bann (Los Angeles: Black Sparrow, 1973), 25. Also in Abrioux, *Ian Hamilton Finlay*, 74.

48. Ian Hamilton Finlay, *FISHING NEWS NEWS*, with drawings by Margot Sandeman (Edinburgh: Wild Hawthorn Press, 1970), unpaginated folded booklet of ten *Fishing News* poems.

49. Ian Hamilton Finlay, *Headlines/Pondlines*, with drawings by John Furnival (Corsham: Pluto Press, 1969), unpaginated. The title page to this folder of prints carries the following quotation from the *Times Literary Supplement*: "After all, the tradition of describing ponds is a largely uncorrupted one; not so with the language of embrace."

50. Ian Hamilton Finlay, "homage to gomringer," poem-print with Ron Costley (Edinburgh: Wild Hawthorn Press, 1972), illustrated in Abrioux, *Ian Hamilton Finlay*, 173. Abrioux also quotes Finlay's comments concerning "The appearance of the warship" (p. 168).

51. Ibid.

52. Stephen Bann, *Ian Hamilton Finlay: An Illustrated Essay* (Edinburgh: Wild Hawthorn Press, 1972), 5.

53. Eugen Gomringer, untitled statement in *Stereo Headphones* 2, no. 3 (spring 1970): unpaginated.

54. John Sharkey, summary of correspondence with Ian Hamilton Finlay, in *Mindplay: An Anthology of British Concrete Poetry*, ed. John Sharkey (London: Lorrimer, 1971), 16.

55. Ian Hamilton Finlay, "Small Is Quite Beautiful" (1976), card with Ron Costley. Illustrated in Abrioux, *Ian Hamilton Finlay*, 96.

56. Stephen Bann refers to the "coarsening" of concrete poetry in his afterword to Ian Hamilton Finlay's *Honey by the Water*, 51. The Canadian concrete poet b. p. nichol discusses the "fascinating new shapes" of late concrete poetry in an untitled statement in *Stereo Headphones* 2, no. 3 (Spring 1970): unpaginated.

57. Eugen Gomringer, untitled statement in *Stereo Headphones* 2, no. 3 (spring 1970): unpaginated.

58. In "On the Postmodern Barricades: Feminism, Politics, and Theory," in *Postmodernism and Social Theory*, ed. Steven Seidman and David G. Wagner (Oxford: Blackwell, 1992), 89, Linda Nicholson discusses postmodern articulations of various "useful tools available to the modernist, such as big categories like gender, race or oppression." Whereas Nicholson looks at the ways in which conventional postmodern discourse effects "only . . . a shift in how we understand and use such categories," Finlay's work since the mid 1970s constitutes a more challenging verbal-visual meditation upon the fate of such "big categories."

59. Letter to the author, 23 December 1992.

60. Ian Hamilton Finlay, *Tea-leaves & Fishes* (Edinburgh: Wild Hawthorn Press, 1966). This list of "proper subjects" for poetry appears in Stephen Bann's essay "*Tarasque*: An Introduction," in the catalog *Metaphor and Motif: Tarasque Press Exhibition, 1972* (Nottingham: Midland Group Gallery, 1972), unpaginated.

61. Ian Hamilton Finlay, quoted in "Profile: The Private War of Ian Hamilton Finlay," *Guardian*, 5 February 1983, 7. Finlay's "Garden Temple" is illustrated in Abrioux, *Ian Hamilton Finlay*, 59–62.

62. Ian Hamilton Finlay, quoted by Martin Walker, in "Evasion as a work of art," *Guardian,* 5 February 1983, 1, back page.

63. Ian Hamilton Finlay, quoted by Leslie Geddes-Brown, in "Digging in at Little Sparta," *Sunday Times* (London), 7 August 1983.

64. Tim Mason, quoted by Iain Wilson, in "Awaiting a High Noon Showdown with Sheriff's Men," *Glasgow Herald,* 4 February 1983, 3; Ian Hamilton Finlay, *Four Posters Against the Scottish Arts Council* (Edinburgh: Wild Hawthorn Press, 1982).

65. Ian Hamilton Finlay's *A View to the Temple* (1987) is illustrated in the catalog *Ian Hamilton Finlay: Poursuites Révolutionnaires* (Paris: Fondation Cartier pour l'Art Contemporain, 1987), 77–81.

66. Ian Hamilton Finlay, "Proposal for a garden commemorating the French Revolution and the Rights of Man, 1789–1989, Hotel des Menus Plaisirs, Versailles," *Art and Design* 4, nos. 5/6 (1988): 36.

67. Ian Hamilton Finlay, quoted by Kevin Jackson, in "The banner and the banned," *Independent,* 17 June 1989.

68. Fredric Jameson, interviewed by Anders Stephanson, in "Regarding Postmodernism: A Conversation with Fredric Jameson," in *Postmodernism/Jameson/Critique,* ed. Douglas Kellner (Washington, D.C.: Maisonneuve, 1989), 44. My article, "Jameson's Complaint: Video-art and the Intertextual 'Time-wall,'" *Screen* 32 (spring 1991): 16–34, offers a general critique of Jameson's account of postmodern culture.

69. Christopher McIntosh and Katherine Kurs, introduction to Ian Hamilton Finlay issue of *Little Critic* 4 (1988): unpaginated; published by the Victoria Miro Gallery, London.

70. Ian Hamilton Finlay, *OSSO* (second block). Photo: Victoria Miro Gallery, London.

71. Ian Hamilton Finlay, letter to the author, 26 June 1989.

72. Ibid.

73. Ibid.

74. Ian Hamilton Finlay, "Bicentenary Tricolor," poem-print with Gary Hincks (Edinburgh: Wild Hawthorn Press, 1989). Illustrated in Jackson, "The banner and the banned."

75. See, for example, Jean-François Lyotard, *The Postmodern Condition,* trans. R. Durand (Manchester: Manchester University Press, 1986); Roland Barthes, "The Death of the Author"; Fredric Jameson, "Regarding Postmodernism"; Jean Baudrillard, *Simulations,* trans. Beitchman (New York: Semiotexte, 1983). It is significant that Barthes's later essays and writings—particularly *Camera Lucida*—go a long way toward reacknowledging the concept of subjectivity that his earlier essays polemically deny. As Félix Guattari points out in *Chaosmose* (Paris: Galilée, 1992), the "grave error" (p. 16) in Barthes's early thought was its overemphasis upon semiotic convention and its neglect of subjective values. Not surprisingly, Guattari advocates predominantly

"ethical-aesthetic" paradigms (see *Les trois écologies* [Paris: Galilée, 1989], 25)—a notion that perfectly describes the driving force of Finlay's present work.

76. "Stephen Bann, Ian Hamilton Finlay: Instruments of Revolution and Other Works," unpaginated text inserted in Ian Hamilton Finlay, *Instruments of Revolution* (London: ICA, 1992).

77. John Cage, interviewed by Nicholas Zurbrugg, in "Thinking about John Cage" *Eyeline* 19 (winter/spring, 1992): 14.

78. Stephen Bann and Ian Hamilton Finlay, *Instruments of Revolution*, unpaginated.

79. Mike Weaver, "Ian Hamilton Finlay," *Extra Verse* 15 (spring 1965): 19.

CHAPTER SIX

From Myth into History: The Later Poetry of Thom Gunn and Ted Hughes

Paul Giles

Thom Gunn and Ted Hughes were first linked in the public mind through what Gunn later called the "publishing convenience" of a joint *Selected Poems*, published by Faber in 1962, "when we were too young and had too little written for a full-scale *Selected Poems* each."[1] This volume soon became a popular text for English classes in secondary schools, reinforcing the familiar cliché of a composite poet—"Ted Gunn," as Alan Bold described this overly "convenient classification."[2] Gunn, in fact, had first come to prominence slightly earlier than Hughes: his first book of poetry, *Fighting Terms*, was published in 1954, leading him to be nominated one of five "Movement" writers in the *Spectator* article of October 1954 that invented this label. The Movement writers were welcomed here as harbingers of the changing structure in postwar British society, purveyors of a new middle-class spirit of rationalism and common sense, which was seen as a welcome antidote to the obscure, overwrought symbolism of a decadent modernism.[3] For the record, the other writers named by the *Spectator* were Donald Davie, Kingsley Amis, John Wain, and Iris Murdoch; various others, notably Philip Larkin, became identified with the group at a later stage. From the perspective of forty years later, it is obvious enough that this idea of a "Movement" was a journalistic invention that failed to encompass all the complex strands of the writers it chose to appropriate. "I found I was in it before I knew it existed," said Gunn in 1958, "and I have a certain suspicion that it does *not* exist."[4] Still, this Movement phenomenon, however vague or chimerical, did help to bring Gunn and Hughes early public recognition because it served to associate both poets with the mood of impatient egalitarianism that permeated British society in the late 1950s. In this sense, the Movement came to signify a general revolt against aristocracy and gentility in the world of English letters. Gunn clearly chose to make use of the term for his own purposes by entitling his second collection *The Sense of Movement* (1957).

Hughes's first volume, *The Hawk in the Rain*, appeared in the same year as Gunn's second book. If Gunn's own relation to this Movement was always tenuous and ambiguous, Hughes was an even more reluctant participant, and in fact he always took care to firmly dissociate himself from what he saw as the more timid styles of other Movement figures (such as Wain and Amis) who chose to write in an *homme moyen sensuel* vein. Hughes's early work was concerned instead to respond to what A. Alvarez in 1962 called "the dominant public savagery" of the times.[5] *The Hawk in the Rain* features a number of poems where landscapes of suburban repression come into conflict with the more "vicious" energies of animal desire, as in "Secretary," where the young woman cooks a "delicate supper" for her father and brother while her sexuality remains dormant. The word *horizons* echoes around this early Hughes collection, as if to imply a yearning for escape from such a claustrophobic realm, a desire given expression in the jaguar's "enraged" vision of a world beyond the confines of its cage:

> His stride is wildernesses of freedom:
> The world rolls under the long thrust of his heel.
> Over the cage floor the horizons come.[6]

Despite their different points of origin, Hughes's style of romanticism made for some easy critical analogies with the iconoclastic themes of Gunn's early work, where the heroes of such poems as "The Unsettled Motorcyclist's Vision of His Death" and "Elvis Presley" are represented as daring to flaunt the restrictive codes of 1950s domesticity.

Gunn has lived in California since 1954; Hughes spent two years, from 1957 to 1959, teaching in the United States with Sylvia Plath, and it is possible to discover traces of an American influence upon his second book, *Lupercal*, published in 1960. Although the English pikes and otters are vividly delineated here, some poems in *Lupercal* seem more cerebral and self-consciously mythic than Hughes's early work; the book chronicles not only the Roman Lupercalia of the title but also the "Niebelung wolves" in "February," Socrates and Buddha in "The Perfect Forms," and the Protestant martyrs who "had Englished for Elizabeth" in "Nicholas Ferrer." In these archetypal inclinations, we may detect an echo of Northrop Frye's idealized categories of myth, together with Frye's predilection for architectonic synthesis, which were widely discussed by American intellectuals during the late 1950s. Also at work in this collection may be a tinge of that more disembodied, rarefied idiom disseminated by the New England tone of Plath's poetry; Hughes said later that Plath at this time had been a great admirer of Wallace Stevens— who had been "a kind of god to her"—although he himself had been considerably less enthusiastic about Stevens's "magniloquence."[7] Nevertheless, some poems in *Lupercal* do appear to be written in a more abstract manner than we customarily find in Hughes's later work. One of the clearest examples here is "Everyman's Odyssey," which starts out in oracular fashion—"Telemachus, now to remember your coming of age"—and continues to recount the Oedipal conflict of its protagonist in a deliberately impersonal way, drawing upon the Homeric legend to infuse its narrative with archetypal significance:

> Your mother, white, a woe freezing a silence,
> Parried long their impertinence with her shuttle,
> And such after-banquet belching of adulation
> Through your hoop and handball years. O Telemachus
> Remember the day you saw the spears on the wall
> And their great blades shook light at you like the sea.[8]

If the association of Gunn and Hughes became a critical cliché in the 1960s, it has also become a cliché, since then, to insist upon the separate nature of their achievements. The poems produced by Hughes in the years after Plath's death in 1963 seem deliberately to turn away from these international perspectives, preferring to root themselves in the atavistic strength of England's native soil. *Wodwo* (1967) derived its title from *Sir Gawain and the Green Knight*, where wodwos (trolls) are counted among the foes of the medieval warrior. Like the *Gawain* poet, Hughes stresses harsh gutturals and an alliterative rhythm in *Wodwo*, as if to signify his affiliation with a distinctively English poetic tradition. Seamus Heaney suggested such an association in 1977 when he wrote that the life of Hughes's language "is a persistence of the stark outline and vitality of Anglo-Saxon that became the Middle English alliterative tradition and then went underground to sustain the folk poetry, the ballads, and the ebullience of Shakespeare and the Elizabethans."[9] To be sure, the literary analogies outlined by Heaney in themselves imply an ideological agenda. Indeed, the way in which such styles of alliterative verse could be said to constitute "an essential and continuous Englishness," in Brian Doyle's phrase, has recently been a subject of critical interrogation; as Doyle has written, conservative literary journals like the *Review of English Studies* have over the past fifty years attempted to identify some "continuity of spirit" in English poetry from Anglo-Saxon to modern times, and gestures towards the rough-hewn genius of the native tongue are familiar enough strategies within that context.[10] Hughes himself was working with this conception of a nationally specific literary heritage when he wrote of Shakespeare's language as "inspired dialect," nearer to "the vital life of English" than the "bluffing, debonair, frivolous" literary manner of the eighteenth and nineteenth centuries.[11] Along similar lines, the critic Calvin Bedient would doubtless have pleased Hughes by his suggestion that the poet's 1983 collection, *River*, embodies an "alliterative echo of harsh Anglo-Saxon prosody."[12]

From this perspective, the appointment of Hughes to succeed John Betjeman as Poet Laureate on 19 December 1984 was a natural culmination of these attempts on the poet's part to define a myth of Englishness. The judgment made then by the literary editor of the London *Times*, that Hughes was "without a doubt the most anti-Establishment" figure ever "to have become a court official," can be seen as true only in a superficial sense. With his jeremiads about how England has lost its soul to the "spiritless materialism" of industrial civilization, Hughes fits comfortably within the tradition of radical Protestantism, encompassing earlier literary prophets such as Blake, the Brontës, and D. H. Lawrence.[13] I am not, of course, suggesting that Hughes's work literally follows the precepts of what Thomas West called the poet's "Mount Zion Christianity"; indeed, Hughes, like Lawrence, has consistently aligned Christianity with industry as one of the dark, repressive forces attempting to smother the energies of nature. What I am suggesting instead is that Hughes's attacks on what he called the "hell" of modern life have been informed by an ideology of romanticism that is itself framed by metaphors drawn from a nonconformist religious language.[14] Hughes's poetic world, like that of the Puritan communities in his native Yorkshire, is dominated by a myth of the Fall, an imagined descent into worldly artifice and corruption. Part of this infernal mental landscape is, for Hughes, made up of barbarous folk memories from the First World War, a conflict in which his own father was engaged and a frequent subject for his poetry.

This is not to claim that Hughes's work should be seen as aesthetically or socially conservative, any more than that of Blake or Lawrence. Hughes's dark romanticism carries a fiercely oppositional charge, and his poems empathize with pagan underworlds rather than with genteel courtiers, with the wodwos rather than with Sir Gawain. My point is, however, that Hughes elects to identify these radically nonconformist energies with the independent spirit of England itself. Moreover, such glimmers of redemptive light as the poet can discern among these dark satanic mills derive from the possibility of establishing a rooted, pastoral mode linked inextricably with what he takes to be the ancient genius of the race. This is adumbrated in "Pike," a poem from the *Lupercal* collection:

> Stilled legendary depth:
> It was as deep as England. It held
> Pike too immense to stir, so immense and old
> That past nightfall I dared not cast[15]

In *Remains of Elmet* (1979), the poet lauds this remote Celtic kingdom, an "uninhabitable wilderness" that was, as he tells us in a prefatory note, the last area of Britain to fall to the rationalizing Angles. Hence Hughes's "River," in his 1983 collection of that name, might be seen as an image of the tribal continuity, the ceaseless flowing between past and present, that his poetry as a whole seeks to elucidate: "It is a god, and inviolable. / Immortal. And will wash itself of all deaths."[16]

But the other side to this idealization of national identity is a tendency toward xenophobia. In the preface to *Moortown Diary* (1989), Hughes justified his chronicle of this "ancient farming community in North Devon" by asserting: "No industrial development or immigrant population had ever disrupted it."[17] In the original volume *Moortown* (1979), "Postcard from Torquay" reproduces racial fears that remain deep-seated in England by portraying a German tourist, in his "minimal continental sportswear," as a stereotype of Teutonic arrogance: a "Commandant—at home / On the first morning of Occupation."[18]

In the light of Hughes's continuing preoccupation with the mythical significance of England and English literature, it becomes easier to see why Thom Gunn said in 1980 that he now had "almost nothing in common" with Hughes.[19] While Hughes stressed union, Gunn wrote of dissolution, fragmentation; while Hughes chose to root himself in his native landscape, Gunn opted for the alienations of exile. Since the second half of his 1961 collection, *My Sad Captains*, Gunn has usually preferred to write in a style of syllabic verse influenced more by American poets—William Carlos Williams, Marianne Moore, Robert Duncan, Gary Snyder—than by any English models. Gunn himself described this as a movement away from "the passion for definition" toward a "passion for flow." Whereas his earlier poetry of the 1950s strove to define objects and ideas within the boundaries of a tightly controlled and traditional poetic form, his later work of the 1960s and 1970s sought rather to concentrate upon the object itself as it exists prior to any abstraction the poet might wish to superimpose upon it. It would be wrong simply to call the former style Gunn's "English" voice and the latter style "American"; as Blake Morrison pointed out, this syllabic mode was anticipated as early as the poems "Market at Turk" and "Vox Humana" in *The Sense of Movement* (1957).[20] Nevertheless, it is true that Gunn's adopted American environment offered the crucial intellectual framework for this development. In "Flying above California," from the second section of *My Sad Captains*, the poet eulogizes the "limiting candour" of the West Coast,[21] a new world freed from the burdens of accreted meanings and historical significances; in "Iron Landscapes (and the Statue of Liberty)," from *Jack Straw's Castle* (1976), Gunn similarly associates this emblem of American liberty with the "Cool seething incompletion that I love."[22] In addition, Gunn has written some important critical essays on Whitman, Williams, Snyder, and other American poets who have experimented with this more amorphous, open-ended idiom of free verse, rather than confining themselves within the formal parameters of European traditions.

These new directions served to dampen enthusiasm for Gunn's work in England. Whereas Hughes's highly charged descriptions of nature have always been enormously popular among his native folk, Gunn's more elusive, ironic, and cosmopolitan style has engendered critical resistance and, on occasion, moral disapproval. Various English critics have frowned upon Gunn's alleged "abrogation of human concern" and his acquiescence in "the vacant counter-cultural slovenliness of [his] Californian ethic"; they have complained of what they perceived as the "narcissism" and faddishness of these poems, their relaxed immersion in the San Francisco gay scene and drug culture; they have taken issue with what Alan Bold called Gunn's style of "self-indulgent free-association," implicitly setting this against the more empirical, Larkinesque forms that dominated British poetry in the 1960s and 1970s.[23]

Yet Gunn's apparent looseness of texture has never implied mere randomness. In the early 1970s, he took care to describe his world within a precise mythic framework, these myths deriving more from the aspirations of American transcendentalism than from any Anglo-Saxon sources. "Sunlight," the culminating poem in *Moly* (1971), is concerned to reconcile disparate terrestrial phenomena within the universal harmony of nature:

> Water, glass, metal, match light in their raptures,
> Flashing their many answers to the one.
> What captures light belongs to what it captures:
> The whole side of a world facing the sun,
>
> Re-turned to woo the original perfection,
> Giving itself to what created it,
> And wearing green in sign of its subjection.
> It is as if the sun were infinite.[24]

"Sunlight" was still designated by the author in 1989 "my favourite poem by myself," and the reciprocal interaction in this poem between the "many" and the "one" is reminiscent of the kind of idealism promulgated by Emerson and Whitman during the nineteenth century.[25] Gunn here reconsiders his familiar theme of reflexivity within a Neoplatonic context, so that the circulation between different entities, the transition between active and passive modes—"What captures light belongs to what it captures"—become more than mere empty mirrorings, because all these fragments are holistically validated by that "original perfection," an essential or "infinite" source of light. (Note that hyphen in "Re-turned," implying a world turning and turning about.) This is not the black *mise-en-abîme* of Gunn's 1954 poem "Carnal Knowledge," first published in *Fighting Terms*—"You know I know you know I know you know"—but rather a mythic justification of the perennial sense of movement, which here becomes redefined as a perpetual oscillation between accident and essence, the many and the one.[26] Such oscillation is reflected formally in the way "Sunlight" alternates lines of ten and eleven syllables, as if to represent how terrestrial contingencies might always relate to, but can never be entirely subsumed by, the measured order of the iambic pentameter.

At around the same time as Gunn was reworking his themes within an American mythic framework, Hughes was developing darker mythic patterns of his own. Drawing at times upon the structural anthropology he first studied in the archaeology and anthropology tripos at Cambridge twenty years earlier, the poet's work of the early 1970s is centered on the reinvention of large-scale Celtic, Norse, and Eastern legends. *Crow* (1970) and *Cave Birds* (published in its first version in 1975) both involve interlinked sequences of poems that, taken together, make up an architectonic construction delineating a universe rotating upon cycles of predatory and bestial energy. *Crow* creates its own inverted theology, its own parody of Eden and the Christian legends, as it sets about imposing its dark humor upon the primordial natural world. "Two Legends," the first poem in the collection, dispenses with the normal apparatus of writing (such as punctuation) and offers instead a kind of magical incantation:

> Black was the without eye
> Black the within tongue
> Black was the heart
> Black the liver, black the lungs
> Unable to suck in light
> Black the blood in its loud tunnel
> Black the bowels packed in furnace.[27]

Cave Birds, equally macabre, takes place within the narrative setting of a legal trial, with an "imbecile innocent" cockerel finding itself indicted for unspecified crimes against natural law.[28] The cockerel is sentenced to death and is swallowed by a raven before descending to the underworld and being initiated into new life. As Leonard M. Scigaj has observed, *Cave Birds* owes much to Jungian archetypes, especially to Jung's conception of the shape-shifting trickster.[29] Jung's methods of psychotherapy were predicated upon the cleansing experience of putting a patient in touch with "the hinterland of his mind," as Jung himself called it, an archetypal underworld where the dissociated sensibility might come to find itself reintegrated with its own psychic resources. Such a dissolution and rebirth of the self could be seen, in Jungian terms, as a quest, a search for the old philosopher's stone endowed with magical powers of transformation. Just as Jung refracted the traditional myths of alchemy through a psychoanalytic perspective, so Hughes extends Jung's designs in order to describe what he sees as the sickness and unnatural repressions of an entire society.

Hughes has written several times about what he sees as the therapeutic and cathartic aspects of myth, its potential to contain violent and irrational forces that would otherwise be unleashed destructively. This represents the modernist view of the poet as maker, orderer, or mythologizer that we associate more with early-twentieth-century aesthetics; interestingly enough, Hughes in 1964 applauded T. S. Eliot's "Ash Wednesday" on the grounds that this long religious poem would qualify Eliot for the shaman's magic drum. Hughes's shaman, like Eliot's ideal Christian poet or Wallace Stevens's "major man," represents himself as a figure mysteriously chosen to "purify the dialect of the tribe," as Eliot put it in *Little Gidding*, to harness and give mythic expression to the genius of the race.[30] This, of course, is why Hughes was such a natural choice for poet laureate. From a more contemporary postmodernist perspective, such a weighty understanding of the poet's responsibilities might appear both ponderous and portentous: John Ashbery, for example, has spoken of his dislike for what he called the "Blood and Stone" school of Hughes and Larkin, with its "intimation that you're going to get something highly serious that's going to teach you a lesson you *badly need*."[31] Without necessarily condoning Ashbery's judgment, it should be observed that the large body of Hughes's work written specifically for children—*Meet My Folks!* (1961), *The Iron Man* (1968), *Season Songs* (1975), and so on—is consistent with this mythopoeic imperative, as are the drawings by Leonard Baskin that adorn many editions of Hughes's poetry. Baskin's picturesque illustrations provide an emollient correlative to Hughes's language, a way of domesticating the natural world that is analogous to those mythic containments wrought by the poetry itself. Hughes's work for children similarly establishes anthropomorphic likenesses between humankind and nature that are no more than exaggerated reflections of the anthropomorphic impetus in the poet's other volumes. Especially in these epic narratives of the 1970s, Hughes seemed to envision his native land, children and adults alike, as being under the protection of the poet as shaman, a wary father figure empowered to protect his house against the evil spirits outside.

In linguistic terms, one problematic aspect of this approach was its apparent positing of what Lawrence Kramer called "a myth of negative transcendence." As Kramer noted, Hughes's poetry of the 1970s worked against, rather than with, language. Obsessed with what he called "a truth under all the truths," a "terrible" and "harrowing" truth "far beyond human words," Hughes battered against the constraints of representation in an attempt to recover some ultimate, unmediated entity.[32] This tail-chasing attempt to use language in order to cancel language produced elements of black farce in Hughes's poetry of the 1970s, where, as David Lodge pointed out, there are sometimes grotesque incongruities between the savagery of the poet's theme and the hyperbolic, cartoonlike quality of his images. Take this example from *Cave Birds:*

> When I said: 'Civilisation,'
> He began to chop off his fingers and mourn.
> When I said: 'Sanity and again Sanity and above all
>   Sanity,'
> He disembowelled himself with a cross-shaped cut.
> I stopped trying to say anything.[33]

In *Cave Birds*, Hughes seems to be attempting to transform language itself into a form of "negative transcendence" to match the dark transformations he is describing within nature, and this lends the larger works a somewhat hermetic quality, accessible only to the initiated. This is not to deny that Hughes's abnegation of poetic language, the way he collapses sensory events into their starker infrastructure, can often be very powerful. But Hughes's mythological intuitions, like those of William Blake, are often at their most intense and effective when compressed into shorter poems, into what Hughes himself called a "surrealism of folklore."[34] In these more concentrated pieces, the reader can recognize more of a dialogue between the quotidian and the magical, rather than being required to enter a strange world all of the poet's own making. For instance, "Coming Down Through Somerset," from *Moortown*, is predicated upon the same principles of alchemy and transformation that we find in Hughes's larger mythic enterprises—the badger, killed by a passing car, is already turning into its own skeleton—but the impact here is sharply and directly focused rather than mysteriously occult:

> A slain badger. August dust-heat. Beautiful,
> Beautiful, warm, secret beast. Bedded him
> Passenger, bleeding from the nose. Brought him close
> Into my life. Now he lies on the beam
> Torn from a great building. Beam waiting two years
> To be built into new building. Summer coat
> Not worth skinning off him. His skeleton—for the future.
> Fangs, handsome concealed. Flies, drumming,
> Bejewel his transit. Heat wave ushers him hourly
> Towards his underworlds. A grim day of flies
> And sunbathing. Get rid of that badger.[35]

"Coming Down Through Somerset" is powerful because its figurative conceits—the anthropomorphic ritualization of the "Heat wave," the staccato sentences that mimic the dismembered badger—are implicitly played off in the reader's mind against a contingent and widely recognizable situation. In this poem, Hughes's language cuts deeply, and precisely because its linguistic qualities are not dwarfed by otherworldly gods; it remains content to redefine a world rather than to invent one.

Yet that mythical "goal of reconciliation with organic law," the ambition that haunted Hughes's poetry in the 1970s to undercut superficial worldly decorum by reuniting primordial signifier with primeval signified, frequently led to a more self-defeating quest to transcend the limitations of language itself.[36] Kramer's complaint in 1977 about this "myth of negative transcendence" was reechoed a year later by Terry Eagleton, who said that the reader "never has the feeling . . . that Hughes's language self-reflectively takes the measure of its own limits and capabilities." The result of this, argued Eagleton, is that Hughes's poetry "fails to assume any *attitude* to what it speaks of."[37] Such nostalgia for an oracular tongue or essential mode of being that might exist prior to the ironies of signification is seen most clearly in Hughes's dramatic script *Orghast*, a ritualistic exercise performed by Peter Brook's theater company at Persepolis in 1971. Pursuing his theory that poetic language should delve to the heart of the matter in emotional rather than cerebral fashion, Hughes came up with oddities like "BULLORGA OMBOLOM FROR," supposedly an equivalent in "original organic language" to "darkness opens its womb."[38]

What I want to suggest, however, is that during the late 1970s and 1980s, the poetry of both Gunn and Hughes came to exhibit greater self-consciousness about the potential of language. If their early work was characterized by iconoclasm, and their midperiod by the superstructures of myth, we might begin to talk of the late period of Gunn and Hughes as distinguished by an amalgamation of different styles and influences, a synthesis between archetypal resonance and ludic play. Both writers were in their fifties during the 1980s, and it may be only now that we can see the final arc of their poetic careers beginning to take shape. A greater readiness to explore the ludic possibilities of language characterized the work of many "postmodern" writers during these latter years, and—though one would wish to avoid simply sticking on another label—it would be true to say that Gunn and Hughes began around this time to integrate more consciously self-reflexive elements within their poetry.

In the light of these aesthetic developments, it seems in retrospect ironic that Blake Morrison and Andrew Motion should have chosen to exclude Hughes from their 1982 *Penguin Book of Contemporary British Poetry* on the grounds that "decisive shifts of sensibility" had occurred, a "reformation of poetic taste" that permitted contemporary poets "greater imaginative freedom and linguistic daring than the previous poetic generation." This "ludic and literary self-consciousness" was associated by the editors with the Martian school of poetry pioneered by Craig Raine and Christopher Reid, as well as, more generally, with "the spirit of post-modernism." Hughes, meanwhile, was sidelined as "a remarkable writer but no longer the presiding spirit of British poetry."[39] Such summations of new poetic generations are always contrived events, of course, even if they may be useful or necessary fictions. Still, Hughes's 1976 collection *Moon-Whales and Other Moon Poems* anticipates many of the rhetorical characteristics of the Martian school, and shows Hughes already beginning to develop a less doggedly idealistic attitude toward language. Ostensibly written for children, these relaxed poems share not only the defining extraterrestrial metaphor of the Martian writers, but also their playful sensibility, their reliance upon verbal ingenuity to invent a radically defamiliarized cosmos:

> Whatever you want on the moon
> You just draw a line round its outline
> And it lumps into life—there it is.[40]

Another poem, "Moon-Tulips," proclaims how "Tulips on the moon are a kind of military band."[41] One of the most comically and politically effective fables here is "A Moon Man-Hunt," which envisages foxes in red jackets out to hunt the "strolling squire":

> 'Ha Ha!' go all the foxes in unison.
> 'That menace, that noble rural vermin, the gentry, there's one!'
> The dirt flies from their paws and the squire begins hopelessly
> > to run.
>
> But what chance does that wretch have against such an
> > animal?[42]

This kind of paradoxical inversion links Hughes with the agenda proposed by Morrison and Motion for new British poetry of the 1980s: the aim of "making the familiar strange again."[43] Of course, Hughes has never written "Martian" poetry in the purist sense, has never chosen to focus upon the defamiliarized object as an end in itself, in the manner of Craig Raine; but this tricksy playing with aesthetic perspectives is a trait common to the recent work of both writers.

This affinity between Hughes and Raine (Hughes's editor at Faber during the 1980s) was recognized by A. D. Moody, who wrote in 1987 of the
poets' shared interest in translating nature into a realm of analogical "fancy,"
a "use of similes to view the world through alien eyes." Moody, though,
assumed a posture of stern disapproval toward both poets, chastising them
for prioritizing sensational metaphors over "inward knowing and feeling,"
rebuking them for the "arrogance" of trying to "improve on" natural objects and for having "none of Yeats's intellectual ambition to deal directly
with things and to get to their heart."[44] Yet Moody's aesthetic preferences
can be seen as somewhat backward-looking, given that the allure of "Heideggerian presence" in language, as Leonard M. Scigaj called it, became less
pronounced in the work of Hughes and many other writers during the postmodernist 1980s.[45] Rather than seeking to recover some original mythic
plenitude, Hughes has focused more recently upon the disruptions and
differences of history, writing of ecological and environmental issues in *River*,
reporting the decay of the coal industry in *Remains of Elmet*, and dealing
sympathetically with the 1984–85 miners' strike in his long poem "On the
Reservations."

In this latter work, part of *Wolfwatching* (1989), the poet compares the
present-day collapse of mining communities in the north of England to the
extinction of Indians in the American Southwest during the nineteenth
century. Hence, the narrative perspective here is both diachronic and
synchronic, concerned with contingencies that move through time as well
as with mythic analogies that cut across time. The drab social details in this
poem—the Tesco's supermarket, the Torremolinos holiday brochures—all
betoken a more temporal environment than we tended to find in Hughes's
work of the early 1970s, a poetic world that now encompasses history as
well as myth. On one level, this renewed historical concern may be an
example of the newly appointed poet laureate attending to the state of his
kingdom during the Thatcherite 1980s, a time when he was concerned to
chronicle how Lucretia, the goddess of greed, "has overtaken Englishness,"
as the poem bearing her name in *Moortown* describes it.[46] In writing about
the Thatcher years, Hughes's metaphors are reminiscent of the language he
uses in "The Warriors of the North," from the earlier *Wodwo*, which recalls
how acquisitive and ruthless Norse invaders trampled underfoot the Anglo-
Saxon heritage:

> Bringing their frozen swords, their salt-bleached eyes,
>   their salt-bleached hair,
> The snow's stupefied anvils in rows,
> Bringing their envy . . .
> To no end
> But this timely expenditure of themselves,
> A cash-down, beforehand revenge, . . .[47]

Hughes has consistently regarded such a destructive greed for gold as foreign and antipathetic to the "Englishness" of native customs.

On a more aesthetically self-conscious level, though, this shift from pure myth into history is symptomatic of an acknowledgment of linguistic difference, of the necessary failure of language to coincide with that primordial heart of the matter for which the poet seemed to be searching during the 1970s. In "On the Reservations," Hughes distances his miners by using oblique similes, deliberately defamiliarizing the pit folk through a chain of figurative substitutions:

> Here's his tin flattened,
> His helmet. And the actual sun closed
> Into what looks like a bible of coal
> That falls to bits as he lifts it. Very strange.[48]

Strange indeed; by this process of linguistic estrangement, Hughes writes not of a bible of coal but of "what looks like a bible of coal." The alterity and radical displacements of postmodernist language allow Hughes to deal more effectively with the radical displacements and contingencies of history, whose reference points are not the mystifications of legend but the secularized modes of politics. Another small indication of this development is Hughes's dating of his poems in *Moortown Diary* (1989), a volume that reworks the original collection *Moortown* (1979). Whereas the first book appeared atemporal and dehistoricized, the later selection is framed by a very specific timescale, each poem being given a footnote relating its composition to a particular day, month, and year. In addition, a preface and endnotes serve to elucidate the more general historical contexts informing these poems.

Similarly, the excellent poem "Eclipse," from the 1986 collection *Flowers and Insects*, encompasses all of Hughes's dark skills at representing nature but is also more willing to recognize the ontological alienation of the observer from the objects he observes. By foregrounding his own narrative stance, the poet introduces a sense of provisionality, an interrogative tone that avoids any hyperbolic or shamanistic attempt to speak in tongues from a privileged position inside the natural world:

> For half an hour, through a magnifying glass,
> I've watched the spiders making love undisturbed,
> Ignorant of the voyeur, horribly happy
>
> . . . .
>
> They are hidden. Is she devouring him now?
> Or are there still some days of bliss to come
> Before he joins her antiques. They are hidden
> Probably together in the fusty dark,
> Holding forearms, listening to the rain, rejoicing
> As the sun's edge, behind the clouds,
> Comes clear of our shadow.[49]

No doubt one could say something here about the way female power tends to be represented as a force for destruction in Hughes's poetry, a theme Edward Larrissy has remarked upon.[50] From a more technical point of view, though, the colloquial narrative tone in this poem, the enjambment, and the hesitancy of the speaking voice—how many Hughes poems have used the word *probably*?—all betoken a new willingness to acquiesce within the alienated condition of terrestrial difference.

These strategies of difference are evident again in *River*, which foregrounds the arbitrary nature of similitude rather than striving for a Heideggerian unity of being: In "Salmon-taking Times," the poet writes of how the river "is like a shower of petals of eglantine."[51] As Thomas West has observed, the narrative eye here becomes a "*sensual* organ rather than an organ of fore-and-hind-sight," with the textual emphasis falling on "the surface of things, including the surface of the arch organ of duplicity, the eye."[52] Oddly enough, it is possible that the laureateship may have been one of the factors influencing Hughes's recognition of an increasingly ludic, demystified notion of the poet's function. For instance, "The Crown of the Kingdom," a "celebratory pageant" written for Queen Elizabeth II's sixtieth birthday in 1986, plays with its mythic conception of monarchy in a self-conscious, at times even ironic, manner. Although it never descends simply into pastiche, this aesthetic production nevertheless maintains so much distance from its material that the reader necessarily recognizes the elaborate, highly wrought quality of its artifice. The epigraph to the second section of this poem, entitled "An Almost Thornless Crown," observes how "Titania choreographs a ballet, using her attendants"; and this "ballet" turns out to be composed of a variety of flowers ritualistically personified and woven together into a court for the Queen. Thus, of the Rose, for instance, the bard declaims:

> Let her be linked
> With somebody slender and tall, autumnal Balsam,
> The full pitcher trembling, at evening—
> Humid, soul-drinking insect,
> Like a child-bride of Nepal
> In her pinkish-purple sari, slightly too big for her,
> Over-painted by temple harlots.[53]

This acknowledgment of irony and difference leads in the *Wolfwatching* collection toward an increased reliance upon the trope of allegory, a trope grounded upon the reader's recognition of the provisionality of allegory's own textual conceits. To take the most obvious example of allegory: in *The Pilgrim's Progress*, John Bunyan does not offer "Everyman" as a literal person, nor as a "symbol" offering direct access to some abstract entity, but as a manifestly fictional figure that makes sense only when interpreted as an idea working within the context of some wider literary or cultural matrix. Paul de Man argued that "whereas the symbol is founded on an intimate unity between the image that rises up before the senses and the supersensory totality that the image suggests," allegory, by contrast, "designates primarily a distance in relation to its own origin," referring "to a meaning that it does not itself constitute."[54] In this sense, we can see in Hughes's poetry over the past twenty years a gradual shift in style from symbolism toward allegory. In *Crow*, the birds were depicted synecdochically, as an intimate

part of the dark nature they were said to represent. In the title poem of
Wolfwatching, however, we find a more self-conscious highlighting of the
poet's contrived linguistic equivalences between wolf and man, contriv-
ances that serve to underline the ontological lack of identity between these
different entities. In early poems like "The Jaguar" or "An Otter," Hughes's
ambition seemed to be to get inside the skin of the animal concerned; here,
however, he prefers openly to represent the animal as a conceptual idea.
One of the points about this youth with wolfish qualities is that he is not
actually a wolf:

> And here
> Is a young wolf, still intact.
> He knows how to lie, with his head,
> The Asiatic eyes, the gunsights
> Aligned effortlessly in the beam of his power.[55]

The poem goes on to talk of the wolfman's "neurotic boredom" in London,
how his "Patience is suffocating in all those folds / Of deep fur."[56] This kind
of allegorical self-reflexivity, the easy transition between abstract and concrete that is also an implicit acknowledgment of a radical divide between
those entities, opens up spaces in Hughes's work that were absent from his
more hermetic, mythic universes of the 1970s. In "Wolfwatching," we see
dialogues between the human and the animalistic, between the quotidian
and the archetypal, between the verbal sign and its thematic signification.
Eschewing the chimera of wholeness, Hughes's recent work encompasses
processes of transformation, delineating a world where different fields of
energy traverse and intersect with each other, circulating indefinitely without ever attaining completion:

> His eyes
> Keep telling him all this is real
> And that he's a wolf—of all things
> To be in the middle of London, of all
> Futile, hopeless things. Do Arctics
> Whisper on their wave-lengths—fantasy-draughts
> Of escape and freedom? His feet,

> The power-tools, lie in front of him—
> He doesn't know how to use them.[57]

Again, the lack of closure here is significant. Questions are left open, uncertainties and ambiguities are admitted. The lack of clear identity between the human and the animal is what concerns Hughes here, not, as in some earlier poems, their symbolic equation.

Gunn remarked in 1990 that he found *Wolfwatching* "very fine," and he specifically exempted Hughes from what he called "the depressing timidity" currently prevalent "in English poetry."[58] Despite their different poetic themes and circumstances, it is possible to recognize some kindred directions in the late work of Gunn and Hughes. Like Hughes, Gunn has gradually moved away from the phenomenology that characterized his poems of the 1970s: The mythic or Heideggerian self-presence implicit in "Sunlight," for instance, has given way to a greater concentration upon the more contingent, temporal processes of history. Just as Hughes's poems chronicled the collapse of mining communities in Thatcher's England, so Gunn's poems of the 1980s had an eye for the poor and dispossessed of the Reagan years:

> By then you will have noticed those
> Who make up Reagan's proletariat:
> The hungry in their long lines that
> Gangling around two sides of city block
> Are fully formed by ten o'clock
> For meals the good Dominicans will feed
> Without demur to all who need.
> You'll watch the jobless side by side with whores
> Setting a home up out of doors.[59]

This poem was first published in 1985, and its return to the pattern of formal meter and rhyme associated more with Gunn's earliest work suggests a shift away from those open or syllabic forms typical of Gunn's radical and more ostensibly "American" period, the late 1960s and 1970s. To oversimplify for a moment: it is possible to align Gunn's free verse with America, with risk, with freedom from old-world constraints, with myths of innocence and the transcendence of time; whereas Gunn's more formal verse can be linked to a sense of limitation, to traditional European aesthetic models, and (by extension) to an intimation of determinism and the forces of history. In this way, the re-emergence of rhyme and meter in Gunn's recent poetry is necessarily intertwined with a renewed focus upon the passing of time and upon the circumscribed conditions of human mortality. Gunn's haunting poems about the effects of the AIDS epidemic in San Francisco constitute the clearest example of this dark affiliation between historical process and personal loss.

It would be wrong to insist too rigidly on this kind of binary opposition, for what we find more often in Gunn is an internal dialectic, an argument between these different formal modes and systems. We see this kind of crosscurrent in the 1988 poem, "Words For Some Ash," which describes the disintegration of a human body into "a bag of ash," punning on the word *bound* to signify the way an active leap or bound is itself bound, circumscribed, by the inexorable framework of time and death:

> . . . the granules work their way
> Down to unseen streams, and bound
> Briskly in the water's play;
>
> May you lastly reach the shore,
> Joining tide without intent,
> Only worried any more
> By the currents' argument.[60]

The imagery here is of oscillating tides and currents, a "play" of the water that itself implies the linguistic plays and reversals at work within the poem. It might seem ironic that this acknowledgment of mutability, the flow of temporal decay, should be one factor inspiring Gunn's return to more formal styles of elegy, though this should not surprise the reader familiar with the paradoxical tone of much of his work. As Gunn said in a 1989 interview, one particular "forte" of his writing is "filtering some kind of subject-matter through a form associated with its opposite." He elaborated: "It's as though I'm taking street-noises and turning them into a string quartet. And I figure that way one finds out more about the street and one finds out more about the potentiality of the string quartet also."[61] Yet given Gunn's emphasis upon "continuities" within his life and art—"between America and England, between free verse and meter, between vision and everyday consciousness"—it is possible also to see these later poems as a confluence of mutually sustaining influences, both a summation and an extension of different postwar Anglo-American poetic traditions.[62]

For Gunn, the phenomenological attractions of urban American landscapes continue to be powerful. In a 1990 essay, he praised Whitman's idiom of "prelapsarian freshness," and some sense of that Whitmanian specificity, the concrete existence of objects prior to any conceptual categories that might reductively be imposed on them, remains still in Gunn's poetry.[63] This accounts for his admiration of Robert Duncan and other American poets who have disregarded the polite fictions of aesthetic decorum; it accounts also for the poetic improvisations of *The Passages of Joy* (1982) and *Undesirables* (1988), with their snapshots of San Francisco street life and their existential valorization of what is self-defining, risky, tough. But in Gunn's most recent poetry, this toughness and bravery finds itself compelled to undertake a negotiation with limits: "Courtesies of the Interregnum," first published in 1989 and appearing subsequently in his magnificent collection *The Man with Night Sweats* (1992), pays tribute to a friend stricken with AIDS who "gallantly" maintains his social civility and charm even in the midst of impending darkness. Again, this poem is set in formal rhyme and meter, and it is as though the arbitrary but seemingly inevitable demarcations of these poetic parameters serve as an aesthetic re-creation of the boundaries of mortality. The poem stylistically encompasses that tension between autonomy and submission, active "bravery" as against a passive acquiescence in death, which this poem is describing:

> And he now, athlete-like, triumphs at length,
> Though with not physical but social strength
> Precisely exerted. He who might well cry
> Reaches through such informal courtesy
> To values grasped and shaped out as he goes,
> Of which the last is bravery, for he knows
> That even as he gets them in his grip
> Context itself starts dizzyingly to slip.[64]

"Courtesies of the Interregnum" shows Gunn using rhyming iambic pentameters to establish a poetic world of duality and balance, where opposites can be played off against each other. Many of Gunn's poems written in the late 1980s and early 1990s make more overt references to images of mirroring or to Chinese boxes, and it is as if these textual figures of paradox, play, and reversal come to imply a larger vision of the world where no object or idea can remain undisturbed by its contrary. One example of this is "An Operation" (1991), which describes an elaborate sting operation:

> A couple of policemen dressed
>   In plain-clothes best,
> Like auto dealers pushing forty,
>   Straight and yet sporty,
> Sat, one on show and one confined
>   To a room behind
> The storefront rented in pretence . . .
>   The hidden cop
> Taped the transactions of the crooks
>   Who filled the books
> The other kept, practical, blunt,
>   Front of a front.[65]

As the poem develops, this description of double-dealing comes to take on a larger conceptual significance. For Gunn, such a scene of displacement and reversal becomes a metaphor for the larger paradoxes of human life, a notion addressed explicitly in the more abstract tone of the last stanza:

> And if you wait,
> Tilting your chair almost at spill,
>   A sort of thrill
> Steals upward to the skin maybe,
>   Till you are free
> To stretch within an innocence
>   Born from constraints.

This image of the chair tilting, swinging precariously between one possibility and another, epitomizes the way contrary impulses are brought together and sometimes balanced off against each other within Gunn's poetic world. In epistemological terms, such interaction between competing forces results in landscapes of perpetual destabilization and radical ambiguity.

In Gunn's later poems, these active and reactive forces can be found working at a formal as well as a thematic level. In *The Man with Night Sweats* (and subsequently), Gunn blends that phenomenological particularity developed in *The Passages of Joy* and in his other "American" works with the styles of self-conscious allegory and traditional meter that we associate more with his early "English" verse. "An Operation" is a good example of this duality, fusing as it does concrete description (the sting operation) with those larger meditations on ontological paradox toward the end of the poem. "Courtesies of the Interregnum" similarly uses the chronometric regularity of poetic form to disrupt the self-possessed quality of phenomenological particularity, to introduce within this poetic world a sense of historical objectification and, finally, death. Still, Gunn also exploits the residual power of that seemingly irreducible phenomenology to draw attention to the artificial and ultimately insufficient nature of the allegorical designs that his texts describe. In this way, Gunn specializes in creating self-conscious allegories, allegories that never quite fit together, as in the poem "Cafeteria in Boston," from *The Man with Night Sweats*: "I stomached him, him of the flabby stomach, / Though it was getting harder to keep down."[66] Here the focus swings between the abstract and the physical, between the metaphorical and the biological implications of "stomaching" something. The pun becomes a microcosm of that more general conflict at work in this poem between the radical otherness of the café's tacky "red formica" and the scavenging ambitions of the poet's allegorical intellect. Within this scene, an element of self-parody intervenes: The technique of shot/reverse shot, familiar from the language of cinema, is turned back upon the narrator so as to make the poet himself an object within the landscape he has described. By foregrounding his own aesthetic perspective in this way, Gunn self-consciously exposes the fabricated style of his own inventions.

Yet these metaphorical halls of mirrors never involve simple narcissism or empty postmodernist gaming. Gunn wrote in 1990 of what he called the complacency of some "new formalist" poets, with their tendency to scoff at "'subject,' placing the term between quotation marks as if referring to some laughable affectation."[67] Gunn's ludic patterns, by contrast, always seem under threat of being weighed down by heavier purposes; indeed, the piquancy of these playful styles often derives from a sense of friction, the impression that some force here can barely be restrained or is bursting to get out. Gunn remarked in a 1990 essay how much Elizabeth Bishop used to admire Joseph Cornell's artistic boxes, and he went on to describe how Bishop's poetry, like that of Andrew Marvell, used the idea of a box "to take unmanageable life and make it manageable by reducing it in scale." Gunn added that he himself also considered the box "a wonderful form" for aesthetic expression, comparing this process of miniaturization to "a board-game like Monopoly," which "is oddly comforting in its containment, and yet just as oddly discomfiting in its implications of the excluded. It only hints at what cannot be contained within its limits."[68] Many of Gunn's own recent poems resemble Bishop's in that they cherish formal enclosure and escape from this enclosure simultaneously: in Gunn's world, the idea of liberation depends paradoxically upon the idea of confinement.

Similar explorations of the provisional, self-canceling nature of allegory have also characterized some of Hughes's poetry of the 1980s, as we have seen, and there are also interesting similarities between Gunn and contemporary American poets like John Ashbery. However, the most obvious English analogues to Gunn's cerebral style are to be found among the metaphysical poets of the seventeenth century. Gunn has written admiringly about the uses of paradox in the poetry of Fulke Greville, who "never allows his feeling to eliminate his mind," and also about the interactions between "artifice" and "sincerity" in Ben Jonson. Gunn remarked of Jonson that "it is the tornness that he does so well"; and this idea of "tornness," a disorienting sense of being pulled in opposite directions at once, is something that recurs often in Gunn's late work.[69] "The J Car," another mordant elegy from *The Man with Night Sweats* commemorating a friend who died of AIDS, is a superb example of these crossed tensions. More fully realized and embodied than his early "English" poetry, yet also more focused and controlled than much of his "American" work of the 1960s and 1970s, "The J Car" intertwines historical detail and the mirrors of reflection to create a work that is most moving for its very evasion or deflection of emotion. The poem does not in fact specifically mention the AIDS epidemic at all, but describes in meticulous detail a meal shared at a German restaurant shortly before the man's death:

> Finishing up the Optimator beer,
> I walked him home through the suburban cool
> By dimming shape of church and Catholic school,
> Only a few white teenagers about.
> After the four blocks he would be tired out . . .
> Unready, disappointed, unachieved,
> He knew he would not write the much-conceived
> Much-hoped-for work now, nor yet help create
> A love he might in full reciprocate.[70]

Love and work surrender to AIDS. But rather than simply recounting his friend's illness, the narrator displaces that object into a structure of retrospective meditation that is itself framed by the cool impersonality of rhyming iambic pentameters. The symmetry of this rhyme betokens an inevitability that, crossed with the narrator's casual and colloquial tone, produces the kind of dialectic between self-willed freedom and possession by a greater force that is reminiscent of Donne's divine sonnets. Looking back to his early "English" poetry of the 1950s, written almost exclusively in iambic pentameter, Gunn observed that his aim at that time was "to be the John Donne of the twentieth century," and oddly enough, this ambition now seems to have become realized.[71] Gunn's poetic career has turned full circle: the existential drive for self-definition that helped propel him toward an American poetic idiom has been harmonized with the aesthetic traditions of his British youth.

In 1974, recalling his adolescence in England, Gunn spoke of himself as having a "suburban muse." It is interesting to see how this description in "The J Car" of a "suburban" San Francisco, a landscape of ordered inconsequence and anticlimax, seems to carry an echo of the parks and enclosed spaces of his London days, as recalled in earlier poems like "Autobiography" and "Hampstead: The Horse Chestnut Trees."[72] For Gunn, this suburban muse betokens not only a geographic location, but also a poetic style and state of mind, an in-between world that is not positively one thing or the other. This idea of a suburban landscape appears again in the author's 1987 poem "Patch Work," where he implicitly represents his own poetic voice as a "mockingbird" that moves "Above the densely flowering / Suburban plots of May" in deliberately unpretentious fashion, as if acceding to his own marginalization from the symbolic centers of power:

> . . . it appears to us
> Perched on the post that ends a washing-line
> To sing there, as in flight,
> A repertoire of songs that it has heard
> —From other birds, and others of its kind—
> Which it has recombined
> And made its own, . . .[73]

Like his suburban mockingbird, Gunn is unafraid of appearing "derivative," as the poem describes it; like Ben Jonson and the Metaphysical poets, he admires the arts of imitation. Such imitation is not slavish self-abnegation but, rather, involves the abjuration of romantic individualism and quests for pure originality or autonomy. The mockingbird acquiesces instead in necessary limitation and acknowledges how the active will must negotiate with aesthetic and ontological boundaries. In particular, the peculiar poignancy of Gunn's recent poems lies in the way the subject seems to be exiled to the margins or the suburbs of his own formal landscape, to become an incidental object within a world he can no longer transcend or master. We can glimpse in "The J Car" a shadow of the suburban mode of the mid 1950s, but this poem represents the literary idiom of that Movement era transformed into a more powerful aesthetic realm. Many critics in the 1950s charged the Movement writers with a suburban pusillanimity, but Gunn's lasting achievement is to have redefined his suburban muse in global and metaphysical terms. As Andrew Motion observed on the book's publication, *The Man with Night Sweats* includes "some of the best poems anyone has written in English in recent years."[74]

In 1986, Gunn talked of his desire to be, like Jonson, "a various poet"— a versatile and cosmopolitan writer, receptive to different influences and skilled in the execution of different styles.[75] This description might now be apt not only for Gunn but also for Ted Hughes, whose poetry of the 1980s showed an increased flexibility in its manipulation of different literary genres. Like Jonson, one of his predecessors as poet laureate, Hughes has become adroit at writing poems for special occasions; like the Martian poets, his work also shows a heightened self-consciousness in its use of metaphor and simile. Of course, it goes almost without saying that Gunn and Hughes are quite different writers with quite different styles. Yet, as with great poets in previous centuries, it is possible to see how their work has been framed by similar contexts and influences: social, economic, mythic, and so on. The late work of Gunn and Hughes suggests a synthesis of these disparate forces: a willingness on Gunn's part to assimilate material from both the English and the American poetic traditions and an ability on Hughes's part to fuse a ferocious romanticism with a more ironic or allegorical consciousness. While openly admitting the fabricated nature of such categories, it might be interesting nevertheless to suggest literary analogies for Larkin, Hughes and Gunn, three of the most prominent British poets of the second half of the twentieth century. Larkin might be compared to Matthew Arnold, another university wit whose characteristic modes were formalism, irony, and elegy; Hughes might be seen as a rough parallel to Tennyson, another immensely popular writer rooted in the English provinces who became poet laureate by giving mythic expression to an idea of national identity; Gunn might be associated with Robert Browning, a fellow exile whose radical experimentation with poetic forms ran alongside a raffish sexual iconoclasm. "Tennyson and Browning" have been linked together in our century much as "Gunn and Hughes" will doubtless be in the next. They do not in themselves comprise a poetic "movement," nor should they be confined by this label; but they are both great writers who have, over the past forty years, responded differently to similar historical circumstances, and to similar intellectual and aesthetic dilemmas.

Notes

1. Quoted in *Contemporary Authors*, s.v. "Thom Gunn."
2. Alan Bold, *Thom Gunn and Ted Hughes* (Edinburgh: Oliver & Boyd, 1976), 1–2.

3. Blake Morrison, *The Movement: English Poetry and Fiction of the 1950s* (Oxford: Oxford University Press, 1980), 57.

4. Thom Gunn, "A Sense of Movements," *Spectator,* 23 May 1958, 661.

5. A. Alvarez, introduction to *The New Poetry* (1962), reprinted in Alvarez, *Beyond All This Fiddle: Essays 1955–1967* (London: Allen Lane/Penguin, 1968), 40. Hughes remarked on the Movement in an interview with Egbert Faas, "Ted Hughes and *Crow,*" *London Magazine* 10 (January 1971): 10–11.

6. Ted Hughes, "The Jaguar," in *The Hawk in the Rain* (London: Faber & Faber, 1960), 12.

7. Thomas West, *Ted Hughes* (London: Methuen, 1985), 43.

8. Ted Hughes, "Everyman's Odyssey," in *Lupercal* (London: Faber & Faber, 1960), 10.

9. Seamus Heaney, "Artists on Art: Now and in England," *Critical Inquiry* 3 (spring 1977): 472.

10. Brian Doyle, *English and Englishness* (London: Routledge, 1989), 83, 92.

11. Faas, "Ted Hughes and *Crow,*" 13; Keith Sagar, *The Art of Ted Hughes* (Cambridge: Cambridge University Press, 1975), 34.

12. Calvin Bedient, "Ted Hughes's Fearful Greening," *Parnassus: Poetry in Review* 14, no. 1 (1987): 156.

13. See Robert Richman, "A Crow for the Queen," *New Criterion* 3, no. 6 (February 1985): 91; and Faas, "Ted Hughes and *Crow,*" 9.

14. West, *Ted Hughes,* 28; Faas, "Ted Hughes and *Crow,*" 7.

15. Hughes, "Pike," in *Lupercal,* 57.

16. Ted Hughes, "River," in *River* (London: Faber & Faber, 1983), 74.

17. Ted Hughes, *Moortown Diary* (London: Faber & Faber, 1989), vii.

18. Ted Hughes, "Postcard from Torquay," in *Moortown* (London: Faber & Faber, 1979), 97–98.

19. John Haffenden, *Viewpoints: Poets in Conversation with John Haffenden* (London: Faber & Faber, 1981), 54. This interview was first published in *Quarto,* no. 8 (July 1980): 9–11.

20. Quoted in Clive Wilmer, "Definition and Flow: A Personal Reading of Thom Gunn," *PN Review* 5, no. 3 (1978): 55; Morrison, *The Movement,* 275.

21. Thom Gunn, "Flying above California," in *My Sad Captains* (London: Faber & Faber, 1961), 34.

22. Thom Gunn, "Iron Landscapes (and the Statue of Liberty)," in *Jack Straw's Castle* (London: Faber & Faber, 1976), 15.

23. Colin Falck, "Uncertain Violence," *New Review* 3, no. 32 (November 1976): 37–41; Ian Hamilton, "The Call of the Cool," *Times Literary Supplement,* 23 July 1982, 782; Bold, *Thom Gunn and Ted Hughes,* 78.

24. Thom Gunn, "Sunlight," in *Moly* (London: Faber & Faber, 1971), 44.

25. Gunn made this remark during a reading on "Poet of the Month" on BBC Radio 3, September 1989.

26. Thom Gunn, "Carnal Knowledge," in *Fighting Terms* (London: Faber & Faber, 1954), 21.

27. Ted Hughes, "Two Legends," in *Crow* (London: Faber & Faber, 1970), 13.

28. Ted Hughes, "In these fading moments I wanted to say," in *Cave Birds: an alchemical cave drama* (London and Boston: Faber & Faber, 1978), 20.

29. Leonard M. Scigaj, *Ted Hughes* (Boston: Twayne, 1991), 101.

30. Faas, "Ted Hughes and *Crow*," 10; Ted Hughes, review of *Shamanism*, by Mircea Eliade, and *The Sufis,* by Idries Shah, *Listener,* 29 October 1964, 677–78; T. S. Eliot, *The Collected Poems, 1909–1962* (New York: Harcourt Brace Jovanovich, 1963), 204.

31. Piotr Sommer, "John Ashbery in Warsaw," *Quarto,* no. 17 (May 1981): 15.

32. Lawrence Kramer, "The Wodwo Watches the Water Clock: Language in Postmodern British and American Poetry," *Contemporary Literature* 18, no. 3 (summer 1977): 332.

33. Ted Hughes, "After the First Fright," in *Cave Birds,* rev. ed. (London: Faber & Faber, 1962), 10.

34. Hughes used the phrase *surrealism of folklore* in his essay "Vasko Popa," *Tri-Quarterly,* no. 9 (Spring 1967): 204.

35. Hughes, "Coming Down Through Somerset," in *Moortown,* 42.

36. Bedient, "Ted Hughes's Fearful Greening," 150.

37. Terry Eagleton, review of *Gaudete,* by Ted Hughes, *Stand* 19, no. 2 (1978): 78–79.

38. Bold, *Thom Gunn and Ted Hughes,* 128.

39. Blake Morrison and Andrew Motion, introduction to *The Penguin Book of Contemporary British Poetry* (Harmondsworth, England: Penguin, 1982), 11–13.

40. Ted Hughes, "Moony Art," in *Moon-Whales and Other Moon Poems* (New York: Viking, 1976), 50.

41. Hughes, "Moon-Tulips," in *Moon-Whales,* 24.

42. Hughes, "A Moon Man-Hunt," in *Moon-Whales,* 68.

43. Morrison and Motion, *Penguin Book of Contemporary British Poetry,* 12, 215.

44. A. D. Moody, "Telling It Like It's Not: Ted Hughes and Craig Raine," *Yearbook of English Studies* 17 (1987): 166, 173–74.

45. Scigaj, *Ted Hughes,* 138.

46. Hughes, "Lucretia," in *Moortown,* 140.

47. Ted Hughes, "The Warriors of the North," in *Wodwo* (London: Faber & Faber, 1967), 159.

48. Ted Hughes, "On the Reservations," in *Wolfwatching* (London: Faber & Faber, 1989), 49.

49. Ted Hughes, "The Eclipse," in *Flowers and Insects* (London: Faber & Faber, 1986), 46, 51.

50. Edward Larrissy, "Ted Hughes, the Feminine, and *Gaudete*," *Critical Quarterly* 25, no. 2 (summer 1983): 33–41.

51. Hughes, *River*, 34.

52. West, *Ted Hughes*, 116.

53. Ted Hughes, "The Crown of the Kingdom," *Times* (London), 21 April 1986, 16. This poem was subsequently collected in *Rain-Charm for the Duchy, and Other Laureate Poems* (London: Faber & Faber, 1992), 10.

54. Paul de Man, "The Rhetoric of Temporality," in *Blindness and Insight: Essays in the Rhetoric of Contemporary Criticism*, rev. ed. (London: Methuen, 1983), 189, 207.

55. Hughes, "Wolfwatching," in *Wolfwatching*, 13.

56. Ibid., 14.

57. Ibid.

58. Ross, "Thom Gunn," 199.

59. Thom Gunn, "An Invitation from San Francisco to My Brother," *PN Review* 12, no. 1 (1988): 36. This poem was subsequently collected in *The Man with Night Sweats* (London: Faber & Faber, 1992), 8.

60. Thom Gunn, "Words For Some Ash," *Paris Review*, no. 106 (1988): 114. This poem was subsequently collected in *The Man with Night Sweats*, 68.

61. Thom Gunn, "Poet of the Month: Thom Gunn," interview by Clive Wilmer, BBC Radio 3, 3 September 1989.

62. Thom Gunn, "My Life up to Now," in *The Occasions of Poetry* (London: Faber & Faber, 1982), 184.

63. Thom Gunn, "Freedom For All," *Times Literary Supplement*, 5 January 1990, 3.

64. Thom Gunn, "Courtesies of the Interregnum," in *The Man with Night Sweats*, 74.

65. Thom Gunn, "An Operation," *Times Literary Supplement*, 18 January 1991, 4.

66. Thom Gunn, "Cafeteria in Boston," in *The Man with Night Sweats*, 48.

67. Thom Gunn, "Fever in the Morning," *New Republic*, 13 August 1990, 42.

68. Thom Gunn, "In and Out of the Box," *Times Literary Supplement*, 27 July 1990, 791. Joseph Cornell (1903–72) was an American multimedia artist, heavily influenced by the surrealists, best known for designing boxes and collages. These boxes would feature decorative memorabilia and other mundane objects repackaged into striking new poetic configurations.

69. Thom Gunn, "Fulke Greville," in *The Occasions of Poetry*, 75; Gunn, "Ben Jonson," in *The Occasions of Poetry*, 111, 114.

70. Thom Gunn, "The J Car," in *The Man with Night Sweats*, 78.

71. Ross, "Thom Gunn," 196.

72. Thom Gunn, "My Suburban Muse," in *The Occasions of Poetry*, 153–56.

73. Thom Gunn, "Patch Work," *Poetry* 151 (October–November 1987): 63. "Patch Work" is also collected in *The Man with Night Sweats*, 23.

74. Andrew Motion, "Posing Over, Pain Begins," *Observer Review* (London), 9 February 1992, 63.

75. Graham Fawcett, "Thom Gunn's Castle," BBC Radio 3, 4 March 1986.

CHAPTER SEVEN

Poetry of the Committed Individual: Jon Silkin, Tony Harrison, Geoffrey Hill, and the Poets of Postwar Leeds

Romana Huk

Between 1958 and 1960 Jon Silkin revived his literary magazine *Stand*, which in 1952 had been devoted to the kind of work he would later and famously anthologize as *Poetry of the Committed Individual* (1973). Issuing conspicuously out of the north of England—at that time Leeds, where Silkin had moved to take up his position as Gregory Fellow of Poetry at the university—*Stand* drew its considerable energies from the charged leftist spirit of its industrial, working-class backdrop, as well as from the international perspective that animated the campus and certain modes of revisionist socialist thought and literary criticism at that point in time.[1] Flipping through its pages from the 1950s and 1960s retrieves many of the early poems of Silkin's colleagues at Leeds, among them Geoffrey Hill, Tony Harrison, Ken Smith, and Jeffrey Wainwright—all of whom later appeared in *Poetry of the Committed Individual*, and all of whom published short collections of their early work in a series by Northern House, a small publishing enterprise intimately associated with *Stand* magazine.

"Commitment," then, to social issues, might seem to be the obvious link from which an essayist hoping to connect this diverse group of writers could proceed. But the word fragments like a figure in a hall of mirrors when invoked in context—during what Fredric Jameson and others have called the beginnings of that "radical break or *coupure*" at the end of the 1950s[2] with not only the usual list of modernist "grand narratives," visions, and aesthetics but also, and more importantly for our purposes, with what

Raymond Williams would later look back upon as "naive" forms of commitment based on either unrevised, unreflexive ideological stances or Sartrean
notions of the freely choosing, sovereign self.[3] The gathering, not yet fully
articulated crisis of "the subject"—reflected ever more disjointedly in mid-
century linguistic theory and political philosophy as being the product of
competing cultural forces (or less certainly composed by "nature" than
semiotically, by inscription within culture's medium, language)—would
necessarily become the crisis of the poet committed to speaking for the
oppressed or silenced against prevailing power structures, or even about
language itself and its role in perpetuating those structures. It may be, then,
that it is in their *negotiations* with the vexed idea of commitment that these
poets can be said to share in a complex relationship, one that situates them
in a space so conflicted by both traditional and changing notions of the
writer's agency and operations within language that their responses, their
strategies against impasse, come into interesting dialogue with those emerging from theoretical struggles over similar ideas developing at the same
juncture in time. Neither naive nor noncommittal, their work over the last
three decades might be seen to describe an alternative arc into the
"postmodern," one that resists both the stultifying relinquishments and
the more heady effects of what has been negatively dubbed "the postmodern
turn."[4]

I

The complications presented by postmodern turns of thought for
writers whose desire was to earnestly address the social and historical situation have become commonplace to 1990s poets, many of whom have been
made, along with their critics, almost overfamiliar with the entrapments of
language, and in a continually proliferating array of theoretical terms. Such
complications were clearly in the making both before and throughout the
1950s, particularly in Marxist or, to use George Steiner's term, "para-Marx-
ist" discourse.[5] They can be glimpsed en route to their critical juncture in
the evolution of the word *commitment* itself after the war.

Especially telling, perhaps, is the developing critique of Sartre's original
formulation of *engagement* in *Les temps modèrnes*, which issued forth upon

the momentum of the *résistance* and his initially utopian, essentially humanist, existential vision. Coupling this vision with the Marxist leanings he and his collaborator Merleau-Ponty developed during the 1940s, Sartre's definition of commitment and "revolution" in language involved the writer's recognition of his or her freedom "to appeal to the freedom of other men [*sic*]." In other words, what Sartre envisioned were "two freedoms," the writer's and the reader's, whose intercourse would meet in a kind of universalized *jouissance*—an "aesthetic joy" and "transcendent exigency"—in which the present world as "disclosed" by the writer and recreated by the reader could be recognized as a totality in which both are necessary and for which both are responsible.[6] When the world becomes such a shared "task," the individual's "positional enjoyment" is superseded by a collectivized, "nonpositional consciousness"—the result of "the authentification of a strict harmony between subjectivity and objectivity" in the making of "this object of universal confidence and exigency" (*W*, 64–65).

As Antony Easthope has observed, Sartre's critique of empiricism provided "the gate . . . through which poststructuralism emerges," given the distinctions it draws between the "real" and the (linguistically) conceptualized world (*W*, 25). Important too, and relevant to then-gestating postmodern thought, was Sartre's location of the writer as being always inside history—or "always (*toujours déjà?!) inside!*" as Stephen Ungar has put it, claiming as he does that Sartre sounds, in this respect, "like Derrida twenty years before the fact" (*W*, 11). Drawing upon the implications of such convictions, as well as upon developing linguistic theories, Sartre would later revise his ideas about the impact of class upon freedom, as well as critique his own thoughts on the place of poetry in the existential revolution.[7] He had at first dismissed poetry as a medium for the artist's appeal, given its different loyalty to the materiality of words—its tendency not to "*utilize* signs" to go out into the world, but rather to create of them "image[s] of the verbal body": "a face of flesh which *represents* rather than expresses meaning" (*W*, 30–31). Of course, postmodern deconstructions of "meaning" begin with its representation in language, a process that Sartre himself began to effect in "Black Orpheus" (translated in *Stand* in 1961–62) by recognizing that, at least in the case of the postcolonial poet, such re-presentations of language as the tool of dominating cultures had revolutionary potential—they could, he believed, effect an "*auto-da-fé*" of the oppressor's linguistic constraints upon the creation of freed identity and, therefore, help to "reconquer . . . existential unity" (*W*, 306–7). But Sartre's continuing insistence upon the freedom of the writing/reading subject, as well as upon individual unity and agency in the making and changing of human history, would grow less and less tenable as the *"coupure"* approached, bringing such ideas under the darker scrutiny not only of other continental philosophers but also of British thinkers influenced by Marxist/structuralist and cultural theory as it was beginning to develop within the New Left.

A period of what E. P. Thompson would later call "quietism" in England fell in between, pointing up again, however mutely, the role that language was slowly being perceived to play in the overdetermination of the subject.[8] Even Sartre, in a recollective writing, lamented that in 1950 Merleau-Ponty succeeded in "impos[ing] his silence upon [him]"—a silence sworn in response to disillusioning news about the Soviet labor camps and involvements in the Korean hostilities.[9] It was a horrified sense of his own written involvement in the political idealisms that had covered for inhumanities that shut Merleau-Ponty down in the years that followed; as Sartre observed it, speaking from his friend's point of view,

> History had definitely perverted its course. It would continue paralyzed, deflected by its own wastes, until the final fall. Thus, any reasonable words could only lie. Silence, the refusal of complicity, was all that remained.[10]

The idea that "words could only lie" was to obtain currency on a number of levels in England as well, and in camps beyond Marxist ones, during the decade—in Steiner's essays, for example, that documented the "Retreat from the Word" given the indelible imprint of the war's atrocities on language, and later the appropriate "Silence of the Poet" in the face of them;[11] in Samuel Beckett's gaping masterpieces that began to appear on the London stage and in prose works (dedicated, like his plays, to staging language in all its emptiness as being both addictive and oppressive);[12] or even in the aesthetic of the so-called "Movement" in poetry, whose return to Hardyesque "neutral tones," traditional forms, syntactical conventionality, sensible (nonpolemical) themes, and "chaste diction" bespoke, at least in part, a revulsion toward, and perhaps a fear of, anything but the most straitened linguistic expression.[13] The tone, Thompson wrote, was that of a generation that "grew to consciousness amidst the stench of the dead, the stench of the politics of power"—of "a generation which has 'had' all the large optimistic abstractions, and has stopped its ears to the booming 'rhetoric of time.'"[14] Certainly the decade's near obsession with language, silence, and complicity set the context for theoretical explorations coming to form in Europe; it also enormously complicated the issue of what it meant to write a committed art.

Adorno contributed to the angst of postwar writers with his famous assertion that there should be "no poetry after Auschwitz"—a statement that he would not entirely retract even in his 1962 essay on "Commitment" in art. He would instead recast it within his slowly broadening definition of what it means to write in a committed way, about any topic, from a position not only "inside history" but inside its complicitous medium, language. Because the situation presented for him a "paradox," his own call for commitment mimicked it formally, expressing itself in characteristically paradoxical terms: "the abundance of suffering tolerates no forgetting" and therefore "demands the continued existence of art while it prohibits it."[15] The danger of commemorative art's turning into social salve and even a profitable commodity in market societies demanded on the part of the artist a kind of painfully self-conscious resistance that Adorno felt could be manifested only through formal representation of such tendencies and contradictions within the artist's medium itself. Although not fully translated and therefore influential in Britain until the 1970s, Adorno's arguments are, in their concern with "the lability and historicity of language," as well as with the illusory autonomy of the subject,[16] exemplary of the poststructuralist imagination that was then coming to form in poetry, I will argue, as well as in philosophical texts.

In both "Commitment" and "Lyric Poetry and Society," Adorno specifically critiques (and historicizes) Sartre's model of transcendent intersubjective praxis based on a writer's freedom to choose—which, as he argues, demonstrates "no regard for the fact that the very possibility of choosing depends on what can be chosen."[17] Adorno's concerns are with the demands that the material (in this case, language) make upon the unwitting artist; the subject is "more than just a subject," because "language *begets* and joins both [lyric] poetry and society in their innermost

natures" (emphasis added).[18] His formulations went a step beyond orthodox reflection theory and enmeshed *all articulations* (including philosophy)
in the medium, or linguistic legacy, of what he understood to be the bar-
baric and disintegrating "course of the world" under market capitalism—a
world that "permanently puts a pistol to men's heads";[19] he therefore identified as committed art *not* the art of political statement, which he felt
participates naively in the same violence, but rather of "autonomous" works
that demonstrate the effects of that hegemonic structure on their own
building materials. The only hope for the future realization of freedom lay,
for him, in "demythologizing" the present by focusing on "the play of
opposing and conflicting forces which goes on under the surface of every
self-contained theoretical position"[20]—and, when reading poetry, by focusing on "the ways in which various levels of society's inner contradictory
relationships manifest themselves in the poet's speaking."[21] Turning around
Sartre's early disqualifications of poetry, Adorno insisted that poetry's generic concentration on language as material, as "representative of meaning," and as a "structure of the external world" (*W*, 30–31) is valuable because,
in what he would call "negative dialectics," praxis takes its cue from such
structures, becoming "a thoroughgoing critique of forms, . . . a painstaking
and well-nigh permanent destruction of every possible hypostasis of the
various moments of thinking itself."[22] "Truth" lay not in the quasi-mysti-
cal, joint recognitions of subjectivities Sartre described, but rather in the
gaps or "breaks" *(Brüche)* within systematic unities; therefore, he argues,
"[i]t is not the office of art to spotlight alternatives" or to make political
arguments, but rather to foreground existing cognitive hierarchies by coming "to full accord with the language itself, i.e., with what language speaks
with its own tendency."[23] Adorno's conception of artistic autonomy would
undergo critique by others—given that it still, ironically, involved the poet
in "choosing" a kind of formal transcendence over his or her "material
being."[24] But his philosophical *methods* present an example of a developing
strain of poststructuralist practice that, instead of calling for the total abolition of the subjective principle (and, consequently, the idea of artistic commitment), advocated "using the force [or struggle] of the subject to break
through the deception of constitutive identity" in order to reveal the structure of contradiction that forges it.[25] Similar anticipatory responses to gathering pressures to both recommit oneself politically *and* reconceptualize

words like *commitment* and *individual* in phrases like *poetry of the committed individual* are discernible in England as well, though not so much in philosophical texts as in the poems themselves, which are situated between the linguistic and political theories beginning to take divisive textual root there in the 1950s and 1960s.

As *Stand* was being rededicated to committed writing—to "sav[ing] what is valuable in a society that *seems* [as it seemed to Adorno] to be disintegrating"[26]—leftist intellectuals were also undertaking a recommitment in their creation of the New Left, impelled by what Raymond Williams described as "the breakdown of the two major socialist intellectual traditions: the orthodox communist one and the social-democratic tradition . . . both of which seemed evidently to have failed in their original terms and to require radical revision."[27] What "radical" might mean, however, would soon become the subject of debate. The deeply rooted, liberal humanist empiricism or "habit of mind . . . in English philosophy generally," as Williams characterized it, was well represented in the movement and would struggle against theoretical developments that, by the mid 1960s, would involve younger members of the New Left "quite consciously in the European ideological debate"[28] about Althusserian linguistics, political (un)consciousness, and ways of viewing social dynamics—all of which threatened conceptions of the fully choosing and unified self.[29] For many of the habit of mind Williams described, such as E. P. Thompson, coming "out of apathy" meant shaking quietism by taking a firm, *un*selfconscious "stand" again in opposition to, on the one hand, the politically propagated myths of "consensus" and achieved "postcapitalism" in Britain in the 1950s (due to Labour's gravitation to the right after its successes during the Atlee administration) and, on the other, Britain's involvement in bloc politics (or "Natopolitan culture," as Thompson put it),[30] which led to new forms of imperialistic behaviors, specifically in Suez in 1956 and in the development of the bomb. It meant shaking the deep "disillusion in Communism"—which culminated with the Soviet invasion of Hungary, also in 1956—by returning to old-fashioned "moral revolt" and, for Thompson specifically, to familiar and trustworthy paradigms in "the long and tenacious revolutionary tradition of the British commoner,"[31] which he was then at work documenting in a book that would prove important to many writers at Leeds, *The Making of the English Working Class* (1963).[32] His version of New Left recommitment was an attractive one of practical political effort, one that displaced both structuralist and Stalinist determinism with "the belief that the moral imagination can still intervene creatively in human history"—including, of course, through the arts, which the New Left quite significantly gathered into its expanding conception of "politics" and therefore into its debates about political commitment.[33]

"Poetry in our time has failed to state relevant values, or to disclose and define social commitments. . . . If we had better poetry we might have less bad sociology and less empty and mendacious politics."[34] In 1979, in a *Stand* symposium on poetry and "commitment,"[35] Thompson once again quite eloquently and movingly laid a huge burden before the artist, invoking Wordsworth and Coleridge in his plea that poets on the Left resume their position as the unacknowledged legislators charged with recovering "relevant" values, inspiring the apathetic, and infusing their medium with new meaning to counteract ideological "offenses against language" (50). Yet in the same symposium Raymond Williams, increasingly influenced by what Thompson contemptuously identified as the "déraciné . . . Marxist-structuralist Left" (51)—more accurately, by that time, the poststructuralist Left— wrote of such definitions of "commitment" and "values" as "naive," following Adorno in his critique of Sartrean "choice":

> No writer is ever free in that absolute sense. . . . [W]e are all, as writers, significantly situated before we even come to write. We are also, I would say, significantly aligned. We see writing through the resources of our given language, through the inherited forms of our literature, through the institutions in which it is practised. And if this is true of our specific situation as writers, it is also true— often much more deeply than we realize—of our values, our perspectives, our assessments of significance. Indeed it seems to me clear, and valuable, that all of us, as writers, are carrying a much larger freight than our single selves, though if we succeed in making it into ourselves, or ourselves into it—processes of social identification, or of (for some) unproblematic internalisation of our inherited culture—we can appear to speak as sovereign subjects. This is, it seems to me, why we get the common situation in which, "speaking only for myself and in the name of the free individual," many of us succeed only in saying what we all already know. (10)

Rendering both the "universal" and the "sovereign" suspect, as the ideological envisionings of fully achieved social identification rather than the
insight of the individual subject, Williams turns the by-now agonized eye
of the socially committed poet back, "self"-consciously, on his or her work,
promoting in poetry the situation Thompson laments in the newly
deconstructive theoretical sphere where, as he sees it, "value formation
becomes a subordinate and determined exercise, the appropriate sour spoon-
ful of 'demystification' of moralistic ideology. . . . No poetry with any dignity would leave its personal corner to enter the service of that philistinism.
And no poets have" (51).

Of course Thompson was wrong; British poets had indeed begun, certainly by the late 1970s, to demonstrate not only deep reservations about
the role of poetry in "value formation" or social construction of the self, but
also a self-consciousness about the arbitrary and/or overdetermined nature
of their medium, language—a self-consciousness that has become raised by
many as the standard of postmodernism itself. The neglected "experimental" poets of largely small-press fame would be among those who have
attempted to work at the fraught intersection between social and linguistic
consciousnesses. However, influential critics such as Alan Robinson have
tended to propagate another view of developments in this period, theorizing that "instabilities" in British philosophy and culture, which range far
wider than those discussed here, have triggered an "implicit rejection of
engagement" altogether and an adoption of practices that sail over
deconstruction into a "ludic Postmodernism, which exultingly parades its
own artifice and apparent senselessness," subverting the advances of critics
"who would see in poetry more than a game with language."[36] "Reliev[ing]
poetry of any need to be socially significant, and restituting a more modest
goal of ludic diversion"; "frustrat[ing] one's conventional expectations that
poetry should be rhetorically committed"; "glid[ing] from one context to
another with metamorphic glee . . . prevent[ing] any oversolemnity";[37]
"frustrat[ing] the demand for communication"[38]—such projects accomplish
the important task of defamiliarizing us from our medium, allowing us to
see it, perhaps, as material in our own construction. They would, nevertheless, be seen by thinkers like Hassan as evidence of the "wrong turn" of
postmodernism, as characteristic of its "ideological truculence and
demystifying nugacity," its "cognitive dispersals" that he, like many others,

is not sure "meet urgent demands of the age."[39] What is the alternative to "cognitive dispersal" in a climate that renders every linguistic formulation suspect? Hassan's plaintive and uncertain objection echoes like a final vibrato in the long-playing postwar call to commitment—a call that becomes more difficult to make, it seems, let alone answer.

In *Stand*, and at Leeds, many of the conflicting ideas and theoretical impasses brought to focus by such debates about committed writing had already begun to be played out, since the 1950s, in poetry that seems in many ways to have been torn between, on the one hand, sympathy for Thompson's project, a desire for "moral revolt"—for the "creat[ion of] values," as Silkin put it in his 1958 editorial,[40] and even for a late modernist poetry of social vision (retrieved from its Sartrean exile as mere self-reflection)—and, on the other hand, a precociously postmodern suspicion about its own medium, its coercive poetic traditions and subjected speaking voices. Such tension often becomes a critical part of the purposefully disunified focus of these poets' works, giving the lie to any unproblematic speaking of the "sovereign subject" as redescribed by Williams. Still, out of this broken focus their works do direct another kind of "speech"—one committed to readdressing difficult historical and political topics but also aware, at the level of form, of the materiality of language, its inescapable, architectural links to social structures and its role in the construction rather than expression of individuality. With interesting variations on theoretical developments taking shape around them, these poets seem to have formulated, not necessarily through the direct influence of those developments but rather by way of similar response to the exigencies of their historical moment and to crises in conventional and dialectical thinking, their own forms of "negative dialectics" in their poetry—an observation that I attempt to bring into focus in the next section by considering a number of early and more recent poems by several of the most powerful and influential poets then writing at Leeds: Jon Silkin, Geoffrey Hill, and Tony Harrison.

II

In 1958, as Jon Silkin was arriving in Leeds to assume his Gregory Fellowship, his second book of poems appeared: *The Two Freedoms*. In its

title poem, Sartre's envisioning of his own "two freedoms" (*W,* 66) might
be seen to be parabled, though here his dynamic—"my freedom, by revealing itself, reveals the freedom of the other"(*W,* 66)—is inverted, as the
"other," freed, reveals a freedom that the speaker ultimately chooses not to
share:

> There were two birds today
> Broke from their cage and seemed as gold until
>> In the dry sun, their bodies were
> Transfigured; . . .
>
> . . . .
>>>> . . . They were
> Inviolable, with that power and helplessness
>> Which sculpture has. The sunlight
> Smoked on them, gold were their wings, gold feet; gold
>>>>> sounds
>
>> Fled from their throats quickened by
> The winged sun that, for a moment, urged their flesh
>> To the transubstantial freedom
> Ghosts are. They in the sun became the one gold
>> With him in dignity.
> I caught them and put them back into their cage.
>
> . . . .
>
> I shut the cage door, I looked with a cold rage
>> At their stretched screams of pain,
> And I thought again of the stairs down which the world
>> Turns from its prison to
> The cage of the still prison; turns and is caged.[41]

The poem makes its resounding point with a mixture of allusions to modernist authority—in what resonates as an Eliotic image of "each confirm[ing]
a prison" from the last stanzas of "The Waste Land"—and Sartrean philosophy; the speaker closes down "cold[ly]" ("coldness" always signifying emotional death in Silkin's poems) upon this revelation of transfiguration made

available through the power of freedom. Like the "inviolable voice" of Philomela in Eliot's poem, the visual text these birds offer to "the generosity of the reader," as Sartre would put it, is shut as the speaker locks them "safely" into their "iron house," thinking "of [his or her] own / Wings, cut and trimmed by [his or her] own grey God" (*SP*, 16). The two birds—on the surface, the "two freedoms"—reveal the real second freedom to be that of the speaker, whose reverent and beautiful language as initially released in observation of the birds describes a seemingly more liberated spirituality and mode of perception than that returned to in the darkening moment of closure. The poem is quite clearly about existential freedom misused and the consequences for others; the "sculpture," or imaginative work presented by the two birds, is at one and the same time "powerful" or, conversely, "helpless"—"free" or only "escaped." The choice is the speaker's, and the greater authority, subtextually, the poet's.

A subtle development began to become noticeable in the poetry Silkin wrote in Leeds over the next several years. His poems have always been about struggle—most often between the helpless and the dominating—but the struggle of both the poet and his speakers over "what can be chosen," as Adorno put it, was to become more pronounced, as well as more particularly and complexly situated in culture and time. In *The Re-ordering of the Stones* (1961), "The Centre" gives us a speaker whose ancestors are from the "near east" (as are Silkin's own Jewish ancestors) but whose subjected "mind stays / In a place [he] saw little of":

> Geneva. Was it fixed
> I should choose your cool streets
> Hinted of by the south?
> Round this place move
> The ornate schisms, intertwined
> And made fast by the vicious and costly
> Emblem of puissant Europe.
> Is it strong only? It is also
> Absurd. It is a continent
> Caught in its intellect
> At which centre it drops

> Into a great lake;
> Like some bath with its plug out.
>
> (SP, 32)

The speaker's "deconstruction" of Europe's intellectualizations, poised on the "ornate[ly]" covered fault lines of its "vicious" history of ascendence even as the whole goes bathetically down the drain, extend to include him as situated there by conditioning if not by heritage:

> And it is here I am
> Constrained by having both
> Prevailing intensities
> As locked, and as formed
> As the coolness is formed here
> In precision from the clash
> Of oppositions. Such firmness
> Seems pre-determined
> And intertwined to a gap
> That is the weave and the space
> Made by Europe in struggle
> Where choice flickers, but does not choose.
>
> (SP, 33)

Drawn as he is, despite his origins, to "the centre" of Europe in this poem, the speaker demonstrates that he is also involved and immobilized, or again imprisoned, as in "The Two Freedoms," but this time in western culture's aporetic, "vicious and costly" vortex of dominating power relations and their rationalizations—of "too much intellect" (*SP*, 33). The opportunity for "choice" only "flickers" in the "gap" (or Adornoesque "break"): that enabling space made by contradictions in the otherwise firm architecture of "ornate schisms." Their jagged edges are "intertwined / And made fast" with a "coolness" that here again bespeaks a lack of responsiveness, as well as a "pre-determined" rigidity against which the speaker attempts to make a stand. Silkin demonstrates the speaker's own complex/complicit situation formally— particularly in the line break following "and it is here I am." Semantically indeterminate, the phrase as it appears in isolation seems to assert positive or emergent identity—the illusion of "sovereignty"—while at the same time it specifies locational variation; the latter possibility, by the next line, becomes determination, involving "constrain[t]" and the speaker's "always already" effected imprisonment amid the "prevailing intensities" that situate the continent's cultural groups. The repeating use of "as," which at first seemingly compares the rigidity of those locked intensities to the "clash / Of oppositions," could very well be comparing the speaker's self, too, the indeterminate "I," to that formation; subject and social formation dangerously blend outlines in this poem to suggest the contingency of identity. The more important suggestion, however, may be that an enabling "gap," like that which exists in Europe's "intellectualizations," exists also within the self—a situation in which individual "choice" is indeed made possible, though it becomes a matter of recognizing one's own *un*freedom and working forward by means of a *negative* dialectic: a breaking up of the "locked" and "formed" unity of selfhood and a reevaluation from starting points in the constellation of one's own internal contradictions and exposed hierarchies of suppositions. The long-noted difficulty of Silkin's language *is* here committed to "disclosure," as Sartre would have it, of the world, but this time it is the world as constructed in language and as revealed through the subjected vision of the struggling speaker. Responding to a situation that is, as Adorno wrote, a paradoxical one involving the necessity to speak despite/about the difficulty of speaking, the poem advocates change, while at the same time it is *formally* expressive of the difficulty of such advocacy, given its own precisely "formed" position in that not only "relatively autonomous" but seemingly tyrannical superstructure that is the "verbal body" of "intelligent Europe."[42]

In a favorable review of this book in *Poetry & Audience*, Geoffrey Hill wrote: "Perhaps [Silkin's] critics have found unpalatable his method of reiteration, the deliberate poise on the verge of tautology, the dogged qualification. . . . The total effect is like a curious amalgam of the forthright and the tentative. . . ."[43] It is not surprising that Hill, unlike "the critics," would appreciate the difficult movement of his colleague's poems, given that Hill's understanding of the "obligation" of the writer is "to enact the drama of reason within the texture of one's own work" because direct statement can never come freely—"our chains rattle," he writes, quoting Coleridge, "even while we are complaining of them."[44] Hill's sensitivity to the dangers inherent in making one's own way through language—through what he would later call "the enemy's country"[45]—was at that time more acute than almost any other poet writing in English. His recognition that "etymology is history"[46] made him a wakeful inhabitant of Jameson's "prisonhouse of language" early in the day of such theorizings—certainly by the time he published his first book-length collection of poems written between 1952 and 1959, *For the Unfallen*. His strategies for working "responsibly" with such suspect materials differ quite dramatically from Silkin's, but the dialogue discernible between their works is useful in trying to understand the context for committed writing as it was being set in Leeds.

The "drama of reason" that Hill's poems display has been, since the mid 1950s or so, less often cast as the "drama of one"—of the personal lyric voice—that characterizes a number of Silkin's poems; in the latter, as Hill has noted, revealing contradictions are most often pointed up when "public myth is at odds with private fact."[47] Certainly Hill's much discussed "September Song"[48] comes immediately to mind as a possible exception to such a rule; yet even in this poem's seemingly very personal struggle to commemorate a Jewish child—born, as the epigraph tells us, a single day after Hill's own birthday and deported to the death camps—"private fact" is exactly what vanishes, for both the child *and* his/her commemorator who realizes, parenthetically,

> (I have made
> an elegy for myself it
> is true)

What might be "true" or "real" experience in the poem becomes an elusive half-fact—the vague referent of the "it"—slipping parenthetically and otherwise out of the text. The account of the child may be true, and true too, therefore, is the "elegy" made here, but the suggestion that the child's experience has been appropriated as the speaker's own, or as poetry's "subject"—just as Adorno feared it might—stops the poem short with a nonetheless problematically dismissive "This is plenty. This is more than enough."

"This" is held with seeming bewilderment in the speaker's hands; this effect of language—whom does it belong to or describe? History as transformed by poetic convention shapes the contorted lyric voice of the poem; in a kind of twisted confirmation of Sartre's initial dismissal of poetry as the genre whose every word "sends back to the poet his own image, like a mirror" (*W*, 37), Hill returns the speaker to "self" here, though it becomes an illusory self seen through a glass, darkly. Subjectivity is displaced into history and vice versa, with language and poetic form foregrounded as the transformative mediator for "personal" experience and its expression.

Any conventional performance of lyric expressivism becomes all but impossible in Hill's poems, which are much more frequently spoken in a strangely choral voice, even when the personal pronoun is present—as though culture itself were speaking, or an "I/We" whose choices of form and response are so heavily overdetermined by cultural possibilities that volition becomes the nonissue at issue, flickering in the gaps opened by contradictions in conventionalities. The "true commitment" of the poet, as Hill puts it, sounding like Adorno, is to the "vertical richness" of his or her medium—"to mak[ing] history and politics and religion speak for themselves through the strata of language."[49] He proceeds, even in his prose, through what he describes as a "negative" progress amid options that require the poet to "return upon himself"—an act that involves focusing on "one's own preconceived notions, prejudices, self-contradictions and errors."[50] In this way, he comes to what Adorno described as "full accord with what language speaks with its own tendency," yet he dramatizes the "breaks" that underlie the systematic (and at times brutalizing) creation of such unities through discourse. In "A Pastoral," for example, written a little over a decade after the war's end, Hill convenes several traditional and emergent linguistic modes in a parodic enactment of how they "work" to restore cultural equilibrium:

> Mobile, immaculate and austere,
> The Pities, their fingers in every wound,
> Assess the injured on the obscured frontier;
> Cleanse with a kind of artistry the ground
> Shared by War. Consultants in new tongues
> Prove synonymous our separated wrongs.

We celebrate, fluently and at ease.
Traditional Furies, having thrust, hovered,
Now decently enough sustain Peace.
The unedifying nude dead are soon covered.
Survivors, still given to wandering, find
Their old loves, painted and re-aligned—

Queer, familiar, fostered by superb graft
On treasured foundations, these ideal features!
Men can move with purpose again, or drift,
According to direction. Here are statues
Darkened by laurel; and evergreen names;
Evidently-veiled griefs; impervious tombs.[51]

The "austere" and harmonic form of the pastoral, a traditional postwar poetic solution, does its heavy duty here with obscene swiftness, "assess[ing]" and "cleans[ing] with a kind of artistry" the "soon-covered," unthinkable suffering evidenced by the carnage. To accompany it are customary nationalistic metonymies that rather violently "graft" the particular dead's experience into "ideal[ized]" figurative discourses, here imaged forth as war memorials (including the poem itself), or "treasured foundations" on (and for) which their transformed features are made to stand.[52] "[N]ew tongues" emerge, also, belonging to "[c]onsultants," or experts, professionals by now on war, the biggest business of the twentieth century—a theme Hill explores more deeply in "Commerce and Society," a sequence in the same volume. Here, the presence of the consultants appropriates the "Pities[']" "assess[ments]," "paint[ing]," and "re-align[ments]" into a commodifying discourse that also casts the artist who would so "repaint" the scene in suspicious light; "for [these victims]," Adorno wrote, "are used to create something, works of art, that are thrown to the consumption of a world which destroyed them."[53] Hill's beautifully rendered form and rhyme scheme, initially thought of by some critics as a link between him and the Movement, serve instead the end of indicting themselves as such upholstery; here the rhyme "drifts," like the wanderers, into distant dissonance in the last stanza, as the form displays its achievement of its contradictory goal of seemingly commemorating but only covering up the war experience. The "separated wrongs" of the period from which world culture might learn are instead, like the "unedifying dead," *unified* in a mass grave of platitudinous generality; "[h]ere the statues" are "[d]arkened by laurel," or by the obfuscations of pastoral art's universalizations. The use of the collective personal pronoun, again, unlike that in Movement poetry, invokes not so much a sense of community among us as readers as it does our complicity; "we" have, along with the poet, traditionally "celebrated fluently and at ease" through such discursive "artistry," moving ahead "[a]ccording to [its] direction" and leaving behind, in an oxymoron, a central contradiction that locks within it that which was, ostensibly, the poem's purpose to take up: the war's "[e]vidently-veiled griefs."

It is to the hyphen in the oxymoron, the experience/history lost between available discourses, that Hill's poetry often leads like a "cognitive map," historicizing and spatializing the directions and avoidances of language.[54] In this way, he takes a stand on the question of "the silence of the poet" in the decade of dilemmatic speaking by committing his own complicitous speech to the purposes of "locat[ing]," as Steiner would write several years later, "as exactly as record and imagination are able, the measure of unknowing, indifference, complicity, commission which relates the contemporary or survivor to the slain."[55] Although Hill's discursive negotiations may seem, to some, dangerously close to becoming a "very cold, intellectual activity,"[56] ill-suited to addressing the Holocaust or the war, Silkin has remained among those who have recognized a committed presence in Hill's "ferocity"—the "sense of outrage" that underlies his poems' combination of disparate elements and that is never wholly qualified by what Silkin also much admires, their "self-auditing compaction."[57] Hill's at that time unfashionable poems did not avoid the unspeakable, as did those of the Movement (for "[commitment] was", as Williams noted, "an argument of what to write about" as much as anything else),[58] nor did they translate it into "personal" expression, as did poems by the emerging "confessionalist" poets of the 1960s (whose work Hill would of course be "sceptical" of),[59] nor did they indulge in "the mannered introduction of the sordid" and of death as a "respectable convention," as Jon Glover, another poet then writing at Leeds, perceived the London "Group" as doing, with "little detectable pressure of feeling" and as "a substitute for any commitment to social problems."[60] Glover, Wainwright, Smith, and other poets who emerged in the

1960s, having studied under Hill and Silkin, perceived themselves as being "committed" poets—and even felt that such commitment described the "eidolon of Leeds University"[61]—but they remember also Hill's paradoxical and nontrendy advice to his students: "The poet is someone for whom words are difficult."[62]

Silkin's work, focused as it has been on Jewish experience—both in specific historical terms and as emblematic of the wide range of persecutions and exclusions endemic to western culture—was similarly out of step with dominant trends in British poetry in the 1950s; in 1954 his first book, *The Peaceable Kingdom*, with its "thick-textured" study of victimization, suffering, silences, and survival in exile was, in Hill's words, "wildly unfashionable" because of its appearance during the advent of the Movement's influence.[63] Hill located in Silkin's verse, as Silkin would in Hill's, a like "fierceness,"[64] though one emanating from a slightly different location— one on the margins of Hill's Church of England-catechized, Oxford-educated positioning—and thus one less fully identified with traditional power structures. A Jew and, at one point, a manual laborer, Silkin begins his "cognitive map" in an elsewhere that he often struggles to chart, proceeding in what he has called a kind of "process" poetry that, in its working away from traditional forms and through contradictions, "stands by a kind of analogy for revolution."[65] Though both often lead readers to discursive gaps and silences, it is in their selection of starting points that Hill and Silkin most differ; Silkin's insistence that personal experience affords at least some slippery ground for resistance against the margin's "assimilation" within a dominant culture[66]—a conceptual issue still today undergoing heated debate within feminist as well as minority cultural theory—at times causes the "confusion" some critics on the Left have registered between political commitment in Silkin's work and "impassioned personal statement."[67] If Hill might be said to have gained a deeper awareness of the Jewish perspective on history through Silkin's presence at Leeds,[68] it might also be said that Hill's problematization of "personalism"—"the whole notion of the simple, sensuous and passionate"[69]—contributed to the "self-auditing compaction" that has increasingly, as in "The Centre," complicated Silkin's poetry, its "drama of reason."

Others at Leeds contributed to Silkin's development during this period, most notably Tony Harrison, with whom Silkin remembers working while he was completing *The Re-ordering of the Stones*. Harrison, then a graduate student at Leeds, and another colleague, Terry Brindley, offered Silkin comments that "made [him] aware of [his] tendency toward rhetoric, and writing 'feelings about feelings.'" "[T]heir idea of history was harder, grittier, and more painful than polished like myth" which, Silkin recalls, they had become "wary" of; "people at Leeds were more concerned with what was real, and not with pursuing some reconciliation with or some easy understanding of what is difficult."[70] Silkin's work, which had been drawn from the outset to the beautiful reconciliatory images in Isaiah and to mythic metaphors of arks and neo-Lawrencian ships—as well as to narratives of diasporic rootlessness, journey, and renewable earth—would, in the early 1960s, begin to strike a deeper counterpoint within demythologized landscapes. For example, in "The Coldness," the first poem in the two-part "Astringencies"—a poem he believes he could not have written before going up to Leeds[71]—Silkin's historical focus is on York, the uncommemorated site of the mass suicide of an entire community of eight hundred Jews before a hostile Christian mob. Measuring the gap their absence creates in York, and the consequences of the city's having defined itself against that absence, even against its memory, becomes the desired/impossible task of the speaker—though one with a negatively descriptive "moral":

> Where the printing-works buttress a church
> And the northern river like moss
> Robes herself slowly through
> The cold township of York,
> More slowly than usual
> For a cold northern river,
> You see the citizens
> Indulging stately pleasures,
> Like swans. . . .
>
> .   .   .   .   .   .
>
> What consciousness is there of the cold
> Heart, with its spaces?
> For nothing penetrates
> More than admitted absence.
> The heart in warmth, even, cannot

Close its gaps. . . .

. . . .

All Europe is touched
With some of frigid York,
As York is now by Europe.

(*SP*, 27–28)

Silkin's speaker suggests that even when "warm" or responsive, human consciousness cannot "close its gaps"—those portions of history unlived or misremembered because one group persecuted another out of existence and/ or because, as the first line has it, "printing-works buttress" institutions of power, leaving the experience of others unrecorded in language. Yet the absence of Jews and synagogues in York *is*, like the "other" against which deconstructive theory's dominating culture defines itself, present; it *is* "An assertion persistent / As a gross tumour" (*SP*, 27), *has* an effect, *is* the cause, the speaker speculates, for "the coldness" of a place "deaden[ed]" to its own past (*SP*, 28). "André Schwarz-Bart chose the martyrdom at York as the starting-point of the long road to Auschwitz in *Les dernier des justes*," as Efraim Sicher reminds us;[72] Silkin reminds us of the same connection in the final three lines excerpted above. Yet always concerned to "imply the need for change," for action,[73] Silkin does allow his speaker to speculate about the possibility of "some moving to / A northern purgation" if only "one / Among them" (the citizens of York) "[c]ould touch the dignity" of the dead— "could feel" (*SP*, 28). The model that seems to be offered, as in "The Centre," is one of beginning within one's own internal gaps—"coldnesses"—in order to readdress history's empty spaces and their effects; the poem formally enacts this interrogative movement, this "historicization" of feeling (or lack thereof), from the local to the larger western cultural picture. It even seeks to reembody and redignify the lost community by imagining the absent workers, though the vivid images of stonemasons, printers, and "[t]aut, flaxen plumbers" appear in the form of a question: "[w]here are" they? (*SP*, 28). Limitations on individual agency signaled by such lack of access, and by the poem's inaugural presences of Althusserian "ideological state apparatuses" like the Church and printingworks, deeply complicate the poem's call to action; what emerges from the poem's contradictions and impasses is, again, an Adornoesque paradox: the palpable presence of absence, of both the impossibility and imperative for acknowledgment and response, and a consequent alertness to what the second part of the poem offers, deconstructively, as the way of the world:

> Where everything that is
> Is agony, in this sense:
> That things war to survive.
> Pain is complex, something akin
> To stone with veins of colour
> In it, that cross and cross
> But never reconcile
> Into one swab of colour
> Or the stone that contains them.
>
> (*SP*, 29)

Because identification of "things"—nations, selves—has always involved definition *against* others, everything that seemingly "is," unified and with its own identity, is actually an "agony," as the undermining line break tells us, of conflict, of lost voices, of gaps.

Silkin would continue to commit his work to exposing such exclusionary processes and to advocating change in the form of an awareness of the costs of (self-) definition, though with increasing attention to the ways in which a writer's use of language can cause "absences" as real as those physical ones in York's history. He later dramatizes this idea most clearly in "Killhope Wheel" (1974), a poem situated in the industrial landscape of northern England. In it his speaker enters a shipyard near the abandoned, nineteenth-century ore-washing wheel of the title, hoping to infuse the dark site of historical working-class misery with some dignity or, as R. K. Meiners argues, a romantic "aura"—that proud, responsive presence Benjamin understood to be critiqued in the work of Baudelaire.[74] Instead, he watches one worker slip, "fall the depth of the hold," "look at [the speaker], and look away" in a painful opening of that space between the poet's poeticizing constructions of the experience at hand and the actual one fated to remain "outside history" and inaccessible to the poem.[75] The remainder of the sequence dwells upon the history buried beneath its text—a history engineered by forces like those symbolized in the forty-foot Killhope Wheel, which seems to exude a relentlessly turning, larger-than-life, mechanistic power that dehumanizes labor, "washing" as it did the "crushed" and "pounded" ore of the dirt associated with the miners, now forgotten "under the ground" (*SP*, 91–92). "A want of sound hangs / in a drop of moisture from the wheel" in a figure of those swept away by its force, along with any evidence of their work. The water becomes—as it does in many poems from this book, *The Principle of Water*—a highly complex image, and one with which the speaker, standing before the sign that allows him free entry to this place of historical misery, punishment, and virtual enslavement, begins to identify:

> Why does a board, tacked to wood,
> concerning my being free to visit
> nourish my useless pain?
>
> Like water. I am its water, dispersed
> in the ground I came from; and have footage
> on these hills, stripped of lead,
>
> which the sheep crop, insensibly white.
> The mist soaks their cries into them.
>
> (*SP*, 91)

The speaker *becomes* the water that, like the wooden sign, nourishes his or her own pain. In other words, the poem suggests that the speaker, like these elements—wood and water—of renewable earth, is made up of the human drama that has gone to ground, though he or she at the same time has been "dispersed," with elements lost in the same way that the region has lost its lead or that history has lost the unrecountable lives and experienced injustices of the working-class scenario of the poem; thus we are told, in a double entendre, that the speaker "can't work out what [he or she has] / come here for" (*SP*, 91). The laws and agents of dispersion become an almost oppressive force in the poem, "soak[ing the sheep's] cries into them," washing the less-articulate utterances of experience from the surviving products of the cycle—among them ore, language, and the poem itself.

A paradox is again presented in this, as in all of Silkin's most complicated works: the water, for all its "cleansing" properties, also "pushes / within a moment of the quick of you, bituminous / and rank" (*SP*, 90); both water and self are implicated, at the line break, of carrying on the polluted effects of historical practice, however unwittingly—as must language too, in poststructuralist terms, and therefore, of course, poetic practice as well. The latter is, in this sense, like the soil under the house in the first poem of the sequence, "Tree"; it too was "disabled" and "rank," and "could enable nothing, nothing / opened in it" (*SP*, 89). Like the speaker in that at first seemingly unrelated poem, Silkin attempts to "plant a tree" or to bring life into the "house" or linguistic structure of his sequence by opening it out from its context to forms and materials that destroy its conventional unities: a "barrel" "dragged in off rocks" (or the poem's rough-hewn, "process" form as vessel), earth mixed with "peat dug from a lake" (or preserved bits of the past), and "dung [he] crumbled in" (or the unpoetic "shit" of experience that he both adds and finds himself dispersing within, as well). Like the man-size "five foot" tree, the poem's redrawings of lost human experience can take only tenuous root in the breaks between such disparate and contrived elements; this is the understanding with which the final dramatic monologue from a "Platelayer" must be read as well. Although there is much the poet and readers "can't tell" about this figure, as the final line of the poem makes clear, it is also clear that the wish of the poet is for this voice, like the tree, "for what it is, to live beyond [him]" (*SP*, 95, 90)—to add another kind of textual voice, fashioned out of the contradictions of its context, to the linguistic preserves of history. In "Killhope Wheel," Silkin demonstrates his career-long desire to combine the discursive mode (which, as he wrote in his introduction to *Poetry of the Committed Individual*, he feels is essential to a "socially-orientated" art) and the imagistic (or "hermetic") mode in his poetry; the former historicizes in this poem, whereas the latter "thinks against" it, establishing a negative dialectic in response to his need to confront history by opening spaces that, as the earlier quotation from "Astringencies" acknowledges, will "never [be] reconcile[d]."

The many irreconcilables in Tony Harrison's "harder" view of history, particularly the contemporary history of his own working-class background in postwar Leeds, have from the start embodied one of the most important points of his poetry; they, on one level at least, constitute in themselves a critique of what had since the 1955 election been represented, even by

Labour's moderate leaders, as Britain's receding need for working-class writing and radicalism given its supposed progress toward a conflict-free, classless society. Like Hill, Harrison conducts much of his argument on the subtle level of discourse, which polices class boundaries and cultural exclusions even as it proclaims, as Thompson and others lamented, "consensus." As Rick Rylance has shown, Harrison uses the many "languages" of his disunified selves, past and present —"scholarship boy," accomplished classicist, working-class poet, "British" professor in Africa, "northern" writer in England, and so on—to reveal their contradictions, and to point up "the drama of expression with a language pressured by problems of power."[76] His poems' traditional forms, filled with hard-hitting, colloquial language, demonstrate that pressure, though they also, unlike Hill's, demonstrate his increasing desire to provide access to his poems for a wider readership; he recalls helpful debates about such issues with James Simmons and Wole Soyinka, who were also students at Leeds at the time and who would move toward songwriting and playwriting to reach larger, more "popular" audiences.[77] He remembers differing with Silkin a good deal, given his own "obsess[ions] with form" and the latter's belief in the social power of "pity" and "qualities of feeling"; what he shares with Silkin is a commitment to readdressing the absences in history from his own personal, once-marginalized standpoint, and to speaking for the inarticulate, whose experience his own approximates—to "rescuing from silence the class into which he was born."[78]

There is, then, a confusion or tension between impulses in Harrison's poetry. On the one hand, as Rylance puts it, is the impulse to write, in the voice of his class, "'a poetry from below' . . . continuous with both the 'history from below' of social historians like E. P. Thompson," (*ON*, 120), as well as with the arguments of Richard Hoggart (another Leeds alumnus) concerning the loss of working-class values and community through co-optive education and myths of classlessness; on the other hand is the impulse to foreground the preemptions and illusions of the very language and traditions he uses to make such arguments. Rylance writes that the force of the former impulse causes Harrison's work to be "different" from that of other postmodernists, given that it is "not happily absorbed into poststructuralist theory" (*ON*, 115, 126), just as Thompson's "culturalism," with its "emphasis on human agency and individual experience" (*ON*, 127), was not easily absorbed into the Althusserian Marxism of the younger members of the

New Left. Viewed from only a slightly different angle, the ways in which Harrison has formally and increasingly problematized his own expressions from within his "particular social and literary context[s]" (*ON*, 116), instead of naively leaving them behind—as Adorno believed one might—appear to have enhanced the possibilities of a poststructuralist reading of his work. At the same time, they have allowed him to remain committed to articulating the problems and experience, as discursively constructed, of his disempowered class.

In a 1960 review of D. J. Enright's *Some Men Are Brothers*, Harrison relays his thoughts on Enright's unambitious, "reportage" poems, his "committed picaresque," in part by pitting the latter's justifications of his art against the arguments of Bonamy Dobrée, the influential chair of the School of English at Leeds, as articulated in Dobrée's 1952–53 Clark Lectures, *The Broken Cistern* (London: Cohen and West, 1954).[79] In them, Dobrée dealt with the absence of "great public themes" in poetry; the young Harrison seems to stand by that complaint in his review, lamenting in late modernist fashion the contemporary lack of "daring" to "enlarge upon" small, fragmented, personal poems or the lack of "uni[fying] . . . imagination": "Faced with the problems Enright tackles [poverty and starvation in foreign lands], we need the product of vision rather than sightseeing."[80] Eleven years later, in his own first book-length collection of poems, *The Loiners* (slang for residents of Leeds), which was published after his return from time spent teaching in Nigeria and Czechoslovakia in the 1960s, Harrison would indeed achieve the kind of enormity of scope that he had called for in poetry, though the "vision" that emerges from this powerful group of interrelated poems and sequences exhibits the effect that the decade's philosophical upheavals had in the meantime had upon conceptions of the "unifying imagination."

The five sections of the book, set variously in the Leeds of Harrison's young adulthood, Africa, South America, Eastern Europe, and Newcastle (where he now lives), do move in a great circle out from the north of England into the world and back again, carrying what at first seem to be motifs of visionary discovery and globalized unity—as is illustrated in the quotation from Thomas Browne's *Religio Medici*, for example, that heads part 2, "There is all Africa and her prodigies in us; we are that bold and adventurous piece of Nature," or in the quotation from John Cleveland that heads part 4, "Correct your maps: Newcastle is Peru!" But that visionary point in which

Harrison says he is "interested," "the point where one can say, 'Newcastle is Peru'" and "when a man like Donne can brood over his woman and say, 'O my America! my new-found-land'"—in other words, the point of overcoming cultural and habitual myopia in order to rediscover the world in the familiar—is exhilarating only for a "very brief time,"[81] and not for the usual or romanticized reasons. Rather, in Harrison's postmodern version of revelation, the ability to break out of boundaries or to see the different parts of the world spin into dizzying similitude swiftly becomes testimony *not* to unifying essentialities but to the pervasiveness of western cultural patterns of discovery, conquest, exploitation, colonization, and/or domination that infiltrate the history and language of places like the mining regions of northern England, as well as Peru, and even of the bedrooms of the poems' speakers/personae, who also exult, like Donne, in the bodies of their lovers as "new-found-lands":

> Discovery! wart, mole, spot
> like outcrops on a snowfield, dot
> the slopes of flesh my fingers ski
> with circular dexterity.
> This moment when my hand strays
> your body like an endless maze,
> returning and returning, you,
> O you; you also are Peru.[82]

Such a moment, from part 4, is meant to be a celebration and, for a brief time, it is; as in the book's central poem, "The Heart of Darkness" (set in an African blackout), making love is the one "unmistakable pulsation" in the highly mediated lives of these voices, and the body of a lover the one "blurred light in the blind / concentric circles of blank mind" (*L*, 47). But, as in Hill's work, the "privacy" of such moments is invaded by cultural overdeterminations; even here, love's circular caresses are continuous with the book's pervasive imagery of circularity in blankness or darkness, which becomes Harrison's secular, deconstructed image of history's progress: against a meaningless backdrop, as in Conrad's novel—the abyss, the "void," *"l'abîme ouvert /* [Pascal] thought was special but is everywhere" (*L*, 22)—constructions of identity and power root themselves in historical/discursive precedents and thus perpetuate their cyclic, eternal return. Caught up, then, not by "human nature" or by any preordained destiny, but rather in the linguistic rhythms of history (quite literally so, in Harrison's Kiplingesque meters and rhyming couplets), the poems' speakers, particularly those visiting former colonies as unwitting representatives of "Empire," "try to break out of one stereotype only to fall into another. . . . [T]he nightmare of history is not only outside but inside under the bed, and enacted in the very forms our sexuality chooses to express itself."[83] Obvious reenactments of European conquest take place in the African section's sexual lootings of the natives, but more subtle suggestions about the intimate ramifications of that legacy occur in tender passages like the one quoted above, in which seemingly innocent images "return" with insidious connections to patterns of conquest and domination in the book as a whole. The amorous pronouncement "you also are Peru" made upon the "endless maze" of his lover's body—an image that connects her female form with the "dark turn[s] of the labyrinth" (*L*, 84) of naked existence, the void upon which "new" old patterns of meaning must be imposed—sends us back to part 2's "Distant Ophir" (a poem written after Fracastorii's sixteenth-century work, *Syphilis*), in which a prophecy is addressed to "Westerners," "self-lumbered [or self-constructed] pilgrims," who "impose" their "new sacraments" of rape, plunder, and domination on existing peoples in "discovered" lands:

> . . . your discoveries will cost
> destructions greater than the siege of Troy,
>
> . . . .
> You'll go on looking, losing more and more
> to the sea, the climate, weapons, ours *and* yours,
> your crimes abroad brought home as civil war.
>
> . . . .
> You'll only find the Old World in the New,
> and you'll rue your *discubrimiento*, rue
> it, rue Africa, rue Cuba, rue Peru!
>
> (*L*, 32)

With such "*discubrimiento*" (discovery) to shadow it in the poem, the lover's vision of his "new-found-land" darkens into a possible analogue for its domination and exploitation translated into sexual terms. Images that directly follow in his drunken train of thought—traveling, like the rest of the poem, in circles—return him to Africa where he, "at ease," watches a native woman doing heavy labor in the hot sun; such complex associations suggest not only the "haunting" of these figures by "the ghosts of imperialism,"[84] but also their unwitting complicity in the perpetuation of its inscription. Penultimately we are left with the speaker's thoughts of how his fingers, lined with coal from laying the evening's fire back in England, "smudge / everything they feel or touch" (L, 85). The coal image, connected inno-cently here with the fire, doubles back through the book to accumulate associations with this "Loiner's" mining hometown, as well as with "the staithes and shipyards of Peru" (L, 84)—making him both a victim, as a native of the industrial north of England, and a victimizer, as an indoctri-nated, traveling representative of the same rapacious western culture that exploits his region and haunts him, as the figure of Queen Victoria, in all of her many iconic forms and residual structures of feeling, haunts The Loiners from first poem to last. Harrison's first book, then, finds a way to speak to the situation of his class and region—to their losses of voice and freedom at the hands of dominant forces within their own culture—while simulta-neously, formally, and discursively demonstrating his own overdeter-mination by the same forces and thus the difficulty of such speech. The very fact that this book of poems roughly follows the course of Harrison's own life, but is infiltrated by history and conducted by a cast of socially recognizable speakers, attests to the invasion of private experience—of "sov-ereignty"—by the sociopolitical realm.

Both Hill and Harrison have, in their use of traditional forms and foregrounded discursive conventions, risked being taken at face value and being diametrically misread. The notorious series of letters concerning Hill's work in the *London Review of Books (LRB)* ("The Case for Geoffrey Hill," 1985–86), which focused to a great extent on the sonnet sequence "An Apology for the Revival of Christian Architecture in England" in *Tenebrae* (1978), serves as a case in point. Constructed as a kind of prismatic, discursive portrait of, as the title would suggest, the nineteenth century's revival of Gothic architecture in the midst of chaotic industrialization and imperialistic ex-pansion, the poem's presentation of the contradictory ways in which such "[w]eightless magnificence upholds the past" alongside images of a "spiritual,

Platonic old England"[85] while its continuance is "bought at a price: not only the sufferings of English labourers but also of Indian peasants," aids Hill in making his subtle "diagnosis" of the "political and sociological reasons for the floating of nostalgia . . . ever since the end of the Great War."[86] In other words, the poem is also, like Harrison's, a demythologization of the *contemporary* "revival" of Victorian values in Britain's postwar, increasingly conservative culture, which has become more and more deeply divided along national, regional, class, and gender lines. Yet, though the work foregrounds language as a material used to build that "architecture" and his own smoothly formal sonnets as complicitous in upholding its "weightless magnificence," Hill and the poem have been accused of (or affirmed as, depending upon the critic) *being* nostalgic and conservative themselves. "Eliot became the accepted spokesperson for a cultural orthodoxy whose terms Hill unquestioningly takes over," writes John Lucas (*LRB,* 3 October 1985) in support of a number of Tom Paulin's assertions, including that Hill is a "chthonic nationalist" (*LRB,* 6 June 1985); his phrasings are, Lucas continues, "unable to break free from the heavy layers of allusion and echo in which the sonnets are cocooned, which the phrases' own literariness endorses, and which the sonnet form itself underpins" (*LRB,* 5 December 1985).

The latter remark is, of course, exactly right—as is Lucas's next statement that the effect of all this is "deadening pastiche"; Hill's language and forms demonstrate their inevitable entrapment in a discursive tradition that Eliot and others not only perpetuated but, given modernism's spatializing, "transhistorical" aesthetics, dehistoricized—a problem turned into sport in postmodern pastiches with their famously outrageous "simulacra," decontextualized quotation, and depthlessness.[87] Hill's pastiche is, in many ways, a study of these effects, but at the same time it inserts historical and marginalized elements, like the three "Short History of India" sonnets and the poor shepherd's sonnet, "Damon's Lament for his Clorinda, Yorkshire 1654," which broaden the picture of how "Platonic England grasp[ed] its tenantry" (*CP,* 158) and financed its architectural whims. Yet in both cases, Hill also makes his point about entrapment by demonstrating the difficulties of calling up such elements from textual traditions that have "[m]a[de] miniatures of the once-monstrous theme" (*CP,* 155) of Indian subjugation, or made literary "masks" like that of Damon (traceable back to Plato) to elegize the little-recorded sufferings of the "real" historical laborers. There-

fore, Hill's production of *his* Yorkshire Damon devolves into pointed comedy as the speaker, having barely finished his conventional shepherd's "we've
flourished simply despite all" speech, suddenly effects a postmodern film
move, a textual "shot/reverse shot" at his creator:

> . . . Why does the air grow cold
>
> in this region of mirrors? And who is this clown
> doffing his mask at the masked threshold
> to selfless raptures that are all his own?

(CP, 153)

As in "September Song," Hill suddenly foregrounds the architectural principles of his own poem, discovering himself "mirrored" *in the text* by his
own character, both of them foolish products of the same idealized, dehistoricized textual traditions. Like the "Quaint Mazes" of the great houses of
the first poem of the sequence, they duplicate, entrap, and lead back only
into themselves for "they," as Eliot famously noted in "Tradition and the
Individual Talent," with another kind of confidence, "are that which we
know."[88] Hill's poem probes the dead ends and discursive cul-de-sacs of what
we know, simultaneously dramatizing *and* resisting both nostalgia and
postmodern turns away from the responsibility to interrogate "history"—
or what the difficulties in doing so reveal about its constructions of the
present.

Harrison's sonnets and otherwise formal poems have been perhaps more
successful in communicating at least their most easily anticipated messages,
given their setting in his own well-known biographical dilemma of having
been socially displaced by his education—a plight not uncommon in postwar, post–Education Act working-class experience and one evocative of a
number of familiar issues, including those of the "Establishment's" co-option
of working-class talent and of the role of language ("Received Pronunciation" versus provincial) in the division of Britain's "two nations." Harrison's
long sonnet sequence, *The School of Eloquence* (1978), has become representative, for many, of his work as a whole because of its frank, accessible
treatment of these issues and its relatively simple operating principles,
explained as they are in what might be the two most-quoted lines in his

oeuvre: "So right, yer buggers, then! We'll occupy / your lousy leasehold poetry!"[89] Though this militant metaphor describes his "tenant's" literary takeover of elite poetic forms with his working-class voice, the same formal practice describes equally well, in the second part of the sequence, the chasm opened by poetry between his parents (or class) and himself. The contradiction is obvious, and fundamental to the point of the sequence; again, as in the case of Hill, critics who direct us to such "shortcomings" articulate the poems' formal thematics most effectively: "[T]here is an inescapable question as to whether Harrison's dynamic isn't also contained and defused by his choice of regular verse forms and whether his appropriation of middle-class culture has not in fact worked in reverse. It is an inescapable dialectic. . . ."[90] It is, indeed, a *negative* one, "a thinking against itself"[91] or, more accurately, a foregrounding of the languages that have constructed his differing "selves" and the barriers between them—all of them either collusive with, or a product of, ruling traditions and their processes of empowerment or impoverishment. Harrison's decision to write in Meredithian sonnets—and therefore link his sequence to the subversive precedent of *Modern Love*[92]—complicates the "diffusion" Woodcock mentions; yet even so, it is still not a matter of "choice," as the latter suggests. Rather, as Jeffrey Wainwright put it in a review of the sonnets in 1979 (the year of the *Stand* symposium on commitment): "It is naive to imagine that poetic convention, like cultural tradition at large, can be ignored and overturned at will. It has penetrated our consciousness too deeply for that, and rather than shirk the implications of this, Harrison takes [it] on. . . ."[93] Without perpetuating the myth of the individual, integrated, sovereign voice, or effecting reconciliation of "dialectical contradiction" when to do so would be to offer his audience "harmonized" fantasy as a substitute for what is "objectively unresolved," if it cannot be objectively described,[94] Harrison demonstrates the need for change by moving negatively through contradiction, offering in *form* what cannot be made by statement. "Dialectical contradiction 'is' not simply; it means," Adorno wrote;[95] nowhere is this complex way of meaning more clearly set into motion than in one of Harrison's latest and most controversial poems, *v.*[96]

v. is more meaningful in what it does not do than in what it "does"; as a result, what it does is "diagnose," as did Hill's poem, the role of language, poetry, and certain imaginations of selfhood in constructions of impasse—such as "this class war" (*v.*, 22). First of all, though set in a Leeds cemetery and modeled, both formally and to some extent thematically, after Thomas Gray's "Elegy Written in a Country Churchyard," the poem does not, like Gray's and other traditional elegies, reconcile the working-class souls it contemplates with either their fate or with their more fortunate countrymen and women, or even with their own class's youthful "skinheads," whose aerosoled epithets on their gravestones provide the poem with both its central focus/conflict and its title. *v.* means "versus" on the stones—as in "LEEDS v. DERBY" (*v.*, 11), one of the footballers' less obscene bits of "aggro," left behind along with the many "shit[s]," "fuck[s]," and "cunt[s]" that enrage Harrison's persona (a dramatized version of one aspect of himself). But *v.* also means "verses" (which involves poetry in the conflict) and, particularly after the war, "victory" and cultural unity. In poststructuralist terms, the sign is perceived to be wholly indeterminate, and the fact that its interpretation or "meaning" is contested, yet dominated by the ruling powers of the poem (represented in part by the educated poet-half of the persona), emerges as one of the critical points made by its unresolved—and for some unsatisfying—ending.

The central contradiction of the poem, the one that exposes the limitations of its form and causes the persona to split into two voices, is reflected in the discrepancy between the persona's stated intentions and the operations of his words. The poem begins in concern for the community's graveyard, whose "subsiding," unkempt stones and positioning over a "worked-out [mining] pit" (*v.*, 9) become figures for its inarticulate souls' eclipse by the industry that consumed them—as it metaphorically consumed Silkin's worker in "Killhope Wheel," fallen "the depth of the hold"; it is also an image of the loss of working-class memory and for the speeding of that loss by "families and friends hav[ing] gone away / for work or fuller lives, like [the poet] from Leeds" (*v.*, 12). Like Thomas Gray, then, the poet's initiatory desire is to be "mindful of the unhonoured dead," and "in these lines their artless tale to relate." But the traditional mode for doing so, as exemplified by Gray, involves imbuing what could not be presently justified—what he calls their "circumscribed . . . virtues," their "Chill Penury"—with "higher" or transcendent meaning; in Gray's poem it becomes reward in heaven for their "simpler innocence," a conscience-salving stereotype. Such reconciliation, or "harmonizing," lifts the historical into realms where

"crucial differences vanish,"[97] relieving the reader of the need to recognize
social injustices, feel outrage, or imagine change. In similar fashion, Harrison's persona, with one of the "grand gestures" that Woodcock feels mar
the poem,[98] demonstrates his collusion with the tradition of his model by
attempting to lift the graffitied "UNITED"—the name of the local football
team—on his parents' own gravestone into higher realms he no longer even
believes in but has "inherited" from tradition as well as from his "dad"

> . . . who'd hoped from 'the beyond'
> a better life than this one, *with* my mother.
>
> Though I don't believe in afterlife at all
> and know it's cheating it's hard *not* to make
> a sort of furtive prayer from this skin's scrawl,
> his UNITED mean 'in Heaven' for their sake,
>
> an accident of meaning to redeem
> an act intended as mere desecration
> and make the thoughtless spraying of his team
> apply to higher things, and to the nation.
>
> > (*v.,* 15)

By reinterpreting the skin's sign for aggressive team- and class-solidarity as
one that signifies metaphysical unity, Harrison's persona not only causes
those "crucial differences [to] vanish," but also robs his class of the "hearing" (*v.,* 19) he originally set out to give them. It is when, shortly after this
point, as he begins offering universalizations for the skinheads' aerosoling—
suggesting that it may be "just a *cri-de-coeur* because man dies" (*v.,* 17)—that
the voice later revealed to be the persona's skinhead alter ego interrupts
him with "*So what's a* cri-de-coeur, *cunt? Can't you speak / the language that
yer mam spoke. Think of 'er!*" The obvious discrepancy between intention
and operation is signaled by the form's breakdown—by the verbal fight that
begins on this peaceful site of traditional elegy—and by the disunified,
discursively constructed self exposed by this internal battle over words. Time-
honored "universalizing"—for many, a virtual requirement within the definition of "poetry"—is revealed to be, when it elides differences, nothing

more than an action as aggressive as any taken by the skinhead; it is domination through the creation of "cover concepts"—"the technique of logical
subsumption for ideological purposes."[99]

Critics' responses to the poem's resolution, or lack thereof, demonstrate
their misunderstanding of Harrison's formal critique of both such conventional textual unifications *and* the achievement of a supposed "personal"
unity of consciousness to compensate for such social divisions. Ken Worpole,
in his very valuable piece of writing on Harrison's sonnet sequence, nevertheless says about *v.*: "Against disintegration he can only offer a new form
of the possessive family circle:

> Home, home to my woman, where the fire's lit
> these still chilly mid-May evenings, home to you,
> and perished vegetation from the pit
> escaping insubstantial up the flue."[100]

But the poem itself problematizes, in countless images, this retreat from the
graveyard home to the poet's wife, renowned operatic singer and actress
Teresa Stratas, whose *Lulu* plays in the background of the stanza Worpole
quotes above. Though both were born into impoverished circumstances,
here the couple represents privileged "high culture," relaxing while in the
hearth burns the coal we have throughout the poem associated with the
working class and with the skinhead, whose earlier words haunt the above
stanza with its image of that coal "escaping insubstantial up the flue":

> *Aspirations, cunt! Folk on t' fucking dole*
> *'ave got about as much scope to aspire*
> *above the shit they're dumped in, cunt, as coal*
> *aspires to be chucked on t' fucking fire.*
>
> (*v.*, 17)

While Harrison's persona returns to his comfortable home where, in the
love he shares with his wife, "opposites seem sometimes unified," (*v.*, 26)
the skinhead's existence goes up in smoke (as well as in reconciliatory,
"insubstantial" poetry); the implication is that it will also go unremembered,
like the legacy of the Leeds graveyard after it falls into the worked-out mining

pit below it. The scene becomes an image of social ills displaced into art (in this instance opera as well as poetry, for *Lulu*, too, is about the disempowered) and set aside by "personal" fulfillment, though they remain burning nonetheless in the hearth/heart of the divided poet. The illusory nature of his "personal solution" has all along been underscored in the poem by the tune hummed by the little boy footballers—"Here Comes the Bride"—as they boot their ball against a hawthorn tree near the graveyard, forcing it to shed its flowers' white petals. This recurring image, one of happy illusion created through violence against one's own place, accompanies the poet throughout his retreat and even into his bedroom, where dying petals from the graveyard fall from the poet's shedded parka, and where "the bride, the bride / [he feels] united to" (*v.*, 31) comes naked to his side. "Turning to love, and sleep's oblivion, I know / what the UNITED that the skin sprayed *has* to mean" (*v.*, 30); in turning away, and changing the "meaning" of the word yet one more time, Harrison's persona displays the irreconcilable nature of his learned maneuverings within language, as well as the ways in which its contradictions continue to haunt him. E. P. Thompson wrote, in response to Auden's "September 1, 1939," that "it is part of the 'human predicament' that love will always be overruled by power," and that "the affirmation of 'love' may appear only as a personal resolution . . .";[101] Harrison further suggests, with his broken, postmodern elegy, that just as language is inscribed by power relations, even the personal sphere is deeply infiltrated by social divisions—it cannot, therefore, be laid as in this scene "to rest."

"It lies in the definition of negative dialectics that it will not come to rest in itself, as if it were total. This is its form of hope."[102] The difficult "form[s] of hope" offered by Harrison, Hill, and Silkin are often quite literally to be found in their poems' forms—in their "returns upon themselves" as effected in their attempts to analyze as well as to represent the discursive "drama of reason" that determines the shape of the social order and those silenced within it. In other words, instead of creating "ludic play" with the empty sign of postmodernism, or concentrating on the impossibility of innocently speaking, or savaging syntax to display despair over its mediation of expression, the "work" done by these poets with their material—language—cannot afford to "frustrate . . . communication," because it attempts to refocus readers on the postmodern crisis of the self as a *social* crisis, directing them to the complex linguistic architecture of difficult historical issues and the role that their own "self"-expression plays in the maintenance of such constructions. By continually doubling back against their own articulated thoughts and the forms of those thoughts, their struggles against both naively speaking *and* "cognitive dispersal" offer forms for change-oriented thinking that never rest—that begin the process of critiquing themselves within their own critiques. As Jeffrey Wainwright affirmed in a *Stand* editorial in 1975, the situation is, as Adorno also put it, one of "paradox"; "[p]aradoxically we need to both accept and reject," Wainwright wrote, all of those limitations inherent in the poet's perspective and medium, even as they cause his/her work to remain continually "unfinished."[103]

The influence of Silkin, Hill, and Harrison upon the poets who would study at Leeds during the 1960s is palpable, particularly in Wainwright's carefully worded, elegantly formed poems, which have often been reminiscent of Hill's in their creation of historical portraiture through the foregrounding of complicit discursive tonalities that "talk over" stark images of cultural violence. It is apparent as well in Ken Smith's colloquial dramatics with their postmodern edge, sounding as they do from the borders of the social mainstream, where they remain intent upon the question: "Who is the 'I' that speaks?"[104]—and how constrained and ephemeral is even that self who nonetheless "want[s]," like a furtive and displaced London "fox" slipping along between culture's fast-dictated successions of images and signs, "a word" for the experience of those who suffer beyond the margins of the cultural text.[105] Though Smith's important long poem *Fox Running* and others among his more recent works, like those set in England's Wormwood Scrubs Prison, best exemplify his strategies for exploring "the myth of civilized society" through the gaps in its construction, it seems fitting to end here with several lines from a much earlier piece, "Grass & Stones," which is dedicated to Jon Silkin, with whom Smith coedited *Stand* during the period at Leeds he refers to as his "apprenticeship."[106] In it Smith brings together Silkin's concerns for responsiveness and "pity" with an early favorite metaphor of his own for the struggle of the artist committed to change in a landscape of "stones"—"imposed things," like structures of thinking, that "crumble slowly"; "measured and cut, they remain where they are put."[107] Like easily destructible but unstoppable grass, the noninnocent desires, forms, and words of the poet reach through gaps in such soil and

into these thin fibre blades,
growing in inches,
seeking minutely where the light is.
Grass experiences, attempting all rocks.
It is sieved out of the soil,
and in its growth reflects
the quality of the earth it lives on.
It must constantly renew itself,
but can be depended on, springing
wherever the razed earth lies bare.

. . . .

Early after the holocaust
it is there, compassionate, active, and demanding.[108]

Notes

1. The internal critique conducted by less-orthodox members of the Left, particularly after the Soviet invasion of Hungary in 1956, opened the "New Left" out to interaction with revisionary continental theorists; this and the translation of European Marxists such as Althusser, Adorno, Gramsci, Lukàcs, Benjamin, and Goldmann in the 1960s contributed to the internationalization of British Marxism. At the University of Leeds itself, the effort was made to bring students from other (particularly Commonwealth) countries to campus, which accounts for the emergence of writers like Wole Soyinka and N'gugi wa Thiong'o from Leeds in the 1950s and 1960s; Soyinka was recently quoted as saying that his teachers in the School of English "opened [his] literary perspective" to a "critical" as opposed to a "doctrinaire" Marxism ("Wole Soyinka talks to Mary David," *Wasafiri* 18 [autumn 1993]: 23). *Stand's* interest in publishing such diverse committed voices and new thinking on the Left was amply demonstrated by the multinational character of its issues and its publication of work like Sartre's *Black Orpheus* (trans. Arthur Gilette, *Stand* 5, no. 4 [1961], and 6, no. 1 [1962]). For discussions of Leeds's history of cosmopolitan thought in the arts and politics see Patrick Parrinder's article "Leeds Intellectuals and the Avant-Garde," *New Formations* 13 (spring 1991): 103–7, and Tom Steele's *Alfred Orage and the Leeds Arts Club* (Aldershot: Scolar Press, 1990).

2. Fredric Jameson, "Postmodernism, or the Cultural Logic of Late Capitalism," *New Left Review* 146 (July–August 1984): 53.

3. Raymond Williams, "Commitment," *Stand* 20, no. 3 (1979): 10.

4. See, for example, Ihab Hassan, *The Postmodern Turn: Essays in Postmodern Theory*

and Culture (Columbus: Ohio State University Press, 1987), xvii. Hassan accuses the liberating force of postmodernism (with its severance of sign and signifier, and so forth) of taking a "wrong turn," of becoming "caught in its own kitsch" and its "borrowed pleasures and trivial disbeliefs."

5. As used in George Steiner's 1958 essay, "Marxism and Literature," in *Language and Silence: Essays on Language, Literature, and the Inhuman* (New York: Atheneum), 310. He uses the term to refer to writers like Adorno and Lukàcs, whose differing views of the role of the arts broke in varying degrees from the Soviet model of political persuasion and "total commitment" (p. 309), as set forth in Lenin's *Novaia Jizn.*

6. Jean-Paul Sartre, *"What is Literature?" and Other Essays* (Cambridge: Harvard University Press, 1988), 63–66. All quotations are from this edition; page numbers are given in the text, prefaced by *W.*

7. See Jean-Paul Sartre's 1960 work *Search for a Method*, trans. Hazel E. Barnes (New York: Knopf, 1963), in which he begins to recognize that class constitutes a determinant in what an individual is able to create.

8. E. P. Thompson et al., eds., *Out of Apathy* (London: New Left Books, Stevens & Sons, 1960), 153.

9. Jean-Paul Sartre, *Situations*, trans. Benita Eisler (New York: George Braziller, 1965), 290.

10. Ibid., 276.

11. References are to "Retreat from the Word" (1961), "The Hollow Miracle" (1959), and "The Silence of the Poet" (1966), all of which can be found in *Language and Silence*.

12. Samuel Beckett's plays *Endgame* and *Waiting for Godot*, as well as his trilogy of novels (*Molloy, Malone Dies, The Unnamable*), are several of his many works that appeared in England in the 1950s; a number of his radio plays, one-acts, and shorter prose works also date from this period.

13. See Donald Davie's *Purity of Diction in English Verse* (particularly his chapter "The Chastity of Poetic Diction") (New York: Oxford University Press, 1953) and his *Thomas Hardy and British Poetry* (London: Routledge & Kegan Paul, 1973). I quote also from a Davie poem, "Remembering the Thirties": "a neutral tone is nowadays preferred"; Davie is of course himself alluding to Hardy's poem, "Neutral Tones."

14. Thompson et al., *Out of Apathy*, 188, 157.

15. Theodoro Adorno, "Commitment," trans. Francis McDonagh, *New Left Review* 87–88 (September–December 1974): 84–85.

16. Peter Dews, "Adorno, Post-Structuralism and the Critique of Identity," *New Left Review* 157 (May–June 1986): 28–44. Dews discusses the long-unremarked affinities between poststructuralist thinkers like Foucault, Lyotard, and Derrida and those who belonged to the first-generation Frankfurt School, especially Adorno.

17. Adorno, "Commitment," 78.

18. Theodor Adorno, "Lyric Poetry and Society," trans. Bruce Mayo, *Telos* 20 (1974): 64.

19. Adorno, "Commitment," 78.

20. See Susan Buck-Morss, *The Origin of Negative Dialectics: Theodor Adorno, Walter Benjamin, and the Frankfurt Institute* (New York and London: Free Press/Macmillan, 1977), 49 ff., for a discussion of Adorno's ideas on non-identity, historical relativity, and the demythifying process. The second quotation on logical breaks is as quoted in ibid., p. 80 (from "Der wunderliche Realist: Über Siegfried Kracauer," in *Noten zur Literatur* [Frankfurt am Main: Suhrkamp Verlag, 1965], 3:84).

21. Adorno, "Lyric Poetry and Society," 65.

22. Fredric Jameson, *Marxism and Form: Twentieth Century Dialectical Theories of Literature* (Princeton: Princeton University Press, 1971), 56.

23. Adorno, "Commitment," 78.

24. Adorno, "Lyric Poetry and Society," 62.

25. Adorno, as quoted in Dews, "Adorno, Post-Structuralism and the Critique of Identity," 36.

26. Jon Silkin, editorial, *Stand* 4, no. 1 (1958): 3–4.

27. Göran Printz-Pâhlson, "Interview with Raymond Williams (1967)," *Comparative Criticism* 11 (1989): 10.

28. Ibid., 11.

29. See Antony Easthope, *British Post-Structuralism since 1968* (London and New York: Routledge, 1988), 2, for an argument placing Williams within "the left-liberal, culturalist and empiricist" mode he critiques here.

30. Thompson et al., *Out of Apathy*, 144 ff.

31. Ibid., 145, 308.

32. Thompson's *The Making of the English Working Class* (London: Gollancz, 1963) provides, for example, important source materials for Tony Harrison's sonnet sequence, *The School of Eloquence*, discussed below. As Ken Smith has remarked in conversation (1988, London), the "ambiance" of Leeds encouraged the reading of histories that attempt to redraw details from suppressed stories, like that of the working class.

33. Seth Moglen, introduction to *Out of Apathy: Voices of the New Left Thirty Years On*, ed. Robin Archer (London: Verso, 1989), 6, quoted from *Universities Left Review* 1 (1957).

34. E. P. Thompson, "Comment," *Stand* 20, no. 2 (1979): 50. Hereafter, page numbers will be given in the text.

35. The word had by then become loose-fitting and fashionable; as Jiri Wyatt put it in the symposium, "Ironically, one of the hallmarks of the Sixties, the call for commitment, has now been taken up by the Right, wholeheartedly by the editors of *PNR*" *(Poetry Nation Review)*, whose project was to "return the culture to the main road" (20).

36. Alan Robinson, *Instabilities in Contemporary British Poetry* (Basingstoke, England: Macmillan, 1988), 7.

37. The first three quotations are from Robinson, *Instabilities*, 32, 49, 121; they refer to poets Christopher Reid, Michael Hofmann, and Tom Paulin, respectively. It should not be assumed from my selections of quotations that Robinson does not deal with "committed" poets; his chapter on Douglas Dunn, in particular, is an elegant treatment of such writing.

38. Antony Easthope and John O. Thompson, eds., *Contemporary Poetry Meets Modern Theory* (Toronto: University of Toronto Press, 1991), 209. In their afterword, the editors suggest that the "best" contemporary poetry takes either of two modes: "a poetry of emotion, confession, plain speech, lived experience, recrimination— where the experience and anger is that of those whom the system marginalizes," and a "poetic practice" of "defamiliarization which is calculated to frustrate the demand for communication, . . . a position perhaps most explicitly set out by advocates of 'Language' poetry." Such categorization seems to leave out a range of postmodern practices, several of which become my focus below.

39. Hassan, *The Postmodern Turn*, 227.

40. Silkin, editorial, *Stand* 4, no. 1 (1958): 3.

41. Jon Silkin, *Selected Poems*, new ed. (London and New York: Routledge, 1988), 15. All quotations are from this edition; hereafter, page numbers will be given in the text, preceded by *SP*.

42. The significance of developing theories concerning the "relative autonomy" of the superstructure, largely indebted to Althusser, is implicit throughout this essay; its basic argument begins to undo the base/superstructure model by proposing that the transformation of materials into products happens at a number of levels, including the literary and theoretical. The conception of the social formation as decentered "process" rather than as "structure" both causes the writing of theory and literature to become more critical kinds of "work" (as well as more complicitous as practices) and erases lines between "center" and "outside," speeding the theoreticization of the subject as effect rather than cause. See Louis Althusser's 1962 essay "Contradiction and overdetermination," in *For Marx* (London: New Left Books, 1977).

43. Geoffrey Hill, "The Poetry of Jon Silkin," *Poetry & Audience* 9, no. 12 (1961–62): 6.

44. Geoffrey Hill, *The Lords of Limit: Essays on Literature and Ideas* (New York: Oxford University Press, 1984), 93, 142.

45. See Hill's *The Enemy's Country: words, contexture, and other circumstances of language* (Oxford: Clarendon, 1991), 7.

46. John Haffenden, *Viewpoints: Poets in Conversation with John Haffenden* (London: Faber & Faber, 1981), 88.

47. Hill, "The Poetry of Jon Silkin," 6.

48. First published in *Stand* 8, no. 4 (1967), then in Geoffrey Hill, *Collected Poems* (Harmondsworth, England: Penguin, 1985), 67.

49. Blake Morrison, "Under Judgement," interview with Geoffrey Hill, *New States-man* 2551 (1980): 214.

50. Hill, *Lords of Limit,* 5, 155. On pages 4 and 5 Hill admires the "strategy" by which Hannah Arendt describes Walter Benjamin's work, which involves using "a great many negative statements"—such as that "he thought poetically, but he was neither a poet nor a philosopher" (from Hannah Arendt, *Men in Dark Times* [Harmondsworth, England: Penguin, 1973]: 153–54). His suggestion is that such procedure is "crucial" to the presentation of his own argument, which moves in similarly "negative" fashion, drawing differences between his idea of poetry as "menace" and the ideas of Baudelaire, or surrealism, or negritude "as polemically invoked by Sartre" in "Black Orpheus." Such characteristic procedures in his prose aid us in understanding Hill's poetry as well, which also must move by pointing up differences between already established and influential categories—for, as Hill says, however "challenging" he intends to be, the condition of discourse is such that he nonetheless "conforms," resisting only through "the positive virtue of negative statements." For the similarities between Benjamin and Adorno, see Buck-Morss, *Origin of Negative Dialectics*.

51. Geoffrey Hill, *For the Unfallen: Poems 1952–1958* (London: André Deutsch, 1959), 56.

52. I quote from *For the Unfallen* instead of the *Collected Poems* here because the exclamation mark in the third stanza is later edited out (a change that perhaps enhances the "impersonal" nature of the line, or its conventionality in nationalistic discourse).

53. Adorno, "Commitment," 85.

54. I mean to suggest here, by using Jameson's concept ("Postmodernism," 91–92), *not* that Hill attempts to "invent and project" the "global cognitive mapping" that Jameson calls for from the "new political art," one that might articulate in Lacan's symbolic dimension the new spatial relations between individual subject and the changed "Real" of multinational capitalism, but rather that, perhaps as a step toward such an enormous project, Hill probes the dark borders of existing "maps," locating spaces made by discursive operations already codified in cultural practice.

55. Steiner, "Postscript," in *Language and Silence,* 157.

56. Morrison, "Under Judgement," 212.

57. Jon Silkin, "The Poetry of Geoffrey Hill," in *Geoffrey Hill,* ed. Harold Bloom (New York: Chelsea House, 1986), 23.

58. Williams, "Commitment," 9.

59. Morrison, "Under Judgement," 212.

60. Jon Glover, "'Penguin Modern Poets 6' and 'Group Anthology,'" *Sixty-One* 5, no. 1 (October 1964): 24.

61. J. J. Healy and R. Parthasarathy, eds., *Poetry from Leeds* (Calcutta: Writers Workshop Books, 1968), 1.

62. Conversation with Jon Glover, summer 1989.

63. Hill, "The Poetry of Jon Silkin," 4.

64. Ibid., 7.

65. Jon Silkin and Anthony Thwaite, "No Politics, No Poetry?—a Tape," *Stand* 6, no. 2 (1963): 14.

66. In "Anglo-Jewish Poetry," *Jewish Quarterly* Special Edition, spring 1967, 22–24, Silkin discusses assimilation as an act of aggression, of "pressure exerted intimately" on diasporic communities by large, nationalistic ones unable to view their own composition as "a complex affair" (23).

67. Alan Munton, "Understanding the Left," *Stand* 21, no. 1 (1979): 44.

68. Conversation with Jon Glover, 1989.

69. Morrison, "Under Judgement," 212.

70. Conversation with Jon Silkin, 1988.

71. Ibid.

72. Efraim Sicher, *Beyond Marginality: Anglo-Jewish Literature after the Holocaust* (Albany: State University of New York Press, 1985), 147.

73. Silkin and Thwaite, "No Politics, No Poetry?," 16.

74. See R. K. Meiners, "Mourning for Our Selves and for Poetry: The Lyric after Auschwitz," *Centennial Review* 35, no. 3 (fall 1991): 545–90. In his rich and complex discussion of the "lyric after Auschwitz," Meiners suggests that Silkin's aim in this poem is like that Benjamin perceived in Baudelaire's work: to "keep steadily in view the processes whereby poetry was disenchanted from the aura while continuing as lyric" (p. 560). To perceive the "aura" of an object, as Benjamin writes (*Charles Baudelaire: A Lyric Poet in the Era of High Capitalism*, trans. Harry Zohn [London: New Left Books, 1973]), is "to invest it with the ability to look at us in return"; in Silkin's poem, the "object," or the "worker," literally "look[s] away" (Benjamin, *Charles Baudelaire*, 148; Meiners, "Mourning," 559; Silkin, *Selected Poems*, 90).

75. I allude here to Eavan Boland's sequence of poems from her book by the same title (*Outside History* [Manchester: Carcanet, 1990]). In her treatment of the same kind of desire—in her case, to recover the extradiscursive experience of the women named or imagined in the poem—Boland effects recognitions similar to those described here.

76. Rick Rylance, "On Not Being Milton," in *Tony Harrison*, ed. Neil Astley (Newcastle upon Tyne: Bloodaxe Books, 1991), 124. All quotations are from this edition; page numbers are given in the text, preceded by *ON*. The essay is reprinted as "Tony Harrison's Languages" in Easthope and Thompson, *Contemporary Poetry Meets Modern Theory*, 53–67.

77. Conversation with Tony Harrison, 1988. The quotations that follow are also from this informal interview.

78. Peter Lennon, "Taking People to Poetry," *Times* (London), 21 December 1984, 14.

79. Tony Harrison, "Some Men Are Brothers," *Stand* 4, no. 4 (1960–61): 50, 49.

80. Ibid., 51.

81. C. E. Lamb, "Tony Harrison," in *Dictionary of Literary Biography: 40 Poets of Great Britain and Ireland since 1960,* ed. Vincent Sherry (Detroit: Gale Research, 1985), 160.

82. Tony Harrison, *The Loiners* (London: London Magazine Editions, 1970), 86. All quotations are from this text; page numbers will be given in the text, preceded by *L.*

83. From the uncorrected proof of *The Loiners,* with blurbs and descriptions. Tony Harrison Collection, Brotherton Library, University of Leeds.

84. Uncorrected proof (see note 83).

85. Geoffrey Hill, *Collected Poems* (Harmondsworth, England: Penguin, 1985), 162, 152. All quotations are from this edition; hereafter, page numbers will be given in the text, prefaced by *CP.*

86. Haffenden, *Viewpoints,* 93.

87. See Jameson, "Postmodernism, or the Cultural Logic of Late Capitalism," 66.

88. *Selected Prose of T. S. Eliot,* ed. Frank Kermode (New York: Farrar, Straus & Giroux, 1975), 40.

89. Tony Harrison, *Selected Poems,* 2d ed. (London: Penguin, 1987), 123.

90. Bruce Woodcock, "Classical Vandalism: Tony Harrison's Invective," *Critical Quarterly* 32, no. 2 (summer 1990): 55.

91. Theodor Adorno, *Negative Dialectics,* trans. E. B. Ashton (London: Routledge & Kegan Paul, 1973), 365.

92. See Stephen Regan's introduction to his edition of George Meredith's *Modern Love* (Peterborough, England: Daisy Books, 1988) for a discussion of its subversive nature, particularly its critique of the ways in which "the abstract notion of love . . . provided a compensating sense of humanity and moral direction . . . [t]o a society dominated by materialistic and commercial instincts" (p. 8); Regan suggests that the sixteen-line sonnet allows for not only narrative continuity but also avoidance of the "epigrammatic neatness of the traditional form" (p. 13).

93. Jeffrey Wainwright, "The Silence Round All Poetry," *Poetry Review* 69, no. 1 (July 1979): 59.

94. Adorno, *Negative Dialectics,* 152–53.

95. Ibid., 153.

96. Tony Harrison, *v.,* new ed. (Newcastle upon Tyne, England: Bloodaxe Books, 1989). All quotations are from this edition; page numbers will be given in the text, preceded by *v.*

97. Adorno, *Negative Dialectics,* 152.

98. Woodcock, "Classical Vandalism," 62.

99. Adorno, *Negative Dialectics,* 152.

100. Ken Worpole, "Scholarship Boy: The Poetry of Tony Harrison," in Astley, *Tony Harrison,* 73.

101. Thompson et al., *Out of Apathy,* 153.

102. Adorno, *Negative Dialectics,* 406.

103. Jeffrey Wainwright, editorial, *Stand* 17, no. 1 (1975): 6.

104. Conversation with Ken Smith, 1989.

105. Ken Smith, *Fox Running* (Newcastle upon Tyne, England: Bloodaxe Books, 1981), 19.

106. Conversation with Ken Smith, 1989.

107. Ken Smith, *The Pity* (London: Jonathan Cape, 1967), 18.

108. Ibid., 19.

CHAPTER EIGHT

"Upon the Slippery Place";
or, In the Shit:
Geoffrey Hill's Writing and the
Failures of Postmodern Memory

R. K. Meiners

I

In this essay I wish to discuss the writing of Geoffrey Hill in contexts where his writing has not usually been placed. It is going to require
using some different perspectives from those ordinarily brought to his work
and perhaps some questionable decorum. The strain on decorum begins
with the title, but what bothers me more than its rudeness is that the re-
straints of a short essay give little opportunity to look closely at Hill's best
poems or to trace the development of his work. But others have done much
of that work,[1] and I have elsewhere written about Hill,[2] so on this occasion
I will move into a different sort of argument.

Of all the problems Hill's work presents the reader, I think the greatest
is the question of "'the sublime' in the old sense." That phrase is appropriated from the first quatrain of Pound's *Hugh Selwyn Mauberley*, within a text
ambiguously inscribed "E. P. Ode Pour L'Election de Son Sepulchre," in order
to remind the subsequent reader of some of the ironic and complex ways
that older ideals of art trouble the eponymous Mauberley's efforts. Those "older
ideals" trouble modernism generally, but Pound remains for the English
tradition such a decisive and intractable case of the difficulties of making
it new that he is particularly relevant. He is relevant to no one more than
to Hill, who has returned repeatedly to Pound's return upon "the tradition," seeing there the emblematic moment of modernist destabilization

221

and appropriation, as well as a prefiguring of the ways in which postmodernism has claimed to disclose modernism's disclosures. Hill's writing ignores the more customary politics of postmodern critique of modernism, not because it is anachronistic and quite satisfied with the old ways of sublimity or excellence (which is older than sublimity), but because it refuses to settle for a critique predicated on the suspicion of ontology and epistemology, which itself endlessly replicates modernist suspicion. For modernism (wherever one marks its advent) insisted on the incremental sedimentation of figures within the archive, an insistence that simultaneously valorizes history and compromises hermeneutics, both anticipating the fecundity of the postmodern replication and dissemination of signification and providing endless occasions for later instruction in the skeptical unmasking of the ideologies of interpretation. There are repeated moments of such discovery of instability in the text of modernism; one of the most resonant in the present context is the meditation on history in Eliot's "Gerontion" (contemporary with Pound's *Mauberley*), with its commanding interrogation: "After such knowledge, what forgiveness?"

Hill's most recent book of prose, *The Enemy's Country*, everywhere assumes the modernist enterprise and the subsequent historicizing of its historicism.[3] Although the first four essays are entirely given over to early writing—Wyatt, Bacon, Donne, Wotton, Dryden, and others—the book pivots on the final essay, a consideration of Pound's "Envoi (1919)" and the exemplary problems of *Hugh Selwyn Mauberley*. Similarly, *The Lords of Limit*, although often given to the examination of the earlier tradition and its transformations in the nineteenth century, had previously taken its dominant tonality from the final essay, "Our Word is Our Bond," where the persistence of the political and the ethical, their recrudescence in the language and problems of art in modernism, culminated in the example of Pound.[4] The later essay examines the impacted and replete beauties of "that song of Lawes" and forces the issue of what any subsequent, more knowing postmodernist estimation[5] might conclude about Mauberley's hesitations between the epigrammatic and the epic, about the poem's sardonic review of a fully commodified aesthetic, or the way in which the *Mauberley* text anticipates the contradictions of the anguished review in *The Pisan Cantos* of the descent of its language through its impacted rhetorics. The attempt to come to terms with Pound contains within itself an appraisal of the commanding difficulty of late modernism's rethinking of its own enterprise, the possibilities for a poetry in its wake, or, indeed, the problems to be faced by any subsequent estimation of poetic virtue.

The final epigraph to Hill's *Collected Poems* comes from Pound: "In the gloom, the gold gathers the light against it."[6] Having taken that for its example,[7] the text of Hill's poetry is joined by *The Enemy's Country*, where, as elsewhere in his prose, those conditions are probed where poetry in the world's languages has its gold subject to the stock exchange. The language in which poetry has been made is the same language in which its beauties are casually and obtusely estimated, and the language of poetry and criticism is also the language of political grandeur, brute indifference, and irreducible cruelty. If the persistence of poetry within the enemy's country and the judgment of its importance is therefore subject to a certain arbitrariness, the appropriate response to that is what it has always been, *merde alors!*—that, and a continued scrutiny of the terms of judgment.[8]

II

"Our own coarse colloquialism," as Hill registers it in his scrutiny of John Dryden's "To the Memory of Mr. Oldham," was "apparently not current before the mid-nineteenth century." In "Dryden's Prize-Song" Hill is chiefly interested in "the intelligence at bay," a phrase he borrows from Pound and characteristically extends to describe the work of finding responsible language (see, for example, "Redeeming the Time") in and of the lexicon of the world's business, confronting its rhetorics, making poetry, and judging the ways in which poetry is bonded within the languages of social obligation. "In the shit" is our own coarse colloquialism, but it may nevertheless "fairly describe Dryden's feeling about the general run of his worldly luck," and it cannot be separated from the kind of art that fabricated "To the Memory of Mr. Oldham," an art that is demonstrated "by the stylishness with which it both maintains the decorum of 'indulgence' and implies the cost that decorum extorts from 'curb'd' genius."[9] Hill is, in this passage, dissecting Dryden's adaptation of a portion of Book V of the *Aeneid* for his own purposes.[10] But the fall of Nisus on what Dryden tactfully calls the "slippery place," and what Hill glosses as "the dung and blood" of sacrificial animals, is something more than a learned reference going back to the Oxford syllabus: it is the figurative (and sometimes literal) siting of the locale of much of Hill's own writing. That writing, whether in prose or poetry, is everywhere preoccupied with the ways in which writing is located and locates itself in the nodes of civic power and the ways in which the world's business, with all of its "cruelty and indifference," is revealed in and shadowed by "the very recalcitrance of language."[11] This preoccupation with the recalcitrance of language, its entanglement with the slippery business of the world and with the proximity of the citadels of excellence to the abattoir, of grandeur to ordure, has led Hill to cultivate the paronomastic muse as no other writer of our time, and to establish the master tropes of catachresis and oxymoron within a rhetoric in which the guiding principle is "extremes meet"—latterly, in Hill's practice, taken even more from Coleridge and Hopkins than from Blake. It has led him to subjects and themes that have seemed improbable according to the cultural scenarios of much consciously postmodern practice: to the examination of Robert Southwell and Elizabethan equivocation, to a defense of the responsibility of Swift's poetry, including the scatological texts, to a sonnet sequence like "Funeral Music," which evokes the Wars of the Roses and the proximity of high humanist learning with the rhetorical display of intellectualized torture and ceremonial execution on the mortal body, to a preoccupation with martyrdom, endurance, nostalgia, and the baffled persistence in the entrapments of language and the imprisonment of poets from Boethius to Pound, and to a whole range of concerns, here entered under the (coarse) shorthand of "in the shit."

One must take care in quoting Hill—even more than the usual care required by textual scruple. It is not the kind of care required in quoting writers like Benjamin and Adorno, where even quite long quotations may misrepresent through the special partiality that comes from the omission of the merest trace suddenly transformed in a dialectical reversal; it is rather that Hill himself is so scrupulous in the use of texts, so fastidiously insistent upon the way "his" words emerge from the circumstances of their histories and the uses to which they have been put in the judgments of others. To make matters more difficult, he anticipates his critics' scruples:

It could be argued that in saying "we are at least given some ground for" [he has been speaking of Nashe, of Wotton, of Bacon's 'Tartar's bow' and the twisting of words back on their user] I concede the weakness of my position. I have never supposed that I was arguing from a position of strength. My concern is with "words, contexture, and other circumstances of language," with language, judgement, and circumstance; not only the ways in which judgement is conveyed through language but also the difficulty of clearing the terms of judgement amid the mass of circumstance, the pressures of contingency.[12]

Among the most pressing of the contingencies in reading Hill is coming to terms with the mass of circumstance in which he locates the language of both his critical arguments and his poems. No writer is more insistent upon the proposition that "[w]hat we call the writer's 'distinctive voice' is a registering of different voices."[13]

But even when taking into account such representation of different voices, and the difficulty in "clearing" the terms of judgment (Clearing them how and of what? Does judgment follow clarity?), and acknowledging that "in the shit" strains decorum, it nevertheless seems appropriate as a description of the space in which Hill's writing is grounded. For amidst all the more customary terms in which judgment has been made upon Hill's writing, and the citing of its stringency, its formality, its spirituality, its sensuality, its passionate intensity and high seriousness, its historicity, its obsessive lexicality, probing of martyrdom and devotion, its fastidious intelligence, its replete beauties,[14] its "immaculate music"[15] (one is saying here, on the contrary, that its "music" is very maculated indeed), Hill's readers should note how obsessive a theme can be traced through the vocabulary of mire, mud, muck, gore, blood, dung, piss, shit, and the extended lexicon of fundamental matters. This is to name but a few nouns. When one adds to it the extensive, equivocal verbs of evacuation and defecation that enrich this writing like "a golden and stinking blaze,"[16] and allies with this terminology the closely affiliated vocabularies of, on the one hand, pain, suffering, and extremity and, on the other, mastery and connoisseurship, one is justified in saying that these are circumstances that require notice, even if the conclusion that is reached is that they "appear self-stultifyingly perverse."[17]

Such vocabularies are an essential part of what may be called the pedagogy of Hill's writing, its "power to let those things be heard which ideology conceals,"[18] in this case the ideology of artistic privilege within the
world's business, including the "meaty conduit of blood" and "mutterings,
blasphemies, and cries for help."[19] It is not that Hill does not privilege poetry.
On the contrary. But in his case it is usually "the endurance of poets" in the
face of political authority and civil duress that is praised. No one who has
read Hill thoroughly would deny—certainly I would not deny—the whole
dimension of his writing, and particularly his poetry, that must be entered
under the headings of active intellect, poetic beauty, rhetorical grandeur,
and other appropriately ideal categories: but when Hill quotes the Ciceronian
apothegm that "claims that it is an error of judgment for statesmen to think
and act as if they were living 'in Platonis πολιτεία' and not 'in Romuli
faece,'"[20] one may be sure that "statesmen" stands metonymically for "poets" as well, as both are among the practitioners of "immersed" knowledges.
For Hill, in these matters as in others, is a Coleridgean. His moral, political,
and linguistic consciousness has been educated at length in Coleridge's prose,
with its refusals to divide and specialize the languages of cultural intelligence and with its passion for desynonymizing the impacted vocabularies
of moral relationship; and he is perhaps the greatest master since Samuel
Taylor Coleridge of the workings of the defecated reason.[21] The reader of
Coleridge may respond that in this usage, found as early as the opening of
the notorious "Essay on Fasts" in *The Watchman,* where, epigraphic bowels
sounding as a harp, Coleridge was speaking of the absence of refined reason
in parliamentary debate, he intended to signify a reason purified from the
dregs of accidentality; of course he was, but Coleridge seldom meant less
than all the available meanings of his *weighted* vocabulary, and in this case
"defecated" was as weighted as Hill's deployment of "in the shit." "Our own
coarse colloquialism" it may be, but Hill turns such a reproachful eye on the
presumptuous "our" of routine "complacent" locution[22] that we may judge
that, even in quotation marks and assigned to the registry of Dryden's
"voice," it is a weighted phrase, if not part of a "cultural scenario," then,
as previously noted, pedagogical. And the burden of that pedagogy is that
the traditional poetic virtues—eloquence, rhetorical power, formal beauty,
authenticity, cleansed vision, a language "simple, sensuous, passionate" (the
list could be greatly extended, gathering contradictions and possibilities as

it grew, and including everything Pound meant by *phanopoeia, melopoeia,* and *logopoeia*)[23]—are never simply virtuous. They are bought at a price, and the scale on which the price is reckoned always begins with the "dung and blood" of those who and that which have been sacrificed. This is a reading and practice of poetry that insists that sublimity and eloquence always carry with them the "grunts and shrieks" of pain and suffering, that rhetorical power is always shadowed by the implacable cruelties of the more overt social forms of power, and that even the finest achievements of art, the "perfect drawing of a heart's dream" and "wrought art's perfection,"[24] including those that come out of the dream of "Platonic England," have been "long since bought and sold" and that we must not "underrate the cost of that."[25]

III

Geoffrey Hill's distrust of the notion of a poetic "voice" is nearly as deep as his suspicion of commonplace notions concerning the poet's mastery of language. Although Hill has nowhere taken notice of the flood of postmodernist theoretical argument engaged in the deconstruction of the romantic-modernist poetic self and its deflected "voices" assigned to textual personalities (or their putative obverse, as in Eliot's famous courting of impersonality), there is a powerful way in which he is coeval with such argument and simultaneously, in ways theoreticians have yet to grasp, makes much of the argument obsolete, irrelevant, and even naive. One cannot imagine Hill foregrounding or thematizing the decentering of the self, the treachery of signification, the complicity of enlightenment Reason with agendas of cultural supremacism, the enclosure of suppressed voices in the narratives of authority such, for example, as one finds in the American "Language" poets, because he has no need to do so. It is not that he is unconcerned with such matters, and there are ways in which he works more closely with the romantic and modernist paradigms than many of his more self-consciously postmodern contemporaries: it is rather that he has already engaged the questions of the dissemination of languages in social and poetic orders at such a level that any overt move into an engagement with recent theory would be, from the perspective of his poetry, regressive. When one has learned as deeply from modernism as Hill has, there can be no question of repeating it unknowingly, of entering into the relationship of inverted complicity with the pedagogy of the great modernists after the fashion of many of his contemporaries. To make such a claim is to insist on seeing Hill's writing very differently from the ways in which it has often been seen. It is emphatically to deny that he is "conservative" in any of the customary ways, or that he can be conscientiously appropriated to rearguard exercises in cultural nostalgia.

John Bayley has obliquely addressed some of these questions, and although Bayley's understanding of Hill is very different from my own, he is certainly correct to insist on Hill's uniqueness among contemporary poets. He argues that there is in Hill no personal voice, no trace of that transcendent poetic self that, as Bayley observes (quoting Geoffrey Hartman), has been "eclipsed" by the rigorous textuality of poststructuralist criticism.[26] It is quite true, as Bayley argues, that Hill is not at all like, for instance, such an overtly epistemological poet as John Ashbery; neither, one should add, can one imagine Hill writing in anything like the mode of such consciously postmodern writers as American poets Charles Bernstein or Susan Howe, or English writer Tom Raworth. The "discovery of the entity-status of language" or "a different critical understanding of the implications of this new textual space" are not matters with which one can imagine Hill being much concerned; nor even with the "psychic imperative" to "dismantle the grammar of control and the syntax of command": not because they are unimportant, but because his engagement with the consequences of modernism and his understanding of the textual and moral responsibilities of postmodern writing, and "the values of poetic work itself,"[27] take place in such a different mode of engagement and radicalization that it is difficult to compare Hill's practice with that of others. It is not necessary to accept in its entirety Bayley's version of Hill's isolation to acknowledge that there is some force in his claim that the "most significant thing about Hill is his solitary position on the contemporary poetic scene," that "[n]ot least among Geoffrey Hill's curious virtues as a poet is that in reading him we have no sense of an art other than his own."[28]

Bayley has a gift for the uncannily apt phrase; it is one of the qualities that makes him such a virtuoso reviewer. Here it is the "curious virtues" that are curiously apt, not so much to describe Hill's poetry as to describe its reception, the responses of its critics. The "curious" observation of Hill's "solitary position," accompanied by objections to his aestheticizing of the ethical, or by admiration of his stoical representations of the intractable, or by an irritated rejection of his mandarin ironies as irrelevant to an authentic contemporary poetry, is a standard feature of much of the criticism his work has received. The last of these responses is characteristic of a certain kind of deliberately "American" criticism in the late developments of a Whitman-Williams tradition; it is also typical of that sort of English writing that decries the insularity of modern English poetry and looks enviously toward France or the United States, or toward any place where more ample possibilities of theory and less stodgy kinds of poetic modernity might be found. This response can usually be found accompanying sidelong glances at what is reprehended as the descent of a thin-lipped, anal-retentive wit stretching deplorably from Housman to Larkin and questionably claiming Hardy as its genius loci.

At this point, I will turn briefly to a recent essay by John Barrell on the poetry of Tom Raworth. Barrell, whose work I admire, here stands, perhaps unjustly, as a surrogate for an entire range of argument about the development of romantic, modern, and postmodern modes of cultural production in the English tradition, including the question of whether the very notion of "English modernism" in writing is a contradiction in terms. Beginning with Shelley's "The Triumph of Life," a text nearly as dear to deconstructionist theory as Poe's "The Purloined Letter," Barrell considers the way in which a major romantic-modern poetic tradition might be seen to turn around matters of language, syntax, "coherent and continuous identity," and other philosophical commonplaces:

> Issues like these, of epistemology, subjectivity, and language, are everywhere the concern of English poetry from William Wordsworth, say, to Arthur Hugh Clough, where they are understood as central to the issue, among others, of the authority of poetry and of the poet. They are the concerns also of the early twentieth-century modernism that hardly happened to poetry in Britain, or that happened only in the works of writers who, precisely because their concerns were the concerns of modernism, have been represented in Britain as marginal and isolated figures—isolated in the

same sense as the Continent is isolated by channel fogs. Issues like
these are nowhere to be found in what many of the most influential institutions of British literary culture represent as the most
important poetry now being written. They are kept out by a series
of arguments—that they are undecidable and therefore not worth
discussing, that they empty poetry of its human content, that they
are properly the province of philosophers and not of poets, that
they are elitist preoccupations which can never engage a wider
public. All these arguments do something to explain why poetry
in Britain has become such a trivial affair.[29]

Barrell goes on to quote Colin MacCabe on "the 'conservatism' of the 'English voice' which survives by refusing to inspect the conditions of its own
existence," a voice that complacently ignores questions of origin, centrality, and "the immediacy of speech."[30] Although Barrell nowhere mentions
the writing of Geoffrey Hill, and leaves it open to conjecture whether in this
scenario Hill's writing would also be entered under the head of "such a
trivial affair," the typical postmodern agenda is very clear in Barrell's summation.

It should also be clear that Hill is very close to this literary and cultural
agenda, yet also very far removed from it. As I have argued, no one currently writing in English has taken the example of modernism (whether or
not, as Barrell insists, it "hardly happened to poetry in Britain") more seriously than Hill; no writer has worked more closely to its equivocal rhetorics and fractured narratives. No one has taken the issues of "subjectivity"
and "language" learned in the pedagogy of modernism more obsessively
into the practices of his own writing. If his poetry does not engage such
issues in such an overtly "epistemological" fashion as Barrell perceives in
Raworth's writing, then that is because epistemology is itself an arena under
contestation, not merely because "British literary culture" or any other official custodian has declared it "elitist" or "properly the province of philosophers," but also because the discourse of knowledge is as much "upon the
slippery place" and as permeated with blood and dung as any other human
discourse that has fastidiously arrogated to itself the right to pronounce
upon the conditions of subjectivity. Like poetry, it is an embedded discourse.
The consuming historical and linguistic anxiety that has led Hill to return,

time and again, to the "circumstances of language" is everywhere subsequent to the modernist enterprise; if it fails to go on into the mimesis of subjectivity following *différance*, to undertake "the politics of subjectivity" and "the politics of syntax,"[31] that is because those issues must themselves be met on grounds that engage the politics and ethics of historical language at a different level. As Hill has said, the sort of metapoetics in which he is interested and with which he engages always involves the struggle with immersed knowledges and the insistence that poetry at such a level "is immersed in the knowledge that it is so immersed."[32] When Hill laconically remarks (quoting the *Oxford English Dictionary*) that "[i]t is perhaps necessary to remark that, when I speak of 'meta-poetry,' I do not mean 'the philosophical study of the nature of poetic language or statements,'"[33] one can observe him putting distance between himself and more typical postmodern arguments and practices and simultaneously refusing to exempt his art from any of the ethical and political difficulties consequent to the demise of modernism.

Just as Barrell's arguments are here being forced to stand in for a larger representation of recent critical argument, so at this point one of Hill's short poems from *Tenebrae* will be made into an exemplar of the manner in which his texts are typically engaged with these complex, embedded difficulties. It is not one of his best-known or most celebrated poems, but it can represent some of the procedures of the more famous work:

TERRIBILIS EST LOCUS ISTE:
Gauguin and the Pont-Aven School

Briefly they are amazed. The marigold-fields
mell and shudder and the travellers,
in sudden exile burdened with remote
hieratic gestures, journey to no end

beyond the vivid severance of each day,
strangeness at doors, a different solitude
between the mirror and the window, marked
visible absences, colours of the mind,

marginal angels lightning-sketched in red
chalk on the month's accounts or marigolds
in paint runnily embossed, or the renounced
self-portrait with a seraph and a storm.[34]

Hill is perhaps not so deeply involved with the history of painting as he is
with music,[35] but this little text forms an exemplary allegory that is central
to the enterprise of his writing. It brings into an abrupt perspective the
work of Gauguin, an artist deeply immersed in absorbing the first rush of
modernism from Daumier to van Gogh, Baudelaire to Mallarmé. Together
with the detail from Gauguin's *The Vision after the Sermon* reproduced on
the dust jacket of Hill's *Collected Poems*, Hill's poem is something like a study
of that process which Fredric Jameson has called "the eclipse of the referent," or "that ontological marginalization which structuralism and poststructuralism have described as a 'decentering' where the ego becomes little more
than an 'effect of structure.'"[36]

There is no "ego" in Hill's text, save in that "renounced self-portrait,"
which is as marginalized as the angels in the notebook, the self textualized,
observed, flattened into runny, unmodulated pigments. The vestiges of a
self are dispersed into the space "between the mirror and the window,"
where the zone of "art" absorbs and dissembles the objects and resources
of the tradition. Hill's title (*Vulgate*; Genesis 28:17), with the Gauguin figures
appropriated on the dust jacket, conflates the episodes of Jacob at Bethel
and at Peniel, acts of covenant and of naming, promising, and wrestling:
hieratic gestures, foundational narratives, the vanished ladder to the gate
of heaven. The dust jacket itself keeps only the wrestlers, struggling in the
blood-red field, staggering under the unseen gaze. Gauguin's own gazers,
which outline and constitute the field of vision and its contestants, are shorn
away; his problematic representation is problematically represented.[37] Hill
foreshortens Gauguin as Gauguin foreshortened the movement from im-
pressionism to symbolism. His text appropriates and criticizes both the
modernist appropriation of hieratic narratives and the postmodern equal-
izing and replicating of the appropriated narratives of reproduction. "Briefly
they are amazed": they are amazed briefly; and, briefly, they are amazed,
caught in a posthistoric eternal present in which the "quaint mazes" of

historical nostalgia and postmodern savoring of "marginal angels" sketched through the quotidian outline this self-portrait of renunciation.[38]

There is a late Gauguin painting, *Nature morte avec "L'Espérance" de Puvis* ("Still Life with 'Hope' after Puvis") that appropriates one of Puvis de Charvannes's allegorical still lifes (as he had appropriated many figures and compositions from Puvis and others—thus the routine charges of plagiarism). Puvis's "Hope" is a nude young woman, innocent, eyes directly meeting the viewer's gaze, bloom in outstretched hand. In Gauguin she is placed in the background, face averted, features expunged; she hangs behind a still life of flowers "in paint runnily embossed," themselves standing in a jardiniere from which Gauguin's characteristic images of Polynesian deities turn hollow-eyed stares toward the viewer. Hill's poems, especially in the later work stretching from the often-maligned poems of *Tenebrae*, and particularly "An Apology for the Revival of Christian Architecture in England," through *The Mystery of the Charity of Charles Péguy*, similarly stand back from both modernist appropriations of the disseminated images of power and from postmodernist scrutinies of these curious exercises in nostalgia masking as irony. They are virtuoso exercises in looking back through the modern tradition toward the ideals of rhetorical justice, classical irony, and a language "simple, sensuous, and passionate," and in seeing this tradition in complicity with the narratives of political and economic modernity. Hill's objections to the ordinary kinds of conservatism are well taken and, considering much of the reception of his writing, should be more often remembered: "Modern Conservatism, which is Whiggery rampant, could be beneficially instructed by radical Toryism, but of course won't let itself be. Conservatives conserve nothing."[39] But there is a sense in which the procedures of his writing are a conservatism with a vengeance. If his writing seems remote from more usual contemporary concerns, if it is often mistaken for traditionalist nostalgia, for a late version of pastoral, then the mistake is in the apprehension and not in the execution. As Hill said on another occasion:

> If one writes lyrics of which nostalgia is an essential element, naïve or malicious critics will say that the nostalgia must be one's own. There are, however, good political and sociological reasons for the

floating of nostalgia: there's been an elegiac tinge to the air of this country ever since the end of the Great War. To be accused of exhibiting a symptom when, to the best of my ability, I'm offering a diagnosis appears to be one of the numerous injustices which one must suffer with as much equanimity as possible.[40]

There is an important way in which John Bayley is correct. For better and for worse, Hill *is* unlike anyone else now writing. If he can only be considered, as I have been arguing, within the contexts of postmodern appropriations of the romantic-modern tradition, then neither does his writing "sound" like more typical postmodernism nor are his concerns, including his concern for language, worked out in more customary ways. If Raworth is, as John Barrell argues, quoting Andrew Lawson, "the most politically acute and direct poet writing in Britain now," then Hill is the most indirectly political poet now writing, his obliqueness a function of his distrust of the slippage in the vocabularies of acuteness and directness. Nor is it particularly difficult to imagine Hill agreeing with Lawson's angry description of "the techno-Dada experiment of Capital called 'Culture' . . . [which] mutilates human beings, bartering values, warping speech,"[41] for such sentiments in Hill go as far back as "Of Commerce and Society," which stands at the emotional and thematic center of *For the Unfallen:*

> Europe, the much-scarred, much-scoured terrain,
> Its attested liberties, home-produce,
> Labelled and looking up, invites use,
> Stuffed with artistry and substantial gain:
>
> Shrunken, magnified (nest, holocaust)
> Not half innocent and not half undone;
> Profiting from custom: its replete strewn
> Cities such ample monuments to lost
>
> Nations and generations . . .[42]

If that seems now a bit dated, it is nonetheless worth rereading in the Europe of the 1990s. It comes directly out of Hill's reading of Allen Tate. A text like

"Of Commerce and Society" is deeply informed by Tate's ironic lyrics, but Hill was even more affected by the "Ode to the Confederate Dead," which he read politically as well as poetically. Tate's soldiers, Hill wrote in an early essay, were "like Milton's angels, who cannot be injured. Parting before the blow, they flew together again. The self-healing properties of Capitalism are, of course, renowned."[43]

If Hill's procedures are radically different from those of his contemporaries, the reasons may be found in where he begins and what his poetry has continued to undertake. It's not that *where* Hill starts is different from where many other young writers born in the early 1930s started. He at first started with the reading of Yeats, Eliot, Pound, and Hopkins, a formula straight out of Leavis's *New Bearings in English Poetry*. For the same reasons an entire generation was to discover, some at greater depth than others, those examples were too large, simultaneously too easy to replicate and quite impossible to repeat. Yeats's mythography, the frozen stasis of Eliot's historical vision in the *Quartets*—England, here, now, never, always—were seductive but impossible. Pound's complex exercises in making it new were a more difficult and productive example, as Hill's protracted returns to Pound indicate. But few writers of his generation took Allen Tate as seriously as Hill did.

In Hill, what there was to be learned from Tate's writing underwent a sea-change by being regrounded in the dark and bloody ground of the English past and its texts. The violence of Tate's rhetoric always demanded a more immediate access to the riches and barbarities of European history than the displacement through the Old South yielded, as his poems from the early 1940s showed.

In an interview Hill remarked that he carried Oscar Williams's *Little Treasury of Modern Verse* all over Worcestershire as a teenager.[44] One would wager that few texts in the Williams anthology affected the young poet so deeply as Tate's "Ode to the Confederate Dead." The "Ode" has never received anything like the criticism it deserves (it is utterly mystifying to see anthologists printing it, together with snippets from "Narcissus as Narcissus" as footnotes). Regional, "classical" (in Tate's characteristic linkages of those terms), with both Pindaric and late Virgilian phrases, when it has been read at all it has largely been seen as hopelessly tinged with Southern exoticism, waiting to be sublated into Lowell's "For the Union Dead." But it is a far more crucial text than that; the "Ode" was one of the definitive poems of the 1930s, deeply involved with the collapse of modernist historicism. It is *the* poem that attempts to define what is happening in the depths of language, what it feels like to submit the decorums of historical and political convention to modernist iconoclasm after the icon of modernism has ceased to bear much charm or efficacy, which may be said to be *the* major problem of the generation of Tate, Hart Crane, and Yvor Winters. Fifty years on, much of Hill's poetry, especially the work from *Tenebrae* to *The Mystery of the Charity of Charles Péguy*, undertakes a later version of the task, and much of it awaits a criticism sufficiently undaunted by the recent theoretical fetishization of the languages of memory and the desire to be read, as Hill remarks of the difficulties of *Mauberley*, as if "the absolute is brought back to become a part of the relative and the conditional, the not quite it and the not quite not it."[45] If Hill could have read in the early 1950s the very late Tate essay "Poetry Modern and Unmodern," where Tate retrospectively described "a style that could be developed from the conversational-ironic in the direction of high rhetoric,"[46] he might have found a formula to serve as an epigraph for the beginnings of his own poetic work; as it is, poem after poem in Hill's early career veers close to Tate's rhetoric, always moving away as if it were necessary to get beyond the isolation that so often haunted Tate's work, to find ways both to comprehend and to judge it.

As this rapid summary indicates, pages of examples should follow, arguments about the ways in which Hill's characteristic structures—paratactic nominative phrases, obsessive paronomasia, radically rhetorical punctuation, the entire stubborn texture of his writing—develop and modulate, doubled by the broken narratives of praise and longing. Instead, this essay will close with a brief turn to *Mercian Hymns* xxv:

> Brooding on the eightieth letter of *Fors Clavigera*,
>> I speak this in memory of my grandmother, whose
>> childhood and prime womanhood were spent in the
>> nailer's darg.
>
> The nailshop stood back of the cottage, by the fold.
>> It reeked stale mineral sweat. Sparks had furred

its low roof. In dawn-light the troughed water
floated a damson-bloom of dust—

not to be shaken by posthumous clamour. It is one
thing to celebrate the 'quick forge', another
to cradle a face hare-lipped by the searing wire.

Brooding on the eightieth letter of *Fors Clavigera*,
I speak this in memory of my grandmother, whose
childhood and prime womanhood were spent in the
nailer's darg.[47]

Most of what "goes into" a text like this has to be assumed: the construction
of Offa, Ruskin, late-Victorian aestheticism, the problematics of "work" as
complicated in postindustrial discourse, personal memory, the modernist-
symbolist images of blooming dust on the lighted water with its whiff of
"Burnt Norton," "Little Gidding," and dozens of other passages, Words-
worthian "spots of time"; the text is so imbedded that the list could be
indefinitely prolonged. All of its rhetorical possibilities are separated from
personal desire and memory, on the one hand, and the ironies of the
deconstructionist harrowing of signification, on the other, by the refusal to
be "shaken by posthumous clamour."

This "posthumous clamour" includes much more than the decorum
that monitors the passage of grief and desire into art; it includes the immense postmodern rhetoric of the defense of poetry, which is always and
everywhere defensive. Enormously subtle arguments are mounted with great
labor in order to defend a resource of immense imagined utility (liberal arts,
moral armor, whatever), only to discover that the defensive battle is already
lost and is being fought with the wrong weapons, that it all has happened
over and over again, the field is soaked with the blood of the combatants,
and no one believes in odes to either the victors or the vanquished. Virtue
is acquired only by pretending the battle is being fought for the first time,
that the issue hasn't been decided, and that the temptation to defense isn't
an indulgence, that there are always newly materialized icons. All strategies
in this battle can be outwitted; nothing wins all the time. It is only a conservatism that knows that you can't conserve a resource that was never

imagined within the frantic exigencies of utility in the first place (as in Walter Benjamin's theology), that knows that the demolition of the unguarded resources that others summon to their own defense can't be required in a game in which you hold their hearts' desires in your own hands as well.

This names the site on which Hill's struggles are also fought. But the twenty-fifth *Mercian Hymn*, from deep within this struggle, directs a radically subversive gaze back both at those, like the shorn-away Gauguin viewers, who don't quite know that in their gazing they constitute the struggle and at those who do know that, and who know besides that the struggle is already over and took place elsewhere. Hill's grandmother in the twenty-fifth hymn stands for the knowledge that no one ever knows enough, that the struggle occurs here as well as before and elsewhere. It may be the enemy's country and the enemy's language, but that doesn't mean you don't walk through it and keep on speaking and writing.

Notes

1. See, for example, Henry Hart, *The Poetry of Geoffrey Hill* (Carbondale: Southern Illinois University Press, 1986); Peter Robinson, ed., *Geoffrey Hill: Essays on His Work* (Milton Keynes, U.K.: Open University Press, 1985); Vincent Sherry, *The Uncommon Tongue: The Poetry and Criticism of Geoffrey Hill* (Ann Arbor: University of Michigan Press, 1987). All of these contain extensive bibliographies of Hill's work and criticism of Hill. Jon Silkin's writings on Hill come out of a long, problematic encounter between the two poets; see both Silkin's "War and the Pity" in the Robinson volume and his earlier "The Poetry of Geoffrey Hill," *Iowa Review* 3 (1972): 108–28. Christopher Ricks has also written extensively on Hill; see his essay in Robinson and essays in *The Force of Poetry* (Oxford: Clarendon Press, 1984). Among the many critics of Hill, I have found the essays of John Bayley, Eric Griffiths, Jeremy Hooker, Gabriel Pearson, Peter Robinson, and Jeffrey Wainwright useful. I owe a particular debt to Merle Brown's *Double Lyric* (New York: Columbia University Press, 1980), full of its own brilliance and eccentricities, as well as to his other writings, produced in a much-too-short career.

2. R. K. Meiners, "Mourning for Our Selves and for Poetry: The Lyric after Auschwitz," *Centennial Review* 35, no. 3 (fall 1991): 545–90. R. K. Meiners, "The Fourth Voice," in *The Poet and the Language*, ed. W. A. Johnson and R. K. Meiners (East Lansing: Michigan State University Press, 1979), 35–58.

3. Geoffrey Hill, *The Enemy's Country: words, contexture, and other circumstances of language* (Stanford, Calif.: Stanford University Press, 1991).

4. Geoffrey Hill, *The Lords of Limit: Essays on Literature and Ideas* (London: André Deutsch, 1984).

5. Postmodernism comes in many forms; *postmodernisms* is a better term, but it is no part of this essay's intention to discriminate among the various forms. What postmodernisms share, insofar as that nomenclature is consciously claimed, is to have understood the power of modernism. Insofar as that power is scrutinized, replicated, and dispersed, it is reified into that sort of game that we, the players, have always already seen through, and thus it is played again.

6. Ezra Pound, "Canto XI," in *The Cantos (1–95)* (New York: New Directions, 1956), 51.

7. "Take that for your example!" is a phrase from "The Mystery of the Charity of Charles Péguy," in Geoffrey Hill, *Collected Poems* (New York: Oxford University Press, 1986), 196.

8. See Hill, *Enemy's Country*, 81.

9. Ibid., 76–77.

10. Hill himself might prefer to use Donne's *cribrate* to describe the process: "'Cribrate,' meaning 'to sift,' and 'cribration,' meaning 'sifting,' are not words that have filtered through into common usage. Their meaning is that matters can be successfully refined and reduced but they obstruct their own claim" ("The Tartar's Bow and the Bow of Ulysses," in *Enemy's Country*, 32). This entire passage, pivoting on some of Donne's awkward, obsessive, and essential vocabulary, is useful as an example of the care with which Hill turns and re-turns language, whether in his own writing or in examination of that of others.

11. Geoffrey Hill, "'The Conscious Mind's Intelligible Structure': A Debate," *Agenda* 4, no. 1 (1971–72): 14–23, 21.

12. Hill, *Enemy's Country*, 31.

13. Ibid., 80.

14. I am particularly thinking here of a theme in Jon Silkin's "War and the Pity," where Silkin argues for the superiority of the poetry of *King Log*, and even of *For the Unfallen*, over later work. He writes, "in *Tenebrae* beauty is triumphant, beauty that is the rage of art" (see Robinson, *Geoffrey Hill*, 117). This ascription of "beauty" to Hill's later work is not, coming from Silkin, meant as praise. Silkin is suspicious of "beauty," suspicious of "the aesthetic," suspicious of the ways he believes them to have been courted in Hill's writing and of what they have cost. I have discussed these matters more extensively in "Mourning for Ourselves and for Poetry."

15. This is from a *Guardian* review by Michael Longley; Hill's publisher prints it as a blurb on the dust jacket of *Tenebrae*. I do not mean to quarrel overly much with others' honorifics, except insofar as they seem symptomatic.

16. Hill, *Mercian Hymns* xii, in *Collected Poems*, 116.

17. Hill, *Enemy's Country*, xi.

18. A phrase from Theodor Adorno's "Lyric Poetry and Society," trans. Bruce Mayo, *Telos* 20 (1974): 56–71. I will not pursue the utility of Adorno in a discussion of Hill's writing in this essay. (See "Mourning for Our Selves and for Poetry," *Centennial Review* 35, no. 3 (1991): 545–90. Adorno's efforts to reclaim an oppositional, radical power for aesthetic experience, simultaneously artistic and political (and neither), form the last, and in some ways most challenging, element of his dialectic. The return of the aesthetic as critique establishes a field of possibility that Hill's poetry shares with Adorno's writing, though their procedures are very different. Adorno's *Aesthetic Theory* was published posthumously; although unfinished, it is still compelling, formidable, and contradictory in ways that only Adorno could be.

19. The phrases are from "Funeral Music, 1" and "Funeral Music: An Essay"; both texts are in *Collected Poems*.

20. Hill, *Enemy's Country*, 41.

21. The relationship between Hill and Coleridge is profound and complex, and to trace it would require an extended argument that cannot be developed here; Hill has, to adapt some of his own words that I have previously cited from quite another context, "sounded" Coleridge's "words in depth" as part of a tutelage in the "recalcitrance of language," in which one may find a chief emblem of the "cruelty and indifference" of the "primary objective world" (see "The Conscious Mind's Intelligible Structure," 21). Although I have here considerably shifted Hill's argument, there can be no question of his long attention to Coleridge, to "the quality of disinterested stoicism with which this habitually self-pitying man was able to bring his own broken life and aspirations into the focus of meditation" (Hill, *Lords of Limit,* 12). This judgment, from "Poetry as 'Menace' and 'Atonement,'" may form a useful place for interested readers to begin; they should also consult such texts as "Redeeming the Time," "'Perplexed Persistence': the Exemplary Failure of T. H. Green," and "Our Word is Our Bond."

22. Hill, *Enemy's Country*, 105–6. This entire long endnote, concerned with *compleasance, complacence*, and the "intimate relationship of power with appeasement," must be read as an illustration of the force with which Hill examines the impacted forces and cultural politics of apparently casual language. The disapproval with which Hill regards "the way in which Professors Bradbury and Bigsby take possession of 'our' and 'ours'" in their remarks in a preface to a series on contemporary writers, including the observation that "we live in a major creative time" and that writers such as Margaret Drabble and John Le Carré are "most important writers," is sufficient to make any critic cautious. When Hill continues, "Margaret Drabble and John Le Carré do not figure among the most important writers of my time," one notes that it is time to reassess one's entire cultural scenario, as in "'*your* time made

placable to *our* cultural scenario.'" That, of course, includes the presumption involved in constructing the cultural scenario of this essay.

23. The possible implications of this terminology as they work through the complex etiologies and difficult contexts of the "beauty" and "simplicity" of Pound's "Envoi (1919)" to *Hugh Selwyn Mauberley* form a substantial part of the last chapter of *The Enemy's Country*. The long endnote on 132–33 is, in itself, both a masterful summary of conflicting interpretations of the Pound text and a skeptical anatomy of what Hill justly summarizes as "anxious scholarship" attempting to deal with an "'interpretive crisis'" (p. 84). *Mauberley* has from the beginning been a key text in modernism, and has long functioned as a diacritical moment in studying the development of Pound's writing.

24. Ivor Gurney's phrases in "War Books," a poem included in *The Collected Poems of Ivor Gurney*, ed. P. J. Kavanagh (Oxford: Oxford University Press, 1982), 196. See also Geoffrey Hill, "Gurney's Hobby," *Essays in Criticism* 34, no. 2 (1984): 97–128.

25. "Platonic England" is Hill's quotation of Coleridge, inscribed as the epigraph to "An Apology for the Revival of Christian Architecture in England" *(Tenebrae)* and repeated several times in the sequence; "long since bought and sold" comes from "The Laurel Axe," the ninth poem in the sequence. "Underrate the cost of that" are the closing words of "Dryden's Prize-Song" (*Enemy's Country*, 82): "When the poet has been 'provok'd' into magnanimity we should not, in justice, underrate the cost of that." *Provok'd* is Dryden's word; *magnanimity* is one rhetorical response in the face of the complex mediations of "decorum" and "the world's business."

This complex doubling in Hill, which I am here somewhat questionably thinking of as a dialectic of the shit and the sublime, is a theme and practice of great power that extends throughout his poetry, from the poems in *For the Unfallen* to the scene of Péguy's death. In various ways, and under a variety of rubrics, Hill's best critics (see note 1, above) have tried to deal with this confrontation of contradictories, and I can't develop it further here. One of the more interesting of the criticisms of Hill in this context is Jon Silkin's importation of the war/pity doublet, developed from Silkin's meditations on Owen and war poetry generally; but for Silkin, Hill finally loses himself in "replete beauty." I disagree.

26. John Bayley, in Robinson, *Geoffrey Hill*, 189.

27. These phrases come from Charles Bernstein's text, "The Great War and Postmodern Memory," *Postmodern Culture* 1, no. 2 (January 1990), Raleigh, North Carolina, PMC@NCSUVM.BITNET, and they are intended to serve here as sort of shorthand indication of some of the major concerns that have impelled the "Language" poets. Bernstein and others have, rightly, questioned the lumping of many very different writers into a category called "Language Poetry." Citing this text will exemplify one of the ways in which discussions of the postmodern force reconsideration. There is no real way to cite the page numbers for this reference because

Postmodern Culture is an electronic journal and arrived in my computer via e-mail, so the page numbers are entirely a function of my printer's settings. John Unsworth, one of *Postmodern Culture*'s editors, remarked to me (also via e-mail), after I had queried concerning the proper ways to cite an electronic text: "We had to tell the MLA folks about this—they wouldn't index even the hard copy of PMC we have been sending them, until we provided them with the form: they're not exactly wild with enthusiasm at the prospect of retooling for e-journals."

28. Bayley, in Robinson, *Geoffrey Hill*, 195.

29. John Barrell, "Subject and Sentence: The Poetry of Tom Raworth," *Critical Inquiry* 17, no. 2 (1991): 388.

30. Ibid., 389.

31. Ibid., 408.

32. Hill, *Enemy's Country*, 60.

33. Ibid., 125.

34. Geoffrey Hill, "TERRIBILIS EST LOCUS ISTE: Gauguin and the Pont-Aven School," in *Collected Poems*, 168.

35. Hill's deep involvement with music is implicit in much of his writing. For his own discussion of some of the issues involved, see his interview with John Haffenden in *Viewpoints: Poets in Conversation with John Haffenden* (London: Faber & Faber, 1981), 91ff.

36. Fredric Jameson, "Baudelaire As Modernist and Postmodernist: The Dissolution of the Referent and the Artificial 'Sublime,'" in *Lyric Poetry beyond New Criticism*, ed. Chaviva Hosek and Patricia Parker (Ithaca: Cornell University Press, 1985), 248, 262.

37. A crucial interpretive occasion should probably not be allowed to pivot on so collaborative and transient a text as a dust-jacket illustration, particularly because I do not know how actively Hill himself was engaged in the production. I assume that he approved the design, that the cropping of Gauguin's image was purposeful, and, of course, that Hill's understanding of Gauguin's work is based upon the passionate meditation that informs all his research. In any case, the pictorial representation accords so closely with the poetic text, and both are so compacted with the modes of historicism and appropriation that seem to me central to Hill's art, that any hermeneutical risk seems worth assuming.

38. "Quaint Mazes" is the title of one poem in Hill's sequence "An Apology for the Revival of Christian Architecture in England." See Vincent Sherry's very different reading of this poem in *The Uncommon Tongue: The Poetry and Criticism of Geoffrey Hill* (Ann Arbor: University of Michigan Press, 1987), 180–81.

39. Haffenden, *Viewpoints*, 86.

40. Ibid., 93.

41. Barrell, "Subject and Sentence," 408.

42. Geoffrey Hill, "Of Commerce and Society," in *Collected Poems*, 47.

43. Geoffrey Hill, "The Poetry of Allen Tate," *Geste* (Leeds) 3, no. 3 (1958): 10. Quoted by Peter Robinson in *Geoffrey Hill*, 211.

44. Haffenden, *Viewpoints*, 78.

45. Hill, *Enemy's Country*, 101.

46. Allen Tate, *Essays of Four Decades* (Chicago: Swallow Press, 1968), 226.

47. Hill, *Mercian Hymns* xxv, in *Collected Poems*, 129.

CHAPTER NINE

"Look for the Doing Words": Carol Ann Duffy and Questions of Convention

Linda Kinnahan

Memory's caged bird won't fly. These days
we are adjectives, nouns. In moments of grace
we were verbs, the secret of poems, talented.
A thin skin lies on language. We stare
deep in the eyes of strangers, look for the doing words.
—Carol Ann Duffy, "Moments of Grace"

As an American critic interested in experimental writing by women, I'm often struck by the difficulty I've encountered in finding British women who write experimental poetry. Although American and Canadian women are entering a second successive generation of linguistic innovations, no doubt energized by a first generation's reclamation of an enabling tradition (Gertrude Stein, H.D., Mina Loy, Laura Riding, Lorine Neidecker, and so on), women writing experimentally in Great Britain seem, at least from these far removes of Pittsburgh, to be few and isolated. However, the example of Carol Anne Duffy, a Scottish-born and English-raised woman, a feminist and a lesbian, whose poetic page at first seems relatively conventional, leads me to muse upon what we mean by "experimental" in a North American context and what might be experienced as experimental in a late-twentieth-century British context. To look at a page of Duffy's poetry, one would not initially (or perhaps finally) associate it with the disjunctive, typographically disruptive structures one comes to expect in opening a book by Susan Howe, for example, or by Lyn Hejinian.

On first reading, the poems seem to remain within fairly regular conventions of prosody and form, drawing particularly upon traditions of the dramatic monologue and the lyric. However, Duffy's poetic forms continually interrogate themselves, asking of language structures questions that reflect current theoretical concerns and intersect with language-centered poetries in America, whereas her adherence to a more accessible form marks a significant engagement with social discourse. Her poetry leads me to ask whether it is possible or valuable to rethink the operations of linguistically experimental poetry in such a way that "experimental" includes a linguistically traditional (on the surface) syntax and a form that enacts a process of self-deconstruction.

Since the late 1970s in America, interactions of poetic practice and contemporary theory have increasingly characterized a line of postmodern innovation descending from the language-oriented modernism of such writers as Gertrude Stein, William Carlos Williams, Louis Zukofsky, and Laura Riding Jackson. Especially with the introduction of theories of poststructuralism and postmodernism to this side of the Atlantic, poets like Charles Bernstein, Ron Silliman, Kathleen Fraser, Susan Howe, and others have undertaken, to varying degrees, the interrogations of linguistic structures that these theories provoke. Through contemporary psychoanalytic and deconstructive theory, poets and critics alike have been given new tools for retreading the earlier experiments of canonically marginalized poets (Stein is a prime example) and for discovering a century-long tradition of poetic processes that have disrupted the conventional unity of sign and signifier. Contemporary practitioners of language-centered poetry are often loosely grouped together as "Language" poets, exhibiting a poetry typified by disjunctive and broken syntax that plays upon indeterminacies of meaning.[1] Linda Reinfeld tells us that Language poetry examines "the effects of formal logical and linguistic structures on our thinking, it demonstrates how those structures can determine what we see and how we behave."[2] Drawing upon and responding (at times contentiously) to poststructural theories of language, American and Canadian language-centered poetry "works in terms of 'diminished reference'" and repudiates a "whole tradition of writing about remembered experiences of the lyric self, turning attention instead to the . . . condition of language as medium."[3]

Too often, discussion of language poetries, by critics and by poets alike, has broken along lines of gender to involve primarily the male practitioners. The first book-length study of L=A=N=G=U=A=G=E poetry, for example, by David Hartley, concentrates on six male poets. Consequently, the discussion of the "structures" that determine us has often ignored gender or has subsumed it within other ideological structures (particularly economics) or, as some would argue, has abstracted it out of existence. In the past few years, the gender politics of experimental poetry have been brought into view through attention to women poets, especially to those women poets whose innovations foreground feminist thought and theory in relationship to language and poststructuralism. The work of current women writers interested in language innovation suggests, to me at least, that experimentalism in America is gendered in its various responses to such issues as lyric, voice, and audience. For many of these women, the Language poets' characteristic resistance to linguistic structures and conventions and the "sceptical interrogation of the subject" have everything to do with gender,[4] and they often see their work in terms of a larger feminist project to reveal relationships between structures of language and power, particularly as these shape constructions of gender and affect the material lives of women.[5] This engagement of poetic and theoretical concerns with a social and feminist discourse leads these women poets to ask different questions (than many of the male poets) of conventions they have inherited, of the meaning of personal experience and voice, and of the audience they are addressing.[6] For a poet like Kathleen Fraser, whose theoretical orientation derives from American and French feminists, the condemnation of the lyric voice by Language poets almost automatically marginalizes her experiments with the lyric. This exclusion threatens possibilities of a feminist revision of voice and replicates the rationalist (and masculinist) banishment of emotion as "too feminine." For someone like Susan Howe, who continually *problematizes* reference but does not abandon it, the insistence upon an extreme *diminishment* of or refusal of reference risks erasing history as a crucial context for understanding the referential structures of language. Even though the work of women experimentalists, like Howe and Fraser, appears more disruptive on the surface than Duffy's relatively conventional retention of the referent and her adherence to accessible prosodic structures, a relationship exists between the British poet and her American contemporaries in their investigations of gender-specific ideologies of the discursive structures we call poetic form. Like these American women, Duffy approaches both convention and referentiality as tools to use in revealing their very constructedness and indeterminacy. In this way, Duffy's seemingly nonexperimental adherence to poetic conventions both reaches an audience and enacts deeply unsettling linguistic experiments. For a British woman to both use and subvert form within an obsessively male-dominated tradition is perhaps more experimental than we in America at first recognize. For Americans, the conventional inclusion of the nineteenth-century poet Emily Dickinson orients us toward thinking of gender and language experimentation even within the confines of the most conservatively male-centered versions of our national literature. In a way that might be less available to British writers cognizant of their own national tradition, Dickinson's radical linguistic innovations provide important models for twentieth-century American women experimentalists who employ language disruption to question the gendering of tradition and language. Although Duffy's work might seem relatively traditional in form to those of us accustomed to a national canon that includes a figure like Dickinson, we can think of it as exemplifying an experimental postmodernism described by British cultural critic Janet Wolff as a "notion of the postmodern as informed, critical cultural practices which engage with tradition in order to subvert it," an engagement she sees as particularly characteristic of "postmodernism in feminist art practice."[7]

A student of philosophy at Liverpool University in the mid-to-late seventies, Duffy brings questions of modern philosophy to bear upon her poetic medium and its forms and functions. As a feminist attentive to divisions of power along lines of gender, class, race, and nationality, she writes a poetry that continually contextualizes this fusion of the poetic and philosophical within the social. In the only substantial essay written on Duffy, despite her growing reputation in Britain, Jane E. Thomas provides an invaluable reading of the impact of contemporary literary theory on her poetry, both of which investigate "the extent to which language constructs rather than reflects meaning." At the same time, Duffy's work is deeply "concerned with the interrogation of gender norms" and "also confronts racial intolerance, religious bigotry, the nuclear nightmare and the political indifference exhibited by the Thatcher administration toward the unemployed and the underprivileged."[8] This social emphasis, I would like to argue, is intrinsically connected to the communicable forms of dramatic monologue, narrative, and lyric she often chooses. My concern is with examining the

experimental interaction between these forms and the deconstructive notions of language Duffy's poetry investigates.

Through raising the question of Duffy's use of conventional forms within
the context of American discussions of "oppositional" language-centered
ruptures of form, I hope to build upon the foundation Thomas provides in
her discussion of Duffy's relationship to poststructural theory. Her poems
often insist upon the contextuality of meaning, exploring language's role
in the production and maintenance of dominant ideologies and charting
the complex interdependence of signs and structures of authority linked to
regulatory practices of race, gender, class, and nationalistic or religious belief.
Within these structures, produced through language, the individual consciousness or subject is shaped. As Thomas explains:

> Any individual who seeks to participate in the social order into
> which it is born can only express and define itself using the par-
> ticular language system formulated by that social order if it is to
> become recognizable both to itself and to other members of that
> order. In this way language can be said to construct or "speak" the
> individual rather than the other way around in that the terms the
> individual uses to define itself, or the subject positions it adopts,
> are pre-existing socially constructed signs with particular ideologi-
> cal implications. They dictate the terms of the individual's subjec-
> tivity.[9]

Even though I will argue in the discussion of "Standing Female Nude" that
Duffy's poetry suggests a possible model of agency—as developing in the
interaction between individual and structure—that Thomas's brief explana-
tion of poststructural subjectivity disallows in its focus on exterior structures, I would agree that these concerns with language, subjectivity, and
authority run through the volumes of poetry Duffy has published since the
mid-1980s: *Standing Female Nude* (1985), *Selling Manhattan* (1987), *The Other
Country* (1990), and *Mean Time* (1993). In considering the congruence of a
poststructural orientation with conventional forms of prosodic progression,
I will first turn to American discussions of convention.

As a representative spokesperson for an oppositional poetics of disrupted
syntax and diminished reference, Charles Bernstein argues that "writing

conventions play a fundamental role in the legitimation of communicative acts. They determine what is allowed into a particular specific discourse: what is accepted as sensible or appropriate or within the bounds of morality." In this way, "convention is a central means by which authority is made credible."[10] Therefore, conventions are suspect, not in and of themselves but in the authority arising from the concealment of the assumptions and biases underlying their construction; in other words, an acceptance of convention as natural, transparent, or timeless—which is how we are customarily encouraged to accept and employ literary convention—encourages a blindness to its shaping by a particular time or ideology.

Similarly, Ron Silliman endorses the contention that "the ideological production of a natural, commonsense 'world' (the world of an unproblematic realism) depends on the illusion of . . . the transparency of language."[11] Severe disjunction of language disallows such transparency, disrupting the naturalized linkage of word to world and, for Silliman, suggests an oppositional writing that problematizes our notions of a world prior to language or of a self capable of "true" and unmediated perception of the world. This "self" and the subsequent reification of experience marks, for Bernstein, the Romantic inheritance. A Romantic "poetics of sincerity," or a lyric claim to pure experience recoverable through memory and representable through language, actually works to conceal its origins in history and ideology: "the poet's lyric address to the human-eternal, to the Imagination, that seems to allow the poem to appear to transcend the partiality of its origin. Thus the poet is able to speak for the 'human' by refusing markers that would pull against the universality of 'his address' . . ."[12] This Romantic ideology leads, in the twentieth century, to New Critical and formalist approaches to art that seek a unity of contradiction that allows the autonomous artifact a transcendence from its social/historical origins and mediations. The conventions of lyric and narrative are implicated in this process of legitimating transcendent authority (which thus disguises the human hand in constructing authority).

At issue here is the question of subjectivity. Bernstein and Silliman, like Derrida or Althusser or Kristeva, reject the metaphysics of presence that supports the humanist concept of the self as unified, self-directed, and self-contained. For this self, experience provides the foundation for knowledge, which develops from the self's reasoned interaction with the world. In terms of this paradigm, the subject is the site from which knowledge originates, and experience is received in pure form by the knower. Poststructural theories, of course, have identified this paradigm as a construct that operates to conceal the workings of ideology upon the individual and her perception of reality. As Althusser would argue, experience always comes to us in already mediated form, and facts themselves can never be seen as "pure," outside of language or culture. Diana Fuss clarifies this distinction:

> In the classical, Aristotelian view, experience is the doorway to the apprehension of essence; experience is understood as a real and immediate presence and therefore as a reliable means of knowing. In the poststructuralist, Althusserian view, experience is a product of ideology. It is a sign mediated by other signs.[13]

In rejecting the humanist subject, many language-centered poets are disdainful of the lyric sensibility, which looks to experience as a "test of knowledge" to support the subject in its "fantasy of autonomy and control."[14] Rather than a self who has access to "truth" through experience and who can recollect or represent it in language, the self of these poetries is unstable and even unidentifiably dissolved within a play of language that emphasizes indeterminacy of meaning and refuses representation.

Is a poetry of indeterminacy necessarily oppositional? And, conversely, is a poetry of convention necessarily not? Erica Hunt, an African American poet, asks us to consider our relationship to the poetic conventions Bernstein and Silliman condemn, and this consideration leads to the question of the poem's social existence. Agreeing with Bernstein that "conventional poetics might . . . be construed as the way ideology, 'master narratives,' are threaded into the text, in content and genre," she points out that while dominant modes of discourse "contain us," we are "simultaneously bearers of the code of containment." We develop a "quasidependent quality": "we get stuck with the old codes even as we try to negate them."[15] Duffy's poetry repeatedly registers this sense of quasi dependence upon learned codes, such as the daughter's "code I learnt at my mother's knee" of silence and self-censorship. Consciousness of complicity with and positionality within linguistic codes makes possible the oppositional word, the language that "embarrassed them" by breaking with the code—yet one is still within it.[16]

Without this consciousness, Erica Hunt seems to imply, practitioners of language innovation are not necessarily oppositional to the authoritative structures encompassing and involving poetic convention: "[T]here is nothing inherent in language-centered projects that gives them immunity from a partiality that reproduces the controlling ideas of dominant culture. . . . There are . . . serious shortcomings to any opposition that asserts its technical victories and removes itself from other oppositional projects on the grounds of pursuing new possibilities of consciousness."[17]

Hunt's points hold particular relevance for the interaction of oppositional poetics, conventional form, and deconstructive insight in Duffy's work; the relevance is most clearly evident, I would argue, in the introduction of audience into this interaction, a move that focuses us upon the poem's social existence. What is the relationship between the experimental poem and a social audience? At what point does innovation preclude social communication, rendering the poem a private act, as autonomous in assumption as the disdained Romantic lyric? These are vexed and complicated questions, which I cannot begin to address fully here but which lead us to a critical juncture in Duffy's poetry—the retaining of convention simultaneous with the deconstruction of ideological forms. What may disguise her poetry as relatively conventional—narrative, dramatic monologue, lyric— can be regarded as an enactment of form's partiality and historicity while also providing access for an audience familiar with navigating the conventions of narrative or lyric. It is in the navigation, however, that possibilities for deconstructive activity on the part of the reader occur. Erica Hunt again provides an important contextualizing point for considering Duffy's experimentalism: "One troubling aspect of privileging language as the primary site to torque new meaning and possibility is that it is severed from the political question of for whom new meaning is produced."[18]

It is with the question of audience that we can now move to a closer discussion of Duffy's work. Her work has been well received in Britain, winning the 1983 National Poetry Competition, the Scottish Arts Council Award for Merit in 1985, the Somerset Maugham Award in 1988, and the Dylan Thomas Award in 1989, among others. Her poetry is imaginative, her command of language, tone, and timing remarkable; commentators like the "diversity" of her styles, and she is especially commended for her dramatic monologues, an honored form within the British tradition. What is interesting to me are the conventional terms and assumptions marking the rhetoric used to describe her work by reviewers. Peter Porter, for example, is quoted on the back cover of *Selling Manhattan* as praising Duffy for being a "very pure poet" who possesses a "crusading sensibility" but refuses "to surrender any touch of art to the urgency of its cause." In all fairness to Porter, this excerpt is presented out of context; nevertheless, what assumptions underlie the choice of this quotation to package for consumption a book of poetry? The pure poet, it seems, is the one who transcends the mucky world of "crusades," whose voice is not limited or made partial by her social reality, whose art rises above its very origins.

Duffy's work meets the requirement of a crafted art, leading to such evaluations as Porter's. At the same time, the very project of her poetry challenges the assured notions of truth, art, and poetic transcendence underlying Porter's praise. Language is her subject, and its structures her concerns. The ideological functions of language in the production of meaning are explored even though a clear syntactical coherence is maintained in many of her narratives, dramatic monologues, and lyrics. However, we can look *first* to poems that operate more disjunctively at the level of syntax and form and can begin to establish some of the connections between language, cultural meaning, and subjectivity that reemerge throughout her work.

"Translating the English" is a virtual collage of phrases describing "the English," calling into question the process of representation as a form of ideological work. Beginning "Welcome to my country!," the poem proceeds to catalog aspects of England's past and present:

> Welcome to my country! We have here Edwina Currie
> and The Sun newspaper. Much excitement.
> Also the weather has been most improving
> even in February. Daffodils. (Wordsworth. Up North.) If
>   you like
> Shakespeare or even Opera we have too the Black Market.
> For two hundred quids we are talking Les Miserables,
> nods being as good as winks. Don't eat the eggs.
> Wheel-clamp. Dogs. Vagrants. A tour of our wonderful
> capital city is not to be missed. The Fergie,
> The Princess Di and the football hooligan, truly you will

like it here, Squire. Also we can be talking crack, smack
and Carling Black Label if we are so inclined. Don't
drink the H$_2$O. All very proud we now have
a green Prime Minister. What colour yours? Binbags.
You will be knowing of Charles Dickens and Terry Wogan
and Scotland. All this can be arranged for cash no questions.
Ireland not on. Fish and chips and the Official Secrets Act
second to none. Here we go. We are liking
a smashing good time like estate agents and Neighbours,
also Brookside for we are allowed four Channels.
How many you have? Last night of Proms.[19]

Paratactically arranged, each phrase stands equally with others, although it is suggested that in the official version of "the English," a more hierarchically structured discourse would subordinate or eliminate the less savory details, such as "plenty rape" (in the final lines) or "Ireland not on." The parataxis works to "translate" the official version of England—the nationalism of "my country"—into a form encouraging us to make connections between Shakespeare or Opera and the Black Market. Although an "I," or more precisely a "my," speaks this poem, it is neither unified nor singular. Rather, the poem seems spoken or produced by various discourses: tourism, nationalism, high culturalism, journalism, the vernacular. The effect of this parataxis of image and discourse is to focus attention upon the exclusion that must be enacted in the process of idealizing "my country," or of constructing a tradition of nationalism. While the paratactic version of "Plenty culture" here includes "child abuse . . . ten pints and plenty rape," the official version of "my country," interwoven throughout the text with the unofficial, would rely upon Shakespeare and daffodils in Wordsworth country. The jarring quality of the paratactic arrangement suggests that an alternative and more soothing hypotactic structure would attain its harmony through an order subordinating and excluding tangential or unimportant items. Similarly, nationalistic pride in both past and present must select out certain conflicting items to sustain itself. The act of representation—of translation—always involves selection and arrangement that is, the poem suggests, ideologically interested. The idea of culture or high art as separate from this ideologically messy world is satirized in the final lines:

> . . . Plenty culture you will be agreeing.
> Also history and buildings. The Houses of Lords. Docklands.
> Many thrills and high interest rates for own good. Muggers.
> Much lead in petrol. Filth. Rule Britannia and child abuse.
> Electronic tagging. Boss, ten pints and plenty rape. Queen Mum.
> Channel Tunnel. You get there fast no problem to my country
> my country my country welcome welcome welcome.
>
> (*OC*, 11)

Imperialism and child abuse collide, as do progress (the tunnel) and filth and pollution, or the royalty and rape. The final repetition of "my country," echoed from the first line, asks us to consider what this customarily proud statement of nationality has to do with environmental and human oppression. Patriotism, within an aristocratic and imperialist inheritance, must bracket out economic disparity, misogyny, colonization—and yet, all of these discourses intersect and are even interdependent. The code of "Rule Britannia," of imperialist domination, translates itself on a familial level into child abuse. The self, the "my," is dispersed among these codes, these discourses, and even the possessive power insinuated by the grammatical form of first person is thrown into instability.

The status of the self within the discursive production of cultural structures is a major concern in Duffy's poetry. This concern often extends to the familial, as in "We Remember Your Childhood Well" (*OC*, 24), which questions the operation of personal memory in either knowing a "true" self or in re-presenting "true" experience. The idea of "facts" or evidence as a foundation for knowledge, and of memory as the retriever of facts, is contradicted by the poem's focus upon the power dynamics involved in the control of facts. In this instance, child abuse is concealed and silenced by the adults in power:

> Nobody hurt you. Nobody turned off the light and argued
> with somebody else all night. The bad man on the moors
> was only a movie you saw. Nobody locked the door.
>
> Your questions were answered fully. No. That didn't occur.
>
> (*OC*, 24)

Is there a true set of facts, a pure experience to return to? How does one construct a narrative of self when facts are ideologically manipulated? As the speaker tells the poem's "you," "What you recall are impressions; we have the facts. We called the tune." (*OC*, 24). The poem articulates a constructionist theory of experience in which experience "is never as unified, as knowable, as universal, and as stable as we presume it to be" and "empirical facts are always ideological productions."[20]

Although the truth of facts is here interrogated, the poem is not a nihilistic surrender to indeterminacy. What is significant is the exposure of the operations of power through the control of "facts" and the illusion that "facts" are "truth." Power works here to construct a narrative by blurring fact and fiction while claiming the authority of fact. Every fact, the poem suggests, is embedded within ideological or power interests that affect its representation, even those facts that one "knows." This does not condemn experience or memory as a source of knowledge but points up its insufficiency as the foundation or origin of knowledge or selfhood. No facts come to us pure. Awareness, however, of their mediated quality helps us to see the constructed nature of a narrative—even of personal history, of "your childhood"—and, hence, to come to a new understanding of it and one's "self."

Within Duffy's poetry, the meaning of art is also a construction and is shown to be produced in relationship to economics, the discourse of the body, and the regulatory structures of gender, race, and class. Institutional structures—explicitly including poetic forms and conventions—are revealed as working to conceal meaning's contextual dependence upon time and place by excluding contradictory material. For Duffy, this contradictory material tends to be the stuff of the real world or the "causes" Porter ironically praises her for transcending, including social conditions and transgressive realms of desire, particularly lesbian eroticism and the lesbian body. Additionally, her work's refusal of language transparency emerges as a continual and self-conscious attentiveness to the subject's position within language, to meaning's contextual production, to experience's discursive formation. Thus, a form like the narrative is used to reflect upon its own assumptions of pure experience, present through language; in this way, notions of a prediscursive experience or of representational truth inhering in form are problematized by the manipulation of poetic form to question itself.

"Standing Female Nude," the title poem of Duffy's 1985 volume, exemplifies this tension. As a dramatic monologue, the poem features a single speaker, an artist's model, speaking within the specific situation of readying to leave the studio after six hours of posing, being paid, and being shown the painting. In the course of the poem, we learn details of the lives of both painter and model: Both are poor; they seem to be in France; he is being heralded as a "genius." The key feature of a dramatic monologue insists, however, that we learn more than mere details. We should learn also of the speaker's private, distinctive character and temperament, inadvertently revealed through her speech. The focus should be, in good Robert Browning fashion, upon this lyric speaker or self whose essence is revealed in the arrangement of her words, her tone, her silences. In Duffy's hands, this arrangement serves to actually undermine the assumption of a distinctive, essential self by locating subjectivity within socioeconomic and linguistic networks. The main feature of the conventional dramatic monologue—the speaking lyric self—undergoes a deconstruction that reveals the ideological foundations (particularly in class and gender) of the idea of the private self. The poem follows in its entirety:

> Six hours like this for a few francs.
> Belly nipple arse in the window light,
> he drains the colour from me. Further to the right,
> Madame. And do try to be still.
> I shall be represented analytically and hung
> in great museums. The bourgeoisie will coo
> at such an image of a river-whore. They call it Art.
>
> Maybe. He is concerned with volume, space.
> I with the next meal. You're getting thin,
> Madame, this is not good. My breasts hang
> slightly low, the studio is cold. In the tea-leaves
> I can see the Queen of England gazing
> on my shape. Magnificent, she murmurs
> moving on. It makes me laugh. His name
>
> is Georges. They tell me he's a genius.
> There are times he does not concentrate

and stiffens for my warmth. Men think of their mothers.
He possesses me on canvas as he dips the brush
repeatedly into the paint. Little man,
you've not the money for the arts I sell.
Both poor, we make our living how we can.

I ask him Why do you do this? Because
I have to. There's no choice. Don't talk.
My smile confuses him. These artists
take themselves too seriously. At night I fill myself
with wine and dance around the bars. When it's finished
he shows me proudly, lights a cigarette. I say
Twelve francs and get my shawl. It does not look like me.[21]

The poem involves several levels of representation: the poem's representation of the model; the model's representation of her experience; the artist's representation of the model; the museum's representation of the painting— or, as the poem tells us, of Art, with a capital *A*. The initial stanza brings these levels into our consideration. The "self" presumed by the dramatic monologue is dispersed here within various discourses: economics and class, the body, Art. She is defined by the bourgeoisie who "coo" at her image, interpreting her as a "river-whore" and defining themselves through difference from her. To the artist, her body is a site conflating commodification and desire; we learn that he sometimes loses his concentration and "stiffens for my warmth." Unable to possess her physically (for, she tells us in a moment of economic determination, her arts are unaffordable to him), "He possesses [her] on canvas." Whose "self" is this? His possession, of course, becomes the possession of the museum and the middle class; Art as commodity is an extension of middle-class ideology.

Artistic representation objectifies the woman just as patriarchal economic structures objectify her as a commodity to be bought, sold, possessed. She will be "represented analytically and hung / in great museums"; her body is translated into "volume, space." In a particularly ambiguous set of lines, the distinction between the human individual and the representation is deliberately and complexly confused: "In the tea-leaves / I can see the Queen of England gazing / on my shape. Magnificent, she murmurs / moving on." The tea-leaves suggest, on the one hand, that she is imagining the future, when the Queen will view her "shape." The representative act has rendered her a "magnificent" shape to be possessed, even by the power of the gaze; it has also exoticized or romanticized her through distancing the material conditions of her life from the work and world of high "Art." The *image* is "magnificent"; the *woman* would most likely be scorned in such an environment. The tea-leaves also suggest, in a more literal fashion, that the Queen herself becomes such a shape within the milieu of popular culture. The Queen's image is customarily reproduced on the inside bottom of tea-cups and is mass-marketed as a souvenir.[22] The image of the Queen gazes upward from the teacup at "my shape"—is this the model or the painting? This confusion of reproduced images and individuals makes it impossible to locate the "self" here, or to find a self free of representation, mediation, or commodification. For women, whether poor models or queens, this confusion is particularly apt, given a long tradition of the exchange of women in patriarchal societies and the regulatory structures that "represent" women, even to themselves. In these lines we also see the collapsing of high and popular art, for the painting becomes an object for the marketplace, just as the cup has been. The myth of the individual genius and the unique creation ("they tell me he's a genius") helps to keep the boundary between the high and the low intact, but the poem illuminates the illusoriness of this boundary by suggesting its participation in bourgeois institutions.

The speaker's representation is bought, sold, possessed, gazed upon. The speaker herself is, as well, a literal commodity, selling her body for the money to survive. Society condemns her way of selling while celebrating the artist's; in this way, a morality that seeks to control women's bodies also conceals the ways in which the marketing of women is institutionalized— in this instance, through art. But the convention of the dramatic monologue pushes us to ask, how does a commodified object then "speak"?

The poem suggests that the "self" and its language is always grounded in material circumstances and that representation only creates the illusion of a unified, autonomous speaking subject. In the final lines, the nude model comments upon the artist's representation of her: "When it's finished / he shows me proudly, lights a cigarette. I say / Twelve francs and get my shawl. It does not look like me." The poem ends with a clichéd response, so familiar that we are apt to overlook its possible complexity. It is tempting, from a humanist perspective, to read this final line as a triumph for the speaker, an assertion of a self, a "me" that the artist and the system cannot assimilate and possess, a "me" that escapes the tyranny of representation, a "me" that is essentially unique and coherent and cannot be replicated.

In offering an alternate reading, I encourage a closer look at the line in this poem, the word choices, and the structure. The penultimate line breaks on "I say," seeming to emphasize the self as speaker. But in the final line, the first words, "Twelve francs," and the final words, "like me," call to each other through their mirrored placement. Bracketing the last line, a monetary amount and a personal pronoun act as reflections across the line and back through the poem. The "me" of the poem is a self shaped by economic systems of exchange and by a set of discourses (moral, aesthetic, and so on) that keeps this system in place. Rather than evoking an essentialized self or enacting a reification that excludes the material and discursive constituents of the "self," the dramatic monologue subverts its own conventional expectations and assumptions in dispersing the self. The final "me" remains re-presented and commodified even by the poem itself, a self-conscious maneuver implied by the emphasis upon representation in the final three words. The speaker's earlier comments, such as "I shall be represented analytically," initiate this emphasis long before the final line.

And so we come back to the poem's form and to the "self" represented in the dramatic monologue, the assumption of a speaking subject the form assumes. Just as the poem insists upon the arbitrary nature of language—the painting is art because "They call it Art"—it also links the process of labeling to authoritative status. The "speaking subject" of the monologue is positioned within this process, ultimately a process of power that seems to rob her of speech and subjectivity: the female nude is written/spoken/painted/represented through this process, her body defined by the material value it attains. And yet, for the spoken or represented subject, the act of speaking assumed by the form of the dramatic monologue creates the possibility of a certain refusal of representation through subversion, not through escape. This suggests a claim to subjectivity or to agency, a "me," at the same time that the subject's construction is placed within socioeconomic forces. The dramatic monologue enacts its own dependence upon an ideology of representation while pointing to its origins in material systems of economic and sexual power: Art with a capital *A* is not transcendent but

absolutely immanent in origin. The objectification of the female body is
positioned within these ideological structures, but the speaking subject remains suggestively cognizant of the discourses (of art, of economics) that
shape her representation. Agency is possible through the cognizant negotiation of the structures within which she is situated, a process involving at
once conflicting and multiple positions for the self. This reconfiguration of
the dramatic monologue's representation of subjectivity suggests the possibilities for reconfigurations of the female self arising from recognition of
the ideological investment within any "representation" of the subject, including one's own self-representation.

As Jane Thomas argues, for Duffy, "it is language which constructs the
individual's subjectivity in ways which are ideologically specific. The positions which are available to us to identify with—even the sign 'Woman'
itself—structure our sense of selves."[23] This positionality in language becomes more explicitly explored in *The Other Country* through poems asserting an increasingly self-conscious linkage between acts of language and
operations of power within authoritative structures. The emphasis in this
volume, as in the earlier books, is on the relationship between meaning and
dominant forms of power; however, the intensified focus upon singular
words, syntactical patterns, and contextual meaning highlights more clearly
the ideological constituents of discursive systems that conventional forms
help to conceal. Rather than disrupting language structures, Duffy draws
upon and disrupts the ideological basis of the forms she employs, as in
"Words, Wide Night," which counterpoints the shaping of experience by
language with the lyric's assumption of private expression. The poem begins with clear reference to the lyric tradition—the isolated self, mourning
distance from a lover: "Somewhere on the other side of this wide night /
and the distance between us, I am thinking of you. / The room is turning
slowly away from the moon."[24] This third line suggests a hyperbolic lyric
self. As central consciousness, its movement (signified by the room) pre-
dominates. Yet this hyperbole is suggestively silly in its effort to poeticize
or to construct the poem around the self. The next stanza reveals the construction of desire through language, a constructedness the room/moon
line has moved us toward considering: "This is pleasurable. Or shall I cross
that out and say / it is sad? In one of the tenses I singing [*sic*] / an impossible
song of desire that you cannot hear." The grammatical play of the second

line positions the "I" and its "singing" adjacent to a grammatical term, "tenses." Which tense of "I" sings in the lyric? How does the particular tense of I sing "desire" that can arbitrarily be labeled pleasurable or sad? The final lines refuse the lyric equation of self-expression and truth: "For I am in love with you and this / is what is like or what it is like in words." Experience is never prediscursive or entirely present; how we think we experience and how we represent experience is always "like," always in language, always ideologically mediated.

It is this recognition of a positionality within language, and within convention and tradition, that links Duffy's poetry to that of American experimentalists. Meaning, even of the individual word, depends on position in time and place. "River" asks us to think of what Thomas calls "the disparity between our individual interests and the discourses available to us." What would happen to our sense of self if we were to recognize our positionality in language? The poem envisions a woman, "At the turn of the river" where "the language changes," where the river crosses into a different country. The "sign / in a new language brash on a tree" alerts the woman to linguistic shifts, and "She feels she is somewhere else, intensely, simply because / of words." If a sense of self is contingent upon words, what happens when their meanings shift; how is subjectivity altered through a destabilization of transparent norms of language? "What would it mean to you if you could be / with her there, dangling your own hands in the water, where blue and silver fish dart away over stone, / stoon, stein, like the meanings of things, vanish?" (OC, 53).

In Steinian fashion (an allusive meaning generated by the contextual word play), the meanings of things vanish as meaning is shown to depend upon context and position, so that the material word attains meaning only within a system of difference. Such awareness does not annihilate the self, but suggests the self who can "write on a postcard," cognizant of its particular position and of the regulatory discourses impinging upon that position: "If you were really there what would you write on a postcard, / or on the sand, near where the river runs into the sea?" Language, like the postcard, is an act of communication and needs forms or containers so that communication can occur; at the same time, the place of inscription, the position of the inscriber, makes language subject to the waters of change and erasure.

Duffy's poetry, in many ways, is about form as a container of language. Poems manipulate forms to reveal their own presuppositions; poems speak about forms. In *Mean Time*, her latest volume, poems like "Litany" and "Confession" point to particular forms or codes of speech as ways of excluding what is contradictory, embarrassing, improper. The housewives gathered in "Litany" talk to one another but "language embarrassed them" and the silent gestures say more than their words.[25] Silence is "the code" learned from the mother, and when the daughter breaks the code by saying "*A boy in the playground . . . told me / to fuck off*" (*MT*, 9), she experiences subversive delight before the mother demands she apologize (in good form) and then washes her mouth out with soap. In "Confession," the young girl is able to partake in the Catholic sacrament and to "recite transgression in the manner approved" (*MT*, 15), although the sacramental form is subsumed by the priest's imagined thoughts, which conflict with the "manner approved":

Come away into this dark cell and tell
your sins to a hidden man your guardian angel
works your conscience like a glove-puppet It
smells in here doesn't it does it smell
like a coffin how would you know C'mon
out with them sins those little maggoty things
that wriggle in the soul . . . *Bless me Father . . .*

                        (*MT*, 15; Duffy's ellipses)

Through interspersing the proper form (the language of confession) with the "improper" thoughts of the priest, this poem, like others by Duffy, invites us to consider the ways in which forms operate to draw boundaries, to conceal incongruities, and to produce the illusions of order and reality. The gendering of confessor and priest additionally emphasizes the regulatory importance of forms, in a historically masculine culture, to position the female as submissive. In the poem, the male's power arises from the female confessor's adherence to a particular discourse. His inward thoughts, syntactically run together with the confessor's prayer, are presented as an unspoken but integral part of the confessional form as a gendered discourse. While the confessional form covers over and conceals the priest's own "confession" through its assumption of the holy man's authority within a religious

order, the poem's linguistic progression works to illustrate the interdependence of the two discourses seemingly in conflict but suggestively operating
in cooperation to sustain the hierarchical power of the masculine position.

Moreover, we are always reminded that the poem, even when translating experience for us, is words. Words are always "like." In "Like Earning
a Living," the speaker asks "What's an elephant like?" We never get an
answer, for "there just aren't words for it" (MT, 17). The meaning of "elephant" depends upon our arrangement of words in articulating or constructing a meaning. Meaning is predicated upon arrangement, just as the
final lines differ in meaning through the movement of one word: "Like
earning a living. / Earning a living like." In Duffy's poetry, "like" often
signifies the gap between word and thing, a gap that the poem "Caul" takes
as its subject in a postmodern response to a Poundian modernism that valued
direct treatment of the "thing":

> No, I don't remember the thing itself.
> I remember the word.
> Amnion, inner membrane, *caul.*
> I'll never be drowned.
>
> . . . .
> I'm all that is left of then. It spools
> itself out like a film
> a talented friend can recall
> using speech along.
>
> The light of a candle seen in a caul
> eased from my crown that day,
> when all but this living noun
> was taken away.
>
>   (MT, 22)

Memory occurs through language. Memory is of experiences. Experience is
a sign mediated by other signs. Does this make experience, memory, and,
ultimately, the self meaningless? Is this the nihilism so often leveled as criticism at poststructuralist interrogations of the humanist, autonomous self?

The phrase *living noun* is intriguing in regard to these questions because it suggests an interaction of language and experience in a self aware of its constructedness, or of its own grammar we might say. Here, in closing, I would like to circle back around to the American poet Susan Howe and her resistance to a tendency among Language poets to condemn the "living" or experiential "I" in this interaction. Even though she questions the lyric sensibility's equation of experience with knowledge, Howe does not want to abstract experience out of existence. In a discussion with a group of Language poets, included in Bernstein's *The Politics of Poetic Form*, Howe is asked by Alan Davies about her poetic project with history as a reclamation of "what really happened." He comments, "Somebody used the term 'real event.' I never really encountered one myself *[laughter]*." Susan Howe replies:

> Of course I can't *really* bring back a particular time. That's true. Or it's true if you think of time as moving in a particular direction— forward you say. But what if then *is* now. I hope my work here and elsewhere demonstrates something about the mystery of time. And I do not believe you never encountered a *real* event. Come on. That sounds so theoretical! Have you ever been really hungry? Did the dentist ever hit a nerve when he was giving you a filling? Have you ever had someone you love die? Did the Holocaust never *really* happen? Did we never *really* drop an atomic bomb on Hiroshima?[26]

Howe suggests here that experience, although the product of social histories, relations, and discourses, is still experienced. To sensitize ourselves to the ideological production of experience, to be attentive to the structures shaping our experiencing of experience, does not negate experience as a resource or as a reality. Howe's words strike me as those of a woman speaking who is cognizant of the disappearance of women's words and realities from our cultural texts. For many experimental women writers, there is an expressed need to retain "real events," and an "I" who experiences them, while revising the masculine model of the lyric self and his pure experience. Language is a part of this revision.

Carol Anne Duffy's proposition of a "living noun" relates closely, I think, to Howe's insistence on lived experience as real even as it is traversed with historical and discursive tracings or is produced through ideological systems. The final two stanzas of "Moments of Grace" (*MT,* 26) expand upon

the self as a "living noun" and upon a need to *experience* experience as both
in and out of language, both in and out of codes:

> Memory's caged bird won't fly. These days
> we are adjectives, nouns. In moments of grace
> we were verbs, the secret of poems, talented.
> A thin skin lies on the language. We stare
> deep in the eyes of strangers, look for the doing words.
>
> Now I smell you peeling an orange in the other room.
> Now I take off my watch, let a minute unravel
> in my hands, listen and look as I do so,
> and mild loss opens my lips like *No*.
> Passing, you kiss the back of my neck. A blessing.
>
> (*MT*, 26)

With its reference to the "caged bird" of memory, the poem allusively dis-
engages its articulation of experience from a Romantic notion of truth and
transcendence. The nightingale will not escape the world through art's
beauty, nor will memory escape language. We are subjects within discursive
structures, and we "look for the doing words" in our interactions with others.
Even the most personal of emotions, loss, is recognizable through language,
through the way it opens the mouth to speak a word *like* it. Loss will not
be fully present in the word; the personal experience of the lyric is mediated
always through language. And yet this does not mean the experience is not
"real"; the workings of language are both oppressive and a "blessing," a site
of contact and interaction. The self, the "living noun," is kissed on the neck
and tells us what it is like. For Duffy, the "like" is where we operate as humans
in language. It is a place not of nihilism but of exploration into the structures of the self, the grammar of the world.

Notes

1. Language (or L=A=N=G=U=A=G=E) poetry developed following the introduction in 1978 of a new magazine, *L=A=N=G=U=A=G=E*, edited by Charles Bernstein

and Bruce Andrews, which was published until 1981. Interested in theory and poetry, and especially in contemporary Marxist and poststructural thought, the group of writers published in the magazine included such poets as Lyn Hejinian, Hannah Weiner, Ron Silliman, Clark Coolidge, Bob Perelman, Tina Darragh, Carla Harriman, Steve McCaffery, Ray DiPalma, and Barrett Watten. Two anthologies associated with this movement are *The L=A=N=G=U=A=G=E Book*, ed. Bruce Andrews and Charles Bernstein (Carbondale: Southern Illinois Press, 1984) and *"Language" Poetries: An Anthology*, ed. Doug Messerli (New York: New Directions, 1987). A more recent anthology of experimental writers, including a high proportion of women, is *What is inside, what is outside*, ed. Leslie Scalapino (Oakland, Calif.: O Books, 1991). To date, two book-length studies of Language poetry have appeared: George Hartley's *Textual Politics and the Language Poets* (Bloomington: Indiana University Press, 1989) and Linda Reinfeld's *Language Poetry: Writing as Rescue* (Baton Rouge: Louisiana State University Press, 1992).

2. Reinfeld, *Language Poetry*, 4.

3. Peter Nicholls, "Difference Spreading: From Gertrude Stein to L=A=N=G=U=A=G=E Poetry," in *Contemporary Poetry Meets Modern Theory*, ed. Antony Easthope and John O. Thompson (Toronto: University of Toronto Press, 1991), 116, 120.

4. Ibid., 124.

5. Here I am thinking not only of Fraser and Howe, but also of Leslie Scalapino, Rachel Blau DuPlessis, Bev Dahlen, and others.

6. The journal *HOW(ever)* (which ended in 1992), edited by Kathleen Fraser, provided a forum for experimental women writers to publish their own work and to comment on previous women experimentalists. Its five volumes are a rich resource for anyone interested in a tradition of linguistic innovation and women.

7. Janet Wolff, *Feminine Sentences: Essays on Women and Culture* (Berkeley: University of California Press, 1990), 94.

8. Jane E. Thomas, "'The Intolerable Wrestle with Words': The Poetry of Carol Ann Duffy," *Bête Noire* 6 (winter 1988): 78.

9. Ibid., 79.

10. Charles Bernstein, "Comedy and the Poetics of Political Form," in *The Politics of Poetic Form*, ed. Charles Bernstein (New York: Roof, 1990), 236.

11. In Nicholls, "Difference Spreading," 122.

12. Bernstein, "Comedy," 238.

13. Diana Fuss, *Essentially Speaking: Feminism, Nature, and Difference* (New York: Routledge, 1989), 114.

14. Ibid.

15. Erica Hunt, "Notes for an Oppositional Poetics," in Bernstein, *Politics of Poetic Form*, 199–200.

16. Carol Ann Duffy, "Litany," in *Mean Time* (London: Anvil Press, 1993), 9. All

quotations are from this edition; hereafter, page numbers will be given in the text, preceded by *MT*.

17. Hunt, "Notes," 204.

18. Ibid.

19. Carol Ann Duffy, "Translating the English, 1989," in *The Other Country* (London: Anvil Press, 1990), 11. All quotations are from this edition; hereafter, page numbers will be given in the text, preceded by *OC*.

20. Fuss, *Essentially Speaking*, 114.

21. Carol Ann Duffy, "Standing Female Nude," in *Standing Female Nude* (London: Anvil Press, 1985), 46. All quotations are from this edition; page numbers will not be given because the poem is all on one page.

22. Thanks to my wise, well-traveled, tea-drinking colleague Anne Brannen for this observation.

23. Thomas, "The Intolerable Wrestle," 85.

24. Carol Ann Duffy, "Words, Wide Night," in *The Other Country*, 47. Because the whole poem appears on one page, page numbers will not be given in the text.

25. Duffy, "Litany," 9.

26. Susan Howe, "Encloser," in Bernstein, *Politics of Poetic Form*, 194.

CHAPTER TEN

Postfeminist Poetry?:
"one more word
for balls"

Vicki Bertram

There is nothing remotely new about postfeminist poetry.[1] There is no recognizable group of poets who call themselves the "Post-Feminist Movement." So far as I am aware, the term has only actually been used in connection with poetry once—in Carol Rumens's anthology, *Making for the Open: The Chatto Book of Post-Feminist Poetry 1964–1984*.[2] Nevertheless, the attitudes implicit in the phrase are characteristic of most mainstream contemporary writing about women's poetry. I shall argue that, for a variety of reasons, we are no nearer having a satisfactory context within and against which poetry by women can be read and enjoyed than we were in the 1950s. Distorted accounts of the scale and impact of "feminist poetry," coupled with a lack of feminist research into contemporary poetry in Britain, and the tendency in what little there is to get tangled in peripheral issues, are all partially responsible. They also play their part in what is actually a much broader failure to provide a comprehensive critique of the dominant liberal humanist aesthetic.[3] I shall examine the workings of this aesthetic in a couple of mainstream women-only anthologies before offering a more specific analysis of the troubled debates surrounding the relevance of gender in (women's) poetry.

In 1985 *Making for the Open*, a new anthology of women poets edited by Carol Rumens, appeared. In her brief introduction, Rumens explained the rationale behind the collection. Although she welcomed the recent appearance of so many editions of women's poetry, she was disappointed by the quality of the poems. Enthusiastic feminist commitment had "led to the elevation of the message at the expense of the medium" (1985, xv). More-traditional women poets, whose work was not explicitly feminist, were being marginalized by the women's presses and their reputations sullied by association with the ranters. Rumens's anthology marked the arrival of a new phase: the calmer waters of postfeminism. Foolish prejudices against women poets are a thing of the past, she assures us; women are at last out there "in the open," serious poetic practitioners alongside the men. She was not exactly tactful in her criticisms:

> Those writers concerned with "the stern art of poetry" as an end in itself have tended to be swamped by the noisy amateurs proclaiming that women, too, have a voice. This anthology is different from its predecessors in that the poems proclaim only themselves. That women have a voice, and the right to be heard, goes without saying. (1985, xv)

With this crude image of engulfment, she rubbishes the achievements of earlier anthologies. Rather than attacking the work of specific poets, she opts for a sweeping dismissal so vague that it cannot easily be challenged: It is impossible to refute such a generalized criticism without knowing which poets qualify for the label "noisy amateurs." A further effect of Rumens's lively turn-of-phrase is that it magnifies the scale of events. These noisy amateurs could be an army massed outside the Poetry Society H.Q., preparing to storm the buildings. Such exaggerated but vague allusions to what is represented as a cohesive brand of feminist poets bent on revolution are a common feature of debates around women poets. This kind of colorful rhetoric has created a legendary phenomenon, neatly dubbed "The Hysterical Women's Movement" by poet-critic Sylvia Kantaris.[4]

In calling her selection "post-feminist," Rumens implies the return of calm objectivity in the aftermath of women's anger. Postfeminism is "a metaphysical rather than historical concept";[5] it is a psychological state of mind signaling "mental freedom." According to Rumens, this blissful liberty is an essential qualification for "poets of quality": "Language can be used authentically (and poetry is language at its most authentic) only by those whose existence, whose *being* is authentic."[6] After the excesses of feminist anger, she implies, it is time for a return to level-headed common sense. This anxious insistence on calm neutrality is reminiscent of Virginia Woolf's conviction—even as she herself contradicted it—that: "[i]t is fatal for a woman to lay the least stress on any grievance; to plead even with justice any cause; in any way to speak consciously as a woman."[7] The trouble is that Rumens cannot quite decide what it is about the poetry of these noisy amateurs that makes it so disappointing. She claims that it is a lack of attention to craft and technique, but content and tone clearly also play their part. Her use of the adjective "noisy" hints at a lack of dignity and decorum, a certain boisterous—even shrill?—quality that sits uneasily beside the smooth objectivity of "mental freedom." She insists that poems about "specifically female experiences" have not been excluded "provided they are genuine poems,"[8] but that there are actually very few in the collection. In the revised introduction to the second edition she tries to clarify matters: "*Making for the Open* is not a work of opposition to feminism but it undeniably opposes the feminist *aesthetic* in its extremer forms."[9]

Again, no examples of this feminist aesthetic are given, but what Rumens understands by it is pretty clear. In their most radical guise, feminist aesthetics apparently combine a challenge to what is considered "appropriate" subject matter with an attempt "to overturn the whole notion of quality, to reject all criteria of what makes a poem 'a poem.'" The latent conservatism of Rumens's aesthetic now becomes explicit: "Within the mutabilities of fashion and convention, etc., there will always be certain essential characteristics fundamental to poetry" (1987, xv). She only gives one example of these essential characteristics—rhythm. Rhyme is dispensable—it is "a superficial device, a useful convention," but without rhythm "there can be no enchantment, no reassurance, no shock" (1987, xv). It could also be argued that there can be no words without rhythm, but that would be to ignore the specific kind of rhythm Rumens has in mind—the regular rhythms of conventionally crafted poetry.

Rumens's conservatism extends to the kind of people she expects to write poetry. Just as the poem itself will never change, neither will the poets who write it: It is the "middle i.e. writing classes" (1985, xv) who have reached the gentle plains of metaphysical freedom, and Rumens does not appear to even consider the possibility that writers may emerge from outside the middle classes. She spends her introduction to the second edition searching for technical "essential characteristics" in order to avoid acknowledging that her aesthetic—far from being neutral and timeless—is in actual fact partial and political, the product of specific literary and cultural forces. There is nothing everlasting about it, although she tries hard to prove that there is. She explains that she has selected "genuine" poems with "verbal intensity": poems that "proclaim only themselves"; "authentic" poetry that does not "betray its own integrity as art." Her guiding aim throughout the project has been to emphasize the relationship between artistic and human rights, and the necessity for freedom. "Poetry is an act of concern . . . for the many forms of human truth."[10]

All these appeals betray the liberal humanist ideology informing Rumens's supposedly objective selection of "poets of quality." *Making for the Open* generated considerable opposition, particularly on account of its tendentious introduction, but it would be a mistake to think that Rumens's position was atypical or extreme. On the contrary, what is remarkable about the project is her clear articulation of the ideology that usually remains concealed. Reviewing the book for the *Times Literary Supplement*, Michael Hofmann accurately described its tone as "studiously unpolemical and, in certain quarters, highly controversial."[11] The certain quarters were, of course, feminist.

Two years after *Making for the Open*'s first publication, *The Faber Book of Twentieth Century Women's Poetry* appeared, edited by Fleur Adcock.[12] Rumens and Adcock are probably the two best-known and most-admired women poets in Britain—fitting choices as editors of such prestigious publications. Chatto & Windus and Faber & Faber had leapt onto the bandwagon of women-only anthologies fairly late in the day once they realized there was money to be made. Paradoxically, their timing gave them an advantage. Coming after the earlier publications by women's presses, and drawing on the clout of their publishers as reputable, long-established companies, these two collections implicitly claimed to be definitive. Now that the chaotic activity of the Women's Movement had run its course, Rumens and Adcock would venture out into the ravaged landscape to rescue and preserve the finest flowers of poetic achievement.

They had similar ideas about women's poetry. Both rejected the idea of a women's poetic tradition, arguing that the only thing women poets had in common was their shared experience of past prejudice. Adcock puts the case particularly strongly:

> If I have a theory about the tradition informing their poetry it is
> that there is no particular tradition: there have been poets, and
> they have been individuals, and a few of them have influenced a
> few others. . . . [I]f "women's poetry" were a special genre, a minor
> and recognizably different offshoot from the main process, it might
> make sense to see it as a unity, but as things are, women have been
> involved in the currents and movements as little or as much as
> men, and have been as various.[13]

The collections thus carry a slight whiff of righteous worthiness, as though
they were just the result of rather unexciting acts of atonement: the publication of those who were left out before, the also-rans—hardly a compelling connecting thread around which to construct a sympathetic and productive ambience for the poems. The strength of an anthology lies in its
capacity to provide a shared context for the poems within. In declaring at
the outset that there is no positive rationale for their anthologies, Adcock
and Rumens effectively undermine the possibility of any such woman-centered context emerging.

The type of poem favored by both editors still suffers from the disease
of "gentility" diagnosed by Alvarez, the perennial weakness of the English
lyric.[14] Meditative, solitary, and detached, but practical, brief, and, above
all, sensible, this poem will avoid passion at all costs, turning to the distancing effects of irony with a sigh of relief. Adcock's list of dislikes is fairly
representative: thumbs down for "incantatory poetry," mysticism, anything
surreal, and the minimalist style she associates with "Creative Writing Programs of the American universities." But the greatest scorn is reserved for
"'primal scream' writing—slabs of raw experience untransformed by any
attempt at ordering and selection."[15] Typically, no examples are given—
readers are left to make their own inferences.

I am not accusing Adcock or Rumens of being unsympathetic to women
poets. As Rumens emphasizes, what she is opposed to is what she considers
to be an extreme feminist aesthetic. But in their easy dismissal of alternatives, both editors seem naively optimistic about the flexibility of traditional
English poetic aesthetics. They subscribe to the belief that art and politics
should inhabit separate spheres, and that great art transcends the individual's
local experience to offer universal truths. They ignore the fact that the

concept of universality is implicitly gendered; it is *male* experience (and invariably white, middle-class, male experience) that has been, and still is, passed off as universal.[16]

To qualify as a great poet, a woman must attain this universality, overcoming the limitations of her gender in the process. Of course this is never stated explicitly, but it becomes quite clear when the criteria for literary evaluation are examined. An example is irresistible: Martin Booth, in discussing modern and contemporary women poets, speaks of Patricia Beer, commenting that "her work is best described as safe. It takes no risks and is rooted firmly in a security that chauvinists might say is typical of women who are happy and safe in a home, a marriage and a round of life in which they know themselves."[17] Hardly surprisingly, after this he cannot find much else to say about it and passes on swiftly. He is more enthusiastic about Stevie Smith. Her vision is "bizarre, macabre, witty, mystical, strange, wonderful and exotic," but apparently she is not a *woman poet*, she is "an enigma."[18] An interesting semantic shift has occurred. *Poetess*, laden down by negative connotations of sentimental weepiness, has fallen out of use, presumably as a gesture of enlightened respect for female practitioners. But *woman poet*, its replacement, is here devalued in the same way; it is used to imply limited range, vision, audience. Thus Sylvia Plath is "not a female poet, but just a poet," because Booth likes her work: "She wrote from the core of the modern woman's soul and, since so many males also took wholeheartedly to her poetry, she did a vast amount for the female cause."[19] He is, at least, beguilingly frank. Plath struck a popular chord because she wrote uncompromisingly of suicide and death "in a violent world to people for whom the bloody violence was fast becoming a sign of the times."[20] What lucky timing—lucky that men could relate to her poetry. The "woman's soul" (a limitation in itself) can only be transcended when there is something to interest the men, too. Men can hardly be expected to be gripped by women's souls. They tend to be a little dull ("happy and safe"). The soul of man is, of course, of infinite depth and fascination, and centuries of poetic investigation have yet to plumb even its shallower waters. It seems that only a few women poets succeed in transcending the limiting specificities of their condition and in finding a metaphor that both expresses that debased other term, *the female*, as well as being broad and vague enough to encompass some "universal" (male?) anxiety. The few who succeed usually jettison or veil any gender-specific metaphors in order to evade accusations of narrowness and insularity.

So it is easy to see why the older generation of women poets may have preferred to be simply poets. It is perhaps more puzzling that the vast majority of younger ones still shy away from the idea of being known as a woman poet. This is Carol Ann Duffy's view on the matter:

> For quite a long time even into this decade we've been allowed certain areas of subject matter, like children, what bastards men are, looms: all these things that appear in late 1970s, early 1980s women's anthologies. But I haven't got any children and I don't define myself entirely as a woman; I'm not interested in weaving.[21]

Why doesn't Duffy define herself entirely as a woman? What is it about the category that is so limiting? *Woman* seems to mean heterosexuality and motherhood to her. But whatever its particular referents in individual cases, being a woman clearly means something quite specific, in a way that being a man does not. And, as Duffy sharply observes, femaleness still circumscribes subject matter, even in these apparently postfeminist days. Female subject matter is equated with domestic life, with the personal and subjective realms of experience. As Louise Bernikow put it bluntly back in 1979:

> Women's lives bore men. The reality of those lives, especially the embarrassing subject of women's bodies, frightens men. Male approval, the condition of a poet's survival, is withheld when a woman shapes her poetry from the very material that contradicts and threatens male reality.[22]

This is stark, but difficult to refute. Indeed, it is a fairly apt description of A. A. Kelly's response to recent poetry by Irish women. Introducing the anthology, Kelly apologizes for the limitations of contemporary women poets: "They are often self-regarding, and too conscious of their female function."[23] It is tempting to ask whose definition of a woman's "function" is being used here, but more disturbing still is Kelly's impatient and reductively literal reading of such work: "Contraception, rape, abortion and female circumcision are highly emotive and controversial issues about which women find it hard to be objective. . . . Women poets now dare to write explicitly about their bodies. A glut of this subject, too explicitly expressed, should lessen as female metaphor becomes innate rather than innovative; . . . Female metaphor is still insecure. Female taboos still permeate the subconscious." "Whose subconscious?" is a tantalizing question, but I shall leave it aside and pass quietly over the insults to consider the important issue Kelly raises about metaphor. Ought metaphors to communicate a universal insight? Eavan Boland writes herself round in a circle over this one:

> A lot of what we now call "feminine experiences," or "women's experiences," or "women's issues," within poetry, are in fact, if people would only look at them closely, powerful metaphors for types of humiliation, types of silence, that are there throughout human experience. But you need to unlock the metaphor and you can't do it by feminizing the material. You can only do it by humanizing it.[24]

In other words, a woman's experience, in order to be accepted as a metaphor for human experience, must be "humanized"—the female element rendered invisible. In the process of humanizing female experience, gender is bypassed because humanism occludes gender difference and imposes a masculine subject. This paradox lies at the heart of Boland's project and explains why any attempt to place women poets centrally in the literary tradition will fail to shift its male-centered perspective.

This hidden agenda also explains why Adcock and Rumens feel sensitive about the absence of male poets from their anthologies. Rumens apologizes for the "limiting factor" and imagines a future version that includes poems by men, too.[25] Such sensitivity to the partial nature of a single-sex anthology is remarkable. You don't find it the other way round in any of the "general" anthologies, despite the paltry and oddly consistent 5 to 8 percent representation of women poets.[26] Clearly conscious—on some level—that specifically female subject matter is not universal, they steer clear of it. This explains the relative absence of such material from these "authoritative" women's anthologies. Even when the occasional exception does get included, the dominant tone will work to muffle its distinctiveness.[27] Having internalized a liberal humanist aesthetic, the woman reader is likely to react negatively to poetry that articulates specifically female experience.[28]

In spite of these efforts to avoid controversy, to choose poems that conform to traditional criteria of poetic excellence and to treat suitably "universal" themes, the mere existence of a women-only publication is apparently sufficient to provoke hostility. One of the reasons given for anxiety about, and disapproval of, separatist anthologizing is that separatism implies censorship. Tension in this area has of course increased over the last decade with the emergence of that liberal bugbear, Political Correctness. In a piece published in 1983, Judith Kazantzis reflected wryly on the relationship between her feminist politics and her writing:

> I would not claim, nor wish to claim, that the more personal poems I write are all grounded in high feminism. Some are about country life, and I send them to *Country Life*, others are about fucking and possibly sexist and these I might send to male editors and gauchely assume that *Spare Rib* readers—for whom I have reviewed women's poetry for some years—won't come across them.[29]

Such levity would be frowned upon today. A more typical tone is that of Sally Minogue in her 1990 article about feminism and poetry. Minogue is anxious about the dangers of feminist prescriptivism:

> The power of these unarticulated rules [concerning what a "feminist poem" should be like], combined with a feminist writer's fear of being found politically suspect, could . . . have a profound influence on future poetry, and not necessarily just that written by self-announced and self-perceived feminists. All female poets could be affected.[30]

I will return to Minogue's article later; what is interesting (and characteristic) here is the acute sensitivity to a hypothetical set of unwritten rules. It seems odd to assume that poets will readily censor their thoughts in the way she fears. It is more likely that the clashes and tensions between principles and desire, between the public and private realms of experience, might prove fertile territory for creativity.

Minogue attributes a coherent, well-defined strategy of absolute separatism to an anonymous group of poets. Eavan Boland seems to have met the same women:

> Separatist prescriptions demand that women be true to the historical angers which under-write the Woman's Movement [sic]; that they cast aside pre-existing literary traditions; that they evolve not only their own writing, but the criteria by which to judge it . . . the gradual emphasis on the appropriate subject matter and the correct feelings has become as constricting and corrupt within Feminism as within Romanticism.[31]

Minogue's essay is over fifty pages long; yet not once does she give an example of a poet who advocates this form of separatism.

So unsubstantiated claims about the extremist behavior of feminist poets are widespread. They can result in some extraordinarily confused prejudices. In an enthusiastic review of Carol Ann Duffy's work, the critic Jane E. Thomas remarks: "Although she is a lesbian and a feminist she displays none of the self-congratulatory essentialism commonly associated with such a stance."[32] With which particular stance? Is she talking of lesbian *poets*, of feminist *poets*, or of the political stance of lesbian feminism? Does Thomas herself share this common association or intend to critique it? This is not mere nitpicking; these are not trivial questions. The conflation of complex and actually quite separate strands of female experience and ideology effectively protects the liberal humanist aesthetic from *any* challenge—political, philosophical, or whatever. The problem is one of taking categories of poetry—black, lesbian, feminist—overliterally, as though they offered a uniform vision rather than a strategic collectivity. There is a fine but crucial distinction between transgressing categories as a self-conscious, deliberate strategy and unknowingly erasing them altogether.[33]

The lack of feminist scholarship about contemporary women's poetry means that there is no one to refute these inaccuracies and to correct the misleading impression they give. Even out of what has been published, very few studies tackle the vexed question of aesthetics. The three that do explore this area tend to concentrate on North American poetry, not on poetry currently being written and published in Britain.[34] Nevertheless, it is worth looking briefly at their work.

As Minogue recognizes, the problem with trying to develop a new aesthetic is that it all too easily ends up being defined against the old one: it becomes everything the old one is not. This is what happens in the first of these studies, *Feminism and Poetry*. Montefiore is trying to isolate a woman's poetic tradition. She decides that content is the most important element in identifying such a tradition. Poems that concentrate on women's experiences and women's lives—whether real, historical women, or mythical figures—would be central to it. On the other hand, she finds the concept deeply problematic:

> [A]s a critical construct, the notion of a woman's tradition is difficult because it seems to demand that women's poetry be conceived purely in its own terms. This demand proves unrealistic, partly because of its implied essentialism, partly because when women's poems are closely examined, it usually appears that women poets are engaged with patriarchal tradition, if only by way of opposing it.[35]

There is, however, no reason why women's poetry need be regarded "purely in its own terms"—in other words, as a separatist venture, as this seems to imply. Why cannot women's poetry be seen to interact with men's poetry, partaking of the same traditions, but also to operate in a different sphere? The problem would be to prevent the different perspectives in women's poetry from being absorbed into, and erased by, patriarchal norms. But it is not impossible to keep the focus on women's poetry, while nevertheless comparing it with poetry by men.[36] Montefiore insists, however, on drawing a stark dichotomy between the patriarchal tradition and an entirely separate women's tradition—a simplistic idea that she cannot support.

Rumens displays a similarly obtuse understanding of the available alternatives. She realizes that one of the drawbacks of women-only collections is they might inadvertently reinforce women's marginal position within (or, perhaps more accurately, without) the poetic tradition. But instead of seeing the decision to publish these earlier women's anthologies as a positive step toward evolving a new context that might overlap in places with the mainstream canon, she reads it as a declaration of arrogant autonomy. She makes this (to her) foolhardy separatism part of the justification for her own more mainstream, conventional anthology. When she began choosing poems, she says,

> . . . there was no anthology, to my knowledge, of women poets which presented its writers as central to the literary tradition. They were apparently either in scornful opposition to it as an exclusively male phenomenon, whose skills and insights were worthless to them, or they simply did not exist.[37]

"[T]hey" presumably means women poets who wanted to situate themselves centrally within "the" literary tradition. Rumens calls this separatism, but carving out a different context through concentrating on women poets is not the same thing as putting the entire mass of Western literature through the shredder. Rumens conflates this attempt to develop alternative spheres with stereotypes of dungareed separatists making a bonfire of their copies of Shakespeare. What both Montefiore and Rumens find peculiarly hard to grasp is the simple idea that new insights may be encouraged by adopting a new perspective, just as plowing the soil stimulates new growth.

Minogue's essay, "Prescriptions and Proscriptions: Feminist Criticism and Contemporary Poetry," reveals a similarly literal and reductive conception of feminist interventions. She bases much of her essay on the testimony of Jan Clausen, a North American poet who has grappled with what it means to be a "feminist poet," and on what a feminist aesthetic entails. As we have already seen, Minogue fears that feminism impoverishes imaginative freedom:

> If women are not allowed a *free* voice to explore and express whatsoever they please, how can they develop as poets? For it seems to me that the great tragedy of the thrust of feminist criticism lies in the way it proscribes certain areas of thought, certain ways of writing. . . . Would a contemporary feminist have dared to write such a poem as "My life had stood—a loaded gun"? The aggressively phallic

> nature of the imagery together with the passivity of the first and
> last stanzas might well be ruled out before they got to the page.[38]

Once again, we get no examples of this unfortunately thrusting feminist criticism. Quite aside from the odd notion that poets are willingly going to police their thoughts, eradicating telltale signs of anything politically unsound, Minogue also seems to think that those who do not espouse feminist ideas are free—they have that "mental freedom" Rumens discussed. The rhetoric of "Freedom" is, of course, deeply ingrained in British liberalism; hence the paranoia about censorship and the accompanying blindness to more insidious forms of social control.

Minogue has no time for the crude notion that poetic language and tradition are "male." She is frustrated by the implication that women are disadvantaged by this maleness—just because flowers have traditionally been used to symbolize female sexuality, this does not mean they cannot be reclaimed or subverted: "A tradition is a tradition: just that. It is not inviolable, unchangeable."[39] Yet in terms of readers' interpretations, it is actually extremely difficult to effect such changes. I touched on this problem earlier, in connection with universality, and quoted from the introduction to an anthology of Irish women's poetry. Apologizing for the number of poems about bodies and physical experiences, the editor, A. A. Kelly, gave the impression that such material would gradually become more acceptable, "as female metaphor becomes innate rather than innovative; . . . Female metaphor is still insecure. Female taboos still permeate the subconscious."[40] Within an androcentric poetic tradition, how can we nurture the growth of female-centered metaphors? This is precisely where context, to return to the original issue, is so important. A sympathetic context can facilitate recognition of interconnections that otherwise might remain unnoticed. The clearest way to demonstrate this is by comparing two very different women-only anthologies. The first—*Making for the Open*—eschews the notion of a woman-centered aesthetic, preferring to simply select the best poems around: "an anthology, if it is to be readable, must have some limiting factor, that of gender being as good a one as any."[41] The second anthology, *The Bloodaxe Book of Contemporary Women Poets: Eleven British Writers,* signals its more positive approach with its front cover—a painting of a woman weaving. In

her introduction, the editor, Jeni Couzyn, comments on entrenched prejudice against women poets, noting the insulting stereotypes ("Mrs Dedication," "Miss Eccentric Spinster," and "Mad Girl") used to label those who
persevere despite such resistance.[42] Her selection celebrates what might best
be called a feminine aesthetic. Each poet's work is prefaced by an autobiographical piece in which she discusses, among other issues, the relevance
of gender to her writing. Opinions differ radically, but the context remains:
gender is firmly on the agenda for anyone who cares to explore its significance. With these prose extracts, photographs of the poets, and an introduction that explores the subversive content of women's poetry across
centuries, this anthology encourages the reader to make connections between poems and poets. There is enormous variety of style and tone—Stevie
Smith, Elizabeth Jennings, and Sylvia Plath hardly offer uniformity—but
within such diversity there are also common strategies, themes, and perspectives.

Of course, however carefully open and nondoctrinaire it may be, some
readers will still resist the woman-centered ethos of an anthology. In his
review of these two anthologies, Michael Hofmann notes that, in his opinion, the best poem in the book "is not on any feminist subject at all." He
is referring to Denise Levertov's "A Tree Telling of Orpheus," which he reads
as epitomizing the gender transcendence Rumens desires: "That imaginative empathy with a neuter object looks 'open' in a way that would gladden
Carol Rumens," he comments.[43] Reviewing the same two anthologies, Stevie
Davies (a feminist critic) also discusses this poem. For her the narrative voice
"identifies itself . . . as a woman-Orpheus."[44] She detects the presence of
subtle parallels with female resistance and reads the poem as a parable about
the rupturing of ancient, deep-rooted traditions. The same poem yields
different insights for different readers. Davies is enthusiastic about the
Couzyn anthology; she recognizes the potential it makes available for a
consideration of female aesthetics. Hofmann resists this invitation, preferring to read the poem and its metaphors traditionally. The tree is a tree—
"a neuter object." Yet it surely must take more effort to ignore the rever-
berations of surrounding poems in the collection than it would if he came
across Levertov's poem in an anthology of contemporary American (men's)
poetry. Without collections of poetry that foreground female experience,
the chance to develop enriching alternatives to androcentric readings is

lost. Placed alongside one another, poems that rework traditional symbols can feed off each other; latent meanings can gather resonance from surrounding poems. The context can help to create a richer perspective for the reader, an echo chamber of fragments and images, leading to a more expansively pluralist vision.

So discussions of women's poetry pursue three lines of investigation that seem, at best, unhelpful: attempts to define a feminist aesthetic; arguments about the importance of accessibility, in order to avoid the "elitist" label associated with poetry; and the search for evaluative criteria. Each leads ultimately to a dead end and distracts attention from more fruitful explorations. I shall look briefly at each in turn.

The effort to define a "feminist" poem, poetic, or aesthetic is tantamount to accepting the oppositional category constructed by the very system one is attempting to move beyond. The problem is not with the term "feminist," so much as with the pressure to define an *essence* of what it is in poetry, as if the magic ingredient could be spotted and labeled. This definition is then taken as prescriptive or monolithic and is attacked as essentialist.[45] It is not surprising that Duffy and many others reject the label "woman poet," because it too is inevitably constructed against the norm of (male) poet. Attempts to isolate precisely what is "feminist" about a poem also ignore the fluid instability of interpretation, whereby meanings are shaped by interactions between reader and poem.

The second misguided area of concern focuses on anxieties about elitism. One of the "unwritten rules" of feminist poetry cited by Minogue is that it should be "accessible in form and content."[46] After several years of teaching contemporary poetry, I can no longer confidently determine the degree of difficulty that a given poem poses to its readers. Some readers find the precise economy of Grace Nichols bewildering, even though the vocabulary is easy for them. Some revel in Medbh McGuckian's heavily descriptive lyrics—from lines dripping with complex images they grasp a crisp picture immediately—whereas others are thrown by her unconventional grammar and syntax. There does not seem to be any way of predicting these different responses; they bear little relation to the reader's "intelligence." The idea that there can be an absolute measure of difficulty is impossible to sustain. Once again, what is really happening is that feminist poetry is being constructed in opposition to the dense, allusive qualities of the academy poem. In reality, strictures about accessibility depend on what kind of audience a poet is seeking. There are women writing all across the spectrum of poetic activity for very different audiences.

The third issue that dominates debate is the search for evaluative criteria for women's poetry.[47] Criticism about the novel is not so obsessed with the question of value, probably because the world of fiction is market led: If a book sells well, it is almost by definition (particularly in the current climate of cultural studies) "valuable" and therefore worthy of study. The market has taken over the evaluative role of the critic. But poetry does not generate so much money or interest. Its audience is smaller, a tight-knit community; its authorities are correspondingly more powerful. They like the chance to determine the "best" poets. As O'Rourke points out: "Excellence in our culture, like quality, is always arrived at through scarcity."[48] Out of the hundreds of poets writing and being published, only a few are "worthy" of serious study. But there are more interesting questions to ask of a poem, as she insists:

> I question the view of literature which sees response first and foremost in terms of hierarchical judgement. Faced with questions of judgement, I don't rush out to fit the template of excellence over my poems and see how close the fit is. I ask who has drawn up these standards, and why? Will they include or exclude this poet— help to explain why they write as they do about this subject? Is there space for my pleasure as a reader?
>
> Like many other feminist critics I want to extend the boundaries of literature: bring it down to earth, include the vernacular and extend the numbers of people poetry speaks to, and for, and about. Such an impulse is at odds with a drive to narrow down, to define what is good through the exclusion of most of what exists at all.[49]

This move away from the narrowness of conventional critique offers a new way forward that is centered on greater sensitivity to the interactions between reader (or listener) and poem. A willingness to keep asking questions about aesthetics symbolizes the openness of this approach—a more innovative openness than that suggested by the cover of Rumens's "open" future.[50]

To conclude, I would suggest that the poems in *Making for the Open* are not "postfeminist" at all. The term, and Rumens's gender-free future, does them a grave disservice. It is not the poems but the continuing acceptance of a gender-blind, apolitical, neo-Romantic aesthetic that impedes the development of more vigorous debate around women's poetry.

There are, however, many signs for hope, and there are hints that the liberal humanist orthodoxy might be waning. *Poetry Review*, the official magazine of the National Poetry Society, has become a much more lively, adventurous forum over the last few years under the editorship of Peter Forbes. Special thematic issues acknowledge the interface between poetry and events in the "real" world. Topics featured recently include poetry and politics, Eastern European poetry, and poetry and education. Its reviews are becoming slightly more enthusiastic about innovations, from performance poetry to a bilingual Bengali/English edition of poems and short stories.[51]

There appear to be more high-profile women in poetry than ever before, and many are not from the traditional white middle-class Oxbridge background. Sujata Bhatt, Jackie Kay, and Liz Lochhead are three examples who are interesting also in terms of their complicated relationships with "Englishness." For younger women emerging as poets, there are plenty of role models and lots of work to read. *Writing Women*, the Newcastle-based journal, continues to flourish. Female tutors are well-represented in Arvon Foundation and similar creative writing courses. The judges of the 1993 Arvon International Poetry Competition are all women. The sheer variety of poetry written by women is at last being acknowledged, and the presence of satirists like Fiona Pitt-Kethley and Wendy Cope makes it easy to refute the old insult that women do not have a sense of humor. The most recent anthology of contemporary British poetry breaks the mold by including seventeen female poets to thirty-eight male.[52]

It seems fitting to conclude with Elizabeth Bishop's well-known statement about the role of gender in poetry. Bishop did not wish her poetry to appear in women-only anthologies. Rumens had to take it out of the second edition of *Making for the Open* on the request of the executor. Adcock managed to get permission to include some poems, as long as she printed

Bishop's disclaimer: "Undoubtedly gender does play an important part in the making of any art, but art is art and to separate writings, paintings, musical compositions, etc., into two sexes is to emphasize values in them that are not art."[53]

What I have tried to do is to explore the elusive "values" that Elizabeth Bishop relegates, rather uneasily, to a different arena—the arena that is "not art." It is not surprising that she does this, because she is comparing like with unlike: "Values" are, self-evidently, not the same thing as "art." "Art is art," she insists, as if she hoped that repetition would compel assent and knock on the head any debate about that teasing question "What is art?" The circle is thus firmly closed. But it is, I suggest, actually much more exciting to explore the "values . . . that are not art." Contemporary women's poetry forces the circle open, leading us out into a more explosive and exhilarating future than the dull blue sterility suggested by Rumens's "open" postfeminist road.

Notes

1. The subtitle of my essay, "one more word for balls," is from Sylvia Kantaris's "The Change." The poem is a sardonic response to derogatory comments about the kind of poetry written by "[t]he emotionally upset adolescent or middle-aged woman." Its epigraph, a quotation from Robin Skelton's *The Practice of Poetry*, emphasizes the ludicrous incongruity of middle-aged women writing poetry: "The spectacle is often both absurd and bewildering." Kantaris's poem offers a tongue-in-cheek reflection on the progress of a woman poet from the heady passions of her teenage through to her menopausal years, noting wryly that whatever stage of life she might be in, "woman" is invariably equated with overblown emotionality. Her sharp critique ends with the doubly ironic observation that only in old age will she finally "grasp the fact that in all fundamentals / poetry is one more word for balls." The poem is published in *Purple and Green: Poems by 33 Women Poets* (London: Rivelin Grapheme Press, 1985), 76. It is also in Kantaris's individual collection, *The Sea at the Door* (London: Secker & Warburg, 1985), 51.

2. Carol Rumens, ed. *Making for the Open: The Chatto Book of Post-Feminist Poetry 1964–1984* (London: Chatto & Windus, 1985). It was revised and reprinted in 1987. In the introduction to this second edition, Rumens tried to answer the angry criticisms provoked by her earlier tone. References in parentheses indicate which edition is being quoted from.

3. This failure to critique liberal humanist aesthetics is a feature of poetry criticism in Britain. Even the more theoretically sophisticated critics like Terry Eagleton revert to traditional humanist modes when reviewing poetry. For years, experimental poets have been complaining about the poetry establishment's failure to devote time or attention to their more radical approach. See, for example, Antony Easthope's article, "Why most contemporary poetry is so bad and how post-structuralism may be able to help," *PN Review 48*, vol. 12, no. 4 (1985): 36–38. Eric Mottram has championed the cause of these neglected poets, and recent publications from Paladin attempt to win recognition for their work. There are many women poets engaged in such experimental poetry—Maggie O'Sullivan, Geraldine Monk, and Denise Riley are three of the best known. There are signs that their work is beginning to receive attention from some feminist journals. See, for example, Wendy Mulford's article, "'Curved, Odd . . . Irregular': A Vision of Contemporary Poetry by Women," *Women: A Cultural Review* 1, no. 3 (winter 1990): 261–75. For the purposes of this article I shall concentrate on the more mainstream poetry selected for inclusion in the establishment publishers' "women's anthologies."

4. Kantaris finally lost patience with this popular habit of making derogatory references to anonymous poets. Infuriated by yet another review that relied on such an unsubstantiated version of the recent past, she wrote to the *Times Literary Supplement*: "Every poetic movement in our past and recent history seems to have been fully documented, with one exception: The Hysterical Women's Movement (1963–80). We know this movement existed because reviewers frequently mention it in relation to women poets who appear to have reacted against it . . . I . . . am only interested to know the names of the poets who have been . . . harshly castigated by Ian Hamilton as 'post-Plath hysterics' or 'muscular harpies of the Adrienne Rich school.' . . . These are only two amongst many examples of reviews and critical articles which measure the poets under consideration against The Hysterical Women's Movement, but in none of them are we given the names of members of that movement, or titles of the books they wrote. All we know is that their voices were almost uniformly 'shrill' or 'strident'" (*Times Literary Supplement,* 19 August 1983, 882). Her letter sparked off a lively debate, but none of the letters successfully addressed Kantaris's contention that this Hysterical Women's Movement was a largely fictional creation.

5. Rumens, *Making for the Open* (1987), xvii.

6. Rumens, *Making for the Open* (1985), xvi.

7. Virginia Woolf, *A Room of One's Own* (London & St. Albans: Granada, 1977), 99. Rumens, like Woolf, clearly fears that anger will pollute the purity of creative work. There are interesting parallels with nineteenth-century debates about the place of politics in poetry. Mrs. William Sharp, editing an anthology of women's poetry in 1887, was eager to prove that "it is as possible to form an anthology of 'pure poetry' from the writings of women as from those of men." Sharp's assertion that women

also write 'pure poetry' is particularly interesting; it suggests that the growth of the Victorian women's movement stimulated politically motivated protest poetry akin to that of what Kantaris dubs "The Hysterical Women's Movement," which is so frequently castigated today. *Holloway Jingles*, a collection of poetry by imprisoned suffragettes, is unlikely to have been a one-off phenomenon; no doubt many other "feminist" anthologies lie tucked away in second-hand bookshops throughout Britain.

8.   Rumens, *Making for the Open* (1985), xvii.

9.   Rumens, *Making for the Open* (1987), xiv.

10.   Ibid., xviii.

11.   Michael Hofmann, "Hopes and Resentments," *Times Literary Supplement*, 29 November 1985, 1370.

12.   Fleur Adcock, ed., *The Faber Book of Twentieth Century Women's Poetry* (London: Faber & Faber, 1987).

13.   Ibid., 1.

14.   In the introduction to his idiosyncratic selection of contemporary British poetry, Alvarez commented that "the concept of gentility still reigns supreme." He went on to explain what he meant by this term: "[G]entility is a belief that life is always more or less orderly, people always more or less polite, their emotions and habits more or less decent and more or less controllable; that God, in short, is more or less good." Writing in 1962, Alvarez noted that "[i]t is a stance which is becoming increasingly precarious to maintain. That the English have succeeded for so long owes a good deal to the fact that England is an island; it is, literally, insulated from the rest of the world" (*The New Poetry* [London: Penguin, 1962], 25). Contrary to his expectations, gentility's hold over creative minds in Britain has not proved to be too precarious. In a trenchant attack on the conservatism of English poetry, David Dabydeen asserts that the charge is still relevant. He goes further, suggesting that glib complacency is—and always has been—the hallmark of English verse, with its history of "colonizing the experience of others for the gratification of their own literary sensibilities" ("On Not Being Milton: Nigger Talk in England Today," in *The State of the Language*, ed. Christopher Ricks and Leonard Michaels [London: Faber & Faber, 1990], 11).

15.   Adcock, *Faber Book of Twentieth Century Women's Poetry*, 13.

16.   Strange as it may seem, it is not even safe to assume that the editor is entirely responsible for the selection of poems in her own anthology. Craig Raine, editor-in-chief at Faber, deleted "some 20%" of Adcock's final manuscript. Adcock writes that Raine "had a considerable amount of control over the contents—mostly in a negative way (he vetted my choices, and deleted some 20% of my selections), but also in that he insisted on the large representation of the 'Big 3' (left to myself I'd have included rather less Moore and Plath, although we agreed about Bishop). Every poem in the

book was chosen by me, but so were a number which aren't in it!" (personal correspondence, 13 August 1988).

17. Martin Booth, *British Poetry 1964–84: Driving through the Barricades* (London:
Routledge & Kegan Paul, 1985), 190.

18. Ibid., 191.

19. Ibid., 190.

20. Ibid., 188.

21. Andrew MacAllister, "An Interview with Carol Ann Duffy," *Bête Noire* 6 (winter
1988): 72.

22. Louise Bernikow, ed., *The World Split Open: Four Centuries of Women Poets in
England and America 1552-1950* (New York: Vintage, 1974; London: Women's Press,
1979), 6–7.

23. A. A. Kelly, ed., *Pillars of the House: An Anthology of Verse by Irish Women from
1690 to the Present* (Dublin: Wolfhound Press, 1987). All quotations taken from the
introduction.

24. Interview with Eavan Boland, in *Sleeping with Monsters: Conversations with
Scottish and Irish Women Poets*, ed. Rebecca E. Wilson and Gillean Somerville-Arjat
(Edinburgh: Polygon, 1990), 80. For a useful analysis of the problems of Boland's
aesthetic, see Clair Wills's essay, "Contemporary Irish Women Poets: The Privatisation
of Myth," in *Diverse Voices: Essays on Twentieth-Century Women Writers in English*, ed.
Harriet Devine Jump (Hemel Hempstead: Harvester Wheatsheaf, 1991), 248–72. In
the light of Kelly's pessimism, it is heartening to consider Caroline Halliday's observations on the striking originality of metaphors used by contemporary lesbian poets.
She notes a new freedom and confidence in their work, which translates into more
daring, vivid forms of imagery: "There is a difference between the use of these images
and the concern being expressed in 1979–80 in a London discussion of 'Writing about
Sex,' over 'how to say it.' The images have been changing, from fern fronds to wild
garlic, from cradles of petals to mussels raw in the strainer. The change marks a dramatic
increase in the freedom with which lesbians are viewing their bodies, and their poetry.
The images change our notions of ourselves, recognising their accuracy with excitement and some shock" ("'The Naked Majesty of God': Contemporary Lesbian Erotic
Poetry," in *Lesbian and Gay Writing: An Anthology of Critical Essays*, ed. Mark Lilly
(London: Macmillan, 1990), 93.

25. Rumens, *Making for the Open* (1985), xviii.

26. Joanna Russ comments on the consistency of this statistic across a wide range
of anthologies in *How To Suppress Women's Writing* (London: Women's Press, 1983),
79. Rebecca O'Rourke offers some more recent examples of the huge imbalance in
supposedly mixed-sex, general anthologies, in "Mediums, Messages and Noisy
Amateurs," *Women: A Cultural Review* 1, no. 3 (winter 1990): 275–86. She also looks
at the ratio of men to women in the current poetry lists of some of the larger poetry

publishers. Bloodaxe has the highest ratio with fifty-one men to nineteen women; Faber has fifty-nine men to nine women; Carcanet seventy-six men to twelve women; Chatto ten men to three women (statistics taken from p. 281). My own research suggests that these ratios remain the same in recent Caribbean anthologies, too.

27. Stevie Davies, reviewing Rumens's anthology alongside Jeni Couzyn's *Bloodaxe Book of Contemporary Women Poets*, comments on the "flattening effect of the rationalization of the poets' voices by the principle of editorial selection." She goes on to observe how even the characteristically radical protest of Adrienne Rich appears muted by Rumens's careful choice of poems and by the surrounding atmosphere of the anthology ("Extending The Territory," *PN Review 49*, vol. 12, no. 5 [1986]: 49).

28. See Suzanne Juhasz, "The Critic as Feminist: Reflections on Women's Poetry, Feminism, and the Art of Criticism," for fuller discussion of this phenomenon (*Women's Studies* 5 (1977): 113–27).

29. Judith Kazantzis, "The Errant Unicorn," in *On Gender and Writing*, ed. Michèlene Wandor (London: Pandora Press, 1983), 25.

30. Sally Minogue, "Prescriptions and Proscriptions: Feminist Criticism and Contemporary Poetry," in *Problems for Feminist Criticism*, ed. Sally Minogue (London: Routledge, 1990), 191.

31. Eavan Boland, "The Woman Poet: Her Dilemma," *Stand* (winter 1986–87): 44.

32. Jane E. Thomas, "'The Intolerable Wrestle With Words': The Poetry of Carol Ann Duffy," *Bête Noire* 6 (winter 1988): 78-88.

33. Gillian Allnutt subscribes to the former position. Introducing her selection, "Quote Feminist Unquote Poetry" (in *the new british poetry*, ed. Gillian Allnutt et al. [London: Paladin, 1988], 77), she writes: "To put any sociologically descriptive tag— be it black, working-class, gay, lesbian or feminist—in front of poetry, is to limit its possibilities. To me, poetry must be one of the few areas of language use where it is acceptable, indeed obligatory, to try and break up the boxes we ordinarily think in . . ." Allnutt expresses the hope that poetry can transcend political categories. Such communication across these constructed categories is desirable, but it is also important to keep hold of more mundane materialist matters. Similarly (in "Blood, Bread and Poetry: The Location of the Poet," in *Selected Prose 1979-85* [London: Virago, 1987], 178), Adrienne Rich warns against "the falsely mystical view of art that assumes a kind of supernatural inspiration, a possession by universal forces unrelated to questions of power and privilege or the artist's relation to bread and blood."

34. See Jan Montefiore, *Feminism and Poetry: Language, Experience, Identity in Women's Writing* (London: Pandora Press, 1987); Minogue, *Problems for Feminist Criticism*. Liz Yorke's study is the most promising, but it focuses entirely on North American poets: *Impertinent Voices: Subversive Strategies in Contemporary Women's Poetry* (London: Routledge, 1991).

35. Montefiore, *Feminism and Poetry*, 95–96.

36. Marge Piercy gestures towards this approach in the preface to *Early Ripening: American Women's Poetry Now* (London: Pandora Press, 1987). She writes: "Women poets have created a large body of contemporary work that I think must change the assessment and finally the shape of all of the writing of our era. It is really about time to do an anthology of poetry that includes male poets in that same landscape and looks at them in the perspective of the exciting work that women are producing" (p. 2). Reviewing the anthology in the United Kingdom, Lawrence Sail assumes that this is merely a reversal of sexist practices, enquiring daintily, "is there a hint here of wheels turning full circle?" (*Stand* 30, no. 3 [summer 1989]: 80). Judging by this reaction, the full radical impact of revisiting men's poetry from the perspective of women needs to be spelled out rather more carefully if the point is to be grasped by mainstream critics.

37. Rumens, *Making for the Open* (1987), xvi.

38. Minogue, "Prescriptions and Proscriptions," 213, 220.

39. Ibid., p. 224.

40. Kelly, *Pillars of the House*, 9.

41. Rumens, *Making for the Open* (1985), xviii.

42. Jeni Couzyn, ed., *The Bloodaxe Book of Contemporary Women Poets: Eleven British Writers* (Newcastle: Bloodaxe, 1985), 15.

43. Hofmann, "Hopes and Resentments," 1370.

44. Davies, "Extending The Territory," 32.

45. This is precisely what Clair Wills does in reviewing a number of recent women poets in the "Among their Selves," *Times Literary Supplement,* 24 June 1988, 715: "If the notion of a distinctively female poetic voice was ever seriously entertained, it is unquestionably undermined by the variety of forms and range of styles in these six recent volumes." It is worth pointing out that it was not feminist critics who started the habit of grouping women together for reviews. All they have done is to try to make something positive from a loose gathering that is currently used only, as above, to mock notions of solidarity or similarities. As Ostriker notes, "the useful generic labels, 'American poets' or 'French poets' do not generate the same scepticism; no one expects them to demonstrate uniformity." See Alicia Suskin Ostriker's *Stealing the Language: The Emergence of Women's Poetry in America* (London: Women's Press, 1986), 9.

46. Minogue, "Prescriptions and Proscriptions," 191.

47. Rumens's assumption that "feminist" poetry is indifferent to evaluative criteria seems to be widely shared. In "Quote Feminist Unquote Poetry," Gillian Allnutt suggests that it is "still synonymous with mere propaganda" (p. 77), and Sally Minogue, in "Prescriptions and Proscriptions," appears to think one of the defining characteristics of feminist poetry is that "it should be unconcerned with criticism, or should view criticism as patriarchally based and therefore suspect" (p. 191).

48. In "Mediums, Messages and Noisy Amateurs" (p. 280), O'Rourke offers some more recent examples of the huge imbalance in supposedly mixed-sex, general anthologies.

49. Ibid.

50. Stevie Davies discusses the unpromising implications of the cover of *Making for the Open*: "The cover-design presents the Open as an unpeopled blue world traversed by a geometrically straight road. Its signpost, an uninscribed white arrow, directs the eye to a uniformly flat horizon over which the sun hangs low. The ungendered world predicted by the Introduction resembles a vacated planet, lacking a dynamic of creation, sealed in its own unanimity, without boundaries or enclosures" ("Extending The Territory," 30). See Suzanne Juhasz for further exploration of feminist reading strategies that challenge conventional aesthetics: "The traditional critic is one who accepts the rules of both traditional literature and traditional criticism and applies them to whatever poem comes before him or her. The feminist critic does not so readily accept any tradition. She (or he) is thus in a better position to judge the work on its own terms; to be more sensitive to the fact that it may have its own terms, terms which she may never have encountered before: to be interested in new terms" ("The Critic as Feminist: Reflections on Women's Poetry, Feminism, and the Art of Criticism," *Women's Studies* 5 [1977]: 118).

51. Debjani Chatterjee and Rashida Islam, eds., *Barbed Lines* (Sheffield: Yorkshire Art Circus and Bengali Women's Support group, 1990). Seema Jena reviews this in *Poetry Review* 83, no. 1 (Spring 1993): 24.

52. Michael Hulse, David Kennedy, and David Morley, eds., *The New Poetry* (Newcastle: Bloodaxe, 1993). I only hope my optimism about the precarious state of unexamined liberal humanist approaches to poetry will not prove as premature as Alvarez's prophecy on the demise of the disease of gentility in English poetry.

53. Adcock, *Faber Book of Twentieth Century Women's Poetry*, 9.

CHAPTER ELEVEN

Bass History is A-Moving: Black Men's Poetry in Britain

Alastair Niven

Defining national identities has been one of the major preoccupations of postcolonial discourse. In 1947 a ship called *Windrush* left Jamaica, carrying the first generation of "immigrants" to Great Britain. In an atmosphere of postwar reconstruction, it was obvious in Britain itself that these immigrants would give necessary assistance in the development of the new dispensations for the National Health Service, transport, and urban development that the Attlee government had been elected to bring about. Few people looked ahead to the time when an increasingly pressured economy would create mass unemployment, to the consequences of losing an empire, or to the tensions that are endemic in a multicultural society. Had they done so, they might still have thought positively about the implications of the social upheaval that migration on a large scale would effect. Britain had never been a monocultural land. Its language, although now used worldwide, was a composite of many origins, among them Latin, Norse, Teutonic, French, Italian, and latterly Hindustani. Its role in European history had often been to receive minorities who had become disaffected or economically deprived in their own lands—Jews, Huguenots, and Irish, for example. The quadripartite political structure of the United Kingdom was itself evidence of indigenous diversification. Immigrants from the Caribbean or from the Indian subcontinent could be forgiven for believing that they were coming to a land of legendary hospitality with a proven capacity to absorb new groups of peoples.

This is not the place to test whether that expectation was justified.

293

Indeed, there is great need to gather together the reminiscences of the *Windrush* generation, both those from the West Indies and those from Asia, to see if the past fifty years of their lives have been lived as they thought they might be when they first arrived in Britain. It is enough to remember that racial disharmony has sometimes disfigured the political and social landscape in this period and that some parliamentarians, such as Enoch Powell and Winston Churchill's eponymous grandson, have sought to fan it in disingenuous attempts to speak up for a spurious notion of white British homogeneity. The fact of the matter is that postwar immigration provided another layer in the ongoing historical process of British multiculturalism. It occurred, however, at a moment when a self-regarding myth of what constituted British greatness was in terminal decay. This myth had been necessary to the maintenance of imperialism and had been creatively appropriated by Churchill in the Second World War. It depended upon a unitary concept of Britishness. Racial difference was anathema to it.

The first writers among the new arrivals did not seek to define themselves in terms of national identity. Paradoxically, the matter needed to be considered only when signs of rejection appeared in their host community. A note of anticipation of what the new life might hold, however, is there from early on, as we detect in E. A. Markham's poem "Inheritance," written in the late 1950s:

> The topless native
> of our ship trusts
> her blue eyes
> for she knows already
> how this trip will end.
>
> And I half-believe
> her, barely doubt
> the dog-eared
> evidence from a diary
> she will publish.
>
> She says it all: she
> knows the man I'm

on my way to be. My
predecessors have armed her
with my secrets.[1]

The poem synthesizes the experience of the *Windrush*-style arrivant, who will abandon his traditional culture in the new society he is about to enter with sea memories of voyages long before, stretching back to the slave ships. The "topless native" is both the rejected woman of the Caribbean island from which the "I" of the poem has departed and a mythic presence like the figure on the prow of an eighteenth-century ship. A sense of recurrent history pervades Markham's poem, as though his own generation half expects to reincarnate slave histories of earlier times.

If, therefore, such writers speak for a generation that anticipates its own rejection even as it moves away from its roots, then it follows that they might not seek to define themselves in any kind of national terms, British or West Indian. The concept *black British poetry* is predicated on a sense of belonging to, or striving to belong to, even while seeking its redefinition, a national entity called "Britain." Because in the aftermath of empire communities fragment and migrate, before possibly reconstituting themselves in other orders and dispensations, it may be purposeless to speak of them with the old labels. Certainly in the last twenty years there has been much unresolved debate about terminology, with the term *black* often ceasing to be applied only to peoples of some African descent. Frequently it has been transmogrified into *Black* and has been allowed to encompass the Asian diaspora (from the Indian subcontinent and China). I follow the view that *Black* should be read no more literally as a description of race or color than *Augustan* is of style or origin.

When in his influential anthology *News For Babylon* (1984) James Berry collects together examples of what he designated "West Indian–British" poetry, he cites no examples from writers of an older generation than his own (he was born in 1924). He does, however, pay tribute to Francis Williams, a Jamaican taken up by the Duke of Montagu and educated at Cambridge University as part of a typical aristocratic social experiment of the time to learn if a black person "given the right circumstances could acquit himself as creditably as a white man." Williams's Latin ode to Governor of Jamaica George Haldane was printed in Edward Long's *History of Jamaica* in

1774 and reveals someone utterly at home in the educated literary conventions of the time. Does one call such a work a minor example of English Augustanism or a foundation brick of the Caribbean cultural edifice? Similarly, are Henry Derozio and Toru Dutt, Indian poets admired in nineteenth-century Britain, elegant reflectors of contemporary taste or swimmers striking out from the colonial coastland in a first attempt to assert an independent cultural identity? I think it is fair to say that none of the pioneering pre-twentieth-century names in Caribbean or Indian subcontinent poetry had any notable impact on the leading West Indian, Indian, or black British poets of today. With the emergence of Claude McKay, A. J. Seymour, and Louise Bennett that began to change, because these poets had discovered not only an independent attitude but also indigenously rooted language and forms. The same was true of Sarojini Naidu and Sri Aurobindo in India. It remains the case, however, that it is far more difficult to trace in either the Caribbean or the Indian ancestries of black British poetry a lineage of influence comparable to that which informs most prominent white British poetry of the modern period. This is partly because black expressiveness is more inherently oral than white, which, with rare exceptions, has lost much significant contact with balladry, song, or folk material. It is also, however, evidence of the deracination that lies behind so much black British writing. "I have crossed an ocean," says Grace Nichols in her poem "Epilogue," "I have lost my tongue / from the root of the old / one / a new one has sprung."[2]

James Berry, who arrived from a Jamaican rural background (via the United States) in 1948, is generally considered in Britain to be the doyen of black poets. He has been officially recognized by the state with the somewhat ironically named Order of the British Empire, and his literary awards include first prize among thirty thousand entries for the 1981 National Poetry Competition. His winning poem, "Fantasy of an African Boy," begins by articulating that sense of displacement and otherness that almost all Caribbean writers perceive at the heart of their societies:

> Such a peculiar lot
> we are, we people
> without money, in daylong
> yearlong sunlight, knowing
> money is somewhere, somewhere.[3]

This is the dream of émigrés over many decades. Berry's poem purports to be the imaginings of an African boy starved of nutrition and education— "We can't read money for books. Yet without it we don't . . . open gates in other countries"—but it works just as well as for any desperate person driven to contemplate departure from the country of their birth. Berry has proved to be not only a prolific poet (his collections include *Chain of Days* [1985], *Fractured Circles* [1979], *When I Dance* [1988], and two sequences published together as *Lucy's Letters and Loving* [1982]) but also a noted children's writer and, latterly, a novelist. He has even turned his hand to verse drama with *Song of a Bluefoot Traveller* (1993), based on the theme of his anthology of poetry by West Indians in Britain, *Bluefoot Traveller* (1976).

James Berry, like so many of the poets considered in this article, is a superb renderer of his own verse. The oral characteristic of much black British poetry obviously derives from traditions inherent in African orature. In Berry's work it sometimes manifests itself in sheer entertainment:

> You so full of you
> fe me
> I lose miself
> fe you
> Boonoonoonoos gal
> you so roun an sweet[4]

It makes Berry a delightful writer for children, and although his best endeavors in this field have tended to be in fiction (*A Thief in the Village and Other Stories*, for example, won the prestigious Smarties Prize for Children's Writing), he has proved in *When I Dance*, a collection of poems substantially aimed at young people, that he has an excellent ear for the nuances of youth.

> Next week I'll leave school.
> Next week, nil, fulltime—
> me—for good!
>
> Yonks now
> nobody bothered.
> No teacher scrawled 'work harder.'

They'd twigged on.
Their words were whispers
to a rock. So
They gave up on me . . .[5]

It is in the Lucy poems, perhaps consciously named in homage to
Wordsworth, that James Berry distills for a generation of displaced Caribbean people in England their nostalgia and sense of loss. The earliest of
these were published in the mid 1970s and were immediately popular in a
vein reminiscent of the creolized English intimacies of Louise Bennett, who
as a performer and writer had been the strongest local influence upon as-
pirant poets of Berry's generation. In his introduction to *Lucy's Letters* Berry
writes, "I try to let Lucy be herself. I try to let her be as I sense her, hear her
and know her. I try not to impose my own ideals and points of view on
her."[6] Lucy has settled in London but does not want to sever her ties with
her home village, where her correspondent Leela cannot receive too much
news from the metropolis. We have only Lucy's side of the letter exchange,
but it is evident that Leela herself is a tantalizing character desperate for
gossip from the great city ("An' Leela, darlin', no, I never / meet the Queen
in flesh").[7] Lucy speaks for a generation of increasingly bewildered Caribbean people who have had to accept that their children have different
perspectives from themselves: "They different breed, me dear . . . Westindies
is jus' a place parents / born."[8] Furthermore, the impersonality of the city
frequently contrasts with the fertility and generosity of the island village,
to which Lucy occasionally returns on holiday:

Leela, I really a sponge
you know, for traffic noise,
for work noise, for halfway
intentions, for halfway smiles,
for clockwatchin' and col' weather.
I hope you don' think I gone
too fat when we meet.
I booked up to come an' soak
the children in daylight.[9]

Chain of Days marked a new maturing of Berry's work. For a start, it was published by Oxford University Press, much earlier work having been under the imprint of New Beacon Books. This kind of shift has bedeviled smaller publishers for many years. They see their best talents poached by houses that can pay the author better and can promote publications more effectively. For the writer this presents a dilemma, for the ethos of the mainstream press is likely to be less committed to a context of appropriate related work within which their own poems can fit. It is an important matter to consider in the case of black writers especially. They have often been sidelined by the established literary press, which tends to disregard publications emanating from nonmainstream sources. This cycle of marginalization of authors from minority backgrounds can be broken, as James Berry has proved, but it may be that a truly radical writer in either ideas or forms would be unable to make the concessions that are usually required if a mainstream publisher is to be involved. I raise this matter here because it would be impossible to write about Berry without admitting that his approachability, tolerance, and humane understanding, all prevalent features of his poetry, have led some to regard him almost as an Uncle Tom figure in the black literary scene in Britain. It is a wholly unjust view, but almost inevitably when a black writer manages to attain the degree of recognition that marks Berry, some will say that it has been on other people's terms.

In *Chain of Days* there are poems far moved from matters of race and deracination, often written about states of mind ("Reconsidering") or being ("A Companionship"). The title poem is a reverie about lost youth and remembered parents—"A joy is trapped in me"[10]—and it is notable for its generalized social and cultural setting: "On a summer road under swinging palms / a chain of days showed me bewildered." Though the poem is long, it shows Berry's new concentration of language, precise, evocative, and sometimes almost crystalline: "I meet my mother's new-born in the secret / birth room strong with asafetida."[11] In this collection Berry also looks at many sides of the post-colonial world, which is always his major subject matter. Here are many echoes of black history, scenes from contemporary black life in Britain, among the Rastafarians for example, and a confident range of tones and forms. Berry shows himself to be the most versatile of the black poets currently at work in Britain. A short poem, "Two Black

Labourers on a London Building Site," sums up the humorous social detail
and underlying cultural dislocation that are at the heart of much of Berry's
writing:

> Been a train crash.
>   Wha'?
> Yeh—tube crash.
>   Who the driver?
> Not a black man.
>   Not a black man?
> I check that firs'.
>   Thank Almighty God.
> 'Bout thirty people dead.
>   Thirty people dead?
> Looks maybe more.
>   Maybe more?
> Maybe more.
>   An' black man didn' drive?
> No. Black man didn' drive.[12]

I have heard James Berry read this poem to audiences on many occasions,
and it has never failed either to amuse or to chasten them, for in its elementary humor lies embedded the neurosis of an immigrant culture that has
grown used to being the butt of racial prejudice.

James Berry was one of several Caribbean writers who first made the
presence of black poetry felt in Britain during the 1950s. Several of them
returned from time to time to the West Indies for replenishment. Some,
such as the playwright and theater director Jimi Rand, who originated in
Barbados, were to establish higher profiles in other genres. Jamil Ali from
Guyana has made a mark as a scriptwriter, and Faustin Charles from Trinidad
as a critic and fiction writer, though both are poets who take off from the
foundations laid by Berry.

Of the older generation of black poets who have come to Britain from
the Caribbean, E. A. Markham and A. L. Hendriks have been outstanding.
Markham has held many writing attachments in universities (most recently
for two years at the University of Ulster, where his own minority back-

ground—he was born in Montserrat—struck particular nerve ends in the internecine complexities of Northern Ireland). Markham has been a prolific poet and has been published in leading poetry journals such as *Ambit*, of which he is an assistant editor, and by prominent poetry publishers such as Anvil Press, which attempt no special espousal of black authors. One emphasizes this because so many of the poets considered here have felt "ghettoized" by the circumstances of British literary publishing. Markham, like Berry, has been an important influence, not only on account of his own poetry but because of his editing and anthologizing work. His most recent contribution has been *Hinterland: Caribbean Poetry from the West Indies and Britain*, in which doyens of the Caribbean poetry world, such as Louise Bennett, Martin Carter, and Derek Walcott, are placed alongside not only Markham himself and Berry, but younger players in the British landscape such as Fred D'Aguiar and Linton Kwesi Johnson.

In *Human Rites: Selected Poems 1970–1982*, E. A. Markham demonstrated one of the widest ranges among contemporary poets working in Britain. In a sequence of early poems centered on a poetic alter ego called Lambchops, Markham is often very funny and quite forgetful of racial nuances. Here are the opening lines of "Lambchop's Ally":

> Now is the summer of his disrespect.
> He passes oncoming women on the left
> disdaining a glance at the hopeful strip
>
> of breast—he's been five hours now past
> indignity, and still carries before him
> (like a fireman's ladder at full stretch)
>
> the weight of his first printed poem—
> an arrow in the crowd.[13]

Much of the poetry concerns love or explorations of Markham's Caribbean origins. This continues to be so in his recent collection, *Towards the End of a Century*. In many of Markham's poems one is unaware that the author is black. These are the tender or observant utterances of a writer obsessed first of all with delicacies of language rather than with historical injustices.

(Who said it must end here?)
The hymn fades out: they look up
from their knees at her,
loose-flowing, a tightness
of flesh or tension, mocking . . .

Dead lips can't speak her intention.[14]

These lines are from a short poem about a new widow, who is both comic and pathetic. Markham's writing is always poised, but it is often more private or ironic than Berry's and perhaps for this reason has never gained the same following. His subject is often poetry itself, or the art of writing it.

A. L. Hendriks (1922–92) was so itinerant that it is questionable whether he should be included in this study. Jamaican by origin, and indeed at one time chairman of the Jamaican Arts Council, he lived for long periods in England and at the time of his death had just moved to the south coast from rural Bedfordshire. His work appeared regularly in the standard poetry magazines, and eight collections in all were published before he died. Although in a poem such as "Jamaican Small Gal"[15] he could use creolized English with conviction, his verse is usually fastidious and often referential. The same is true of John La Rose, who came to England in the 1950s and became a key player in the Caribbean Artists Movement (recently documented by Anne Walmsley).[16] Perhaps because as the founder and mainstay of New Beacon Books La Rose has been so potent an influence in the development of indigenous black publishing and bookselling in Britain, his own writing has been overshadowed by that of the authors he himself discovered or promoted. He is, though, a fine poet, as his poem "Connecting Link," with its distant echoes of slave history, bears out:

> The lineal connection
> Between space and time
> Tangles like ship's rope
>
> No coils unwind
> But stretch their stench
> To unobtained oblivion

Torment,
Twined in an underbrush
Of corroding custom,
Unwinds itself in inky blood lettings
Unstatisticated.

Memory
Mounts its past
In muddled pride.[17]

The generation of Berry, Hendriks, and La Rose was succeeded by that of E. A. Markham and Faustin Charles. They in turn have seen come forward a new generation of poets who have mainly known Britain, rather than the Caribbean, as their home. Few poets in Britain of any origin have more fervent followings than do Linton Kwesi Johnson and Benjamin Zephaniah. David Dabydeen and Fred D'Aguiar are popular with younger audiences, though theirs is a more consciously literary tradition, effective orally but evidently aware of printed traditions in both Caribbean and English poetry. There is also the phenomenon of poets, such as Lemn Sissay and John Lyons, who have notable regional followings, though reputation to some extent eludes them in London or in the national publications.

Anger and comedy go hand in hand in the work of many of the leading black British poets, often in an intimidating manner. Linton Kwesi Johnson, who came to urban England from rural Jamaica when he was eleven years old, has one of the largest popular followings, but it is almost exclusively among black people. I have seen him hold a full theater rapt as he recites poems that appear banal on the printed page. The performance element is crucial, lending ironic overtones to words that could otherwise seem only exhortatory to black people or threatening to whites, such as those words repeatedly used from the title of a poem like "Time to Explode."[18]

Six years ago Benjamin Zephaniah, a black poet born in England, whose dub rhythms and entertaining personality have made him seem at times almost a part of the show-business world, became the butt of some press mockery when he applied for a fellowship at a Cambridge University college. His application failed for reasons that were not entirely risible, but it became clear that those in the university who pronounced adversely upon his work did so without any knowledge of its Caribbean roots. They paid exclusive regard to the effect of a fixed printed text, because European literary criticism has now raised that above all other values. The oral origins and musical links of Zephaniah's work, or the rapport with a live audience, which he achieves ahead of almost any white British poet, counted for nothing. All that his Cambridge judges could see were simplistic rhymes and a discomforting social aggression:

> I decided to take a walk to meet some friends,
> I was standing at the door, I was talking to a girl,
> I told her that I write,
> she said I must recite,
> and then I saw a fight.
> There was many, they looked like skinheads,
> they were shouting 'National Front, National Front,'
> they were shouting killa, killa, kill a blackman.
> they were shouting kill a blackman lover.[19]

Perhaps the incomprehension of Leavis-trained Cambridge academics when they are faced with such confrontational verse will cause few sleepless nights in the black literary community, but it means that black writers in this vein are in danger of marginalizing themselves by creating an artistic ghetto in which outsiders have no place. This process is positively welcomed by some younger black critics—by Kwesi Owusu and Amon Saba Saakana, for example. Owusu's ideological commitment to populist and radical literature at least seeks to define a clear aesthetic for black British writing, in which orature and the links with Africa have primacy. It is not surprising that, with the Senegalese poet-critic Ahmed Sheikh, he set up Afrikan Dawn, a performance group of poets who throughout most of the 1980s made regular *griot*-style appearances in Britain and elsewhere, with musical accompaniment. They consciously sought to continue the tradition of the West African *griot*, who has a defined function in the community to be a poet storyteller. The model for this approach to poetry is, paradoxically, an intellectual one and lies in Nigeria, where a generation of younger critics led by Chinweizu has thrown down challenges both to the Eurocentrically trained academic community and to the supposed elitism of the poet and dramatist Wole Soyinka. The patron of such a view is the Kenyan writer (thought not a poet) Ngugi wa Thiong'o, who, though he has, for political reasons, lived in Britain and the United States since 1979, has never become part of the black British or black American literary scene. Owusu's articulate but highly political stance has a hard core of adherents, but it is difficult to see it seeping easily into the attitudes of schoolteachers, librarians, and reviewers, who will be responsible for enlarging the educated person's awareness of black British writing.

Somewhere between the two exclusivities of the Gutenberg-obsessed Cambridge view and the neo-Marxism of Owusu lies a critical path that will allow orally derived works of contemporary poetry, often expressed in nonmetropolitan forms of English, to be appreciated alongside conventionally acceptable works. David Dabydeen manifests confidence in both modes. As the author of *Hogarth's Blacks*, an erudite study of the placing of black people in eighteenth-century English art, and of two novels, the second of which, *Disappearance,* is particularly acute about degenerative historical processes, Dabydeen has shown himself to be, when appropriate, an elegant and penetrating analyst. In *Slave Song*, however, which won the Commonwealth Poetry Prize in 1985, and in *Coolie Odyssey*, which came out in 1988 by way of marking the 150th anniversary of the presence of an Indian population in the Caribbean, Dabydeen frequently adopts a creole form of English that articulates much of the frustrated anguish of suppressed peoples. Here is an excerpt from one of the most pained poems in *Slave Song*, "Love Song":

> Black men cover wid estate ash
> E ead haad an dry like a calabash,
> Dut in e nose-hole, in e ear-hole,
> Dut in e soul, in e battie-hole.

> All
> day
> sun
> bun
> tongue
> bun

all
day
troat
cut
haat
hut
wuk na dun, na dun, na dun!
Hack! Hack! Hack! Hack!
Cutlass slip an cut me cack![20]

The monotony of cane-cutting is caught in the staccato lines along with the historic indignity of the black slave's predicament. The fourteen poems that made up *Slave Song* were published with extensive notes and translations (ten years later it seems less likely that such conscientious explications would be required); in writing of the above lines, the author refers to "the deep self-disgust of the second stanza in which the cane-cutter recognizes by contrast his own existence in scorching daylight filth."[21] Yet the poem is truly a "Love Song," redolent with tenderness:

Moon-eye
Blue like blue-saki wing,
Silk fracktumble an splash on me face like wata-fall
an yuh dance an yuh call
In de night.[22]

Dabydeen's poetry has great versatility, for he moved from the linked sequence of *Slave Song* to a more miscellaneous collection in *Coolie Odyssey*. Here the language is not always creolized.

His mother dropped a new child every year
And all affection was crowded out.
His mother was a sackful of crabs in her womb, scratching
Up, mashing
Up, clawing
For air,

Now you must surely see
Why he seeks
The wide space and sole portion of your heart
In which to be singularly free.[23]

Dabydeen originated in Guyana, an astonishingly productive country in literary terms. It has been the birthplace of Grace Nichols, Wilson Harris, Fred D'Aguiar, John Agard, and Marc Matthews, to say nothing of the major poets Martin Carter, Jan Carew, and, by adoption, Ian McDonald, all of whom remained in Guyana. Harris is chiefly known as a philosophical and metaphysical novelist and essayist; his twentieth novel appeared in 1993. He has often been nominated for the Nobel Prize, and it is perhaps only his intellectual impenetrability for the ordinary reader that has prevented him from receiving it, for his fiction is the most formally ambitious Caribbean writing that exists. It is commonplace to say that his prose is poetic, but less frequently recognized is the poetry he wrote early in his career. In *Eternity to Season*, published in Georgetown in 1954 but reissued in London by New Beacon Books in 1978 as a conscious act of heritage building, he set out embryonically the agenda for his great sequence of novels exploring the Guyanese hinterland and pre-Columbian concepts of time. Settled in Britain for nearly forty years, Harris rarely returned directly to poetry, and as a consequence he might not fit too easily into this essay. His influence on Dabydeen (whose *Disappearance* is written as an echoing critique of Harris's *The Secret Ladder*) and on D'Aguiar is readily acknowledged by both, the latter dedicating his poem "Frail Deposits" (in *British Subjects*) to Harris, whose company on a visit back to Guyana is recalled within it.

Fred D'Aguiar at the time of this writing is resident in America, but his work as poet and dramatist has been firmly based in England since the days of his secondary school education there. His first collection, *Mama Dot* (1985), was largely about Guyana, a coming-to-terms with the poet's past. In *Airy Hall* (1989) he interconnects Guyana and Britain. In the long poem "1492," published at the time of the Columbus quincentenary, his theme is colonialism. It is in the punningly titled 1993 volume *British Subjects* that D'Aguiar most directly examines what it is like to be black in Britain, though two years before, in the historically eye-opening and theatrically adventurous

play *A Jamaican Airman Foresees His Death,* he had done so through the eyes
of West Indian servicemen based there during the Second World War. The
ambivalence of his response to Britain is obvious in a poem such as "Home":

> These days whenever I stay away too long,
> anything I happen to clap eyes on,
> (that red telephone box) somehow makes me
> miss here more than anything I can name.
>
> My heart performs a jazzy drum solo
> when the crow's feet on the 747
> scrape down at heathrow. H.M. Customs . . .
> I resign to the usual inquisition,
>
> telling me with Surrey loam caked
> on the tongue, home is always elsewhere.
> I take it like an English middleweight
> with a questionable chin, knowing
>
> my passport photo's too open-faced,
> haircut wrong (an afro) for the decade;
> the stamp, British Citizen not bold enough
> for my liking and too much for theirs.[24]

British Subjects is in some respects the most mature group of poems about
Britain that any black poet has yet produced. Many moods are expressed,
and there are moments of almost surreal humor, as when the poet imagines
his color has drained from him onto pillows in British guest houses
("Colour"), or when he satirically observes "Thirteen Views of a Penis." The
poems are historically alert ("At the Grave of an Unknown African") and
deeply dependent on the presence of water—the sea at Whitley Bay and the
River Thames, in particular. D'Aguiar understands the central paradox of
the British personality, that it is both insular and harmonizing, as though
isolated by the waves yet part of the international flow of a great river.

John Agard is one of the most popular poets in Britain. I can think of
no richer performer among the new generation of writers, not all of them

black, who regard oral communication with an audience as every bit as important as the publishing of texts. Agard has perfect timing and is by turns funny, tender, and assertive, and he couples linguistic energy with a directness of utterance that appeals to all age groups. Many of his best poems are for children. For years he has been much in demand to give poetry workshops and to recite aloud to young people at the Commonwealth Institute in London, at the South Bank Centre where he held a residency throughout 1993, or in schools up and down the country. His mockery of white lifestyles and his delight in the absurdities of human pretension are evident in many of his best poems. A favorite with audiences is "Finders Keepers":

> This morning on the way to Charing Cross
> I found a stiff upper lip
> lying there on the train seat
>
> Finders Keepers
> I was tempted to scream
>
> But something about that stiff upper lip
> left me speechless
>
> It looked so abandoned so unloved
> like a frozen glove
> nobody bothers to pick up
>
> I could not bear to hand in
> that stiff upper lip
> to the Lost & Found
>
> So I made a place for it
> in the lining of my coat pocket
>
> and I said
> Come with me to the Third World
>
> You go thaw off.

This poem appears in *Mangoes and Bullets: Selected and New Poems 1972–84*.[25] Agard is the author of several collections both for adults and for children. He often appears at live readings with his wife, Grace Nichols. He is, however, almost totally ignored in critical journals by erudite commentators on modern poetry. As Benjamin Zephaniah found when applying to Cambridge University, there is a gulf between popular and academic perceptions of quality.

Marc Matthews has been settled in Britain only since 1984, and his subject matter is usually Guyanese. He is one of many black poets working in Britain whose work tends to be known in exclusive, and mainly Caribbean, circles. There are many such writers who, unlike Berry, Markham, D'Aguiar, Dabydeen, and Agard, remain impounded in a cultural ghetto. It is not always clear whether this is by intention or whether blame should lie with the failure of literary reviewers to go outside the standard poetry journals and familiar publishers' lists. The work of Amon Saba Saakana, previously known as Sebastian Clarke, is an example of this isolating process. In *Tones & Colours*, published in 1985 by his own publishing company, Karnak House, he even celebrates it:

> I is the king
> in this land-memory of myself:
> a screaming impassioned eye
> blood-kissed & blessed with ancient stirrings[26]

Saakana is attuned to Rastafarianism, the roots of which are in Ethiopia. Lemn Sissay is a Manchester-based "performance poet" whose parentage is Ethiopian. Though his work has its best effect when heard aloud, he has nevertheless by the age of twenty-six published three collections, of which the most recent, *Rebel without Applause* (1992), is rhythmically confident throughout and often very telling in its perception of the black person's daily existence in Britain:

> I don't need an occupation
> for basic rights to be taken away.
> I don't need an occupation
> to visit cells for a day.[27]

The story of male black British poetry is not exclusively derived from Caribbean or African origins. There are, however, far more poets with such roots than a short article can discuss. It is intriguing to know that several of the best black poets have very strong regional reputations and would indeed be claimed with pride as local poets even though their national reputation is modest. Lemn Sissay is one such example, but Levi Tafari in Liverpool, John Lyons in Manchester, and several others who also fall into this category suggest that black poetry in Britain is not just a London presence.

Writers whose roots are in the Indian subcontinent have made far less impact on British poetry than their African Caribbean counterparts. If this were an essay on black British fiction, then perhaps the case would be different. The dominating talent of Salman Rushdie would alone repair the balance, assisted by the likes of Kamala Markandaya, Farrukh Dhondy, and Amit Chaudhuri. One of the greatest of Indian writers, the historian and essayist Nirad C. Chaudhuri, has lived in Oxford for over twenty years and at the age of ninety-six continues to write prolifically in both English and Bengali. In the past, key writers such as the novelist Mulk Raj Anand or the critic Thurairajah Tambimuttu, who derived from Sri Lankan origins, lived long periods in Britain. Indeed, Tambimuttu wrote a poem entitled "Natarajan" for T. S. Eliot's sixtieth birthday and as early as 1941 had produced a verse collection called *Out of This War.* Neither in the past nor today, however, have many Asian poets of the first rank worked in Britain for long periods. Some have claimed that Vikram Seth, author of an award-winning collection of poems, *The Humble Administrator's Garden,* as well as *The Golden Gate,* a novel written in the form of a sonnet sequence, is a contributor to British writing because he visits Britain frequently and is a highly sophisticated stylist, but he is resolutely Indian by domicile and culture.

Mahmood Jamal is a filmmaker with some following as a poet. H. O. Nazareth also works in media-related concerns. Both are Indian poets capable of great vividness of image, as the following excerpts from their work demonstrate:

> My first son died
> when the cyclone struck.

I found his bone in the rubble.
Here it is under my pillow;
it talks to me when I am lonely.[28]

When he feels old
and something of a failure,
(saying 'Life was good though',
and saying 'Not much I could do')
and the sun insists on being brilliant,
Lobo contemplates dying, poetry,
and the kitchen table too.[29]

Neither poet, though their work is arrestingly direct, has written much about being resident in Britain. Mahmood Jamal has the more solid track record as a poet, for he has several collections to his name, ranging from a first appearance in the privately printed *Buddha's Death* to *Silence Inside a Gun's Mouth*, where his themes often have to do with racism and imperialism. His is an overtly political voice at times. This is not so with Prabhu Guptara, whose collections *Beginnings* and *Continuations* were published in Calcutta before he even contemplated settling in England, where he has made a mark as a cultural commentator. Indian poetry in English has produced major talents in the mother country—Nissim Ezekiel, Arun Kolatkar, A. K. Ramanujan, Jayanta Mahapatra, and many others. There are notable poets in Pakistan, Sri Lanka, and Bangladesh. In Britain itself there are interesting writers working in subcontinent languages—Saqi Farooqui in Urdu, for example. There are simply not yet, however, leading poets in Britain working in English with Indian subcontinent backgrounds, though Debjani Chatterjee and Sujata Bhatt (resident in Germany but published in Britain, where she often visits) suggest that women's voices will be heard the loudest.

Black British poetry in Britain, from whatever sources it derives, faces acute problems of gaining recognition by the arbiters of quality—the editors of leading literary journals, the chain booksellers, those who set examination syllabi in schools and colleges, those who buy books for libraries out of tight budgets. Its energy, even if strongest when the background is Caribbean, is so vibrant that one must assume that it will grow in reputation and acceptance. It will then perhaps be redundant to call it "black" at all.

Derek Walcott, after all, has commented that no one ever called him a black poet until he received the Nobel Prize, whereupon it became obligatory!

This essay has dealt only with male writers. Their gender is apparent in much of what they write, but I do not see it as the determining characteristic of the movement in which most of them feel they belong. That is clearly determined much more by race and cultural origins. Black poetry in Britain is now so strong a presence, so seeped into the mainstream of our literary life, that I hope this essay will be read as a celebration.

Notes

1. E. A. Markham, "Inheritance," in *Human Rites: Selected Poems 1970–1982* (London: Anvil, 1984), 20.

2. Grace Nichols, "Epilogue," in *i is a long memoried woman* (London: Karnak House, 1983), 80.

3. James Berry, *Chain of Days* (Oxford and New York: Oxford University Press, 1985), 18.

4. James Berry, "Boonoonoonoos," in *Fractured Circles* (London and Port of Spain: New Beacon Books, 1979), 30.

5. James Berry, "Getting Nowhere," in *When I Dance: Poems by James Berry*, illus. Sonia Boyce (London: Hamish Hamilton, 1988), 77.

6. James Berry, *Lucy's Letters and Loving* (London and Port of Spain: New Beacon Books, 1982), 9.

7. Ibid., 41.

8. Ibid., 49.

9. Ibid., 40.

10. Berry, *Chain of Days*, 4.

11. Ibid., 7.

12. Ibid., 28.

13. E. A. Markham, "Lambchop's Ally," in *Human Rites*, 109.

14. E. A. Markham, "A Challenge," in *Towards the End of a Century* (London: Anvil, 1989), 22.

15. A. L. Hendriks, *To Speak Simply: Selected Poems, 1961–86* (Surrey: Hippopotamas Press, 1988), 85.

16. Anne Walmsley, *The Caribbean Artists Movement: A Literary and Cultural History 1966–72* (London: New Beacon, 1992).

17. Antony (John) La Rose, "Connecting Link," in *Foundations* (London and Port of Spain: New Beacon Books, 1966), 13.

18. [We were unable to obtain permission to reproduce the quotation selected by the essayist. We refer readers instead directly to the poem in the following book. *Eds.*] Linton Kwesi Johnson, "Time to Explode," in *Dread Beat and Blood*, intr. Andrew Salkey (London: Bogle L'Ouverture, 1975), 38.

19.　Benjamin Zephaniah, "Call It What You Like!" in *City Psalms* (Newcastle upon Tyne, England: Bloodaxe Books, 1992), 41–42.

20. David Dabydeen, "Love Song," in *Slave Song* (Mundelstrup, Denmark: Dangaroo Press, 1984), 31.

21. Ibid., 57.

22. Ibid., 31.

23. David Dabydeen, *Coolie Odyssey* (Coventry: Dangaroo Press, 1988), 42.

24. Fred D'Aguiar, "Home," in *British Subjects* (Newcastle upon Tyne, England: Bloodaxe Books, 1993), 14.

25. John Agard, "Finders Keepers," in *Mangoes and Bullets: Selected and New Poems 1972–84* (London and Sydney: Pluto Press, 1985), 45.

26. Amon Saba Saakana, "Tapestry," in *Tones & Colours* (London: Karnak House, 1985), 13.

27. Lemn Sissay, "Occupations," in *Rebel Without Applause* (Newcastle upon Tyne, England: Bloodaxe, 1992), 18.

28. Mahmood Jamal, "A Peasant in Bengal," in *Silence Inside a Gun's Mouth* (London: Kala Press, 1984), 25.

29. H. O. Nazareth, "For Future Reference," in *Lobo* (London: Penumbra, 1984), 67.

CHAPTER TWELVE

Accent and Identity:
Women Poets of
Many Parts

C. L. Innes

> The cardinal winds have brought us here,
> Now battered, now buoyant, we survived.
> What mattered most was getting it clear:
> no longer strangers, we have arrived.
>
> —Debjani Chatterjee, "Arrival"

For readers in England, "multicultural" poetry tends to come in anthologies; it is associated with group identities and group enterprises. Anthologies of black British poetry followed some paces behind the anthologies of African and Caribbean poetry that were produced in the 1960s and 1970s by British-based publishers such as Heinemann and Longman, chiefly with African and Caribbean educational markets in mind. But these early collections were also picked up by the few tertiary and secondary educational institutions in Britain that sought to introduce multicultural curricula, partly in response to the existence of a generation of schoolchildren of Caribbean and African descent. It was not long before some of that generation began to write poetry too, while at the same time a number of those first immigrants who had come to work or to study in Britain in the fifties accepted, even if too many white British people did not, that they had come to stay. Of these, the two best-known poets were James Berry and E. A. Markham.[1] Berry emigrated from Jamaica in 1948 and edited two influential anthologies, *Bluefoot Traveller* (1976) and *News for Babylon* (1984), before winning the prestigious National Poetry Award for his *Collected Poems* in 1988. Markham, who had left Montserrat in the 1950s, has written and edited nearly a dozen volumes of poems and short stories. Both Berry and Markham were at one time editors of the minority arts magazine *Artrage*, which published poetry as well as reviews and notices of visual and performance arts.

Within British educational institutions, the term multicultural was really a code for two cultures, white and black, each perceived in fairly monolithic terms. So far as poetry was concerned, there was the standard canon of English authors, from Chaucer to Donne, Milton, Wordsworth, Keats, Eliot, Hughes, and Larkin. (Yeats might also be included as an English poet.) Then there was "multicultural" poetry, represented by one of the anthologies mentioned above, or possibly by a small selection of photocopied poems, and probably mainly African Caribbean/British. Despite their presence and considerable success in the United Kingdom, poets of Asian, Irish, Australian, New Zealand, or Canadian backgrounds rarely got a look-in. And women, it seemed, belonged on neither side of the divide, at least not before the 1980s, when Sylvia Plath began to appear on some school syllabi and James Berry's anthology of forty "West Indian–British" poets, *News for Babylon*, included four women—Grace Nichols, Valerie Bloom, Amryl Johnson, and Accabre Huntley.

It is in this context that the first collections of poetry by black British women appeared. Doubly or, indeed, triply excluded (for black women writers rarely appeared even in the anthologies of women's poetry that the pressure of feminism began to introduce in the 1970s), the poems they contained often addressed themselves to that sense of exclusion on grounds of gender and race perpetrated by black men as well as by white men and white women. Silenced or unheard because they were women and not white, black women demanded a hearing and spoke from the authority of bodily and personal experience and appearance. Although the first anthologies of poetry by women of color also declare a group identity, they differ from those devoted to black male poets in that they include Asian authors as well as those of African and Caribbean descent. For the black male poets, the implicit audience is generally neither race nor gender specific; many of the women poets acknowledge the support of women's writing collectives, whose presence is sometimes felt in the way that poems are explicitly directed to a black female audience and assume a shared experience.

The first such anthology, *A Dangerous Knowing*, published by the Sheba Collective in 1985, featured Barbara Burford, Gabriela Pearse, Grace Nichols, and Jackie Kay. All four of these poets are of African Caribbean or African British descent, but the preface to the collection is written by two Asian women, Pratibha Parma and Sona Osman. The title of the collection is taken from a phrase included in one of Barbara Burford's poems:

> Woman
> guard well your mystery:
> Your own creative fruitfulness.
> It is a bloody, an ancient,
> and a dangerous knowing,
> Beset with chimeras.
> But it is the design
> drawn on your bones;
> the song hidden under your tongue;
> the landscape painted
> on the inside of your skin.[2]

Burford's poems celebrate the poet's identity as woman—as mother, lover, sister. Color and culture as markers of difference do not have a place in her poems here; and she draws on Greek legend, rather than on Caribbean or African traditions, to proclaim her newfound assurance as a woman poet, as in "Sisterwrite":

> I've done it.
> Persephone has bought
> two glowing ears of wheat
> to take down into the
> marital hades.
> Just two thin iconoclastic
> books of verse.
> But now, Persephone knows
> where the cornucopia lives.
> She no longer eats from

Pluto's hand.
Is she getting ready to
bite it?[3]

The other three poets in *A Dangerous Knowing* similarly see their identity as women as primary, but they also acknowledge in varying ways and degrees the significance of culture and color in contributing to their sense of self. Thus, Gabriela Pearse, born in Colombia of a Trinidadian mother and an English father, speaks in "Autobiography" of the history of conquest and missionary zeal that lies behind her incarnation in the sixties:

I am to be the brown bridge
that builds a trust.

My black my white
dissolve.
A third language later
I come in to the cold
from calypso warmth
to learn.[4]

The poetry of Grace Nichols and Jackie Kay will be explored in some detail later in this chapter; for now it is worth noting that although they share the desire to celebrate and write about their identity as women, they also attend to differences in history, culture, and voice. Such attention affords them identities not as archetypal women, or generalized descendants of the colonial experience, but as carriers of a specifically Caribbean female history (in Grace Nichols's poetry) or a specifically black Scots female identity (in Jackie Kay's poetry).

But two subsequent anthologies, *Watchers and Seekers* (1987) and *Charting the Journey* (1988),[5] emphasize solidarity and the common experience of black British women rather than the diverse experiences that result from differing cultural or regional backgrounds. Shared experience is given structural recognition in both anthologies because the poems are grouped by theme rather than by author. Anger, isolation, hurt, motherhood, being regarded as sexually undesirable, mourning for the loss of black youth, all these feelings are articulated as the lot of black women, and as shared afflictions they are given status that overrides the exploration of an individual author's experience in its many aspects. Thus, although the poets are far more numerous (twenty-six in *Watchers and Seekers*, thirty-nine in *Charting the Journey*) and the backgrounds far more diverse, including Jamaican, Guyanese, Nigerian, Pakistani, Trinidadian, Indian, South African, Palestinian, Ghanaian, and Barbadian, and although the language used varies from "standard English" to Jamaican patois and other varieties of "creole" or "national language," the overriding impression is one not of diversity but of similarity.

In her introduction to *Watchers and Seekers*, Rhonda Cobham notes that the majority of poets in the anthology acknowledge African American poets such as Alice Walker as their inspiration, and certainly that inspiration is manifested in the recurrent themes as well as the style and technique of their poems. Many were unaware of an earlier Jamaican poet who spent considerable time in Britain, Una Marson, whom Cobham sees as a foremother to this younger generation of black British women poets. Before her death in 1965, Marson published several volumes of poetry, was producer of the BBC program, "Calling the Caribbean," and wrote several plays, of which *Pocomania* was the most successful and innovative in its use of "folk" language and tradition. She was also for a time secretary to Haile Selassie and involved in both the International Women's and Pan-Africanist movements. Much of Marson's poetry was constricted by the nineteenth-century and Georgian conventions she associated with the poetic, but the discovery of African American poets such as Langston Hughes and James Weldon Johnson at times freed her from those constrictions and allowed her to give voice to the feelings and circumstances of black women in Britain and Jamaica, using blues and other folk forms. But she wrote at a time when there was little interest in or encouragement for a poetry that was distinctively Caribbean and female, and her work has been largely forgotten.[6]

Another Jamaican woman poet who is still very much alive, Louise Bennett, is better known to the present generation, particularly those members of it who were born in Jamaica. Unlike Marson, whose poetry belongs more clearly to a mainly literary tradition, Louise Bennett is most effective in performance, drawing upon dramatic monologue, ballad, and Jamaican patois to create a series of characters, who comment ironically, humorously, and tellingly on political and social situations. Bennett's readings when she visits London draw enormous audiences, and her satiric "Colonisation in Reverse" has become particularly well known:

> Wat a joyful news, Miss Mattie,
> I feel like me heart gwine burs'
> Jamaica people colonisin'
> Englan in reverse.[7]

As in so many of Louise Bennett's poems, the satire is double-edged, reflecting both on an unquestioning admiration of England by some older Jamaicans and on the mixed feelings of the English, who never dreamed of themselves as being in the position of being colonized.

Of the younger women poets in Britain, Valerie Bloom, who was born and educated in Jamaica, most effectively draws upon the Louise Bennett tradition. Her ballad forms give voice to a variety of Jamaican women, young and old, gently and affectionately bringing them to life in confrontation with each other or with arrogantly sexist young men, enduring travel on Jamaican public transport, selling their goods in the market, writing to their children in Britain. Like Louise Bennett, Valerie Bloom is an excellent performer of her own—and of others'—poetry. Her first collection of poems, *Touch mi! Tell mi!*, was published in 1983.[8] She also writes more directly political poetry set in Britain, which often builds up to a forceful final line, as in "Yuh Hear Bout?":

> Yuh hear bout di people dem arres
> Fi bun dung di Asian people dem house?
> Yuh hear bout di policeman dem lock up
> Fi beat up di black bwoy widout a cause?
> Yuh hear bout di M.P. dem sack because im refuse fi help
> im coloured constituents in a dem fight
>   'gainst deportation?
> Yuh noh hear bout dem?
> Me neida.[9]

In such poems, both the form of language, which might be termed British Jamaican or West Indian (for the differing nation-languages from Trinidad, Guyana, Jamaica, and other Caribbean islands have begun to merge with one another and with other urban idioms and pronunciations in England), and the sense of community, which includes Asian, "black," and "colored," differs significantly from those poems set in Jamaica or that feature a Jamaican of the older generation. Another well-known poem by Valerie Bloom, "For Michael," draws upon the model of dub poetry, a genre originating in the practice of West Indian DJs speaking poetry against a background of music, frequently reggae music. In this genre, Bloom creates her powerful and poignant elegy for the murdered Jamaican dub poet, Mikey Smith, a poet revered by young black people in Britain as well as in the Caribbean.

Bloom's lament picks up the refrain of one of Smith's best-known poems, "Me Cyaan Believe It," in which Smith assumes a woman's voice and speaks on behalf of the suffering of women abused and neglected by Jamaican men. In her turn, Valerie Bloom assumes the voice of the dead male poet and speaks for all his compatriots, male and female, in her sorrow at his loss and at the context of thuggery and political corruption that produced Smith's murder. Valerie Bloom's elegy gives her the occasion to step across the boundaries of the Louise Bennett tradition she had adopted, to take on what has generally been a male preserve, namely dub poetry, and to speak for a whole generation with new authority.[10] The power and sophistication of this work compares not only with Mikey Smith's but also with the poetry of another woman dub poet, Jean Binta Breeze.

As Carolyn Cooper argues in her ground-breaking discussion of criteria for judging performance poetry, dub poetry within the British or international context has all too often turned from a responsible, politically oriented art form to glib entertainment and mere doggerel. She comments that where audiences are not attuned to the nuances of allusions, language, and rhythms of Caribbean oral traditions, "the inter-dependent relationship of performer, word, audience and occasion that invigorates the work of Breeze and Mikey Smith is often compromised in the efforts of less accomplished practitioners who quickly become dubbed out. . . . The search for the exact word and rhythm is abandoned as the dubber settles for the automatic reflex of cliché."[11] In Britain, male dub poets such as Linton Kwesi Johnson, Benjamin Zephaniah, and Matabaruka have become media stars,

entertaining mass multicultural audiences where, as Stewart Brown comments, poets such as Linton Kwesi Johnson, despite the genuineness of their
anger and the relevance of their political protest, are challenged with "the
real danger that the protest, the anger, the fire, become an act, while the
image, the dub/rant/chant/dance become the real substance of the performance."[12]

As with the Black Power movement in the United States, which had
some influence on Caribbean and black British poets in the 1970s and 1980s,
there has been a strong political emphasis on asserting "masculinity": the
rhetoric is often aggressive and "macho." And the performers have been
almost all male. Working first in Jamaica and now for the past few years in
Britain, Jean Binta Breeze has restored new life and new complexity and
subtlety to dub poetry. The title poem of her first volume and record, *Riddym
Ravings and Other Poems*,[13] takes as its persona a "mad" woman whose voice
and plight and commentary question received notions of sanity and the
politics that debase women. Through the use of a variety of women's voices
and contexts, Binta Breeze's poetry challenges the usual voices and stances
of a masculine dub and performance poetry tradition. On stage, record, or
page, she speaks for and to black female experience and encompasses a wide
range of subjects, styles, and tonalities, from the anger and desolation of
the mad woman, speaking her own truths in "Riddym Ravings," to the gentle
and moving affirmation of "Simple Tings":

> de simple tings of life, mi dear
> de simple tings of life
>
> she rocked the rhythms in her chair
> brushed a hand across her hair
> miles of travel in her stare
>
> de simple tings of life
>
> ah hoe mi corn
> and de backache gone
> plant mi peas
> arthritis ease

de simple tings of life
leaning back
she wiped an eye
read the rain signs
in the sky
evening's ashes
in a fireside

de simple tings of life[14]

Jean Binta Breeze's poetry draws mainly on the culture, character, and language of the rural Jamaica she knew as a child and young woman; her recent move to Britain has not as yet begun to make an impact on her writing. The poetry and prose of Grace Nichols, who came to Britain from Guyana in 1977, expresses her experience on both sides of the Atlantic and challenges representations of black women by Caribbean male poets as well as by the white British media.

Grace Nichols's first volume of poetry, *i is a long memoried woman*, won the prestigious Commonwealth Poetry Prize in 1983. This eighty-page volume is a sequence of poems charting the psychic journey of African women torn from their mothers and mother culture and recreating their encounter with slavery and the "New World." By lamenting the loss of the African mother culture, and specifically by appealing to African goddesses such as Ala and Yemanja, her poetic sequence reminds us of them and also ceremonially installs them in the new land. Like the African American poet Audre Lord (in *The Black Unicorn*), Grace Nichols turns to Africa to find in her own ancestral past a community of strong and powerful women, where blackness and femaleness is affirmed rather than marginalized:

I come from a country of strong women
black Oak women who bleed slowly at
the altars of their children
because mother is supreme burden[15]

And in the Caribbean, women dream of a return to that community where their belonging will be proclaimed:

Suddenly, for no reason
though there is reason
plenty
I feel the dizzying
        mid-day
        drum-spell
        come over me
.   .   .   .
Once again
I am talking
words
that come smoothly

Once again
I am in the eyes
of my sisters
they have not
forgotten my name

Osee yei yee yei
Osee yei yee yei

they cry from behind
their evening pots

rejoice!
rejoice!
rejoice!

she is back
she is back
she is back
Waye saa aye saa oo!
Waye saa aye saa oo!

She has done so

> She has done so
> She has done so
>
> Mother behold
> your wilful daughter
>
> Yes the one who ventured
> beyond our village is back
>
> Osee yei yee yei
> Osei yei yee[16]

I have quoted this particular poem at length because it is otherwise difficult to convey the effectiveness with which Nichols captures the impression of the repeated drum beat, the rhythmic invocation of a past that is carried in the instrument itself and that can be repeated and recreated in the Caribbean, so that the past is carried into the present, and the present carries one back into the past. Here too, Nichols invokes the lost language, the names, the words that once "came smoothly" and that now survive only in traces of cadence and intonation. The theme of silencing, of a lost language, and the long and painful creation of a new means of articulation is a recurring one in the sequence and is recapitulated in its "Epilogue":

> I have crossed an ocean
> I have lost my tongue
> from the root of the old
> one
> a new one has sprung[17]

The new tongue is an English-speaking one, and it is also a woman's tongue, giving voice to the silenced and unspoken history of the African women who were kidnapped and transported to the Caribbean. Nichols's use of drum rhythms and her invocation of the culture and context of the African motherland in "Drum-Spell" and other sections of *i is a long memoried woman* suggest that she is setting her poetic sequence beside the work of Kamau Brathwaite, regarded by most critics as one of the Caribbean's two major poets (Derek Walcott being the other). Brathwaite's trilogy, *The Arrivants*, written in the 1960s and first published as a trilogy in 1973, is also a sequence that takes the male spokesman from the physical and spiritual oppression of slavery in the Americas back to Africa in a quest for identity and restored meaning and for glimpses of cultural origins transplanted and renewed in the present. Brathwaite also uses a variety of rhythms, personae, and voices to capture a collective history. But with the memorable exception of "Dust," where he recreates the voices of women from his native Barbados, Brathwaite draws only upon the experiences of men in his first two volumes, *Rites of Passage* and *Masks*, and the gods he invokes are all male gods, including Shango and especially Ogun. In 1977, Brathwaite published *Mother Poem*, which celebrates the language and landscape of his motherland, Barbados, and imitates the voices of Barbadian women. His motherland and the mothers of Barbados await redemption by their sons. Grace Nichols's *i is a long memoried woman* can in part be read as a response to both the trilogy and the subsequent volume, *Mother Poem*. It gives stronger and less passive voices to women, and presents them as active participants in their history. The outer softness and allure of women disguises a hard will to survive and to destroy those who have abused them:

> Know that I smile
> know that I bend
> only the better
> to rise and strike
> again[18]

In contrast, the outer hardness of men disguises their softness, as in "Sugar Cane," one of the several poems in the sequence that reverses the more usual analogy between woman and nature:

> There is something
> about sugar cane
>
> He isn't what
> he seem—

indifferent hard
and sheathed in blades

his waving arms
is a sign for help

his skin thick
only to protect
the juice inside
himself
.   .   .
Growing up
is an art

he don't have
any control of

it is us
who groom and
weed him[19]

Here, and elsewhere in the sequence, Grace Nichols affirms women as artists who take control of male nature and do not merely nurture it but also
fashion it, describe it, and define its significance.

Grace Nichols's first volume can be read in part as addressed to a Caribbean context and audience, to readers familiar with Brathwaite's eloquent
poetic history, whose forms and narratives she takes up, reshapes, and
complements with African Caribbean woman's history. Her two later volumes, *The Fat Black Woman's Poems* and *Lazy Thoughts of a Lazy Woman and
Other Poems*,[20] might be seen as addressing a more specifically British context. Rather like a contemporary version of Chaucer's Wife of Bath, the
persona of the fat black woman responds lustily, assertively, and un-
ashamedly to British (and Western) concepts of feminine beauty and behavior, challenging the judges' preference for the slim and ethereal winners
of Miss World contests, issuing invitations to would-be lovers, dismissing

ballet and the ballroom for the boogie-woogie. Some poems also cheerfully challenge Western intellectual discourse, whose categorizations of African women can be seen as part of an overall project to justify its patriarchal hegemony. Thus "The Assertion" reminds her and us of the power of Asante queens and is followed by a poem that rejects the Aunt Jemima stereotype. She scorns the anthropologists in "Thoughts drifting through the fat black woman's head while having a full bubble bath":

> Steatopygous sky
> Steatopygous sea
> Steatopygous waves
> Steatopygous me
>
> O how I long to place my foot
> on the head of anthropology
>
> to swing my breasts
> in the face of history
>
> to scrub my back
> with the dogma of theology
>
> to put my soap
> in the slimming industry's
> profitsome spoke
>
> Steatopygous sky
> Steatopygous sea
> Steatopygous waves
> Steatopygous me[21]

Steatopygia, the term for "abnormally" protuberant buttocks, was in the nineteenth century considered to be particularly characteristic of "Hottentot" women. Thus the Oxford English Dictionary cites Darwin in its definition of the term: "With many Hottentot women the posterior part of the body projects in a wonderful manner; they are steatopygous."[22] Nichols's use and repetition of the term within her floating reverie and sensual celebration of the body in the context not of the lecture room but of the bathroom, subverts its association with a solemnly scientific and rational discourse. The discourses of anthropology, history, and theology that have sought to define and control women are challenged by "the authority of experience" and are redeployed to become part of a celebration of the "natural"; steatopygia becomes the cosmic norm, rather than the sign of the abnormal and the other. This poem more explicitly addresses the implicit agenda of so much of Nichols's poetics, her view that "poetry, thankfully, is a radical synthesizing force. The erotic isn't separated from the political or the spiritual, and a lot gets said."[23]

In poems like these, Grace Nichols challenges not only Western and Caribbean male traditions, but also a developing tradition of black women's writing, often a feature of the anthologies, that focuses on their suffering and portrays black women chiefly as victims of white male patriarchy. Although her poems frequently acknowledge the alien climate, geography, and culture of England's cities, as well as the racism, Grace Nichols eschews what she perceives as the trap of self-pity:

> refusing to be a model
> of her own affliction
> the fat black woman steers clear
> of circles that lead nowhere[24]

Nor will she allow herself to be trapped, like the bitter women in Sylvia Plath's "Lesbos," in domesticity and housework. *Lazy Thoughts for a Lazy Woman* moves from challenging concepts of femininity that exclude women who are black and joyfully well-fleshed to challenging internalized ideals of the good housewife, obsessed with the care of the house. She invokes not only poets like Brathwaite but also Walt Whitman to celebrate "the reclining body."[25] The poems in this latest volume draw on an increasing range of forms, voices, rhythms, and subjects to express the varieties and complexities of black women's experience and being. As she writes in the poem titled "Of Course When they Ask for Poems About the 'Realities' of Black Women":

I say I can write
no poem big enough
to hold the essence
    of a black woman
    or a white woman
    or a green woman

. . . .

Maybe this poem is to say,
that I like to see
we black women
full-of-we-selves walking

Crushing out
with each dancing step
the twisted self-negating
history
we've inherited
    Crushing out
    with each dancing step[26]

Grace Nichols is the best known of the women poets of Caribbean descent in Britain, but she is by no means alone. Valerie Bloom, who came to Britain from Jamaica, was mentioned earlier. Amryl Johnson, originally from Trinidad, published her first volume of poetry, *A Long Road to Nowhere*, in 1985 and has in the past decade become well known as a performer of her own poetry, which draws effectively on the language, sounds, and imagery of Trinidad as well as of England.[27] Merle Collins, from Grenada, has also become a powerful poet-performer, whose work comments on the politics of Grenada, American intervention, and the lives of black people in Britain.[28] Her poem "No Dialects Please" wittily denounces blinkered and arrogant British attitudes to speech and to other cultures, while demonstrating the range and strength of expression that "dialects" allow.

For British poets of Caribbean descent, there is a choice of "Englishes," which many of them exploit to the full. For those of Asian descent, however, the choice may be between English and another language, and the opposition between the ancestral culture and the new English one may be seen as more clear cut. But the comparative strangeness of English can also be seen as a strength, as Debjani Chatterjee asserts in her prize-winning poem "To the English Language":

> Your words raise spectral songs to haunt me.
> I have subverted your vocabulary
> and mined rebellious corridors of sound.
>
> . . . .
>
> I know you now
> With the persistence that a stranger musters.
>
> . . . .
>
> but I do not come to your rhythms empty-handed
> —the treasures of other traditions are mine,
> so many koh-i-noors to be claimed.[29]

Debjani Chatterjee's assertions are justified and well illustrated in the thirteen poems she includes in *The Sun Rises in the North*, a collection featuring four poets (two male, two female) whose origins are in the "southern" regions of the world, such as South Asia, Africa, and the Caribbean.[30] All four now live in the north of England (Sheffield and Manchester); "the treasures of other traditions they bring" are from India, Trinidad, Afro-America, and Ghana. All four demonstrate their mastery of the language and at the same time make play with its strangeness in order to subvert it.

Chatterjee differs from the other three, however, not only in the range and variety of rhythms and poetic forms she handles with dexterity and wit (see, for example, "The Sneezeling" and "Making Waves"), but also in her assertion of a rich historical and cultural alternative tradition from which to mine her "treasures"—the story of the Sultana Razziya, memories of her childhood home and friends in India, Indira Gandhi's struggle to master another language more alien to her than English, Hindi. Such memories, whether personal or political (and Chatterjee characteristically brings the two together in her poems, whatever their starting point), are rarely viewed from a single perspective or merely "treasured"; each is seen as multifaceted, carrying double-edged messages, which reverberate in the reader's mind after the close of the poem.

Chatterjee's poetry is, as far as I am aware, all written in English. A number of other Asian men and women poets and novelists now resident in Britain write in the languages of the Indian subcontinent, such as Gujarati, Bengali, Urdu, and Hindi. Ketaki Kushari Dyson, however, writes in both English and Bengali, and as a result has suffered because critics and publishers from both areas cannot categorize her simply as either "black British" or "Indian." Yet part of Ketaki Dyson's aim as a writer is to deny such monolithic categories and to insist on the duality and complexity of her cultural identity. Indeed, her critical work expands that understanding of complex cultural influence and makeup. She has published a book-length study of the relationship between Rabindranath Tagore and the Argentinian author Victoria Ocampo. She has also translated Anglo-Saxon alliterative verse into Bengali, as well as poems by D. M. Thomas, David Constantine, and the Argentinian writer Rafael Felipe Otelino. Her most recent publication is a translation of the poetry of Tagore, *I Won't Let You Go: Selected Poems*, which was awarded a Poetry Book Society recommendation in 1991.[31]

Although it is important to record that Ketaki Dyson has received recognition as a poet, novelist, and critic for her writings in Bengali, and has received a number of awards for her contributions to Bengali letters, it is her poetry in English that I must concentrate on here. Her first volume of poetry, *Sap-Wood*,[32] experiments with a range of forms, tones, styles, and subjects, from free-verse or poetic prose meditations on war, conquest, nature, or memories of childhood, to short, epigrammatic rhymed and often light-hearted verses referring to domestic tasks, children, or Alexander the Great's encounter in India with an oracular tree:

> Shun this world's harlotry
> but keep a branch of the speaking tree,
> think poetry,
> live poetry,
> never lose your pot-pourri.[33]

Ketaki Dyson's second volume of poetry in English, *Spaces I Inhabit*, published in 1983,[34] establishes her as an accomplished poet in this language, writing with a new authority and in a voice more recognizably her own. This volume also takes on in a more sustained manner issues of

patriarchal power and language, differences of history and tradition and
their significance, and questions of feminism and feminist poetics and critics (especially in her remarkable poem on Sylvia Plath, "Myths and Monsters," which both empathizes with Plath and expresses dismay at "the
besotted rearguard" that "needs its girls to burn at the pyre"). These poems
do not simply address the issues, but again and again, in a variety of complex and allusive modes, *enact* them. Thus, "Visions of an Indian Woman
in an English Garden" begins with "A hard digging I had of it," which seems
a lighthearted parody of Eliot's "Journey of the Magi," and interweaves
allusions to other Eliot poems and other English poets within a poem that
explores the theme of "a meeting of innocence and boldness, / of art and
nature."[35] What the poem gradually reveals is that neither nature nor art
can ever be innocent, for every flower and plant is laden with associations
from Dyson's reading of English literature as well as from the experience of
India, the norms she brings with her. Through a subtle balance between
surface vision and complex subterranean analogy, the poem demonstrates
a flowering, a rich intermingling, of two cultures and two worlds in combination, the one fertilizing the other. Thus the daffodils "cup-winning,
imperial" remind her in this case not of Wordsworth but of "some lustrous
silk from the looms of Kanchipuram / in India's far south." Analogies with
Birnam Wood and "the rank grass of Bengal" flourish side by side, until the
poet/gardener becomes a new colonizer, imposing order, uprooting and
"extraditing" the dandelions and other "tough natives of the soil," and in
the process entering and exploring a new underworld and dream terrain,
knowledge of which still nourishes the neat "diminutive seedlings" she plants
for the next season. The richness and variety of imagery and language and
the deft maintenance of a fine balance between lighthearted and witty
allusion and a deeper, more somber analogy make this a poem that continues to grow in the reader's consciousness and that demonstrates particularly well Ketaki Dyson's poetic imagination and skill.

"Dialogues" is another poem that works through inversion of associations in order to clear a new space for both writer and reader to inhabit:

> A dialogue in English
> can be difficult for me.

> Like talking to a flighty friend
> while trying to clear a rain-forest.
>
> .   .   .   .
>
> A dialogue in Bengali
> is arrival in that space won from the jungle.
> Hut is thatched, pumpkin planted,
> cow tethered, milk frothy in bowl.
> Child plays in beaten-earth yard,
> naked, without nappies.[36]

Here, the English speaker (and by implication the English language) is male and is associated with territorial conquest, whereas Bengali is associated with the world of women, a world that has been domesticated. (One might compare this analogy with Seamus Heaney's equally problematic description of the "English language and literary tradition as male, the 'matter of Ireland'" as female).[37] As the poem progresses, the "alien" non-English world of the jungle displaces the familiar and becomes the metaphor for the English language, and the English-speaking friend degenerates into a monkey creature who speaks mere gibberish, mocking the listener. Ketaki Dyson here uses imagery and rhythm effectively to express an increasing sense of frustration and alienation that contrasts sharply with the calm of the pastoral scene in Bengal, conveyed in a series of simple everyday scenes that, without becoming banal, express a communal life in harmony with nature. But the wit and effectiveness of the poem also derive from Ketaki Dyson's ability to make her English reader share in her relief in escaping from the alien gibberish of English to what becomes, for both speaker and reader, the normality of Bengali while the reader admires Dyson's absolute control over the English language she uses to express its uncontrollability. The poem is only slightly marred by the rhetorical flourish of its final couplet: "But if in these lines I have made some meanings clear / I shall have overcome. I shall have overcome."[38]

A number of the poems in this volume meditate upon the consequences of patriarchy on the lives of women in India, Europe, and England and summon up mothers, grandmothers, and great-grandmothers. These reveries are evocative, combining loss and affirmation. Other poems, like "Trees" and "Lunacy," are lyrical celebrations of nature, drawing on both European and Asian associations for their similes and metaphors. There are lighthearted verses, haiku, and a fine nine-poem sequence titled "Conversations Between Temple-Dancers," all demonstrating a range of forms, tones, rhythms that make Ketaki Dyson one of the more accomplished poets writing in English today.

Whereas Ketaki Dyson writes as a Bengali-English woman whose work and subject matter fuse and cultivate an interplay between both worlds and Grace Nichols challenges English norms of the feminine by celebrating the many-sidedness of African and Caribbean women's lives, Jackie Kay speaks as a poet whose mother culture and mother tongue are British. But she also writes and speaks as one whose identity is in question, for she is black, child of an unknown British mother and Nigerian father; adopted by Scots parents, she speaks with a Glaswegian accent. Unlike the neutrality of the standard English in which Ketaki Dyson writes or the distinctively creole idioms sometimes used by Grace Nichols, Jackie Kay's distinctive Scots accent and idiom paradoxically identify her as British; in this context, color rather than culture becomes singled out as the mark of difference. In her poetry, alternative cultures and perspectives are conveyed by "voice" much more than by images or stories from a historical past or geographical distance, and with the emphasis on "voice" comes an emphasis on the authority of personal experience; however resonant and suggestive they might be of analogous experiences, her poems speak first of all as autobiography or biography rather than as group or communal history. In performance, Jackie Kay's Scots accent both strengthens and dramatizes her identity as black and British.

Jackie Kay was born in Edinburgh in 1961. Her father was Nigerian and her mother Scottish, and she was adopted when she was a baby by Helen and John Kay, a white Glaswegian couple. Her first volume of poetry, *The Adoption Papers*,[39] is dedicated to her adoptive mother and links the exploration of personal and family identity with the exploration of national and cultural identity; for Jackie Kay, the connection between the nature of motherhood and the nature of motherland is closely linked. Her autobiographical persona never mentions the absent Nigerian father, nor does she refer to Nigerian culture; her color is given as fact rather than as inheritance. But the absent biological mother is a recurring figure in her reveries and dreams, a question for whom many answers are explored.

Jackie Kay acknowledges the influence of the Scots poet and dramatist Liz Lochhead on her style. Her earliest poems typically were structured as dramatic monologues that used Scots urban dialect to construct a series of women characters who are spirited, wry, and often sharply pointed in their commentary on the lives of women and their attitudes to men and society. Like Liz Lochhead, she has also written drama for stage, radio, and television, and her poetic talent seemed in her earlier poems to be essentially a dramatic one, although her later work reveals an intense lyrical mode as well. But her subject matter and her approach to it have always been uniquely her own. *The Adoption Papers* begins with a sequence of eleven poems that have been revised from their earlier composition as monologues into a trio of voices: the child's, the "natural" mother's, and the adoptive mother's. Sometimes the voices intermingle, as in "The Seed," where the child, now pregnant, imagines the feelings of her natural mother during pregnancy. Both the pain of the mother who gives up her child and the pain of the child who seeks to come to terms with that mother's choice and to imagine her then and now are intermingled with the anxious and loving care and the reality of the stalwart sense, understanding, and humor with which the adoptive mother copes with social workers, the racism and ignorance her child encounters, and her child's desire to know about her biological mother:

> I could hear the upset in her voice
> I says *I'm not your real mother,*
> though Christ knows why I said that,
> If I'm not who is, but all my planned speech
> went out the window

> She took me when I'd nowhere to go
> my mammy is the best mammy in the world OK.
> After mammy tell me she wisnae my real mammy
> I was scared to death she was gonnie melt
> or something or mibbe disappear in the dead
> of night and somebody would say she wis a fairy
> godmother. So the next morning I felt her skin
> to check it was flesh, but mibbe it was just
> a good imitation. How could I tell if my mammy

> was a dummy with a voice spoken by someone else?
> So I searches the whole house for clues
> but I never found nothing. Anyhow a day after
> I got my guinea pig and forgot about it.[40]

As a black Scots schoolgirl growing up in the late 1960s, Jackie Kay looked upon her adoptive mother and Liz Lochhead as models of strong and articulate women; she also turned to Bessie Smith, Pearl Bailey, and Angela Davis:

> On my bedroom wall is a big poster
> of Angela Davis who is in prison
> right now for nothing at all
> except she wouldn't put up with stuff.
>
> .   .   .   .
>
> Angela Davis is the only female person
> I've seen (except for a nurse on TV)
> who looks like me. She had big hair like mine
> that grows out instead of down.[41]

The title sequence of Jackie Kay's volume focuses on questions of personal identity within a society that sees African characteristics as abnormal; within that society, the adoptive parents provide an ideal of acceptance in which biological/racial inheritance is acknowledged but makes no difference to loving personal relationships or to the individual's place within the family or community. At the same time, these poems challenge what in Britain are commonly assumed connections between racial and cultural inheritance. A number of other poems in this volume present the reader or listener with similar challenges to assumptions about social and biological norms; they speak for and about lesbian women, male transvestites, single mothers, men dying of AIDS. These poems are tender, poignant, and often painful in their revelations, yet they are given a specificity and complexity of detail that prevent them from becoming sentimental. Many merge the real and surreal in nightmare visions of Britain in the eighties. Thus, the sequence "Severe Gale 8" is an extraordinarily powerful political commentary, where images of hurricane-force winds, artists creating from the debris

of a consumer society, and the poor and homeless combine with recurring
phrases such as "There was no bread." These images and refrains culminate
in the final poem of the sequence, "The Third Hurricane":

> The wind was revolutionary;
> ducks and gulls and Canadian geese
> levitated to catch flying pieces of bread.
> Small children flew higher than hawks,
> their fat little bodies buffeted by Galeforce 8
> moving along at 95 mph.
> Adults stood rooted
> like the trees used to be,
> their arms waving in the wind.
>
> The children flew to Nicaragua Libre
> to the Soviet Union, to South Africa
> just in time to see a man who no longer
> looked like his picture get released;
> after 27 years they sang the anthem
> they learned on the way there.
>
> They bought him a turtle dove
> and took their leave.
>
> When they returned the wind stopped
> and they landed soft as feathers—
> some people were dead, the rest were marching
> all the way down to all the way down to
>
> la la la la laughing.[42]

Among Jackie Kay's most recent work is a television documentary that
combines poetry and film imagery to question the legal system that con-
victed and sentenced a sixty-three-year-old woman to life imprisonment
for killing her husband by stabbing him twice through the heart after years
of physical, mental, and sexual abuse. The sequence of poems uses repeti-

tion of the judge's actual words to convey their masculine bias and sets this against repetition of the woman's imagined thoughts and the refrain "There's no way out, no way out" to convey her sense of panic and entrapment within her marriage. Unlike Kay's earlier free-verse work, which draws on the rhythms and cadence of speech, in the documentary she uses a series of tightly rhymed couplets, quatrains, and closed forms combined with the film images of mannequins and theater-like courtrooms to suggest loss of individuality and character within the ritualistic and dehumanized conventions of the British legal system. Part of a series involving five other contemporary poets, Jackie Kay's contribution to *Words on Film* suggests new directions in such multimedia art, as well as in her own work, although it continues from her long concern with those who have been rejected by a society in which the norms and judgments made by white men are those that dominate.

This essay has dwelled at most length on the work of Grace Nichols, Ketaki Kushari Dyson, and Jackie Kay as poets who write with particular skill and power and who speak from the experience of three different groups of black British women—those whose experience bridges the Caribbean/ African and British worlds, those who have come from Asia to Britain and who often speak from more than one language as well as more than one culture, and those, more often of a younger generation, who have grown up entirely within Britain. What they share in common is an antipathy to what Gayatri Chakravorty Spivak has termed the "totalizing that all great narrative explanations finally bring us face to face with."[43] In different ways and from different standpoints, all three poets challenge, often with subversive wit and humor, essentialist concepts of women and race, or monolithic views of culture, and insist upon the interplay of multiple heritages and voices in a Britain where they "have arrived."

Notes

1.   A number of other well-known poets who have since returned to the Caribbean or have become resident in North America, including (Edward) Kamau Brathwaite and Andrew Salkey, also came to Britain in the 1960s and formed part of the influential Caribbean Artists Movement, of which James Berry was an active member. For

further information about the Caribbean Artists in Britain, see Anne Walmsley, *The Caribbean Artists Movement: A Literary and Cultural History 1966–72* (London: New Beacon, 1992).

2. Barbara Burford, *A Dangerous Knowing: Four Black Women Poets* (London: Sheba Feminist Publishers, 1985), 4.

3. Ibid., 10.

4. Ibid., 33.

5. Rhonda Cobham and Merle Collins, eds., *Watchers and Seekers: Creative Writing by Black Women* (London: Women's Press, 1987; New York: Peter Bedrick Books, 1988); S. Grewal et al., eds., *Charting the Journey: Writings by Black and Third World Women* (London: Sheba Feminist Publishers, 1988).

6. For an exploration of Una Marson's life and writing, see Delia Jarrett-Macaulay's forthcoming study *Una Marson.*

7. Louise Bennett, "Colonisation in Reverse," in *Jamaica Labresh* (Kingston, Jamaica: Sangster's Bookstores, 1966), 179–80.

8. Valerie Bloom, *Touch mi! Tell mi!* (London: Bogle L'Ouverture, 1983).

9. Ibid., 78.

10. For a discussion of dub poetry as a male-dominated scene and her own entry into this scene, see Jean Binta Breeze, "Can a Woman be a Dub Poet?" *Women: A Cultural Review* 1, no. 1 (April 1990): 47–49.

11. Carolyn Cooper, "Words Unbroken by the Beat: The Performance Poetry of Mikey Smith and Jean Binta Breeze," *Wasafiri* 11 (spring 1990): 8.

12. Stewart Brown, "Dub Poetry: Selling Out," *Poetry Wales* 22, no. 2 (1987): 53–54.

13. Jean Binta Breeze, *Riddym Ravings and Other Poems,* ed. Mervyn Morris (London: Karnak House, 1983). Many of these poems are also available on Island Records.

14. Jean Binta Breeze, "Simple Things," in ibid., 33.

15. Grace Nichols, "Web or Kin," in *i is a long memoried woman* (London: Karnak House, 1983), 9.

16. Grace Nichols, "Drum-Spell," in *i is a long memoried woman,* 88–90.

17. Grace Nichols, "Epilogue," in *i is a long memoried woman,* 80.

18. Grace Nichols, "Skin-Teeth," in *i is a long memoried woman,* 50.

19. Grace Nichols, "Sugar Cane," in *i is a long memoried woman,* 32-33.

20. Grace Nichols, *The Fat Black Woman's Poems* (London: Virago, 1984), and *Lazy Thoughts of a Lazy Woman and Other Poems* (London: Virago, 1989).

21. Grace Nichols, "Thoughts drifting through the fat black woman's head while having a full bubble bath," in *The Fat Black Woman's Poems,* 15.

22. Charles Darwin, *The Descent of Man,* 11, xix, 345.

23. Quoted in *Let It Be Told,* ed. Lauretta Negobo (London: Virago, 1988), 103.

24. Grace Nichols, "Trap Evasions," in *Lazy Thoughts of a Lazy Woman,* 14.

25. One might also compare this postcolonial affirmation of "the body reclining" to Les Murray's transportation of Whitman to an Australian context in his poem, "The Quality of Sprawl," in *Selected Poems* (Manchester: Carcanet, 1986), 88.

26. Grace Nichols, "Of Course When They Ask for Poems About the 'Realities' of Black Women," in *Lazy Thoughts of a Lazy Woman,* 52–54.

27. Amryl Johnson, *A Long Road to Nowhere* (London: Virago, 1985). Johnson has also produced her poetry on cassette and has published a prose account of her return to Trinidad and other Caribbean islands (see Amryl Johnson, *Sequins for a Ragged Hem* [London: Virago, 1988]).

28. Merle Collins is a member of African Dawn, a group that performs dramatized poetry fused with African music. She has published her first volume of poetry: *Because the Dawn Breaks* (London: Karia Press, 1985).

29. Debjani Chatterjee, "To the English Language," in *Wasafiri* 13 (spring 1991): 22.

30. *The Sun Rises in the North* (Huddersfield: Smith/Doorstop Press, 1991). The other three poets are Cheryl Martin, John Lyons, and Lemn Sissay.

31. Rabindranath Tagore, *I Won't Let You Go: Selected Poems,* trans. K. Dyson (Newcastle upon Tyne, England: Bloodaxe Books, 1991).

32. Ketaki Dyson, *Sap-Wood* (Calcutta: The Writers' Workshop, 1978).

33. Ketaki Dyson, "Shun this World's Harlotry," in ibid., 20.

34. Ketaki Dyson, *Spaces I Inhabit* (Calcutta: Navana, 1983).

35. Ketaki Dyson, "Visions of an Indian Woman in an English Garden," in ibid., 16.

36. Ketaki Dyson, "Dialogues," in *Spaces I Inhabit,* 70.

37. Seamus Heaney, *Preoccupations* (London: Faber & Faber, 1985), 34.

38. Dyson, "Dialogues," 70.

39. Jackie Kay, *The Adoption Papers* (Newcastle upon Tyne, England: Bloodaxe Books, 1991). *The Adoption Papers* won an Eric Gregory award in 1991.

40. Jackie Kay, "Chapter 6: The Telling Part," in ibid., 21–22.

41. Jackie Kay, "Chapter 7: Black Bottom," in *The Adoption Papers,* 26–27.

42. Jackie Kay, "The Third Hurricane," in *The Adoption Papers,* 38.

43. Gayatri Chakravorty Spivak, *The Post-Colonial Critic,* ed. Sarah Harasym (London: Routledge, 1990), 118.

CHAPTER THIRTEEN

From the Lost Ground:
Liz Lochhead,
Douglas Dunn, and
Contemporary Scottish Poetry

Cairns Craig

I

In his introduction to *The Faber Book of Twentieth-Century Scottish Poetry*, Douglas Dunn notes an oddity about the post–Second World War "generation" of Scottish poets—that it took a long time to come of age:

> W. S. Graham published young, in 1942, but fifteen years were to elapse between *The Nightfishing* . . . and *Malcolm Mooney's Land* (1970). *Riding Lights* (1955), which announced Norman MacCaig's first mature style, appeared when he was in his mid-forties. Edwin Morgan was around the same age when he re-invented his talent by writing the poems that appeared in *The Second Life* (1968). Bearing in mind Sorley MacLean's delayed reputation, and Robert Garioch's, and Derrick Thomson's—outside a handful of readers—the career pattern that seems to be revealed suggests that Scottish poetry underwent a difficult mid-century phase which subsequent success has tended to obscure.[1]

That generation has proved to be one of the most powerful and fecund in Scottish literary history, for one can add to the names Dunn gives those of G. S. Fraser, Sidney Goodsir Smith, George Campbell Hay, Muriel Spark, Hamish Henderson, and George MacKay Brown: all born within three years of the start and the conclusion of the First World War. But few of them were to make any impact as writers until the 1950s, often, indeed, till the 1960s, and the fortunes of those born in the 1920s (William Neill, Iain Crichton Smith, and Alasdair MacLean, for instance) were little better. The fact is that the Second World War proved to be an intense disruption of Scottish literary life because the Scottish Renaissance of the 1920s and 1930s had been founded on a recrudescent Scottish nationalism, a nationalism that was to seem disloyal during a war that the British government was waging on the idea of the "common people"—common both in class and culture.

The emergent post–Second World War generation of Scottish poets were either integrated into a British literary tradition that had no place for the use of the Scottish vernacular (or of Gaelic) or were marginalized into obscurity. Alvarez's influential anthology, *The New Poetry* (1962), includes both MacCaig and Crichton Smith but in its introduction inducts them silently into English writing: "[L]ife in England goes on much as it always has, give or take a few minor changes in the class system. . . . That the English have succeeded for so long owes a good deal to the fact that England is an island; it is, literally, insulated from the rest of the world"[2]— and from Scotland and Wales as well, one supposes! MacCaig and Crichton Smith could be so corralled into the English side of Alvarez's debate between English and American poetry because, in the 1950s, they were producing highly formal poetry whose language was standard English—a poetry that did not *assert* its Scottishness and whose Scottishness could therefore be ignored.

It was in such a context that the young Douglas Dunn, in the early 1960s, could accept that the appropriate place to learn to be a poet was in Hull, under the influence of Philip Larkin. His Scottishness, and his local linguistic inheritance, was not an issue; the fact that he was an outsider only underlined the crucial lessons he learned from Larkin: "the up-to-dateness of observation," the "objective realism."[3] Dunn's first volume, *Terry Street* (1969), echoes Larkin's phrasing and imitates Larkin's stately accounts of the trivia of modern life:

> In small backyards old men's long underwear
> Drips from sagging clotheslines.
> The other stuff they take in bundles to the Bendix.[4]

And Dunn's relation to the people he is dealing with is like Larkin's in *The Whitsun Weddings*, self-ironizing and self-deprecating only to insist the further on the distance between himself and his subjects:

> This time they see me at my windows, among books,
> A specimen under glass, being protected,
> And laugh at me watching them.
> They minuet to Mozart playing loudly
>
> On the afternoon Third. They mock me thus,
> They mime my culture. A landlord stares.
> All he has worked for is being destroyed.[5]

Situated between the landlord and the tenants, Dunn's speaker maintains his distance from both by the solipsism of a "culture" that has no place in their lives or in their community. Like Larkin's jazz, Dunn's culture (in the form of the "Third," the BBC's former radio station for minority, intellectual tastes) is imported and forms a defense from the very world in which his poetry sedulously, but sacrificially, immerses itself. The distance Dunn has traveled since the 1960s is indexed by a poem from *Northlight* (1988), whose title—"Here and There"—is a deliberate recollection of Larkin's "Here," the poem that most influenced Dunn's early writing.[6] Larkin's "Here" represents his response to the parochial world of Hull, a response that involves a self-denigrating acceptance of his place in a world of "A cut-price crowd, urban yet simple, dwelling / Where only salesmen and relations come," and the search for some pastoral ideal that can match his poetic isolation: "Here is unfenced existence: / Facing the sun, untalkative, out of reach."[7] The poet is neither within the community of the place nor fully in touch with the natural world that surrounds it. Dunn, on the other hand, has learned the need for and the power of a community, a community of the voice:

> *'Worse than parochial! Literature*
> *Ought to be everywhere . . .'* Friend, I know that;
> It's why I'm here. My accent feels at home
> In the grocer's and in Tentsmuir Forest.
> Without a Scottish voice, its monostome

> Dictionary, I'm a contortionist—
> Tongue, teeth and larynx swallowing an R's
> Frog-croak and spittle, social agility,
> Its range of fraudulence and repertoires
> Disguising place and nationality.[8]

The emphasis on the emplacement of English writing, English's emplacement in a Scottish tonality, asserts a sense of the oral dimension of poetry
that was entirely lacking in *Terry Street*, and asserts an acceptance of the
poet's place within a community of speakers, which Larkin could not achieve.
For Larkin, the poetic voice suffers submersion in the vernacular only in
order to escape into a realm of purified isolation; for Dunn, the journey is
from the isolated purity of the "Third Programme's" idea of universal "culture" (the "Third" was a bastion of Received Pronunciation) to immersion
in the local.

Dunn's anthology of Scottish poetry is the record of a poet recovering
his poetic inheritance from the obliterating effects of the decade in which
he grew to maturity: It is a sign that Scottish poetry since 1970 has, like
Dunn himself, come home to itself, unwilling to be chastised as provincial
by an English culture whose superiority and centrality it regards as "an
undignified / Anachronism" (*N*, 29).

II

What happened to Scottish poetry in the 1970s, while Dunn was
living in Hull, was a liberation of the voice, an acceptance (even if the poet
was writing in English) that the medium of the poetry was Scottish *speech*
rather than written English or Scots. The most radical assertion of this kind
is found in Tom Leonard's poetry, which voices itself through an orthography designed to capture the intensely regional vernacular of the Glasgow
working classes:

> yir eyes ur
> eh
> a mean yir

> pirrit this wey
> ah a thingk yir
> byewtifl like ehm
>
> fact
> fact a thingk yir
> ach a luvyi thahts
>
> thahts
> jist thi wey it iz like
> thahts ehm
> aw ther iz ti say[9]

"A Summer's Day" harnesses (at least) four different textual and vocal modes to construct a space of intersecting linguistic forces:

1. the vernacular of Glasgow working-class speech, a speech so demotic that, as he puts it in another poem, "even thi Scottish National Dictionary tellt mi' 'ma langage is disgraceful'" (*IV*, 120). The poem mimics the (supposed) inarticulacy of the working man when faced with expressing personal emotion in a sexually charged situation.
2. the author's use of that speech to make assertions that the speaker himself is not conscious of or, at least, not able to articulate in the way implied: thus, by continually leaving "yir" on the end of the line—"fact a thingk yir"—the poem insists on an "existential" reality that language is unable to encompass: it is the "is-ness," "yir-ness" of the beloved (her *thing*ness) that astonishes him.
3. the use of the phonetic transcription to create puns that operate across the boundaries between vernacular and standard speech. The pun on "thing" and "think" can only occur visually, a doubling of the significance of the vernacular expression of a standard word. Thus "a luvyi" combines verbal and nominative forms: the speaker asserts "I love you," while at the same moment the object

of his love is defined by a new noun, "a luvyi" ("a loveyou")
in one and the same moment.

4.   the allusion of the poem by title and theme to Shakespeare's
     Sonnet 18—"shall I compare thee to a summer's day / Thou
     art more lovely and more temperate." Shakespeare's son-
     net insists on the fact that beauty is beyond poetry's de-
     scriptive powers while at the same time insisting that the
     poetry will outlive (and is therefore more significant than)
     the actual beauty: the existential superiority of immediate
     beauty is counteracted by the fact that "in eternal time to
     time thou grow'st: / So long as men can breathe, or eyes
     can see, / So long lives this, and this gives life to thee."
     Leonard's poem makes precisely the opposite assertion.

It is, of course, only as long as "eyes" ("I's") can read *English* that the assertion of Shakespeare's sonnet remains true. The time-transcending power of
the poetry depends on the power of the language and culture to defend
itself against erosion; Leonard, on the other hand, puts his poem on the
side of the existent, on the side of the speechless feminine object of poetic
discourse, who has no choice but to *accept* her existence in time and space
as the ultimate value and whose beauty reduces her lover to a real rather
than a pretended speechlessness. For Leonard, as for the unnamed "object"
("thingk") of Shakespeare's poem, "beauty" is "bye" in the batting of an
"eye"/"I"—or the stutter of an "ehm," and no language is consolation against
that. That is truly "aw there iz ti say."

By siting his own poem within the Shakespearean allusion, Leonard
asserts the *living* value of even the most inarticulate regional speech over
against the fluent articulacy of the literary—or as "Beastie Men" would have
it, "all livin language is sacred / fuck thi lohta thim" (*IV*, 120). Leonard's
poetry allows the poetic voice to range from the demotic to the most literary without having to shed its Scottishness; Shakespeare is integrated into
a Scottish context rather than the Scottish poet having to give up his language for the language of Shakespeare in order to be poetic.

In 1979 that cultural liberation seemed to be put under threat by the
failure of proposals for an equivalent political liberation in the setting up
of a Scottish parliament: without a parliament, many feared, the 1980s—

especially after the Falklands conflict with all its echoes of the Second World War—would be another decade of Scottish reintegration into the British (English) "Geist" that Margaret Thatcher was so insistently recreating. In fact, however, the 1980s were to prove to be a decade of deepening and intensifying awareness of the difference of Scottish culture from English: in art, in music, in philosophy, in literature, a wide range of works appeared asserting that there exists a powerful and very separate tradition in Scotland, one that provided the contemporary creative artist with a strong native resource for the creation of new works. Dunn's anthology of modern Scottish poetry is a late contributor to this dynamic reassertion of the cultural, if not the political, independence of Scotland.

A key poetic work here is Edwin Morgan's *Sonnets from Scotland* (1984), a sequence that constructs a time traveler's history of Scotland from the earliest geological formation of the landmass through to some future time in which an independent Scotland is a distant archaeological discovery. Morgan's poems range from demotic urban Scots to allusive literariness, but do so to assert the natural continuity rather than the opposition of Scotland's divided linguistic inheritance. The "Theory of the Earth" makes poetic Scots and rational English—the division that Scottish culture is often asserted to have suffered from since the eighteenth century—into a single cultural truth:

> James Hutton that true son of fire who said
> to Burns 'Aye, man, the rocks melt wi the sun'
> was sure the age of reason's time was done:
> what but imagination could have read
> granite boulders back to their molten roots?
> . . . They died almost
> together, poet and geologist,
> and lie in wait for hilltop buoys to ring,
> or aw the seas gang dry and Scotland's coast
> dissolve in crinkled sand and pungent mist.[10]

Language(s), land and seascapes, and poetry and science are fused in the fire of an imagination recovering the Scottish past as a *totality* rather than as a series of fragments, as an inner dialectic (and a dialogue of dialects) rather than as a destructive contradiction between the English of the Enlightenment intellectual and the Scots of the plowman poet. Morgan's poem reveals a Scotland no longer in fear of the dilemmas of its past precisely because it has recovered its past(s) from that engulfing Englishness to which Alvarez's introduction to *The New Poetry* testified.

Scotland's vocal liberation, however, was aided by the thrust of Alvarez's argument, because it was in interaction with American and East European writing, as well as from the recognition of the Scottish experiments of the 1920s, that Scottish writers found the techniques to shape a contemporary Scottish voice. Morgan was known in the 1960s as a translator of East European writers before he was widely known as a poet (his translation of Mayakovsky into Scots was the most daring of experiments);[11] he was also recognized as part of a Glasgow "Beat" scene in the late 1950s (see his "Trio" for the influence of Ginsberg); and Tom Leonard has written that it was the example of William Carlos Williams that directed him to a poetry of the voice (see "The Locaust Tree in Flower, and Why It Had Difficulty Flowering in Britain" [*IV*, 95ff.] and his parodic version of "This is Just to Say," written in west of Scotland dialect as "This is Just to Let Yi Know" [*IV*, 37]). The influence of American writing provided, one might say, an alternative center of gravity that released Scottish writers from the hegemonic pull of London, without requiring them, as the English center did, to be integrated hegemonically into another culture.

III

It is appropriate that Liz Lochhead, confronted by the suddenly changed environment of Berlin after the Wall has come down, should use Morgan as her touchstone—"I think who could make sense of it? Morgan could, yes Eddie could, he would. / And that makes me want to try"[12]—for Lochhead, of all contemporary Scottish poets, is the one who has succeeded in making English the medium of a Scottish voice and who, progressively, and particularly through her work in the theater, has broadened the range of her English by extending her capacities in Scots. Without being committed, like Leonard, to an orthography of the vernacular, Lochhead's poems have always been written in a specifically Scottish English—something that is clear when she reads, even if the text on the page appears to be standard English—and she, too, was inspired by American examples.[13]

But Lochhead's interest in the vernacular is not simply a matter of adopting words or adapting sounds: for Lochhead, poetry is the transfiguration of the debased commonplaces of ordinary speech into a revelation of the individual human meanings that it often conceals by the clichéd nature of its idioms. It is in the debased coinage of ordinary speech that Liz Lochhead's poetry finds its inspiration. The title poem of her first collection, *Memo to Myself for Spring*, already shows her negotiating with the banalities of cliché:

> I won't be as mad as March in April,
> April you confidence trickster,
> you very practical
> practical joker—
> your clichéd burgeoning and budding
> calculated
> to set me wandering in a forest of cosmetic counters'
> lyric poetry.[14]

The leftover sayings of an agricultural world are juxtaposed with the trivia of modernity in order to reveal (and revel in) continuities in life that are maintained within the texture of the language itself. This is a technique she uses powerfully in her poems about women in order to imply the unspoken realities behind the language in which they are trapped:

> everybody's mother
> was the original Frigid-
> aire Icequeen clunking out
> the hardstuff in nuggets, mirror—
> silvers and ice-splinters that'd stick
> in your heart.
>
> Absolutely everyone's mother
> was artistic when she was young.

Everyone's mother
was a perfumed presence with pearls, remote
white shoulders when she
bent over in her ball dress
to kiss you in your crib.

Everybody's mother slept with the butcher
for sausages to stuff you with.[15]

Branded by brand names, hemmed in by fearful daughter fantasies, the clichés of women's roles as mothers become an insistent series of myths that generate and regenerate each other, effectively silencing the women themselves. In Lochhead's poem, the mother has no speech of her own—she exists only in the languages of repetition, reminiscence, resistance, and rejection, by which she is defined and in which she is encased. The person behind the role may exist somewhere, but there is no language for that individual existence; it is the achievement of Lochhead's poem that it is precisely the *silence* of individual female existence of which we become aware as the counterbalance to the fecund and witty plethora of voices that it mobilizes. Motherhood as submission to negation is affirmed by the very vitality and prolixity of the clichés by which the mother is defined: "Nobody's mother can't not never do nothing right." The final line summarizes Lochhead's technique, for in its colloquial confusion of negatives it releases multiple possible meanings, depending on how we intone it in speech: "Nobody's mother can't not never do nothing—right?" ("a woman's work is never done—okay?" "Mothers can't change things," spoken aggressively or ironically) creates an entirely different set of implications from the exhausted despair of "Nobody's mother . . . —can't not . . . —never do . . . —nothing right." The written text is a notation that is designed to underwrite many possible voicings, but the voices will never be able to escape from the negative metaphors and images the language imposes on them.

"Everybody's Mother" is from the book *The Grimm Sisters*, in which Lochhead explores contemporary clichés of women's identities and alternative—female—versions of the fairy tales that the Grimm brothers deformed into patriarchal meanings. These are poems that, in siting themselves within the traditions of an oral culture that feminist critics have reclaimed as specifically female, reassert that culture through their own insistent exploitation of the oral and by fusing into the written text the tones and techniques of "performance" poetry. As part of her theatrical work, Lochhead has developed what she calls "recitations" rather than poems: raps and monologues and verse designed to capture contemporary characters and situations. "Bagpipe Muzak, Glasgow 1990," for instance, is a parody of Louis MacNeice's "Bagpipe Music": "The rent-boys preen on Buchanan Street, their boas are made of vulture / It's all go the January sales in the Metropolis of Culture" (BM, 24), and "Glasgow's No Different" features Vicki, the graduate waitress serving in a theme restaurant called "the Hungry 30s." In such recitations Lochhead constructs a complete "voice" as a revelation of a character and a situation, and it is in allowing contemporary female voices to reinhabit old legends and myths that she produces some of her most striking poetic effects. So, in "Beauty & The," the happy fairy-tale transformation is reversed:

> Three days & nights, three patient years,
> you'll win I'm sure.
> But who'd have guessed
> paying your dues would mean
> the whole wham bam menagerie?
>
> Oh, but soon
> (her hair grew lang her breath grew strang)
> you'll
> (little One-Eye for little Three-Eyes, the
> Bearded Lady)
> Yes, sweet Beauty, you'll
> match him
> horror for horror[16]

The use of Scots words—"lang," "strang"—returns the modern into the violent, archetypal world of ballads rather than the genteel world of nineteenth-century fake tale.

Breaking open the falsehoods of female stereotypes and opening up the entrapments of easy exits from contemporary definitions of gender, Lochhead's poems are ironic engagements with the vocabulary of contemporary sexuality and the illusions in which it is cloaked. But like many other Scottish women writers in the 1970s and 1980s, she clearly found her feminist views problematically related to a Scottish identity that was figured as predominantly and aggressively male. "Inter-City" dramatizes a profound alienation from a culture where the word "fuck" has ceased to have even a minimal human or sexual significance:

> Hammered like a bolt
> diagonally through Scotland (my
> small dark country) this
> train's a
> swaying caveful of half-
> seas over oil-men (fuck
> this fuck that fuck
> everything) bound for Aberdeen and
> North Sea Crude.[17]

"My" is sundered from the "small dark country," the two riveted as painfully together as the "half- . . . men" would be if they fulfilled their language and tried to "fuck / everything" in their mechanized world, for the travelers are all "bound" to the dehumanizing crudities of the world economy. The woman (and the artist) has to negate herself in this environment:

> Outside's all
> black absolutely
>
> .   .   .   .   .   .
> Only bits of my own blurred
> back-to-front face and
> my mind elsewhere.
> The artsyfartsy magazine I'm
> not even pretending to read
> wide open
> at a photograph called Portrait of Absence.[18]

Art and femininity have no place in this world, this Scotland that has blacked out the possible country for economic gain. But the poem makes an equation that was to become increasingly significant in Lochhead's dramatization of her own situation: the negated female was not simply a product of a particularly male-oriented national identity—rather, there is a parallelism between the suppressed nation and the repressed feminine; the negation of a female identity becomes an index of a lost national identity; they become emblems of the same suppression, the same silence.

In adopting this image, Lochhead was, in fact, drawing on one of the most potent metaphors of Scotland in cultural descriptions of the country over the past half century. The nature of Scottish culture has been constantly defined in terms of its "absences," its failures to fulfill the normal development pattern of "mature" nations. This is particularly clear in the case of the most influential analyst of Scottish culture in the post–Second World War period, Tom Nairn. Nairn's *The Break-Up of Britain* has been enormously influential in defining the issues in relation to modern Scottish identity, and for Nairn, Scotland's history is defined inexorably in terms of what it *failed* to produce, in terms of "voids," "vacuums," "neuroses":

> [N]o new "intelligentsia" in the relevant sense developed, turning to the Scottish people to try and fight a way out of its intolerable dilemma. Hence Hroch's phases "A" and "B" were alike absent in Scottish development: there was, there could be, no nationalism or its associated romantic culture fully present in that development. There could only be the "void."[19]

In Lochhead's poem, however, the woman is *between* the "artsyfartsy" portrait of absence and an all-too-insistent male language: she is *not* taking in the absence, but her "own blurred / back to front face" superimposed on the "small dark country." By the identification of her own condition with the country's, she makes redemption of the feminine equivalent to redemption of the nation; construction of a *feminine* speech is a means to recovering an obliterated Scottish speech.

It is from her ability to use a distinctively Scottish syntax within the context of an apparently standard vocabulary that much of the power of Lochhead's invention has derived. However, instead of a regional vocabulary (like Leonard's), what she adopts is a *temporal* vocabulary; Lochhead mobilizes words that are specific to passing fashions of modern life and turns them into a modernized equivalent of MacDiarmid's synthetic Scots:

> Down on her hands and knees
> at ten at night on Hogmanay,
> my mother still giving it elbowgrease
> Jiffywaving the vinolay[20]

The first line opens an unspoken cliché—"down on her . . . luck"; the second becomes an incantation to temporality—"*at* ten *at* night *on* . . ."; the third takes a Scottish phrasing—"still giving it" ("giving it laldy" = to go hard at it)—to underscore the dehumanizing effects of labor spent on an impersonal world of objects. "Giving" is transformed from human beneficence ("still giving") into the exhausting effort of the body that, through labor, becomes itself a product—"elbowgrease"—as though out of a bottle or a tin; the final line then makes that object world into the linguistic environment of a temporal trap, with the woman dominated by the things that she has to maintain and locked into the historical time frame within which her—and her poet-daughter's—identity is defined. The New Year demands renovation, transformation—"this midnight must find us / how we would like to be"—but produces only repetition and banality: "A new view of Scotland / with a dangling calendar / is propped under last year's ready to take its place." And yet it is precisely out of acceptance of that banality that human significance must be prized: Mother and Scotland must be redeemed not by a possible transformation into something different but by acceptance of the given:

> And this is where we live.
> There is no time like the
> present for a kiss.

The effects of that abrupt second line, ending on "the," transform cliché into multiple meanings that overwhelm the banal sentimentality of Hogmanay into a stammering realization of the fragility of the time frame that the characters inhabit: at a dramatic level, "no time like the" gives the effect of the voice caught with emotion unable to continue; at a syntactic level, it transforms the definite article into an object, implying their subjection to the plethora of "the" things around them ("On the kitchen table / . . . / the slab of black bun,"); but by that very disjunction of "present" from its definite article, the poem implies a "present" (time/gift) that is outside of ordinary temporality as defined by the object-world: a moment when mother and daughter *are* both present (here offering themselves to each other as gifts) rather than being simply *in* the present. Female solidarity, and the celebration of a shared *presence* in time, makes a human completeness out of the debased culture (Hogmanay and tartan) that Nairn, and others, have bemoaned as symptomatic of the degradation of Scottish culture. Vernacular life is redeemed from the degradation that is all that the elitism of the cultural critic can seem in modern Scotland.

The overwhelming success of Lochhead's poetry lies in the releasing of powerful effects from commonplace speech precisely because she is on the side of the vernacular: unlike Larkin in "Mr. Bleaney" or "Study of Reading Habits," she uses it in order to release the true depth of feeling that its clichés conceal, not to uncover the shallowness of which cliché is a product. Her poetry (and recitations) are, in this sense, insistently populist (and popular): they turn to modern idiom as a true folk literature of the present, and they construct a speech that is the crossing place between an international, and increasingly generational, culture and the insistent assertion of local identity and local speech. Lochhead's poetry stands alongside much of the writing in Britain by others using folk idiom as an assertion of separate cultural identity (West Indian writers in particular), but in utilizing a modernized folk culture as her medium, she (like John Byrne in his television plays) is in fact founding her work on one of the most insistent aspects of Scottish poetic success since the eighteenth century—trusting the voice of the Scottish people to remain Scottish, no matter how much it absorbs of English, or now American, culture.

IV

The influence of Larkin on Dunn is obvious, acknowledged but fundamentally misleading. Dunn's *Terry Street* poems may have received

high critical praise from critics who were very familiar with Larkin and therefore understood the genre in which he was working. But to see Larkin as a
founding influence is mistaken: Dunn's achievement (not unlike Heaney's)
has been to develop his own voice through the absorption of other voices.
In the early work, Larkin has to be balanced against Lowell (probably the
most powerful influence on his work) and (as Dave Smith has noted) James
Wright.[21] In later work, Marvell has to be balanced against the influence of
Yeats, that model of how to take English poetic tradition and relocate it in
another culture. It is clear, too, from the introduction to *The Faber Book of
Twentieth Century Scottish Poetry*, that Dunn has a problematic relationship
with MacDiarmid; it is possible, however, that he is more like MacDiarmid
than he is prepared to admit. MacDiarmid wrote his poetry out of the *trouvés*
of language, whether in his synthetic Scots period or in the late poems that
salt away lengthy quotations from anything he happened to be reading;
equally, Dunn seems to write many of his poems around a rhythmic or
perceptual *trouvé* from other poets, oyster-like in building his personal product from alien grit. Dave Smith points out how Dunn's "Cosmologist" in
Terry Street echoes Wright's "A Blessing" (Dunn: "if water fell on me now
/ I think I would grow"; Wright: "if I stepped out of my body I would break
/ into blossom").[22] More significantly from a Scottish perspective, "St. Kilda's
Parliament: 1879–1979," the poem that enacts Dunn's return to Scotland
in the photographer's recollection of people "Whose be-all and end-all was
an eternal / Casual husbandry upon a toehold / Of Europe" (*SP*, 144), deliberately recollects key terms from one of MacDiarmid's most powerful early
lyrics. Dunn's lines, which emphasize the natural meaning of the island
beneath the human surface—

> It was easy, even then, to imagine
> St Kilda return to its naked self,
> Its archaeology of hazelraw
> And footprints stratified beneath the lichen.
>
> (*SP*, 144)

—echo MacDiarmid's vision of an earth that has lost its human meaning
in "The Eemis Stane," where the poet cannot read the words

> . . . cut oot i' the stane
> Had the fug o' fame
> An' history's hazelraw
> No' yirdit thaim.[23]

MacDiarmid's punning use of "fame" is usually glossed as "lichen," so that "hazelraw" and "lichen" slip easily together to anyone familiar with the poem. The dates in the title of Dunn's poem—1879–1979—acknowledge their concern with Scottish identity: 1979 was the year of the Devolution Referendum, when Scotland was offered and then refused its own parliament after a decade of vigorous political and cultural action. Dunn's poem takes the evacuation of the inhabitants of St. Kilda as a metaphor for the contemporary political defeat: just as the speaker can still read the signs of the island's "naked self" in its fauna, so we can read, as part of the archaeology of Dunn's own language, echoes of one of MacDiarmid's greatest lyrics—as though the cultural beginning of the Scottish nationalist movement in the 1920s is contained and continued into the present in defiance of this moment of political failure.

It is by such negotiations with other poets that Dunn has moved from being a poet with *a* style, to being a poet who grows through his transitions of style. Being in Hull, Dunn may have mimicked Larkin's tone, but the deeper force at work on his verse was American, and in that American influence he was, in fact, following the same pattern as Lochhead and Leonard, if to a very different conclusion.

The stages of the transition can be outlined in *Love or Nothing* (1974) and *Barbarians* (1979). In *Love or Nothing,* the American models lead toward a truly autobiographical poetry rather than toward the observational poetry of *Terry Street.* Thus, for instance, "The Competition" and "Boys with Coats" (both from *Love or Nothing*) are experiments in the characteristic phrasing of Lowell's autobiographical narratives. They construct a mysterious lost world from public but generally unknown place-names ("When I was ten, going to Hamilton / On the Leyland bus named for Eddlewood") that are the context for juxtaposing apparently inconsequential moments of the past against their later significance ("A boy with an aeroplane just like mine / Zoomed at his war games in the seat in front").[24] The final line here has

learned Lowell's lesson of the verbal energy of the personal dissipating itself
into a world of casual objects unequal to the speaker's desires. Autobiography requires the recognition of a place, a region, and that place or region
requires not just a personal history but a public history with which the poet
is engaged. It is that movement through personal history to regional and
national history that *Love or Nothing* begins:

> My poems should be Clyde-built, crude and sure,
> With images of those dole-deployed
> To honour the indomitable Reds . . .

Autobiographical poets have to be regionalists, not just of where they happen to be but of where they come from: "my footprints melt and run. /
They'll follow to my life. I know they must."[25] The "following" is a two-way
process: the past shadows the present even though the present flows forward ("back to London"); the past also carries with it, however, its own
moral imperative—"I know they must"—that the "I" must accept because
of where his feet have tramped from. At this stage, however, Dunn seems
uncertain of the identity that his personal past imposes on his poetic self:
"Realisms" (dedicated to Derek Mahon and matching its verse structure and
strict abstractions to Mahon's "Lives"—which was in turn dedicated to
Seamus Heaney) concludes with a wish that goes back to Larkin's visions
of "unfenced existence" (in "Here"):

> Our cities of shipyards,
> Belfast, Glasgow, fervent closures
> Of protestantism dispensed with—
>
> We never escape them,
> . . . .
> And the dream comes back,
> Again and again, far away
> At the end of roads,
>
> The existential clarity

> Of love and nothing, the peace
> Poets in patched trousers deserve.
>
> > (*SP*, 71–72)

The last line sets the wish for "existential clarity" in mocking tension with the absurdity of poets defined by "patched trousers," as though the desire for transcendence ("at the end of roads") insistently turns into an awareness of a self all-too-securely (if awkwardly) attached to the material world and to the past. It is a tension that is taken up in the poem immediately following it in *Selected Poems*, "Renfrewshire Traveller":

> Home rain, an aerial night-Clyde,
> Spray of recollection
> And my only appropriate welcome
>
> Have I come back?
>
> > (*SP*, 73)

The returning poet is met with archetypal bleakness from his "small dark kingdom": he has only a false identity ("I am Scots, a tartan tin box") and is "full of poison"; like Lochhead in "Inter-City," his nationality is "an ache in a buffet of empty beer-cans." The autobiographical movement involves a potentially terrifying confrontation with an identity that is so restricted and embittered that it can appear as no more than the leftovers of a dying culture—"rust-reminders," as "Sailing with the Fleet" puts it.[26]

In England, Dunn has been regarded as a poet of the political Left; but in the development of the poems in *Love or Nothing* and *Barbarians,* he enacts a classic development in Scottish left-wing thought in the 1970s and 1980s. For many Scots intellectuals, the New Left provided the medium by which they could assert their commitment to working-class politics, while at the same time distancing those politics from the regional (and parochial) commitments of Scottishness. Left politics represented an internationalism that allowed an escape route from the dull, immobile world of Scottish Laborism and connected back to the excitements of potential revolution among the Red Clydesiders of the 1920s. Those left politics, however, were insistently shaped by an English agenda that saw, in the experiences of the English Civil War (see, for example, the work of Christopher Hill) and the "English" Industrial Revolution (see, for example, the work of E. P. Thompson) the fundamental model of class conflict, because England (as Raymond Williams insists in the introduction to *The Country and the City*) was the first to go through the experience of industrialization and so represents a paradigm for all other developed countries.[27] In this context, Scotland might be a politically acceptable environment in terms of its proletarian characteristics, but with its Calvinist heritage and its "absent" culture, it did not provide paradigmatic models of universal patterns of class conflict. In fact, as Tom Nairn insists in *The Break-up of Britain,* Scotland's development could only be seen in this context as "non-standard," leading to a national backwardness "which naturally appears as 'neurosis' in relation to standard models of development."[28] In this New Left model, the "universal" experience is the experience of England's class conflict; to accept that model is to escape from the marginalism and regressiveness of local culture, and it is primarily through that English model that Dunn articulates his self-identity as "barbarian" in the poems of the 1979 volume of that name.

"The Come-on," a poem whose aggression has made it, retrospectively, a kind of anthem for the generation of working-class poets who stormed the citadel of high culture in the 1960s and 1970s, presents us with a speaker who discovers that in the context of "culture" "I am an embarrassment / To myself . . ." (*SP*, 99), and who seeks a way of overthrowing "the kings' sons and guardians" of "a culture of connivance," not by revolution (unless it is Raymond Williams's "long revolution"), but by "cunning"—"We will beat them with decorum, with manners, / As sly as language is."[29] The description of the speaker's background is, however, entirely *acultural* and nonspecific. We enter the poem through an epigraph from Camus, and we enter into a cultural world that is defined by English standards ("black traffic of Oxbridge"); nothing in the poem announces the speaker as from the Scottish rather than the English working class. This focus on a repressive English history and culture is continued in two of the most powerful poems of the volume, "In the Grounds" and "Gardeners," but it is a repression *internal* to English culture rather than between English culture and its peripheries:

We are intransigent, at odds with them.
They see our rabble-dreams as new contempt
For England's art of house and leaf. Condemn
Our clumsiness—you do not know, how, unkempt

And coarse, we hurt a truth with truth, still true
To who we are: barbarians, whose chins
Drool with ale-stinking hair[30]

The power of these poems, however, arises from the fact that Dunn is situating his opposition to English culture within elegant classical forms of English verse. Formally, the poems announce their complete ease with English tradition and with traditions of high culture, even as they assert their alienation from it. It is this dialectic of structure and statement that provides the real drama of these poems: the drama of the poet who has made the tradition his own, only to deny the cultural rights of those who claim that tradition. However powerful and successful these poems, for Dunn to do this was still a kind of ventriloquism: an alienation that does not admit the ground of its own stance voices itself by solidarity with other people's alienation. But the method of a dialectic between a formal order derived from high culture and a point of view essentially vernacular was to be the foundation on which Dunn would build the major achievements of his poetry in the 1980s.

The tension between form and content, and between solidarity and shared experience, is clearest in one of Dunn's most successful poems of this period, "Gardeners." The poem allows the laborers of England in 1789 (those who, according to G. K. Chesterton, have never been allowed to speak in English literature) to voice their condition in a language of abstraction ("tilt this Nature to magnificence / And natural delight") and of formal elegance (ten-line stanzas of couplets enclosed by the rhyme of lines one and five) that belongs to their masters, announcing the parallel between poetry (taken from its makers by the cultural elite) and the English landscape, whose "elegance / Is not our work, but your far tidier Sense" (*SP*, 106). That dialectic, however, though precisely located in history, is placed in a mythic England ("Loamshire 1789"), which is a construction (by way of the country-house poem and Augustan Georgic, later translated into nineteenth-century rural novels like George Eliot's *Adam Bede*) of the very tradition that Dunn is challenging. Like the laborers, Dunn wants both to attack the tradition and to inhabit it:

> Townsmen will wonder, when your house was burned,
> We did not burn your gardens and undo
> What likes of us did for the likes of you;
> We did not raze this garden that we made,
> Although we hanged you somewhere in its shade.
>
> *(SP, 106)*

Dunn has always been attracted by pastoral (see "A Removal from Terry Street": "That man, I wish him well. I wish him grass" [*SP*, 8]), an image that reappears throughout his work.[31] Thus "Gardeners," for example, challenges the social bases of English pastoral only to allow its ordered world to remain, a still-possible context for those who have labored in it, or who have been shut out from it—a still-possible *inheritance* for a poet born into a very different culture.

In the context of the growing self-confidence of Scottish culture in the 1970s, the mode of historical soliloquy that "Gardeners" uses was, like the autobiographical poem, to insistently require that Dunn's writing engage itself with Scottish cultural tradition. It is territory that is opened up by "The Student: Of Renfrewshire, 1820"—

> 'If you want life,' they said, 'you must die first.'
> Thus in a drought of fear Republic died
> On Linen Street, Lawn Street and Causeyside
>
> *(SP, 107)*

—and that develops powerfully in *St Kilda's Parliament* (1981) through "An Address on the Destitution of Scotland" ("It was a long hard road back to this undeclared Republic"), "Witch Girl," and "Washing the Coins" into a resiting of Dunn's poetry, in terms of landscape, history, and theme, in Scotland. From this point forward, Dunn's poetry inhabits not the English republic of letters, but the "undeclared republic" of Scotland, a Scotland that has "come back / From the lost ground of your dismantled lands,"[32] and that will be celebrated in the *Northlight* volume of 1988, despite its failure to declare itself—"wrinkled time's abolished house / Perpetuates a posthumous / Nation"—as "life, love and ground / And intimate welcome," as a landscape and lightscape where "Melodious lost literature / Remembers itself."[33] It is not the language of Scotland that Dunn aligns his poetry with, but the vernacular of place, so that "Eye, nose, skin, ear, / Reverberate on the vernacular."[34]

That public movement back to Scotland was, however, cut across by personal tragedy—the death of Dunn's wife from cancer in March 1981, which was to produce the poems of *Elegies* (1985). Few modern British poets can have met personal suffering with such public self-examination: Dunn described the balancing act required of such poetry in his lecture of 1988, *Importantly Live: Lyricism in Contemporary Poetry*:

> In what is a largely subjective form of poetic art, achieving its victories through an unembarrassed exposure of the first-person singular, anything that contributes to reticence is liable to be damaging. A weakened version of what was actually felt is just as inauthentic as an overstated feeling or a feeling claimed that was never experienced. In a context of poetry, cerebral prissiness is another version of the sentimental.[35]

The balance that Dunn achieves in *Elegies* is a balance based on and yet challenging of the whole poetic tradition within which he had worked: he uses the "realism" that he learned from Larkin and the autobiographical "I" that he learned from Lowell to construct a poetry that negates itself, a poetry whose insistent recording of the actual (the continuing, the existing) is a record of its opposite—absence, memory—and whose assertion of first-person experience becomes a celebration not of isolation but of community.

In *Elegies*, the formal method of realism—essentially a method of contiguity, the juxtapositions of the *existent*—is countered by the power of a memory that recalls what no longer has any place in that all-too-real world. Realism becomes the ghostly shell of an insistent—but unreal—presence:

A dozen sparrows scuttled on the frost.
We watched them play. We stood at the window,
And, if you saw us, then you saw a ghost
In duplicate.[36]

The speaker, left over in the world of the real, is as much of a ghost as the person whom he remembers; the real world is only a frame for the recollection of what is lost. The method of Larkin's realism is mobilized in order to emphasize its limitations:

Sad? Yes. But it was beautiful also.
There was a stillness in the world. Time was out
Walking his dog by the low walls and privet.[37]

The common banalities of the everyday are no longer the focus of an *observing* and distant poet persona: they are the measure of his distance from everyone else as a grieving subject, a subject for whom the most ordinary of objects is suffused with an all-encompassing personal significance. Thus the moment of death is recorded parabolically through three seagulls in a mobile:

Trying to stay awake, I saw love crowned
In tears and wooden birds and candlelight.
She did not wake again. To prove our love
Each gull, each gull, each gull, turned into dove.[38]

The transformation of the objective context into a subjective meaning defies the realism of the early poetry; and yet the focus on objects rather than on emotion acknowledges the "other," rather than the self, as the real source of this transformation. This balancing of the traditions he had been absorbing throughout the 1970s allowed Dunn to achieve—and to surpass—what he was later (perhaps as a projection backwards from his own work) to describe as the effect of some of the best of Larkin's writing: the construction of "realms of existence weirdly beyond contingency and time."[39] In *Elegies*, realism and the method of contiguity is transformed into its own opposite: a challenge by the recuperative imagination to the limitation of life to the boundaries of time and space. In doing so, *Elegies* enacts at a private level exactly the dialectic that the poems of *Barbarians* enact at a public level: the fusion of a poetic decorum from a tradition that gives the sense of control and order juxtaposed against an intensity of personal emotion that continually threatens, but never quite overthrows, that order.

Elegies revealed how far Dunn had traveled from *Terry Street*: the observer of life is a forced participant; the poems dramatize a voice engaged in rather than disengaged from the lives around him; objects are no longer the opaque determinants of other people's unimaginable lives but are the medium of a commonality that allows, however indirectly, a sharing of the burden of life's suffering. The last two stanzas of "Reading Pascal in the Lowlands" enact the painful impossibility of communicating the burden of suffering in language, and yet the poet's isolation becomes a celebration of a shared world, a communality that is encompassing and sustaining in proportion to its ability to absorb and transcend tragedy:

> A swing squeaks in the distance. Runners jog
> Round the perimeter. He is indiscreet.
> His son is eight years old, with months to live.
> His right hand trembles on his cigarette.
> He sees my book, and then he looks at me,
> Knowing me for a stranger. I have said
> I am sorry. What more is there to say?
>
> He is called over to the riverbank.
> I go away, leaving the Park, walking through
> The Golf Course, and then a wood, climbing,
> And then bracken and gorse, sheep pasturage.
> A little town, its estuary, its bridge,
> Its houses, churches, its undramatic streets.
>
> (*SP*, 251)

Dunn here mobilizes the most self-dramatizing of modern poets, W. B. Yeats, to an entirely undramatic purpose: Yeats's pained cry in "Nineteen Hundred and Nineteen" ("Man is in love and loves what vanishes / What more is there to say?") is transformed from prologue to a self-dramatizing assertion

of the tragic but heroic individualism of the poet in the face of death ("some
moralist or mythological poet / Compares the solitary soul to a swan," Yeats
declares, and declares himself "satisfied with that") to an acceptance of the
ordinary, undramatic, and unselfish heroism of suffering among ordinary
people. Yeats demanded that the poet escape solipsism and the pain of loss
by imposing his will upon reality to give it shape and order: "A man in his
own secret meditation / Is lost amid the labyrinth that he has made / In art
or politics";[40] Dunn, however, counters solipsism ("I am light with meditation, religiose / And mystic with a day of solitude") with a poetic perspective in which order will be provided by community ("houses, churches, its
undramatic streets") if only the poet can rise out of himself to see it.[41] The
poet is no longer, like Yeats, the romantic agonist fighting the "filthy tide"
of modernity nor, like Larkin, the disillusioned sufferer of a debased world
where communality is simply banality, but the servant of an essential
humanity that derives from shared community.

However personal the poems of *Elegies*, they are not set apart from the
trajectory of Dunn's journey back to Scotland; that insistence upon
communality—part of the tradition of Scottish Calvinism and Laborism—
was to become part of Dunn's rejection of the individualism of Thatcherism
that he excoriated in his pamphlet on the "poll" tax.[42] And it is the sense of
an achieved—and threatened—communality that dominates *Northlight*, the
volume that celebrates his return to Scotland and his renewed personal life

> In the hollows of home
> I find life, love and ground
> And intimate welcome:
> With you, and these, I'm bound
>   To history.[43]

It is no accident, therefore, that at the center of the collection is a poem
about Edwin Muir, for it was Muir (most prominently in *Scott and Scotland*
in 1936) who challenged the relevance of a Scottish tradition to modern
Scottish writing.

> But this Nothing in which Scott wrote was not merely a spatial
> one: it was a temporal Nothing as well, dotted with a few discon-

nected figures at abrupt intervals: Henryson, Dunbar, Allan Ramsay, Burns, with a rude buttress of ballads and songs to shore them up and keep them from falling. Scott, in other words, lived in a community which was not a community and set himself to carry on a tradition that was not a tradition. . . .[44]

For Muir, the only answer is for the Scottish writer to join English tradition, a route that is only a variant of what Dunn presents in "John Wilson of Greenock," that is, a poet silenced to earn a living and suppressing his celebrations of his native land—"Each night I dreamt of fame as I revised / My praised and printed *Clyde*" (*SP*, 189). Dunn's poem, however, reverses that trajectory and has Muir's poems, written in various parts of Europe, as projections of an intensely Scottish experience:

> Now Edwin Muir walks from the tram to be a clerk
> In Renfrew where the river flows like liquid work
> Past Lobnitz's, a shipyard where his writing fills
> Commercial ledgers with lists of materials.
> Doves on a ledge, a corner of town hall baronial,
> Remind him of the future life he'll live in verses
> Which, one day, he'll write, in towns other than this.[45]

The inversion of temporal perspective in which Muir previews his poetry through a Scottish environment is the application of a surrealism (or fantastic anti-realism) that has been an undercurrent throughout Dunn's poetry (most notably in his homages to the French poets Laforgue and Desnos).[46] Muir writes only ledgers, but is preparing to turn his experience into a different kind of writing somewhere else; that writing will in turn have to be read back into the Scottish context that Muir tried to sunder himself from. By relocating Muir in Scotland, Dunn reveals the opposite direction of his own work: instead of taking Scotland into the foreign, he brings the foreign into Scotland; instead of living through the cataclysms of European history (as Muir did in Germany and Czechoslovakia in the 1930s and again in the late 1940s), he brings an awareness of European and American cultural traditions to root in Scotland.

Dunn's poetry has developed, therefore, through continual inner

dialogues: dialogues between styles, between cultures, between possible identities of the poet. The poet who began by inhabiting alien cultures ends by
domesticating them into the recovered context of his own culture. As with
Tom Leonard or Edwin Morgan, Lochhead and Dunn have developed in a
particularly Scottish synthesis of American, English, and French influences,
honed on the vernacular of contemporary Scottish speech and on the recovered sense of a national past. But whereas Lochhead moves insistently
into a Scottish speech as the essential unity between poet and community,
Dunn draws his Scottish community insistently into poetic artifices drawn
from "classical" cultures. The dialogue with realism that drove Dunn's early
poetry has become a dialogue with formalism, the deliberate assertion of a
classical style in a vernacular. Modern Scottish poetry, however, in its re-
covery of a variety of vernaculars, testifies to the vitality of a poetic culture
that no longer needs to see itself as either insistently self-generating and
autonomous or as inherently broken and fragmentary; that is no longer a
deformed variant of the supposedly organic development of English culture, but is a microcosm of a multilingual, multicultural Europe, which is
the inheritor equally of the classical ideal and of a vernacular idiom:

> Singing in earth and water
> In all our languages.
> Listen. They are reality.[47]

Notes

1. Douglas Dunn, ed., *The Faber Book of Twentieth Century Scottish Poetry* (London: Faber & Faber, 1992), xxxvii.

2. A. Alvarez, *The New Poetry* (Harmondsworth, England: Penguin, 1962), 25.

3. *Under the Influence: Douglas Dunn on Philip Larkin* (Edinburgh: Edinburgh
University Library, 1987), 3, 9.

4. Douglas Dunn, "The Patricians," in *Selected Poems, 1964–83* (London: Faber
& Faber, 1986), 5. All quotations are from this edition, whose title will be abbreviated
to *SP* in the text.

5. Douglas Dunn, "Young Women in Rollers," in *Selected Poems*, 15.

6. See *Under the Influence*, 9.

7. Philip Larkin, *Collected Poems* (London: Faber, 1988), 136.

8. Douglas Dunn, "Here and There," in *Northlight* (London: Faber & Faber, 1988), 28. All quotations are from this edition, whose title will be abbreviated to *N* in the text.

9. Tom Leonard, "A Summer's Day," in *Intimate Voices: Selected Work, 1965–1983* (Newcastle upon Tyne, England: Galloping Dog Press, 1984), 41. All quotations are from this edition, whose title will be abbreviated to *IV* in the text.

10. Edwin Morgan, "Theory of the Earth," in *Sonnets from Scotland*, ed. Edwin Morgan (Glasgow: Mariscat, 1984), 24.

11. Edwin Morgan, *Wi the Haill Voice: 25 Poems by Vladimir Mayakovsky* (Oxford: Carcanet Press, 1972).

12. Liz Lochhead, "5th April 1990," in *Bagpipe Muzak* (Harmondsworth, England: Penguin, 1991), 79. All quotations are from this edition, whose title will be abbreviated to *BM*.

13. See Liz Lochhead, "Letter From New England," in *Dreaming Frankenstein & Collected Poems* (Edinburgh: Polygon, 1984), 12. All quotations are from this edition, whose title will be abbreviated to *DF* in the text.

14. Liz Lochhead, "Memo to Myself for Spring," in *Dreaming Frankenstein*, 158–59.

15. Liz Lochhead, "Everybody's Mother," in *Dreaming Frankenstein*, 94.

16. Liz Lochhead, "Beauty & The," in *Dreaming Frankenstein*, 80.

17. Liz Lochhead, "Inter-City," in *Dreaming Frankenstein*, 33.

18. Ibid.

19. Tom Nairn, "Scotland and Europe," in *The Break-Up of Britain: Crisis and Neo-Nationalism*, 2d ed. (London: Verso, 1977), 119.

20. Liz Lochhead, "View of Scotland/Love Poem," in *Bagpipe Muzak*, 56.

21. See Dave Smith, "Them and Uz," in *Reading Douglas Dunn*, ed. Robert Crawford and David Kinloch (Edinburgh: Edinburgh University Press, 1992), 80–94.

22. Ibid., 85–86.

23. Hugh MacDiarmid, "The Eemis Stane," in *Collected Poems of Hugh MacDiarmid*, ed. Christopher Murray Grieve (New York: Macmillan, 1967), 17.

24. Ibid.

25. Douglas Dunn, "Clydesiders," in *Selected Poems*, 83.

26. Douglas Dunn, "Sailing with the Fleet," in *Selected Poems*, 82.

27. See Raymond Williams, *The Country and the City* (London: Chatto & Windus, 1973), 2: "It ought to be clear that the English experience is especially significant, in that one of the decisive transformations in the relations between country and city occurred there very early and with a thoroughness that is still in some ways unapproached . . ."

28. Nairn, *Break-Up of Britain*, 153.

29. Douglas Dunn, "The Come-on," in *Selected Poems*, 99.

30. Douglas Dunn, "In the Grounds," in *Selected Poems,* 101.

31. Cf. "ungrassed," in Douglas Dunn, "Reading Pascal in the Lowlands," in *Selected Poems,* 251.

32. Douglas Dunn, "Galloway Motor Farm," in *Selected Poems,* 157.

33. Douglas Dunn, "At Falkland Palace," in *Northlight,* 2; Douglas Dunn, "Abernethy," in *Northlight,* 14.

34. Douglas Dunn, "Memory and Imagination," in *Northlight,* 70.

35. Douglas Dunn, *Importantly Live: Lyricism in Contemporary Poetry* (Dundee: Dundee University Occasional Papers, 1, 1988), 12.

36. Douglas Dunn, "France," in *Selected Poems,* 19.

37. Douglas Dunn, "Thirteen Steps and the Thirteenth of March," in *Selected Poems,* 233.

38. Douglas Dunn, "Sandra's Mobile," in *Selected Poems,* 239.

39. Dunn, *Under the Influence,* 3.

40. W. B. Yeats, "Nineteen Hundred and Nineteen," in *Selected Poetry,* ed. A. Norman Jeffares (London: Macmillan, 1967), 120–24.

41. Douglas Dunn, "Reading Pascal in the Lowlands," in *Selected Poems,* 251.

42. See his *Counterblasts* pamphlet, *The Poll Tax: The Fiscal Fake* (London: Chatto & Windus, 1990).

43. Dunn, "At Falkland Palace," 2.

44. Edwin Muir, *Scott and Scotland* (London: Chatto & Windus, 1936), 12.

45. Douglas Dunn, "Muir's Ledgers," in *Northlight,* 37.

46. See David Kinloch, "The Music and the Fruit: Douglas Dunn and France," in Crawford and Kinloch, *Reading Douglas Dunn,* 151–67.

47. Douglas Dunn, "Europa's Lover," in *Selected Poems,* 225.

CHAPTER FOURTEEN

Wales and the Cultural Politics of Identity: Gillian Clarke, Robert Minhinnick, and Jeremy Hooker

Linden Peach

I

A discussion of English-language Welsh poetry must obviously focus upon poetry written by people from Wales (a geographical entity) on subjects relevant to Welsh history and culture. But poetry from Wales includes the work of writers from outside of the country who, having decided to live there, write on subjects relevant to contemporary Wales and rely on Welsh-based journals and publishers for the dissemination of their work.

In the light of the extraordinary diversity and richness of Welsh writing in English, this essay concentrates upon two writers, Gillian Clarke and Robert Minhinnick, who are of Welsh origins but of different generations, and a third, Jeremy Hooker, who is of English origins. Although Hooker is currently living once again in England, much of his best work to date, the work with which this essay is concerned, was written during the eighteen years in which he lived in Wales. He is now also recognized as one of the leading critics writing on English-language Welsh literature.

Much English-language Welsh poetry, at least prior to 1970, as Oliver Reynolds, a native of Cardiff, implied in "Daearyddiaeth" ("Geography"), is essentially rural, due to a considerable extent to the influence of R. S. Thomas.[1] On one level, Gillian Clarke, although also born in Cardiff, belongs to this tradition. Of rural origins on both sides of her family, she literally walks in "Fires on Lln" in R. S. Thomas's footsteps. But on another level, her work makes an original contribution to Welsh poetry. For among the most important influences on Clarke are her strong female ancestors and the fact that she writes both as a Welsh poet and as a woman in a country whose national images are essentially male.[2]

Any discussion of identity in terms of national foundations is, of course, problematic. Traditional concepts of identity have been dislodged from their attachment to restrictive geographical boundaries. New information and communication technologies have created new spatial structures, relations, and orientations. Increasingly, modern identities are being shaped through a process that is both multilayered and international. But, paradoxically, there has been a fresh awareness that all "life-stories . . . have milieux, immediate locales, provocative emplacements which affect thought and action."[3] As far as contemporary writing in Wales is concerned, it is impor- tant to recognize that often this does not mean reclaiming the older mono- lithic and mythological versions of cultural identity.

The dislocation of traditional concepts of identity from their attach- ment to restrictive boundaries and the more polyphonous models that are being increasingly employed in analyzing the significance of milieux and locales have inspired a retheorization of the relationship between social and cultural life, geography, and history. A key theorist in this area, Edward Soja, has pointed out that history and an understanding of how history is made have occupied privileged positions in Western thought at the expense of geography for too long. The latter part of the nineteenth century, he argues, can be seen as the beginning of an era of rising historicism that lasted until at least the 1960s.[4] During this period, the development of identities has tended to be seen as a historical, and only incidentally a geographical, process.

Soja maintains that we need to reclaim a more imaginative and insight- ful awareness of geography and space from this "overdeveloped historical contextualization of social life."[5] "[I]t may be space more than time," he argues, "that hides consequences from us, the 'making of geography' more than 'the making of history' that provides the most revealing tactical and theoretical world."[6] In practice, this means greater recognition of how politics, ideology, and power relations are inscribed into "the apparent innocent spatiality of social life," together with more awareness of the polyphonous nature of cultural identity.[7]

Soja's thesis provides an especially pertinent framework within which to discuss contemporary poetry from Wales because of its abiding concern with the sociopolitical construction of space. Robert Minhinnick's poetry, as we shall see later, provides a sustained focus upon the origins and consequences of displacement and upon the need for "reterritorialization" in postmodern Wales. Jeremy Hooker's work reclaims locales that have been marginalized by the concentration of cultural and socioeconomic power in London and the Home Counties in order to resist a centralized, social conformity. It is Gillian Clarke's work, however, that offers a particularly useful starting point for a discussion of the application of Soja's model to poetry from Wales. In Wales, the ideological deconstruction of space must inevitably privilege issues of gender, for the national image of the country is essentially male.

The space that women have customarily occupied has been marginalized as the roles traditionally assigned them within a male-orientated country have been undervalued. Not surprisingly, women poets in Wales, as in Ireland, anchor their work in spaces that have been the traditional domains of women, such as houses, rooms, and gardens, and in reclaiming a national identity, they are especially anxious to resist the older, monolithic models, which are often male dominated.

Gillian Clarke's major poem, "Letter From A Far Country," like many poems by the Irish writer Medbh McGuckian, employs the everyday domestic environment of women to focus and revalue women's restriction within a patriarchal society, transforming apparent limitation into creative strength. Clarke herself has said of the poem:

> All creative energy is the same. If you bake brown bread and gather bluebells, and paint a picture with a child, the head of steam is taken off that energy, the poem will wait until tomorrow. Think of the last century, the letters women wrote, the journals, the samplers, the embroidery, the bread, the preserves, the quality of efficiency and passion they put into a day's work.[8]

Ostensibly, because the national images of Wales have traditionally marginalized women, the way in which Clarke associates the newfound confidence of women in Wales since 1970 with the reclamation of Welshness appears surprising:

> Then my mother, swamped in a sense of inferiority about being Welsh and trying with all her might to be English. And the next generation rediscovering Welshness and pride in it, which is sometimes parallel to the new confidence of women and the women's movement.[9]

Despite the male-orientated national culture, Clarke is able to flesh out this parallel by invoking in her poetry a number of women ancestors—Mamgu in "Letter From A Far Country," for example, and Marged, in another of her poems—who were exceptionally strong, independently minded individuals. Sally Roberts Jones in *Relative Values* is similarly able to recall strong women in her family; for, despite the importance assigned to men in Welsh history, women have occupied key positions in Welsh families and communities.[10]

Reclaiming the part that Mamgu, Marged, and others like them played in Welsh ancestry involves giving voice to the previously underrecognized achievements of the women members of their families; in this respect the works of Clarke and Jones can be considered feminist projects. Some critics initially felt that "Letter From A Far Country" was a new kind of writing for Clarke because of its focus upon the domestic environment of women. But in its concern to reclaim the condition of being a woman from the male-structured space that in the past has confined and defined it, "Letter From A Far Country" is a development from Clarke's earlier poetry. Much of her work highlights the experience of what it means to be a woman. Her language often has a female orientation that distinguishes it from the male, Romantic tradition, which includes D. H. Lawrence, Ted Hughes, and Seamus Heaney, into which Hooker (mistakenly on this occasion) has tried to shoehorn her.[11] In "Birth," for example, Clarke, as a mother herself, identifies with the animal giving birth:

> ... I could feel the soft sucking
> Of the new-born, the tugging pleasure

Of bruised reordering, the signal
Of milk's incoming tide, and satisfaction
Fall like a clean sheet around us.[12]

The phrase "bruised reordering" highlights not only that giving birth involves pain as well as pleasure, but the way in which a woman's life, body, how she sees herself, and how she is perceived by others are literally restructured by becoming a mother. It is this focus upon the mother rather than the calf that distinguishes "Birth" as a female poem from, for example, Hughes's "The Birth of Rainbow," which, unlike Clarke's poem, emphasizes the struggle of the calf, and from Nigel Jenkins's "First Calving," in which the attitude to the delivery is male, functional, and almost brutal.

Her work highlights the way in which all women, through the roles traditionally assigned to them by biology and society, have had a special proximity to suffering and death. In "Sheep's Skulls," for example, a metaphor reminds us that in working-class, and especially mining, communities it was the task of the women to lay out the bodies of the dead, and this traditional practice is alluded to also in "Taid's Funeral," where the ominously dark incisions in the stalks of daisies are made by a woman's nail. In other poems, such as "Suicide on Pentwyn Bridge," this closeness to suffering assumes a larger significance, becoming a basis upon which women are drawn together.

In reclaiming the experience of women from its marginal position, Clarke takes risks that do not always succeed. Jeremy Hooker, for example, has pointed out that "her concern with birth and death and love, in emotive metaphorical language, risks inflation, and her directness and simplicity risk sentimentality."[13] Equally, the poems in which men and women occupy separate spaces in opposition to each other risk simplification. In "Jac Codi Baw," for example, the male driver of the J.C.B. is overly indifferent to change and destruction, whereas the poet-narrator embraces a nurturing and protective attitude to the past. But poems concerning interaction and conflict within personal relationships, such as those focusing on the relationship between mother and child or on that between two partners, invariably reveal Clarke's strengths as a writer. "Catrin" is successful because of the ways in which the symbols and images in which Clarke naturally thinks do justice to the complexity of the subject matter.

The struggle over the physical umbilical cord in the first part of "Catrin," giving way to a struggle over a metaphorical umbilical cord between mother and teenage daughter in the second part, focuses the reader's attention upon the potential for conflict between a mother and a child as the child begins to discover and occupy her own space. The language—"fighting / you off" and "that old rope, / Tightening about my life"—expresses the intensity of the conflict that is in turn justified, as it were, by the intensity of the daughter's reaction to being called in from skating. This is conveyed, albeit indirectly, in the mother's physical description of her daughter:

> . . . as you stand there
> With your straight, strong, long
> Brown hair and your rosy,
> Defiant glare . . .
>
> (SP, 14)

In another poem, "Swinging," the mother's ambiguous response parallels her daughter's own ambiguous combination of sexual awakening and childlike innocence, which permeates the language of the whole poem. The daughter's swinging is an act of childlike self-comfort, but quickening— "her legs thrusting" (SP, 18)—signifies her increasing, half-understood sexual awareness. In sundress and shorts, she is both child and young female. The whiteness of her "daps" (plimsolls, or running shoes) and the smallness of her limbs suggest innocence and presexuality, but the darkening plimsolls, the reference to her hands between her thighs, and the image of the cut and sodden grass signify the onset of puberty and sexual knowledge.

The shifting metaphors and fragmented, linear narrative of "Letter From A Far Country" focus and explore the complex diversity of roles that constitute the position of the female subject. The arrangement of books on the shelves and the neat ordering of clothes in cupboards and drawers signify the ordering of space. In the course of the poem, the ordering of space dovetails with the larger hegemonic processes of ordering and classification that legitimize the power of men over women, as in the account of the inscriptions on the stones in the graveyard, which privilege the male ancestors. But criticism of the way in which women occupy a more restrictive social space than men is juxtaposed with the creative pleasure that the narrator derives from some of her activities within that space. Indeed, throughout the poem there is an uneasy tension between these two positions. As the narrator flirts with fantasies of escape, the language of the poem strains to maintain its legitimization of the way in which her creativity finds expression in activities that men have traditionally patronized and undervalued:

> The washing machine drones
> in the distance. From time to time
> as it falls silent I fill baskets
> with damp clothes and carry them
> into the garden, hang them out,
> stand back, take pleasure counting
> and listing what I have done.
>
> (*SP*, 52)

"Drones" both signifies the frustration and monotony of the environment and anticipates the honeycomb metaphor that comes later: "I move in and out of the hive / all day, harvesting, ordering" (*SP*, 53). The fulfillment gleaned from the activities is undercut by the temporariness of the reprieve from the machine's drone and the relentlessness of the house's demands. As the poem enlarges its frame of reference and extends its documentation of the patriarchy that has restricted women through history and geography, it becomes more assertively feminist. References to the activities in which the narrator finds creative fulfillment recur like a refrain, but there is an escalating tension between them and the increasingly candid criticism of the way in which women are confined. At one point, fruit in a preserving jar, a product of the kind of domestic activity in which earlier in the poem women find some creative fulfillment, becomes a metaphor for the entrapment of women within their domestic space:

> You can see the fruit pressing
> their little faces against the glass;
> tiny onions imprisoned
> in their preservative juices.
>
> (*SP*, 57)

The image of the onions as imprisoned faces is recalled later in the poem in the description of the woman who commits suicide even though she is seen in the eyes of the men as having everything she could have possibly wanted.[14]

The identification of the twin pillars of Welsh patriarchy—the minister and the father—is juxtaposed in the early part of the poem with the description of women as the ones left behind at home and having to pass time:

> The minstrel boy to the war has gone.
> But the girl stays. To mind things.
> She must keep. And wait. And pass time.
>
> *(SP, 53)*

The phrase "And pass time" suggests that women have time on their hands, but it might also suggest the way in which women pass time in another quite different sense, through the menstrual cycle. As such, it would anticipate later, more explicit references to menstruation, which is, after all, very much a part of the condition of being a woman. The first such reference occurs in the description of the poet-narrator as a young girl entering the male domain of fieldwork—a description that focuses upon the stubble cutting her legs. The entry into the field is regarded as the crossing of a threshold—"I had longed to carry their tea, for the feminine privilege, for the male right to the field" *(SP, 57–58)*—and it is significant that this transition is accompanied by her bleeding. The terms in which that is described are those in which a woman might refer to menstruation: "Even the small task made me bleed!" Later in the poem, the way in which the monthly cycle becomes such an integral part of a woman's identity is signified in the reference to "my cramps and drownings" *(SP, 62)*.

The identification of this monthly cycle with the phases of the moon is given an interesting twist in "Letter From A Far Country" when the poet-narrator complains of the way in which women's lives are determined by the moon. However, this position—"the moon decides my Equinox"—is ambiguous because even though women's identification with the moon involves entrapment on one level, it is liberating on another: "At high tide I am leaving." A particularly interesting development of this interconnecting imagery occurs in the way in which Clarke identifies her male ancestors as being "in league with the moon" (*SP*, 63). In this single phrase, the frustration of "my cramps and drownings" is linked through the lunar cycle to the repressions of patriarchy. The point is not developed as such, but is followed by a description of the pleasure, satisfaction, pain, frustration, and reordering of the mother-child relationship. It occurs in the latter half of the poem, when the poet-narrator appears determined to leave the restrictive, domestic space and is perhaps more an expression of mood than a logical position. However, it does remind us of how the biological condition of being a woman has been used to help locate women within a private, more restrictive, and inferior social space than that occupied by men.

The initial fantasy of escape in "Letter From A Far Country" becomes an increasingly likely possibility as the lure of opportunities for expansive fulfillment becomes stronger. But at the end of the poem, the narrator pulls back, as it were, interrupted by the school bell. The letter is literally written between school bells, and the bell marks an end to the period of time that, at least on this occasion, has allowed the poet-narrator her own space.

The traditional verse that concludes "Letter From A Far Country," after the school bell brings the narrator's writing time to an end, is such a strong restatement of women's traditional roles that within the context of the whole poem it is problematic. It contradicts the independent-mindedness that gathers strength in the course of the work. Of course, the kind of escape that the poem entertains is not possible for many women. But the traditional verse does more than highlight the reality of compromise in many women's lives. It emphasizes the creative fulfillment that the early part of the poem suggests women have found in their domestic roles rather than the more critical stance, which becomes stronger as the poem develops.

Notwithstanding this apparent failure to pursue the feminist implications of "Letter From A Far Country," the female orientation of Clarke's work is an original and important contribution to poetry from Wales, where the national image is essentially male. Of course, the way in which it deconstructs the history and geography of Wales, emphasizing the sociopolitical and ideological dimension of its geography—what Edward Soja calls the "sociospatial dialectic"—is not uncommon among Welsh writers.[15] As we said at the outset, in Wales, a nation that has been colonized, the way in which geography and social life are permeated with politics, ideology, and power relations is a major concern of its writers, although each may approach the issue differently. As in any examination of the cultural identity of a particular national literature, there are inevitable areas of concern: subject matter (particularly the construction of national character) and the literary traditions and other source material on which they draw (and particularly the degree to which they draw on what has been constructed as the national heritage). For example, a recent and important influence upon Clarke has been the "Cofiant," a very distinctive Welsh form rooted in a Welsh recognition of the beauty of genealogy, a beauty not only encapsulated in the rhythm of the Welsh names, but in the rhythm, as it were, of an ancestral line.[16]

The "Cofiant" is an illustration of how for many contemporary Welsh poets the dislocation of identity from traditional boundaries has its counterpoint in "reterritorialization." Clarke's work typifies how in post-1970 English-language Welsh poetry, identity is increasingly perceived as being forged through a convergence of representational, cultural, and national systems at the same time that traditional concepts of identity, as we said at the outset, are being dislodged from their attachment to restrictive boundaries. But it is important to recognize that for many writers such as Clarke, the process of reterritorialization is revisionist insofar as traditional versions of the past—for example, those that deny the part played by women in Welsh cultural life—are themselves scrutinized and revised. The emphasis given to women in Clarke's own "Cofiant" is not coincidental.

II

No Welsh poet is as concerned with the struggle to achieve a sense of identity in the light of displacement from traditional notions of belonging as Robert Minhinnick. And, in his later work, he is the first English-language Welsh poet to explore the difficulties of establishing an identity in postmodern, industrialized Wales. Many of the most successful poems in his early collection, *Native Ground*, focus upon the boundary between displacement and reterritorialization, combining a sense of displacement with a developing awareness of the past and of belonging. In "The House," for example, the loft in which the poet lies suggests the intellectual nature of his displacement, while the torch beam, identifying shapes, signifies the commitment to unearth ancestral lines symbolized by the wires that twist into darkness. The wires as "a crumbling / Skein of red and black" suggest, like the silence of the house, the disintegrating hold of the past.[17] But the red wires signify the "life" and "blood" in which Minhinnick's work, like Clarke's, finds affirmation against an undercurrent of death and darkness.

In the titular poem of the collection, Minhinnick's memory of how as a boy he had no sense of history, "that tangible subject I might love," is reinforced by the estranged nature of what confronts him: the strange rind of the pomegranate, the bent silhouette of his grandfather, and his grandmother's gossip. As a young boy, he is bored by visits to his grandparents. The poem emphasizes his dislocation. Even the fruit he is given to eat is unfamiliar and makes him feel clumsy. Looking back as an adult, he sees his grandparents as representatives of his multilayered past. But as a young boy, he was representative of a generation losing its sense of the past. The honeycombed nature of the fruit that repels him suggests the multilayered or honeycombed past, in which he has no interest. This indifference to history is commensurate with a lack of appreciation of what remains "an ugly jewellery of words"(NG, 9).

The young boy in "Native Ground" stands in sharp contrast to the young poet in "The Strata: To Llywellen Siôn." Whereas the central image of "Native Ground" is one of bored detachment, epitomized in the pinpricking of the pomegranate, that of "The Strata" is one of engaged vision. The difference between the two positions lies in the discovery in "The Strata" of an organic sense of the past encapsulated in the image of "the separate maps of the tree / Of time, each growing from the last" (NG, 17). Minhinnick's language here—"the separate maps"—betrays the spatial nature of his imagination and his sense of the diversity of the past. Each ring—or, in Minhinnick's imagery, "map"—of the tree, like each generation, grows from the past. This image gives coherence to the sense of the past in "The Strata" in contrast to the random view of the past in "Native Ground," which is encapsulated in the key image of the creeping pimpernel "scattered everywhere like confetti." The coherence, however, does not come from reclaiming a traditional, monolithic, or mythologized past. Minhinnick's approach, like Clarke's but with different emphases, is clearly revisionist as the poet-narrator is "able to claim what is mine, / To fashion with blunt words my own design"(NG, 17).

In *Native Ground*, the need "to look around" and "find our own /
Mythology" is given a poetical as well as a personal dimension. "J.P." epitomizes the way in which Minhinnick and many contemporary poets from
the industrialized areas of Wales have developed, even in their writing about
rural areas, a powerful sense of how politics, ideology, and power relations
are inscribed into "the apparent innocent spatiality of social life." "J.P."
highlights the poet-narrator's developing sense of the contrast between the
magistrate's estate and the decaying farms. It also epitomizes how the
emergence of more polyphonous models of cultural identity have encouraged writers to give voice to what has been silenced or underemphasized by
the older, monolithic versions of the past. At the outset of the poem, the
image of the moth suggests the vulnerability and smallness of the young
people as individuals when they come up against the entrenched English
landowner and powerful vested interests, epitomized in the image of the
strong headlights' beam of the Wolsey. But as the poet-narrator begins to
dwell on what colonization (the references to the mansion house and the
magistrate's panama are strategically placed) has denied—"Llangewydd's /
Square mile of history, its cwms and / Slow decaying farms . . ."—the sense
of rebellion becomes stronger: "Even then the idea was alive / Within us:
we belonged; we continued . . ." *(NG,* 43). Within this context, phrases such
as "tribal defiance" and "we stood our ground" are dislodged from their
attachment to a mythologized past in which the Welsh tried to resist the
English invasion and, carrying echoes of that view of Welsh history, are
reemployed in an account of the sociopolitical relations inscribed in the
spatiality of economic and social life in late-twentieth-century Wales.

Native Ground is an exciting collection because of its encapsulation of
the ways in which a number of contemporary Welsh writers offer imaginative and politicized readings of geography and space, demonstrating the
kind of awareness that, as we said at the outset, Soja recommends we reclaim from "an overdeveloped historical contextualization of social life."[18]
It is not an entirely successful collection, however. The lack of a unifying
imagery is indicative of its unclear focus, but in subsequent collections, Minhinnick achieves a surer grasp of his material and particularly of how concepts of identity have become dislodged from their traditional foundations.

In *The Dinosaur Park*, this displacement is located in the transformation from an industrial to a postindustrial society. In this respect, Minhinnick is the first Welsh poet to tackle an aspect of modern life, "regional recycling," that, Soja argues, a greater awareness of the sociospatial nature of space should help us to understand and that has had a particular impact in Wales.[19] Soja's term "regional recycling" describes the way in which an industrial region falls into demise with the decline of its heavy industry but then is "recycled" and restructured through the deployment of new technology and new mobile capital. Wales, a former center of heavy industry, has now become relatively more prosperous as a result of new technology that has also restructured it by shifting the geographical location of its economically successful areas.

Minhinnick approaches "recycled," postmodern Wales from a number of perspectives, including the way in which the growth of an electronic society has led not only to regional restructuring, but a reorientation of cultural and social life. Whereas in *Native Ground* Minhinnick is concerned with the sociospatial construction of space, especially in terms of power relations, in his later work he becomes increasingly concerned with the role of an electronic, microchip society in creating the space that people occupy while the environment and its destruction go increasingly unnoticed.

Each reference to the computer in "The Arcade" in *The Dinosaur Park* emphasizes its ability to seduce and dupe us—the initial "screen" becomes "panels of flickering glass" and eventually, bewitchingly, "glows in green"— so that we no longer expect to be presented with a hold on the external world but are content with the "reality" presented by the electronic images.[20] As John Fiske argues of computer games: it is as if the "excess of concentration produces a loss of self, of the socially constructed subject and its social relations."[21] This loss of "the socially constructed subject" is highlighted in Minhinnick's poem by the image of the child-as-consumer enclosed in a cocoon, an image reinforced by the alliteration that gives a sense of closure to the language: "A serious child cocooned in concentration / As an army reassembles at his touch" (*DP*, 28). The way in which the later image of the player as a sniper refers us back to this initial image of the assembling army itself ironically mirrors the way in which representation has become an interplay of images rather than a means of knowing about the external world.

Of course, as poems within a sequence, "The Resort" (the last resort?) and "The Arcade" should be read in association with the opening poem, and when we read both poems in association with each other, Minhinnick's concern with the way in which young people in contemporary Wales are inhabiting an increasingly self-enclosed space becomes clearer. In the opening poem, the surfers' awareness of their bodies, an awareness that the players in the arcade lack, is emphasized in the accumulation of appropriate verbs— "pitching," "flattering," "stand erect," "balance," "glide," "somersaulted." But despite this stress on activity, the surfers, like the players, are locked into an all-consuming present. In conveying the excitement of surfing, the divergent imagery—"girls grinning like dolphins," "table of dark sand," "roofs of water"—gives the impression that the surfers experience an illusory, hyperreality, encapsulated in Minhinnick's phrase "the summit of a wave" (*DP*, 25).

The surfboard in the opening poem of "The Resort," uniting function and leisure in one relatively cheap commodity, is an index of the way in which culture and capitalism in postindustrial society, and especially in areas identified by Soja as "recycled regions," converge around visible rallying points for fantasy and consumer investment. The negative aspects of this concept are stressed in "On the Sands":

> There is, here and now and nothing else,
> The present sucks us in. For the first time
> I can look around and find a place so strange
> Nothing balances it; there is no context.
>
> (*DP*, 29)

In stressing the present, the first line here significantly repeats the conjunction that children overuse in their insatiable appetite for the immediate, while the stanza literally leads to "nothing." Indeed, a recurring feature of Minhinnick's writing about this aspect of postindustrial society is the realization that although in nineteenth-century bourgeois society objects were seen as things owned, in postmodern society objects are things to be consumed and measured by turnover so that nothing is perceived as either permanent or unique:

> Our ground is blurring
> Losing its angles, but the brand-names push
> Out of the sand their familiar epitaphs.
>
> (*DP*, 12)

Loss of definition and death are combined here in contradistinction to the concept of birth, suggested in the way in which "brand-names" are ironically said to "push." But the sense of emptiness and death that characterizes Minhinnick's writing on modern consumerism is also part of a larger argument about identity: in postindustrial society objects are never allowed to become fixed and stable for longer than is required for people to identify with them and to learn to desire them.[22]

Through emphasizing the player in interaction with the machine, with obvious connotative links to the production line, "The Arcade" stands in contradistinction to the titular poem, "The Dinosaur Park," which is concerned with the demise of heavy industry in Wales. The effect of this contradistinction is to stress what is new in the postindustrial society of Soja's "recycled regions." The milieu to which "The Dinosaur Park" looks back has now been turned upside down. "Age"—"An age might pass"—is a key ambiguity in "The Arcade," suggesting, on one level, the length of time the boy spends pondering his next move but, on another level, implying wasted time and youth. As Fiske reminds us, the metaphor that "time is money" is so central to industrial culture "that a machine that can prove that time is money and, in doing so, 'waste' both has the potential for causing profound social offence."[23] Whereas in industrial society the worker works with a machine, in postindustrial society the player—evincing the leisure-generated interests of postindustrial society—works against it. But even though the computer games allow the player power, it can only be exercised within the paradigm of choices provided by the microchip.

The model of postindustrial society that we find in Minhinnick's work—where fantasy and consumer investment are substitutes for the loss of traditional identities and "realities"—is more overtly politicized in the work of Mike Jenkins, a South Wales contemporary of Minhinnick. For example, the alliteration in "Industrial Museum" from *Invisible Times* emphasizes the idea of a "packaged" reality—"pit-wheels perfectly preserved," "mummified miners"—and provides the satirical edge to the comedy in the line: "their hwyl is higher and hireath higher."[24] As with Minhinnick's criticism of postindustrial society, the horror lies in the way in which people engage knowingly in a kind of make-believe world and in the way in which they so willingly accept the sanitized version of what is depicted. The same point is made succinctly by Tony Curtis in "Thoughts From the Holiday Inn": "They took the coal-miners and put 'em in a coal museum: / And the people drove down, coughed up three quid just to / see 'em."[25]

Poems in Minhinnick's *The Looters* that develop the concern of *The Dinosaur Park* with postindustrial society focus more strongly upon individuals and especially the young. In "Staff," the secretary opening letters and answering the telephone is at the center of the kind of information flow that, because of microchip technology, has become increasingly important, transcending traditional geographical boundaries and creating new spatial structures and relations.[26] As postmodern geographers such as Soja argue, information itself is an important commodity, and the flow of information has restructured the world map. The way in which the voices that the secretary connects and that are seen as only playing around each other typifies the recurring concern in this collection with the lack of connection between people. Modern technology has brought areas of the world that were formerly distant from each other into a new proximity, but within these areas, especially within "recycled regions," spatial proximity between people is no indicator of the closeness of the communication between them.

"Ghost Train" dovetails the lack of personal contact between the purchaser and the young woman who hands out tickets—"No need to talk. / She pushes out the tickets with the change"—with the way in which she appears to live in a packaged, mass media orientated "reality" signified by "her hutch of glass," her paperback novel, and "the headphones pulled down tight" (*L,* 15). The hutch and the fact that the headphones are pulled down tight suggest the enclosure of her "world," whereas the fact that all her senses are kept occupied suggests an information overload. The artificial thrills of the ghost train are emblematic of the solipsistic, postindustrial society that Minhinnick exposes in *The Dinosaur Park.*

Minhinnick's imaginative awareness of space underpins many of the poems in *The Looters.* Indeed, there is a recurring concern with the space that people occupy, which is often a restrictive space: the secretary in "Staff" is in "the cage," the young woman in "Ghost Train," as we said above, occupies a hutch, and the young people in the government training scheme in "YOPS" are marooned in a shed by the rain. Minhinnick emphasizes their frustration by describing them as "teenaged working men" and referring to their "scorched identities" (*L*, 14). The poem is riddled with irony— the teenagers are denied the self-respect of being "working men," and the rain that awaits them at the beginning of the poem is a portent of the unemployment that may lie ahead. They are marooned between education and unemployment.

As in "Ghost Train," the emphasis is upon the restricted space, socially, economically, and physically, that the teenagers occupy, signified here by the closed door and the illusory nature of the spread-eagled poses of the women in the pictures they have cut from pornographic magazines to adorn the walls of the shed. Here and in "Ghost Train," too, the generalized sense of boredom is eventually focused upon a very specific indicator of defiance with violent connotations. Here the "steelies start to tap the leaking boards," while in "Ghost Train":

> . . . from her hutch of glass
> This girl stares out,
> The disc of tickets turning on its spike.
> Her purple nails
> Are filed like arrow heads.

> (*L*, 45)

The disc of tickets suggests the days that the young woman passes in this way, and those others of her generation who have not been able to realize their full creative potential.

The fairground in *The Looters* develops what the arcade in *The Dinosaur Park* was used to suggest: how postindustrial society turns on its head industrial society's dictum that time is money. But the instantaneous nature of postmodern society is given more emphasis. The comparison to a fast-food queue of the people waiting outside the palmist suggests not only the commodification of individual futures but the postindustrial trend toward instant gratification, a point made also in "A Footnote to the History of Bridgend."[27]

Minhinnick's concern with thinking in terms of space as well as history permeates his later work, with its increasing emphasis upon postindustrial Wales as a "recycled region," as much as it underpinned *Native Ground*. Throughout his work, he is concerned with the way in which space is structured and controlled by powerful vested interests. His work does not betray the kind of interest in traditional Welshness that we find in Gillian Clarke's poetry. Minhinnick's reterritorialization is inspired by his Welsh socialism, as is his critique of the more consumer-orientated, postindustrial society of contemporary Wales. His interest in *Native Ground*, epitomized in "J.P.," in how capitalism, which is largely English capitalism, of course, has structured Wales in terms of its geography as well as its history, develops in his later work into his analysis of postindustrial Wales.

III

In "Resistant Voices: Five Young Anglo-Welsh Poets," Jeremy Hooker argues that Minhinnick is one of a number of poets from the industrialized working-class area of Wales who have found inspiration in the worked-out, industrialized Welsh landscape.[28] In this respect, it is possible in Hooker's *Solent Shore* to detect the influence of English-language Welsh poetry. For, just as Hooker finds in the work of Minhinnick and Mike Jenkins an essence of place bound up with its working-class past, he depicts Southampton as "a shore / stripped to its working parts." Although Hooker's work is not as overtly politicized as that of Minhinnick, it shares his emphasis upon spatial relationships within the functional, industrialized environment:

> All is ready for work:
> launches at their moorings,
> small tubs off the pierhead,
> warehouses; and above all
> the cranes, there flying high
> or with pulleys dangling,
> those far back, more spidery.[29]

The language of the poem here, devoid of imagery for a number of its lines and pared down to a minimalist functionalism, encapsulates how the shore line has been structured by economic interests. By contrast, the second part of the poem tends to romanticize the environment, depicting an essence of a place that comes dangerously close to an armchair idealization of the world of tough, manual work:

> No, it is not their function
> to please the eye.
> Yet they do—more so for the common goodness
> of their function, for grace
> extra to a working world
> that neighbours sky and water,
> drawing from all
> some ordinary tribute; . . .
>
> (*SS*, 25)

The ambiguity of "common" and the religious overtones of "grace," "goodness," and "tribute" appear to overload the aesthetic appreciation of the environment. "Solent Winter," on the other hand, is a more successful poem than "On a Photograph of Southampton Docks." Hooker, freed of the difficulty of disentangling his own response from a secondhand aesthetic mediated by the photograph, suggests, as in Minhinnick's work, the political complexities of the Solent shore (*SS*, 24). The yachts, signifying wealth derived from oil and the new leisure-orientated postindustrial society, serve as a counterpoint to the tankers, which are rusty, suggesting the waning of the industrial age from which they come.

Hooker, however, is not really a poet of industrialized areas, and *Solent Shore*, a compilation of poems written over the 1970s, betrays the influence of English-language Welsh poetry in other, more significant ways:

> Deeper the echoes fathom
> Sounding dugouts,
> Stumps of a forest
> Under peat under sea.

> From words I turn
> To an estuary flooded,
> Reflecting branches,
> Gulls frosty against
> A pale, full moon.

(SS, 55)

The woods and the estuary defy any one perspective. These lines epitomize how Hooker's realization of a landscape makes us aware of the complexity of a place while at the same time leaving us conscious of the impossibility of ever capturing what he calls "totality." In Hooker's work, there is a creative tension between an elusive concept of "totality" and the polyphonous forces that constitute space as "place":

> A place is a totality, a place is all that has created it through the process of time, it is the history, the geology, the circumambient environment, and in addition to that, is the connection within a single compass of all those living forces.[30]

His elucidation of the concept of "totality" embraces so much that it leaves the reader with a sense of the impossibility of the concept. Indeed, it is the awareness of the extent and diversity of the forces to which he refers that betrays Hooker's affinity with English-language Welsh poetry. He has admitted in an interview:

> I feel closer to the position of the Anglo-Welsh poets in relation to their subjects, and their attitude and outlook than I do to most, though not all, of my English contemporaries.[31]

In fact, Jeremy Hooker was beginning to develop an approach to poetry and concepts of the role of the poet before he came to Wales that, when he arrived in the country, enabled him to engage sympathetically with its poetry written in English. The approaches and concepts that led Hooker toward Welsh writing were themselves developed, deepened, and directed by it. So much so, that his own rather romantic definition of himself as a "praise poet" is a Welsh one, of the poet as "celebrator, commemorator, praiser of people, and indeed, also of landscape, also of life itself."[32]

Although Hooker's concern with nature, landscape, and community places him in a particular tradition of Welsh poetry that includes R. S. Thomas, he shares a more widespread concern in English-language Welsh poetry with displacement and reterritorialization so that even many of his poems written on English subjects bear the stamp of Welsh poetry. English-language Welsh poetry, for all its tendency to mythologize, furnished Hooker with an alternative model of place to that provided by the English literary tradition in which places are valued "for their local color, as picturesque deviations from the centralized norm," or they become a source for official national and imperial ideas.[33] There is then a strong correlation between the development of an exciting, alternative model of place in his work and his own developing engagement with Wales: the "change from thinking about the place in which I now live as the edge of Western Britain, to the realization that it is the centre of a culture."[34] Indeed, many of his poems mirror very closely in structure and content the process by which he found himself drawn closer and closer into Wales.[35]

Once again Soja's retheorization of the relationship between history, geography, and social life provides a framework within which to discuss Hooker's alternative to the English literary model of space. As we have already said, during the nineteenth century, in Soja's view, the rise of modern capitalism and the onset of empire despatialized historicism and depoliticized space as the objects of critical social discourse.[36] Hooker's "Englishman's Road" (1980) offers a profound understanding of how the cultural politics of space is fundamental, as Minhinnick's poetry demonstrates, to what Soja calls "emancipatory political thought."[37] In Hooker's poem, polyphonous voices are employed to emphasize the different ways in which space, knowledge, and power are interconnected. Augustus Brackenbury's egocentricity, encapsulated in the number of times he employs the first person, alienates him from Wales (mainly "mountain wilderness") and from the indigenous population ("dark, unsmiling faces"), which he perceives as "other." There is no attempt to recognize, let alone engage with, the nation. But his projection of English concepts of landscape—a gentleman's country estate and parkland—upon a Welsh countryside betray the interrelation of land as economic capital, and knowledge and education as cultural capital.[38] Other voices within the poem also enable Hooker to explore the way in which money, power, and knowledge led to the commodification of space and its division into manageable economic units. The squatters of Mynydd Bach recognize that any attempt to disperse and democratize political power must challenge dynastic power embedded in place—"There shall not be any large farms or houses built on / Mynydd Bach but they shall be pulled down"— but fail to appreciate his need for a coordinated, spatial strategy.[39]

As an Englishman, despite the affinity he felt with the Welsh people, Hooker frequently felt like an intruder in Wales. Not surprisingly, "Englishman's Road" exemplifies how Hooker's work is as much concerned with intrusion as alienation. In "Hill Country Rhythms," the poet significantly disturbs a hawk before he discovers the bodiless wings emblematic of the intruder's alienated condition. In "Englishman's Road," Wales as a "circumambient environment" resists attempts of intruders to gain a purchase upon it even though they may disturb it:

> This is settled country, an intricate pattern of farms and
> smallholdings, with Bethel in a hollow. A work wrought
> in rock, vaster and more labored than the pyramids;
> but unfinished. And here these English words play on
> a surface through which they cannot shine, to illuminate
> its heart; they can possess the essence of this place no
> more than the narrow road under the Welsh mountain
> can translate its name.[40]

Yet although Hooker himself perceived Wales as "other," he has an important place within contemporary, English-language Welsh poetry. Not only has his work been profoundly influenced by English-language Welsh writing, but it demonstrates how the work of immigrants can contribute to the definition of the geographically based cultural identity that they wish to enter. Hooker has contributed more to the understanding of English-language Welsh literature as a critic than many Welsh-born scholars. His poetry has served as a vehicle for concerns that have characterized English-language Welsh writing, and he has influenced and encouraged writing in English by Welsh-born authors.

The cultural politics of identity in Wales are complex. In discussing the work of three very different poets concerned with this subject, we have tried to show how the diversity of poetry in contemporary Wales reflects this complexity. Throughout much of English-language Welsh poetry, however, there is an abiding concern with the way in which geography in Wales is inscribed with politics, ideology, and power relations. The retheorization by Edward Soja of the relationship between geography, history, and social life provides a framework within which to discuss this widespread preoccupation in contemporary Welsh writing and, in particular, to understand its various models of reterritorialization.

Notes

1. Oliver Reynolds, *Skevington's Daughter* (London: Faber & Faber, 1985), 64–65.

2. See also, Linden Peach, "Incoming Tides: The Poetry of Gillian Clarke," *New Welsh Review* 1, no. 1 (1988): 75–81, expanded and updated in Linden Peach, *Ancestral Lines: Culture and Identity in the Work of Six Contemporary Poets* (Bridgend, Wales: Seren, 1993); and Deirdre Beddoe, "Images of Welsh Women," in *Wales: The Imagined Nation*, ed. Tony Curtis (Bridgend, Wales: Poetry Wales Press, 1986), 227.

3. Edward Soja, *Postmodern Geographies: The Reassertion of Space in Critical Social Theory* (London: Verso, 1989), 14.

4. Ibid., 4.

5. Ibid., 15.

6. Ibid., 1.

7. Ibid., 6.

8. Susan Butler, ed., *The Common Ground* (Bridgend, Wales: Poetry Wales Press, 1985), 195–96.

9. Ibid., 195.

10. See Sally Roberts Jones, *Relative Values* (Bridgend, Wales: Poetry Wales Press, 1985), 15–16; and Linden Peach, "Family and Inheritance: Sally Roberts Jones," *Poetry Wales* 25 (1990): 40–43.

11. Jeremy Hooker, *The Presence of the Past* (Bridgend, Wales: Poetry Wales Press, 1988), 152.

12. Gillian Clarke, *Selected Poems* (Manchester: Carcanet, 1985), 12. Hereafter, all quotations from this volume will be cited in the text, prefaced by *SP*.

13. Hooker, *Presence of the Past*, 151.

14. See Clarke, *Selected Poems*, 60.

15. Soja, *Postmodern Geographies*, 57–58.

16. Gillian Clarke, *Letting in the Rumour* (Manchester: Carcanet Press, 1989), 68. See also Susan Butler, *The Common Ground*, 197.

17. Robert Minhinnick, *Native Ground* (Swansea, Wales: Triskele Books, 1979), 16. Hereafter, all quotations from this volume will be cited in the text, preceded by *NG*.

18. Soja, *Postmodern Geographies*, 15.

19. Ibid., 172.

20. Robert Minhinnick, "The Arcade," in *The Dinosaur Park* (Bridgend, Wales: Poetry Wales Press, 1985), 28. Hereafter, all quotations will be cited in the text, prefaced by *DP*.

21. John Fiske, *Reading the Popular* (London: Unwin Hyman, 1989), 93.

22. Ibid., 29.

23. Ibid., 81–82.

24. Mike Jenkins, *Invisible Times* (Bridgend, Wales: Poetry Wales Press, 1986), 26–27.

25. Tony Curtis, *The Last Candles* (Bridgend, Wales: Seren Books, 1989), 40.

26. Robert Minhinnick, *The Looters* (Bridgend, Wales: Seren Books, 1989), 55. Hereafter, all quotations from this volume will be cited in the text, preceded by the abbreviation *L*.

27. See Minhinnick, *Looters*, 67.

28. Hooker, *Presence of the Past*, 177–98.

29. Jeremy Hooker, "On a Photograph of Southampton Docks," in *Solent Shore* (Manchester: Carcanet Press, 1978), 25. Hereafter, all quotations will be cited in the text, preceded by *SS*.

30. Butler, *Common Ground*, 203.

31. Ibid., 201.

32. Ibid., 202.

33. Jeremy Hooker, *The Poetry of Place: Essays and Reviews, 1970–1981* (Manchester: Carcanet Press, 1982), 11.

34. Ibid., 173.

35. Ibid.

36. Soja, *Postmodern Geographies*, 10–11.

37. Ibid., 1.

38. Jeremy Hooker, "Englishman's Road," *Anglo-Welsh Review* 65 (1979): 10. The poem is reprinted in Jeremy Hooker, *Englishman's Road* (Manchester: Carcanet New Press, 1980).

39. Ibid., 12.

40. Ibid., 17.

NOTES ON CONTRIBUTORS

James Acheson is Senior Lecturer in English at the University of Canterbury, in Christchurch, New Zealand. He is author of *John Fowles* and *Samuel Beckett's Artistic Theory and Practice: Criticism, Drama and Early Fiction,* coeditor of *Samuel Beckett: Texts for Company,* and editor of *The British and Irish Novel Since 1960* and *British and Irish Drama Since 1960.* A member of the Editorial Board of the *Journal of Beckett Studies,* he has contributed essays to many edited collections and journals.

Vicki Bertram is Lecturer in English Studies at Oxford Brookes University, where she teaches modern and contemporary literature, with a particular focus on international Englishes, and on feminist theory and practice. She is currently writing *Muscling In: A Study of Six Contemporary Women Poets and English Poetic Tradition.* One of her concerns is to narrow the gap between practitioners and academics; with this in mind, she organized the "Woman and Poetry" conference in Oxford in 1994, in which she combined academic papers with public performances by women poets.

Claire Buck is Principal Lecturer in English at the University of North London. She is editor of *The Bloomsbury Guide to Women's Literature,* and author of *H.D. and Freud: Bisexuality and a Feminist Discourse.* Dr. Buck is currently Visiting Scholar in the English Department at Brown University.

Cairns Craig is Lecturer in English at the University of Edinburgh. He is author of *Out of History* and *Yeats, Eliot, Pound, and the Politics of Poetry*. In addition he is general editor of *The History of Scottish Literature* (in four volumes), and editor of the volume on twentieth-century literature. During the eighties he was closely involved with the Scottish arts magazine, *Cencrastus*.

Antony Easthope is Professor of English and Cultural Studies at Manchester Metropolitan University. He has held visiting fellowships at Wolfson College, Oxford, the University of Adelaide, and in 1990, at the Commonwealth Center for the Study of Literary and Cultural Change at the University of Virginia. He is author of *Poetry as Discourse, British Post-Structuralism, Poetry and Phantasy,* and *Literary Into Cultural Studies;* and coeditor (with John Thompson) of *Contemporary Poetry Meets Modern Theory*. In addition, he is author of two forthcoming books, *A Cultural Studies Reader* and *Wordsworth Now and Then.*

Paul Giles is Lecturer in American Studies at the University of Nottingham. He has also taught at Oxford University, Bristol University, Stafford Polytechnic, Reed College, and Portland State University. Dr. Giles is author of *Hart Crane: The Contexts of "The Bridge,"* and of essays on Thom Gunn, Charles Dickens, Jane Austen, F. Scott Fitzgerald, and other writers.

Romana Huk is Associate Professor of English at the University of New Hampshire. She is author of a forthcoming book on Stevie Smith, and has published essays on contemporary British and American poets and poetic dramatists in various collections and journals. She has spent most of her research and sabbatical time in England, studying the intersections between mid- to late-twentieth-century politics, theory, and poetic form; most recently she has begun writing on "experimental" poetries and is organizing Assembling Alternatives, the first large-scale international conference/festival that will discuss/celebrate such work as it is being written in the U.S., U.K., Canada, and Ireland.

C. L. Innes is Professor of Post-Colonial Literatures at the University of Kent at Canterbury, England. She is author of *Chinua Achebe, The Devil's Own*

Mirror: The Irishman and the African in Modern Literature, and *Woman and Nation in Irish Literature and Society, 1880–1935.*

Linda Kinnahan is Assistant Professor of English at Duquesne University, Pittsburgh, Pennsylvania. She is author of *Poetics of the Feminine: Tradition and Authority in William Carlos Williams, Mina Loy, Denise Levertov and Kathleen Fraser.* She has published on Williams, Loy, and Fraser in various journals.

Edward Larrissy is Professor of English at the University of Keele, in Staffordshire, England. He is author of *William Blake* and *Reading Twentieth Century Poetry: The Language of Gender and Objects,* and has contributed poems to various journals. He is currently working on a book on W. B. Yeats.

John Matthias is Professor of English at the University of Notre Dame, Notre Dame, Indiana. He is author of six volumes of poetry, including *Northern Summer: New and Selected Poems* and *A Gathering of Ways.* Professor Matthias has published numerous essays and reviews on contemporary British and American poetry, most of which appear in his recent volume of prose, *Reading Old Friends.* In addition, he has published translations from several languages and has edited *23 Modern British Poets, Selected Works of David Jones,* and *David Jones: Man and Poet.*

R. K. Meiners is Professor of English at Michigan State University and editor of the *Centennial Review.* He is author of *The Last Alternatives: A Study of Allen Tate, Everything to be Endured: An Essay on Robert Lowell and Modern Poetry, Journeying Back to the World,* a collection of poetry, and many essays, poems, and reviews. The essay in this volume is part of a book in progress on the relationships of theoretic and poetic discourses in recent cultural institutions.

Alastair Niven is Literature Director of the Arts Council of Great Britain. He has held academic posts at the Universities of Ghana, Leeds, Stirling, Aarhus, and London, and from 1978 to 1984 he was Director-General of the Africa Centre in London. He is author of two books on D. H. Lawrence, and of studies of Raja Rav, Mulk Raj Anand, and William Golding. From 1979 to

1992 he was editor of the *Journal of Commonwealth Literature,* and has written many articles on Commonwealth literature for such journals as *Ariel, British Book News, Kunapipi,* and *Poetry Review.*

Linden Peach is Professor of English at the Loughborough University of Technology, in Loughborough, England. He is author of *British Influence on the Birth of American Literature, The Prose Writing of Dylan Thomas, Marxism and Culture: Christopher Caudwell* (with David Margolies), and of *Ancestral Lines: Culture and Identity in Six Contemporary British Poets.* Professor Peach has contributed essays to such journals as *Poetry Wales* and *The New Welsh Review,* as well as to various edited collections.

Nicholas Zurbrugg is Professor of English and Cultural Studies in the School of Humanities, De Montfort University, in Leicester, England. He is author of *Beckett and Proust, The Parameters of Postmodernism,* and of essays on such authors as Beckett, Burroughs, Barthes, Baudrillard, and Jameson. From 1969 to 1982 he served as editor and publisher of *Stereo Headphones,* a review of experimental poetry, and he also guest-edited the "Multimedia Text" issue of *Art and Design.*

ACKNOWLEDGMENTS

Agneau 2

3 lines from J. H. Prynne, "Frost and Snow Falling," in *Poems* (Edinburgh: Agneau 2, 1982), 70.
2 lines from J. H. Prynne, "Die a Millionaire (pronounced 'diamonds in the air')," in *Poems* (Edinburgh: Agneau 2, 1982), 13.
11 lines from J. H. Prynne, "Thoughts on the Esterhazy Court Uniform," in *Poems* (Edinburgh: Agneau 2, 1982), 247.
32 lines from J. H. Prynne, "Sketch for a Financial Theory of the Self," in *Poems* (Edinburgh: Agneau 2, 1982), 19–20.
6 lines from J. H. Prynne, "Of Movement Towards a Natural Place," in *Poems* (Edinburgh: Agneau 2, 1982), 221.

Allardyce Barnett

13 lines from Veronica Forrest-Thomson, "Pastoral," in *Collected Poems and Translations* (London, Lewes, and Berkeley: Allardyce Barnett, 1990), 72.
9 lines from Veronica Forrest-Thomson, "Cordelia, or, 'A poem should not mean but be,'" in *Collected Poems and Translations* (London, Lewes, and Berkeley: Allardyce Barnett, 1990), 104.

Anvil Press

31 lines from Carol Ann Duffy, "Translating the English, 1989," in *The Other Country* (London: Anvil Press, 1990), 11.
4 lines from Carol Ann Duffy, "We Remember Your Childhood Well," in *The Other Country* (London: Anvil Press, 1990), 24.
28 lines from Carol Ann Duffy, "Standing Female Nude," in *Standing Female Nude* (London: Anvil Press, 1985), 46.
8 lines from Carol Ann Duffy, "Litany," in *Mean Time* (London: Anvil Press, 1993), 9.

3 lines from Carol Ann Duffy, "Words, Wide Night," in *The Other Country* (London: Anvil Press, 1990), 47.

12 lines from Carol Ann Duffy, "River," in *The Other Country* (London: Anvil Press, 1990), 53.

8 lines from Carol Ann Duffy, "Confession," in *Mean Time* (London: Anvil Press, 1993), 15.

3 lines from Carol Ann Duffy, "Like Earning a Living," in *Mean Time* (London: Anvil Press, 1993), 17.

12 lines from Carol Ann Duffy, "Caul," in *Mean Time* (London: Anvil Press, 1993), 22.

10 lines from Carol Ann Duffy, "Moments of Grace," in *Mean Time* (London: Anvil Press, 1993), 9.

15 lines from E. A. Markham, "Inheritance," in *Human Rites: Selected Poems 1970–1982* (London: Anvil Press, 1984), 20.

8 lines from E. A. Markham, "Lambchop's Ally," in *Human Rites: Selected Poems 1970–1982* (London: Anvil Press, 1984), 109.

6 lines from E. A. Markham, "A Challenge," in *Towards the End of a Century* (London: Anvil Press, 1989), 22.

Astra

23 lines from Astra, "coming out celibate," in *One Foot on the Mountain: An Anthology of British Feminist Poetry, 1969–1979*, ed. Lilian Mohin (London: Onlywomen Press, 1979), 37–38.

Black Sparrow

13 lines from Ian Hamilton Finlay, "Star/Steer," in *Honey by the Water* (Los Angeles: Black Sparrow Press, 1973), 25.

Bloodaxe Books

Reprinted by permission of Bloodaxe Books Ltd from: *The Adoption Papers* by Jackie Kay (Bloodaxe Books, 1991), *City Psalms* by Benjamin Zephaniah (Bloodaxe Books, 1992), *v.* by Tony Harrison (Bloodaxe Books, 1985), *British Subjects* by Fred D'Aguiar (Bloodaxe Books, 1993), *Rebel Without Applause* by Lemn Sissay (Bloodaxe Books, 1992).

18 lines from Jackie Kay, "Chapter 6: The Telling Part," in *The Adoption Papers* (Newcastle upon Tyne, England: Bloodaxe Books, 1991), 21–22.

8 lines from Jackie Kay, "Chapter 7: Black Bottom," in *The Adoption Papers* (Newcastle upon Tyne, England: Bloodaxe Books, 1991), 26–27.

22 lines from Jackie Kay, "The Third Hurricane," in *The Adoption Papers* (Newcastle upon Tyne, England: Bloodaxe Books, 1991), 38.

8 lines from Benjamin Zephanaiah, "Call It What You Like!" in *City Psalms* (Newcastle upon Tyne, England: Bloodaxe Books, 1992), 41–42.

16 lines from Fred D'Aguiar, "Home," in *British Subjects* (Newcastle upon Tyne, England: Bloodaxe Books, 1993), 14.

4 lines from Lemn Sissay, "Occupations," in *Rebel Without Applause* (Newcastle upon Tyne, England: Bloodaxe Books, 1992), 18.

24 lines from Tony Harrison, *v.*, new ed. (Newcastle upon Tyne, England: Bloodaxe Books, 1989), 9, 11, 12, 15, 17, 19, 22, 26, 30, 31.

Bogle L'Ouverture Publishers

10 lines from Valerie Bloom, "Yuh Hear Bout?" in *Touch mi! Tell mi!* (London: Bogle L'Ouverture Publishers, 1983), 78.

Jonathan Cape

14 lines from Ken Smith, *The Pity* (London: Jonathan Cape, 1967), 18–19.

Carcanet

5 lines from Gillian Clarke, "Birth," in *Selected Poems* (Manchester: Carcanet, 1985), 12.

5 lines from Gillian Clarke, "Catrin," in *Selected Poems* (Manchester: Carcanet, 1985), 14.

1 line from Gillian Clarke, "Swinging," in *Selected Poems* (Manchester: Carcanet, 1985), 18.

21 lines from Gillian Clarke, "Letter from a Far Country," in *Selected Poems* (Manchester: Carcanet, 1985), 52.

7 lines from Gillian Clarke, "Birth," in *Selected Poems* (Manchester: Carcanet, 1985), 12.

13 lines from Gillian Clarke, "Drones," in *Selected Poems* (Manchester: Carcanet, 1985), 53, 57–58, 62, 63.

15 lines from Donald Davie, "The Priory of St Saviour, Glendalough," in *Collected Poems* (Manchester: Carcanet, 1990), 60.

12 lines from Donald Davie, "Lancashire," in *Collected Poems* (Manchester: Carcanet, 1990), 258.

12 lines from Donald Davie, "A Winter Talent," in *A Winter Talent and Other Poems* (London: Routledge & Kegan Paul, 1957), 47.

Andrew Crozier

12 lines from Andrew Crozier, "The Veil Poem," in *All Where Each Is* (London and Berkeley: Allardyce Barnett, 1985), 121.

5 lines from Andrew Crozier, "Two Robin Croft," in *All Where Each Is* (London and Berkeley: Allardyce Barnett, 1985), 92.

4 lines from Andrew Crozier, "Pleats," in *All Where Each Is* (London and Berkeley: Allardyce Burnett, 1985), 182.

6 lines from Andrew Crozier, "The Life Class," in *All Where Each Is* (London and Berkeley: Allardyce Barnett, 1985), 139.

2 lines from Andrew Crozier, "High Zero," in *All Where Each Is* (London and Berkeley: Allardyce Barnett, 1985), 222.

4 lines from Andrew Crozier, "The Veil Poem," in *All Where Each Is* (London and Berkeley: Allardyce Barnett, 1985), 120.

6 lines from Andrew Crozier, "February Evenings," in *All Where Each Is* (London and Berkeley: Allardyce Barnett, 1985), 91.

2 lines from Andrew Crozier, "Evaporation of a Dream," in *All Where Each Is* (London and Berkeley: Allardyce Barnett, 1985), 297.

Dangaroo Press

24 lines from David Dabydeen, "Love Song," in *Slave Song* (Mundlestrup, Denmark: Dangaroo Press, 1984), 31.

11 lines from David Dabydeen, *Coolie Odyssey* (Coventry: Dangaroo Press, 1988), 42.

Faber & Faber

3 lines from Ted Hughes, "The Jaguar," in *The Hawk in the Rain* (London: Faber & Faber, 1960), 12.

8 lines from Ted Hughes, "Everyman's Odyssey," in *Lupercal* (London: Faber & Faber, 1960), 10.

4 lines from Ted Hughes, "Pike," in *Lupercal* (London: Faber & Faber, 1960), 57.

2 lines from Ted Hughes, "River," in *River* (London: Faber & Faber, 1983), 74.

7 lines from Ted Hughes, "Postcard from Torquay," in *Moortown* (London: Faber & Faber, 1979), vii, 97–98.

2 lines from Thom Gunn, "Iron Landscapes (and the Statue of Liberty)," in *Jack Straw's Castle* (London: Faber & Faber, 1976), 15, 97–98.

8 lines from Thom Gunn, "Sunlight," in *Moly* (London: Faber & Faber, 1971), 44.

11 lines from Ted Hughes, "Coming Down Through Somerset," in *Moortown* (London: Faber & Faber, 1979), 10.

1 line from Ted Hughes, "Lucretia," in *Moortown* (London: Faber & Faber, 1979), 140.

3 lines from Douglas Dunn, "The Patricians," in *Selected Poems, 1964–83* (London: Faber & Faber, 1986), 5.

7 lines from Douglas Dunn, "Young Women in Rollers," in *Selected Poems, 1964–83* (London: Faber & Faber, 1986), 15.

4 lines from Philip Larkin, "Here," in *Collected Poems* (London: Faber & Faber, 1988), 136.

7 lines from Douglas Dunn, "St Kilda's Parliament, 1879–1979," in *Selected Poems, 1964–83* (London: Faber & Faber, 1986), 144.

5 lines from Douglas Dunn, "Clydesiders," in *Selected Poems, 1964–83* (London: Faber & Faber, 1986), 83.

10 lines from Douglas Dunn, "Realisms," in *Selected Poems, 1964–83* (London: Faber & Faber, 1986), 71–72.

4 lines from Douglas Dunn, "Renfrewshire Traveller," in *Selected Poems, 1964–83* (London: Faber & Faber, 1986), 73.

5 lines from Douglas Dunn, "The Come-on," in *Selected Poems, 1964–83* (London: Faber & Faber, 1986), 99.

7 lines from Douglas Dunn, "In the Grounds," in *Selected Poems, 1964–83* (London: Faber & Faber, 1986), 101.

7 lines from Douglas Dunn, "Gardeners," in *Selected Poems, 1964–83* (London: Faber & Faber, 1986), 106.

2 lines from Douglas Dunn, "Galloway Motor Farm," in *Selected Poems, 1964–83* (London: Faber & Faber, 1986), 157.

3 lines from Douglas Dunn, "Europa's Lover," in *Selected Poems, 1964–83* (London: Faber & Faber, 1986), 225.

3 lines from Douglas Dunn, "The Student: of Renfrewshire, 1820," in *Selected Poems, 1964–83* (London: Faber & Faber, 1986), 157.

13 lines from Douglas Dunn, "Reading Pascal in the Lowlands," in *Selected Poems, 1964–83* (London: Faber & Faber, 1986), 251.

2 lines from Douglas Dunn, "John Wilson of Greenock," in *Selected Poems, 1964–83* (London: Faber & Faber, 1986), 189.

4 lines from Philip Larkin's "Money," in *High Windows* (London: Faber & Faber, 1974), 40.

Faber & Faber/Farrar, Straus, & Giroux

9 lines from Thom Gunn, "An Invitation from San Francisco to My Brother," in *The Man with Night Sweats* (New York: Farrar, Straus, & Giroux, 1992), 8.

8 lines from Thom Gunn, "Words for Some Ash," in *The Man with Night Sweats* (New York: Farrar, Straus, & Giroux, 1992), 68.

8 lines from Thom Gunn, "Courtesies of the Interregnum," in *The Man with Night Sweats* (New York: Farrar, Straus, & Giroux, 1992), 74.

2 lines from Thom Gunn, "Cafeteria in Boston," in *The Man with Night Sweats* (New York: Farrar, Straus, & Giroux, 1992), 48.

9 lines from Thom Gunn, "The J Car," in *The Man with Night Sweats* (New York: Farrar, Straus, & Giroux, 1992), 78.

9 lines from Thom Gunn, "Patch Work," in *The Man with Night Sweats* (New York: Farrar, Straus, & Giroux, 1992), 23.

Faber & Faber/Harper Collins

7 lines from Ted Hughes, "Two Legends," in *Crow* (London: Faber & Faber, 1970), 13.

8 lines from Ted Hughes, "The Warriors of the North," in *Wodwo* (London: Faber & Faber, 1967), 159.

Faber & Faber/Peters, Fraser & Dunlop

4 lines from Douglas Dunn, "France," in *Selected Poems, 1964–83* (London: Faber & Faber, 1986), 19.

3 lines from Douglas Dunn, "Thirteen Steps and the Thirteenth of March," in *Selected Poems, 1964–83* (London: Faber & Faber, 1986), 233.

3 lines from Douglas Dunn, "Sandra's Mobile," in *Selected Poems, 1964–83* (London: Faber & Faber, 1986), 239.

12 lines from Douglas Dunn, "Here and There," *Northlight* (London: Faber & Faber, 1988), 28.

9 lines from Douglas Dunn, "At Falkland Palace," in *Northlight* (London: Faber & Faber, 1988), 2.

4 lines from Douglas Dunn, "Abernethy," in *Northlight* (London: Faber & Faber, 1988), 14.

2 lines from Douglas Dunn, "Memory and Imagination," in *Northlight* (London: Faber & Faber, 1988), 70.

7 lines from Douglas Dunn, "Muir's Ledgers," in *Northlight* (London: Faber & Faber, 1988), 37.

Faber & Faber/Viking

5 lines from Thom Gunn, "After the First Fright," in *Cave Birds*, rev. ed. (London: Faber & Faber, 1962), 10.

Alison Fell

9 lines from Alison Fell, "Girl's gifts," in *One Foot on the Mountain: An Anthology of British Feminist Poetry, 1969–1979*, ed. Lilian Mohin (London: Onlywomen Press, 1979), 12.

Fondation Cartier pour l'Art Contemporain

"A View to the Temple" [photo], in *Ian Hamilton Finlay: 'Poursuites Révolutionnaires'* (Paris: Fondation Cartier pour l'Art Contemporain, 1987), n.p.

Fulcrum Press

65 words from the introductory note to Roy Fisher, *The Cut Pages* (London: Fulcrum, 1971), 6–7.

8 lines from Roy Fisher, *The Cut Pages* (London: Fulcrum, 1971), 13.

6 lines from Ian Hamilton Finlay, "OHMS," in *The Dancers Inherit the Party* (London: Fulcrum, 1969), 13.

4 lines from Ian Hamilton Finlay, "Angles of Stamps," in *The Dancers Inherit the Party* (London: Fulcrum, 1969), 12.

3 lines from Ian Hamilton Finlay, "The One-Horse Town," in *The Dancers Inherit the Party* (London: Fulcrum, 1969), 48.

6 lines from Ian Hamilton Finlay, "Scene," in *The Dancers Inherit the Party* (London: Fulcrum, 1969), 46.

Galloping Dog Press

13 lines from Tom Leonard, "A Summer's Day," in *Intimate Voices: Selected Work, 1965–83* (Newcastle upon Tyne, England: Galloping Dog Press, 1984), 41.

2 lines from Tom Leonard, "Beastie Men," in *Intimate Voices: Selected Work, 1965–83* (Newcastle upon Tyne, England: Galloping Dog Press, 1984), 120.

Caroline Gilfillian

9 lines from Caroline Gilfillian, [Untitled], in *One Foot on the Mountain: An Anthology of British Feminist Poetry, 1969–1979*, ed. Lilian Mohin (London: Onlywomen Press, 1979), 46.

Grosseteste Press

330 words from the interview in Roy Fisher, *19 Poems and an Interview* (Pensett, Staffordshire: Grosseteste Press, 1975), 15, 17, 18.
2 lines from "Diversions," in Roy Fisher, *19 Poems and an Interview* (Pensett, Staffordshire: Grosseteste Press, 1975), 138.

Caroline Halliday

8 lines from Caroline Halliday, "Reading 'Of woman born' by Adrienne Rich," in *One Foot on the Mountain: An Anthology of British Feminist Poetry, 1969–1979*, ed. Lilian Mohin (London: Onlywomen Press, 1979), 58.

Angela Hamblin

18 lines from Angela Hamblin, "To Astra," in *One Foot on the Mountain: An Anthology of British Feminist Poetry, 1969–1979*, ed. Lilian Mohin (London: Onlywomen Press, 1979), 18.

Hamish Hamilton

10 lines from James Berry, "Getting Nowhere," in *When I Dance: Poems by James Berry*, illus. Sonia Boyce (London: Hamish Hamilton, 1988), 77.

Jeremy Hooker

27 lines from Jeremy Hooker, *Solent Shore* (Manchester: Carcanet, 1978), 25.

Kala Press

5 lines from Mahmood Jamal, "A Peasant in Bengal," in *Silence Inside a Gun's Mouth* (London: Kala Press, 1984), 25.

Karnak House

18 lines from Jean Binta Breeze, "Simple Tings," in *Riddym Ravings and Other Poems*, ed. Mervyn Morris (London: Karnak House, 1983), 33.

5 lines from Grace Nichols, "Web or Kin," in *i is a long memoried woman* (London: Karnak House, 1983), 9.

44 lines from Grace Nichols, "Drum-Spell," in *i is a long memoried woman* (London: Karnak House, 1983), 80, 88–90.

19 lines from Grace Nichols, "Sugar Cane," in *i is a long memoried woman* (London: Karnak House, 1983), 32–33.

5 lines from Grace Nichols, "Skin Teeth," in *i is a long memoried woman* (London: Karnak House, 1983), 50.

4 lines from Grace Nichols, "Epilogue," in *i is a long memoried woman* (London: Karnak House, 1983), 80.

4 lines from Amon Saba Saakana, "Tapestry," in *Tones & Colours* (London: Karnak House, 1985), 13.

Judith Kazantzis

4 lines from Judith Kazantzis, "Medea," in *One Foot on the Mountain: An Anthology of British Feminist Poetry, 1969–1979*, ed. Lilian Mohin (London: Onlywomen Press, 1979), 121.

London Magazine Editions

14 lines from Tony Harrison, *The Loiners* (London: London Magazine Editions, 1970), 86.

Mariscat Press

10 lines from "Theory of the Earth," in Edwin Morgan, *Sonnets from Scotland* (Glasgow: Mariscat, 1984), 24.

Navana

8 lines from Ketaki Dyson, "Visions of an Indian Woman in an English Garden," in *Spaces I Inhabit* (Calcutta: Navana, 1983), 16.

12 lines from Ketaki Dyson, "Dialogues," in *Spaces I Inhabit* (Calcutta: Navana, 1983), 70.

New Beacon Books

6 lines from James Berry, "Boonoonoonoos," in *Fractured Circles* (London and Port of Spain: New Beacon Books, 1979), 30.

13 lines from James Berry, *Lucy's Letters and Loving* (London and Port of Spain: New Beacon Books, 1982), 9, 40, 41, 49.

14 lines from Antony (John) La Rose, "Connecting Link," in *Foundations* (London and Port of Spain: New Beacon Books, 1966), 13.

Oxford University Press

By permission of Oxford University Press:
4 lines from Roy Fisher, "Diversions," part 18, in *Poems 1955–87* (Oxford: Oxford University Press, 1988), 138.
159 words from Roy Fisher, "City" [prose], in *Poems 1955–87* (Oxford: Oxford University Press, 1988), 21, 23, 27, 28, 29.
2 lines from Roy Fisher, "The Thing About Joe Sullivan," in *Poems 1955–87* (Oxford: Oxford University Press, 1988), 152.
124 words from Roy Fisher, "The Ship's Orchestra" [prose], in *Poems 1955–87* (Oxford: Oxford University Press, 1988).
16 lines from Roy Fisher, "City" [prose], in *Poems 1955–87* (Oxford: Oxford University Press, 1988), 21, 23, 27, 28, 29.
4 lines from Roy Fisher, "Of the Empirical Self and for Me," in *Poems 1955–87* (Oxford: Oxford University Press, 1988), 125.
24 lines from Roy Fisher, "The Lesson in Composition," in *Poems 1955–87* (Oxford: Oxford University Press, 1988), 125.
8 lines from Roy Fisher, "Introit: 12 November 1958," in *A Furnace* (Oxford and New York: Oxford University Press, 1986), 3.
2 lines from Roy Fisher, "Style," in *Poems 1955–87* (Oxford: Oxford University Press, 1988), 143.
14 words from Roy Fisher, "The Home Pianist's Companion" [prose], in *Poems 1955–87* (Oxford: Oxford University Press, 1988), 168–69.
2 lines from Roy Fisher, "The Home Pianist's Companion," in *Poems 1955–87* (Oxford: Oxford University Press, 1988), 168–69.
23 lines from Roy Fisher, "Handsworth Liberties," part 15, in *Poems 1955–87* (Oxford: Oxford University Press, 1988), 123–24.
10 lines from Roy Fisher, "Correspondence," in *Poems 1955–87* (Oxford: Oxford University Press, 1988), 94–95.
48 words from Roy Fisher, preface to *A Furnace* (Oxford and New York: Oxford University Press, 1986), vii–viii.
23 lines from Roy Fisher, "Introit," in *A Furnace* (Oxford and New York: Oxford University Press, 1986), 3–4.
35 lines from Roy Fisher, "A Furnace," part 2, in *A Furnace* (Oxford and New York: Oxford University Press, 1986), 11–14, 18.
7 lines from James Berry, "Fantasy of an African Boy," in *Chain of Days* (Oxford and New York: Oxford University Press, 1985), 18.
5 lines from James Berry, *Chain of Days* (Oxford and New York: Oxford University Press, 1985), 4, 7.
15 lines from James Berry, "Two Black Labourers on a London Building Site," *Chain of Days* (Oxford and New York: Oxford University Press, 1985), 28.

Paladin

3 lines from J. H. Prynne, "Frost and Snow Falling," in *A Various Art*, ed. Andrew Crozier and Tim Longville (1987; reprinted, London: Paladin, 1990), 242.

11 lines from J. H. Prynne, "Thoughts on the Esterhazy Court Uniform," in *A Various Art*, ed. Andrew Crozier and Tim Longville (1987; reprinted, London: Paladin, 1990), 247–48.

32 lines from J. H. Prynne, "Sketch for a Financial Theory of the Self," in *A Various Art*, ed. Andrew Crozier and Tim Longville (1987; reprinted, London: Paladin, 1990), 233–34.

6 lines from J. H. Prynne, "Of Movement Towards a Natural Place," in *A Various Art*, ed. Andrew Crozier and Tim Longville (1987; reprinted, London: Paladin, 1990), 262.

13 lines from Veronica Forrest-Thomson, "Pastoral," in *A Various Art*, ed. Andrew Crozier and Tim Longville (1987; reprinted, London: Paladin, 1990), 117.

9 lines from Veronica Forrest-Thomson, "Cordelia, or A poem should not mean but be," in *A Various Art*, ed. Andrew Crozier and Tim Longville (1987; reprinted, London: Paladin, 1990), 121.

12 lines from Andrew Crozier, "The Veil Poem," in *A Various Art*, ed. Andrew Crozier and Tim Longville (1987; reprinted, London: Paladin, 1990), 75, 85.

5 lines from Andrew Crozier, "Two Robin Croft," in *A Various Art*, ed. Andrew Crozier and Tim Longville (1987; reprinted, London: Paladin, 1990), 70.

4 lines from Andrew Crozier, "Pleats," in *A Various Art*, ed. Andrew Crozier and Tim Longville (1987; reprinted, London: Paladin, 1990), 82.

6 lines from Andrew Crozier, "The Life Class," in *A Various Art*, ed. Andrew Crozier and Tim Longville (1987; reprinted, London: Paladin, 1990), 76.

4 lines from Andrew Crozier, "High Zero," in *A Various Art*, ed. Andrew Crozier and Tim Longville (1987; reprinted, London: Paladin, 1990), 74, 84.

6 lines from Andrew Crozier, "February Evenings," in *A Various Art*, ed. Andrew Crozier and Tim Longville (1987; reprinted, London: Paladin, 1990), 69.

2 lines from Andrew Crozier, "Evaporation of a Dream," in *A Various Art*, ed. Andrew Crozier and Tim Longville (1987; reprinted, London: Paladin, 1990), 94.

Penguin (U.K.)/Dufor Editions (U.S.)

6 lines from Geoffrey Hill, "Damon's Lament for his Clorinda, Yorkshire 1654," in *Collected Poems* (Harmondsworth, England: Penguin, 1985), 158.

18 lines from Geoffrey Hill, "A Pastoral," in *For the Unfallen: Poems, 1952–1958* (London: André Deutsch, 1959), 56.

Penguin (U.K.)/Oxford University Press (U.S.)

3 lines from Geoffrey Hill, "September Song," in *Collected Poems* (Harmondsworth, England: Penguin, 1985), 67.

1 line from Geoffrey Hill, "An Apology for the Revivial of Christian Architecture in England," in *Collected Poems* (Harmondsworth, England: Penguin, 1985), 86.

Penguin (U.K.)/A. P. Watt

2 lines from Liz Lochhead, "Bagpipe Muzak, Glasgow 1990," in *Bagpipe Muzak* (Harmondsworth, England: Penguin, 1991), 24.

2 lines from Liz Lochhead, "5th April 1990," in *Bagpipe Muzak* (Harmondsworth, England: Penguin, 1991), 79.

11 lines from Liz Lochhead, "View of Scotland/Love Poem," in *Bagpipe Muzak* (Harmondsworth, England: Penguin, 1991), 56.

Penguin (U.K.)/Peters, Fraser & Dunlop

1 line from Tony Harrison, "The School of Eloquence," in *Selected Poems*, 2d ed. (London: Penguin, 1987), 123.

Penguin (U.S.A.)/Olwyn Hughes Literary Agency

7 lines from Ted Hughes, "Moony Art," in *Moon-Whales and Other Moon Poems* (New York: Viking, 1976), 50, 68.
1 line from Ted Hughes, "Moon-Tulips," in *Moon-Whales and Other Moon Poems* (New York: Viking, 1976), 24.

Penumbra Publications

7 lines from H. O. Nazareth, "For Future Reference," in *Lobo* (London: Penumbra Publications, 1984), 67.

Pluto Press

3 lines from Ian Hamilton Finlay, "pebble ROCKS POND" (1969), in *Headlines/Pondlines*, with drawings by John Furnival (Corsham, U.K.: Pluto Press, 1969), n.p.

Poetry Wales Press

6 lines from Robert Minhinnick, "The Arcade," in *The Dinosaur Park* (Bridgend, Wales: Poetry Wales Press, 1985), 28.
2 lines from Robert Minhinnick, "The Resort," in *The Dinosaur Park* (Bridgend, Wales: Poetry Wales Press, 1985), 25.
7 lines from Robert Minhinnick, "On the Sands," in *The Dinosaur Park* (Bridgend, Wales: Poetry Wales Press, 1985), 29.
1 line from Mike Jenkins, "Industrial Museum," in *Invisible Times* (Bridgend, Wales: Poetry Wales Press, 1986), 26–27.

Polygon

8 lines from Liz Lochhead, "Memo to Myself for Spring," in *Dreaming Frankenstein & Collected Poems* (Edinburgh: Polygon, 1984), 158–59.
16 lines from Liz Lochhead, "Everybody's Mother," in *Dreaming Frankenstein & Collected Poems* (Edinburgh: Polygon, 1984), 94.

13 lines from Liz Lochhead, "Beauty & The," in *Dreaming Frankenstein & Collected Poems* (Edinburgh: Polygon, 1984), 80.

20 lines from "Inter-City," in *Dreaming Frankenstein & Collected Poems* (Edinburgh: Polygon, 1984), 33.

Reaktion

16 lines from Ian Hamilton Finlay, "Poster Poem," in Yves Abrioux, *Ian Hamilton Finlay: A Visual Primer* (Edinburgh: Reaktion Books, 1985), 75.

7 lines from Ian Hamilton Finlay, "fir/far," in Yves Abrioux, *Ian Hamilton Finlay: A Visual Primer* (Edinburgh: Reaktion Books, 1985), 86.

13 lines from Ian Hamilton Finlay, "Star/Steer," in Yves Abrioux, *Ian Hamilton Finlay: A Visual Primer* (Edinburgh: Reaktion Books, 1985), 74.

2 lines from Ian Hamilton Finlay, "homage to gomringer," in Yves Abrioux, *Ian Hamilton Finlay: A Visual Primer* (Edinburgh: Reaktion Books, 1985), n.p.

1 line from Ian Hamilton Finlay, "Small is Quite Beautiful" (card with Ron Costley), in Yves Abrioux, *Ian Hamilton Finlay: A Visual Primer* (Edinburgh: Reaktion Books, 1985), 96.

Reed Consumer Books

29 lines from Jon Silkin, "The Coldness," in *Selected Poems,* new ed. (London and New York: Routledge, 1988), 15.

27 lines from Jon Silkin, "The Re-ordering of the Stones," in *Selected Poems,* new ed. (London and New York: Routledge, 1988), 32–33.

12 lines from Jon Silkin, "The Kilhope Wheel," in *Selected Poems,* new ed. (London and New York: Routledge, 1988), 91–92.

Sangster's Bookstores

4 lines from Louise Bennett, "Colonisation in Reverse," in *Jamaica Labresh* (Kingston, Jamaica: Sangster's Bookstores, 1966), 179–80.

Seren

3 lines from Tony Curtis, "Thoughts from the Holiday Inn," in *The Last Candles* (Bridgend, Wales: Seren Books, 1989), 40.

9 lines from Robert Minhinnick, "Ghost Train," in *The Looters* (Bridgend, Wales: Seren Books, 1989), 15, 45.

1 line from Robert Minhinnick, "YOPS," in *The Looters* (Bridgend, Wales: Seren Books, 1989), 14.

Sheba, Feminist Publishers

11 lines from Barbara Burford, "A Dangerous Knowing," in *A Dangerous Knowing: Four Black Women Poets* (London: Sheba, Feminist Publishers, 1985), 4.

13 lines from Barbara Burford, "Sisterwrite," in *A Dangerous Knowing: Four Black Women Poets* (London: Sheba, Feminist Publishers, 1985), 10.

Smith/Doorstop Books

4 lines from Debjani Chatterjee, "Arrival," in *The Sun Rises in the North* (Huddersfield: Smith/ Doorstop Books, 1991), 16.

Studio Books

16 lines from Ian Hamilton Finlay's "Poster Poem," in John Lewis, *Typography/Basic Principles: Influences and Trends Since the Nineteenth Century* (London: Studio Books, 1967), 73.

Alan Swallow

4 lines from J. V. Cunningham, "Montana Pastoral," in *The Exclusions of a Rhyme* (Denver: Alan Swallow, 1960), 37.

Tarasque

13 lines from Ian Hamilton Finlay, "Star/Steer" (Nottingham: Tarasque, 1966), unpaginated folding page.

Thom Gunn

19 lines from Thom Gunn, "An Operation," *Times Literary Supplement* 18 (January 1991): 4.

Triskele Books

2 lines from Robert Minhinnick, "The House," in *Native Ground* (Swansea, Wales: Triskele Books, 1979), 16.
1 line from Robert Minhinnick, *Native Ground* (Swansea, Wales: Triskele Books, 1979), 9.
4 lines from Robert Minhinnick, "The Strata: to Lywellen Siôn," in *Native Ground* (Swansea, Wales: Triskele Books, 1979), 17.
5 lines from Robert Minhinnick, "JP," in *Native Ground* (Swansea, Wales: Triskele Books, 1979), 43.

Victoria Miro Gallery

Ian Hamilton Finlay, "OSSO" [photo], London: Victoria Miro Gallery.

Virago/Curtis Brown

14 lines from Denise Riley, "A note on sex and 'the reclaiming of language'," in *Dry Air* (London: Virago, 1985), 7.
17 lines from Grace Nichols, "Thoughts drifting through the fat black woman's head while having a bubble bath," in *The Fat Black Woman's Poems* (London: Virago, 1984), 15.
4 lines from Grace Nichols, "Trap Evasions," in *Lazy Thoughts of a Lazy Woman and Other Poems* (London: Virago, 1989), 14.
17 lines from Grace Nichols, "Of Course When They Ask for Poems About the 'Realities' of Black Women," in *Lazy Thoughts of a Lazy Woman and Other Poems* (London: Virago, 1989), 52–54.

Wasafiri (Periodical)

8 lines from Debjani Chatterjee, "To the English Language," *Wasafiri* 13 (spring 1991): 22.

Wild Hawthorn Press

6 lines from Ian Hamilton Finlay, "THE ONE HORSE TOWN/Dobbin," in *Stonechats* (Edinburgh: Wild Hawthorn Press, 1967), n.p.
7 lines from Ian Hamilton Finlay, "fir/far," in *Telegrams from My Windmill* (Edinburgh: Wild Hawthorn Press, 1964), n.p.
4 lines from Ian Hamilton Finlay, *FISHING NEWS NEWS,* with drawings by Margot Sandeman (Edinburgh: Wild Hawthorn Press, 1970), n.p.
2 lines from Ian Hamilton Finlay, "homage to gomringer," in *FISHING NEWS NEWS,* with drawings by Margot Sandeman (Edinburgh: Wild Hawthorn Press, 1970), n.p.
Ian Hamilton Finlay and Gary Hincks, "Bicentenary Tricolor" [poem-print] (Edinburgh: Wild Hawthorn Press, 1989).

Women's Press

8 lines from Gabriela Pearse, "Autobiography," in *Watchers and Seekers,* ed. Rhonda Cobham and Merle Collins (London: Women's Press, 1987), 33.

The Writers' Workshop

5 lines from Ketaki Dyson, "Shun this World's Harlotry," in *Sap-Wood* (Calcutta: Writers' Workshop, 1978), 20.

INDEX

415